westermann

Pathway
Approach

Gymnasiale Oberstufe – Einführungsphase

Herausgegeben und erarbeitet von
Iris Edelbrock

Pathway
Approach

Zusatzmaterialien zu Pathway Approach

Für Lehrerinnen und Lehrer:

Teachers' Manual	978-3-14-121503-8
BiBox Einzellizenz für Lehrer/-innen (Dauerlizenz)	WEB-14-121509
BiBox Kollegiumslizenz für Lehrer/-innen (Dauerlizenz)	WEB-14-121510
BiBox Kollegiumslizenz für Lehrer/-innen (1 Schuljahr)	WEB-14-107424

Mehr Informationen über aktuelle Lizenzen finden Sie auf www.bibox.schule.

Für Schülerinnen und Schüler:

Prep & Practice Book	978-3-14-121502-1
BiBox Einzellizenz für Schüler/-innen (1 Schuljahr)	WEB-14-121506

westermann GRUPPE

Druck A[1] / Jahr 2021
Alle Drucke der Serie A sind im Unterricht parallel verwendbar.

Redaktion: Marion Kramer
Sprachliche Betreuung: John Poziemski
Umschlaggestaltung: LIO Design, Foto: Mark Gibson/Alamy Stock Photo
Layout: Alexandra Brand, Paderborn
Druck und Bindung: Westermann Druck GmbH, Georg-Westermann-Allee 66, 38104 Braunschweig

ISBN 978-3-14-**121500**-7

Contents

Level of difficulty	
●○○	basic
●●○	intermediate
●●●	advanced

Webcodes

All audio/-visual material and worksheets are provided on **webcodes**. Access the following website www.westermann.de/webcode and enter the respective code, e. g. WES-121500-001

FOCUS ON ANALYSIS

Growing Up – No Longer Being a Child!

FOCUS ON COMMUNICATION

Youth Culture and Role Models in the Digital Age

FOCUS ON WRITING

Symbols & Skills

Group work, work in a team, work with a partner
→ communication skills

Communication training, e.g. discussion
→ communication skills

M Mediation between English and German
→ mediation skills

Creative writing task
→ writing skills

Presentation of projects
→ speaking skills

@ Internet research
→ intercultural competences

WES-121500-001 Worksheets
→ reading/writing/listening/audio-visual skills

WES-121500-001 Audio files and audio links
→ listening skills

WES-121500-001 Video files and video links
→ audio-visual skills

@ WES-121500-001 Research links
→ intercultural competences

Tasks for advanced students

metaphor* This * sign indicates that the word/term can be found in the Literary Terms Section (pp. 274 ff.).

How to work with the Pathway Approach

Liebe Schülerinnen und Schüler,

der *Pathway Approach* möchte euch in der Vorbereitung auf die Qualifikationsphase unterstützen. In 4 Units bearbeitet ihr die inhaltlichen Schwerpunktthemen des Lehrplans und erwerbt und übt die zentralen Kompetenzen und Fertigkeiten (*Skills*), die ihr für die schriftlichen und mündlichen Prüfungen in der Qualifikationsphase und im Abitur benötigt.

Dabei stehen folgende **Skills** im Vordergrund, die durch ein **Farbleitsystem** am oberen Rand der Seiten gekennzeichnet sind. Die jeweilige Farbe verweist auf die **zentralen Kompetenzen**, die schwerpunktmäßig in dieser Unit geübt werden.

Focus on Comprehension	listening skills reading skills viewing skills	• Hörverstehen • Leseverstehen • Hör-/Sehverstehen
Focus on Analysis	analysis skills	• Text- und Medienkompetenz
Focus on Communication	communication skills speaking skills	• an Gesprächen teilnehmen • zusammenhängendes Sprechen
Focus on Writing	writing skills	• Schreiben

Am **Ende jeder Unit** findest du ein **Mediation *Extra***, das dich im Umgang mit Sprachmittlung schult und kleinschrittig inhaltlich und sprachlich unterstützt.

Jede Unit wird durch eine **Skill Task** (Lernaufgabe) abgerundet, die **projektartig** einen besonderen Skill in den Mittelpunkt stellt und mit der du in der Unit erworbenes Wissen und erlernte Kompetenzen anwenden und erproben kannst.

Aufgabenapparate

Die **farbigen Balken der Aufgabenapparate** folgen einem analogen Farbsystem:
Comprehension – **Analysis** – **Writing/text production/evaluation (Activities)** – **Grammar/Language**

Sie entsprechen dem Farbsystem der **Standardized Terminology for Tasks *(Operatoren)*** (S. 10 – 15).

- Jedem Level (Anforderungsbereich) sind in den Aufgabenapparaten bestimmte **Operatoren** zugeordnet, damit du den Umgang damit üben kannst.
- Der Skill, der mit einem Material schwerpunktmäßig geübt werden soll, ist zusätzlich durch einen Farbkasten hervorgehoben. Untergliedernde **Steps** kennzeichnen diese Aufgaben und bieten dir zusätzliche Unterstützung und Vertiefungsmöglichkeiten.

START-UP ACTIVITIES	Brushing up knowledge, preparing a new topic, introducing the new unit
AWARENESS	Introducing a new text or material, giving an impetus
COMPREHENSION	Tasks for the understanding, comprehension and reproduction of texts/material
ANALYSIS	Tasks for the analysis, examination and interpretation of texts/material
ACTIVITIES	Tasks for further discussion, creative writing, evaluation, presentation, etc.
GRAMMAR / LANGUAGE	Brushing up grammar and language skills, grammar exercises in context

Arbeiten mit den Webcodes

An vielen Aufgaben findest du **Webcodes**, über die du auf **weitere Materialien**, die **online** verfügbar sind, zugreifen kannst. Über die Website www.westermann.de/webcode kannst du, nach Eingabe des entsprechenden Webcodes, auf diese Materialien zugreifen:

WES-121500-001 Aufgaben ergänzende oder vertiefende **Worksheets** helfen dir bei der detaillierten Bearbeitung.

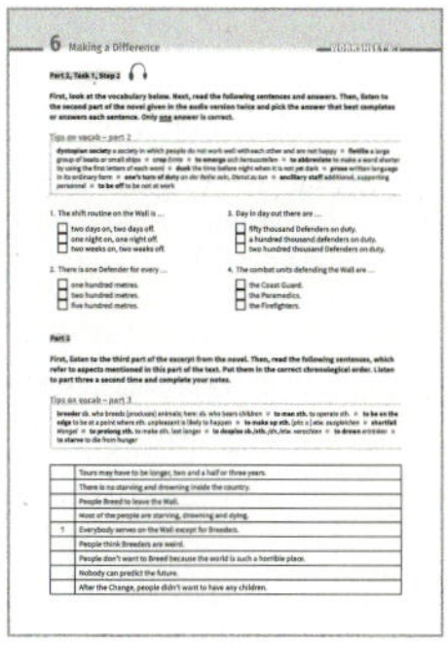

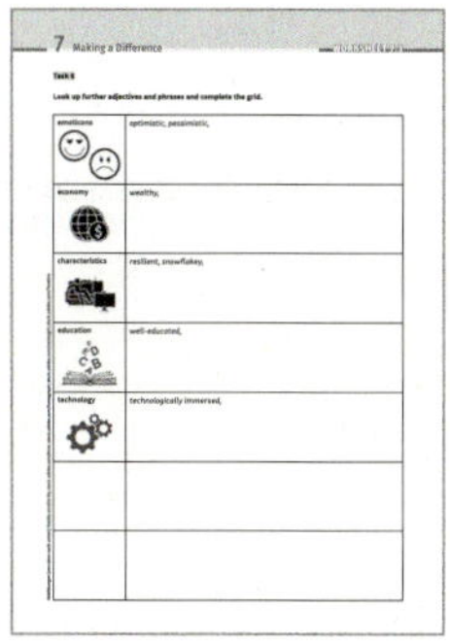

WES-121500-001 Hier stehen **Audio-Dateien** oder **Audio-Links** zur Verfügung, z. B. eine politische Rede, die du für die Bearbeitung der Aufgaben benötigst.

WES-121500-001 Diese Webcodes bieten Video-Dateien oder Video-Links, z. B. einen Filmtrailer, ein Interview, eine *documentary*.

WES-121500-001 Diese Webcodes verweisen auf ***research links***, die dir helfen, weiterführende oder vertiefende Hintergrundinformationen, z. B. für *presentations* oder *discussions* zu finden.

Appendix

Der *Pathway Approach* verfügt über einen umfangreichen **Anhang *(Appendix)*** (S. 223 – 302), der dir eine Vielzahl von **Skills**-Seiten, Hilfen, Beispielen, Vokabeln und eine kleine Grundlagengrammatik an die Hand gibt. Hier findest du kleinschrittige Erklärungen, wie du eine Aufgabe bearbeiten kannst und worauf du besonders achten solltest. Verweise auf den Appendix direkt unter den Aufgaben helfen dir, die passenden Skills-Seiten zu finden.

Skills & Competences
Focus on Skills-,
Focus on Language- und
Focus on Facts-Seiten;
Hilfen zur Textbearbeitung

Literary Terms
Zusammenstellung von Fachvokabular und *Phrases* zur Textbearbeitung und -analyse

Selected Language Features
Sprachliche Besonderheiten und Fallstricke des Englischen

Grammar
Grammar Basics zum Nachschlagen und zur Wiederholung

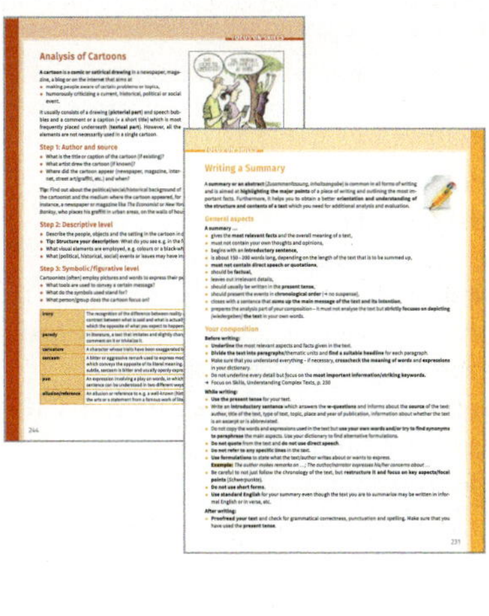

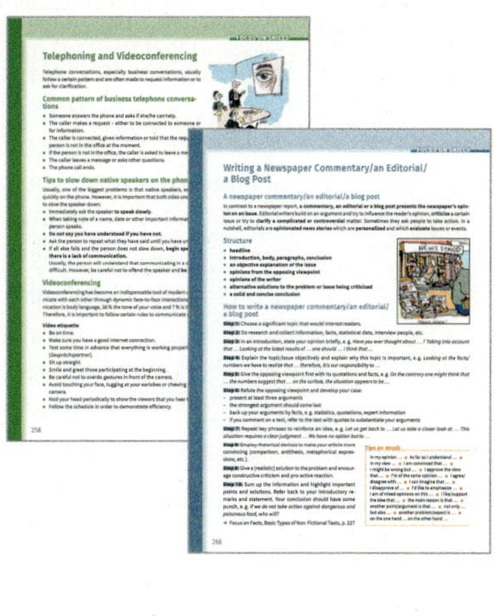

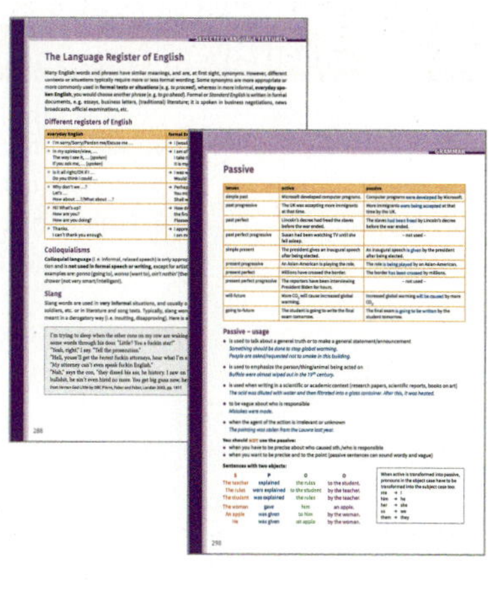

Standardized Terminology for Tasks (*Operatoren*)

In order to enable you to better understand and deal with the tasks in this coursebook, the following list gives you the key words and standardized formulations for tasks (*Operatoren*) used in the German *Zentralabitur*. Each key word is connected with a definition that not only explains the term itself but also shows you what you are expected to do in order to fulfil this task.

Kompetenzbereich: Schreiben

Key word/terminology	Example	Definition	What you are expected to do
Level I: Orientation/comprehension/understanding/reproduction of texts			
define *bestimmen/umreißen/ definieren*	Define the meaning of the term multi-cultural.	give a clear, precise meaning/explanation of a term/idea	• before writing, highlight/underline specific details in the text • you should refer to details but do not write wordy explanations – be as precise and specific as possible • make references to lines in the text but do not quote – paraphrase instead
describe *beschreiben*	Describe the woman's appearance.	give/present an accurate/a detailed account of sth./sb.	
state *angeben/sagen/ Gründe angeben*	State briefly the main development of the ecology movement.	specify clearly	
outline *darstellen*	Outline the author's stance on immigration.	work out the main features, structure or general principles of a topic – but omit minor details	• focus on the structure of the text, e.g. how the author develops his/her line of argument or how a story develops, etc. • divide the text into paragraphs • make references to lines/arguments etc. in the text but do not quote – paraphrase instead
present *darstellen*	Present the situation of Asians in London.	(re-)structure and write down	
point out *beschreiben/erläutern*	Point out the author's main ideas on …	find and explain certain aspects	• focus on the most relevant aspects/ideas/ arguments of the text and avoid details • make references to lines/aspects in the text but do not quote – paraphrase instead
sum up, summarize, write a summary *zusammenfassen*	Summarize the information given in the text about the American Dream.	give a concise account of the main points (→ no details, no direct speech)	• before writing a summary, underline the most relevant aspects in the text – avoid details • use your own words to paraphrase main aspects: – do not quote from the text/do not use direct speech – do not refer to certain lines etc. in the text • be factual and precise → FoS, Writing a Summary, p. 231
Level II: Analysis and re-structuring of texts			
analyse/examine *analysieren/untersuchen*	Analyse the opposing views on immigration presented in the text. Examine the author's use of language.	describe and explain in detail certain aspects and/or features of a text	• focus on the structure of the text and pay attention to details • formulate a connecting sentence (contents → analysis) at the beginning • be as precise as possible by using the correct terms and expressions • use quotations/direct references to lines in the text to prove the accuracy of your analysis → FoS, Analysis of a (Non-)Fictional Text, pp. 235, 237 → Vocabulary for Text Analysis, p. 249 → Connectives and Adverbs, p. 251

Key word/terminology	Example	Definition	What you are expected to do
characterize/write a characterization *charakterisieren/im Detail beschreiben und erklären*	Characterize/Write a characterization of the main character in the play.	analyse the typical features of sb., then describe, explain and interpret the way in which the character(s) is/are presented	• highlight/underline important details about the character and take notes in the margin, using different colours for specific devices • pay attention to details: do not cover everything but focus on the most striking devices/details • use quotations/direct references to lines in the text to prove the accuracy of your analysis → FoS, Characterization of a Figure in Literature, p. 247
contrast *gegenüberstellen*	Contrast the main characters' opposing views on the USA.	emphasize the difference between two or more things	• before writing your text, make a table in two columns and juxtapose views/arguments/evidence that refer(s) to the argument and the counterargument of the matter • refer directly to certain lines/arguments etc. and use quotations and/or refer to lines in the text • collect ideas/arguments and structure them before writing your text
explain *erklären*	Explain the protagonist's obsession with money.	describe and define in detail	• highlight/underline important details in the text and take notes in the margin, using different colours for specific devices • pay attention to details: do not cover everything but focus on the most striking devices/details • refer directly to certain lines/arguments etc. and use quotations and/or refer to lines in the text • be as precise as possible by using the correct terms and expressions → FoS, Analysis of a (Non-)Fictional Text, pp. 235, 237
illustrate *veranschaulichen*	Illustrate the author's use of metaphorical language.	use examples to explain or make clear	• pay attention to details: do not cover everything but focus on the most striking devices/details • choose the most relevant/significant examples from the text for your explanation • use quotations/direct references to lines in the text to prove the accuracy of your analysis
interpret *interpretieren*	Interpret the message the author wishes to convey.	make clear the meaning of sth.	• try to read 'between the lines' and use your background knowledge • do not give wordy explanations and opinions but be as specific and precise as possible • refer directly to certain lines/arguments etc. and use quotations and/or refer to lines in the text
compare *vergleichen*	Compare the views of the two writers on recycling. Compare the behaviour of the women.	point out similarities and/or differences of things/characters/situations	• before writing your comparison, underline the most relevant differences/similarities in the text using different colours • make a table in two columns and compare/juxtapose the different aspects and details • refer directly to certain lines/arguments etc. and use quotations and/or refer to lines in the text

Key word/terminology	Example	Definition	What you are expected to do
Level III: Discussion/evaluation/text production			
comment (on) *Stellung nehmen*	Comment on the statement that the American Dream is over.	state clearly your opinions on a topic and support your views with evidence/arguments/reference to the text(s)	• before writing your text, make a table in two columns and juxtapose views/arguments/evidence that refer(s) to the argument and the counterargument of the matter • give your opinion on the topic but do not be personal – your judgment should be based on evidence and facts • connect aspects/arguments given in the text with your background knowledge and further references • be careful not to just reproduce sth. that you have learned by heart but paraphrase and refer to the most specific/exemplary aspects • finish your text with a concluding sentence → FoS, Basic Types of Non-Fictional Texts, p. 227 → FoL, Conversation and Discussion, p. 254
evaluate *einschätzen/einordnen/bewerten*	Evaluate the author's view on the impact of global migration.	form an opinion after carefully considering a topic/question and presenting advantages and disadvantages	
assess *beurteilen*	Assess the importance of standards in education.	make a judgment after thinking carefully about the points for and against sth.	
discuss* *erörtern*	Discuss the consequences of consumerism as referred to in the text.	investigate or examine by argument; give reasons/examples for and against	• weigh different aspects/arguments and counterarguments of a matter • take different positions/views on an issue • collect ideas/arguments first and structure them before writing your text • finish your text with a conclusion that summarizes the most important aspects • do not express your own opinion but refer to aspects dealt with in the text at hand → FoL, Conversation and Discussion, p. 254
justify *rechtfertigen/begründen*	You are a CEO of a company. Justify your decision to give a microcredit loan to a village in Nigeria.	give reasons for decisions and conclusions	• before writing your text, collect reasons and examples that support your decision • consider the importance/weight of your arguments/reasons and structure them • finish your text with a concluding and summarizing sentence and/or statement → FoL, Conversation and Discussion, p. 254
prove *am Text belegen*	Prove the effects of Western values on developing countries.	give evidence to provide a clear and convincing argumentation	• before writing your text, collect ideas about the respective matter and structure them • give examples and refer to background information but focus on relevant aspects/arguments • do not give wordy explanations and opinions but be as specific and precise as possible • refer directly to certain lines/arguments etc. and use quotations and/or refer to lines in the text → FoS, Basic Types of Non-Fictional Texts, p. 227
reflect on *reflektieren/bedenken*	Reflect on how the author deals with the problem of exploiting workers in sweatshops.	express your thoughts in a carefully considered and balanced way	• before writing, underline/highlight keywords and relevant aspects in the text that you want to use • collect ideas on how you want to respond to the matter • weigh up different aspects/arguments by juxtaposing them in a table • you may state your opinion on the issue but avoid being personal – be factual and precise • finish your text with a concluding and summarizing sentence and/or statement → FoL, Conversation and Discussion, p. 254

Key word/terminology	Example	Definition	What you are expected to do
write (+ text type) *schreiben, verfassen, formulieren*	Write an ending of the story. Write an interior monologue that reflects the character's view of the situation and his/her feelings. Write a letter to the editor in which you discuss the assumption that the American Dream is dead.	produce a text with specific features	• be aware of the specific features of the literary genre and/or type of text you are working with • employ the formal characteristics of the respective text type or genre • put your analysis results and findings in a wider context that also includes aspects you have dealt with in class • make sure that your text is related to the input text and is based on your analysis results → FoS, Continuing a Fictional Text, p. 264 → FoS, Writing a Review, p. 265 → FoS, Writing an Interview, p. 269 → FoS, Writing a Newspaper Article, p. 270 → FoS, Writing a Letter to the Editor, p. 273

* The task "Discuss (in class)" focuses on an oral activity together with a group rather than a written evaluation of a topic.

Kompetenzbereich: Sprachmittlung

Key word/terminology	Example	Definition	What you are expected to do
explain *erklären/ verdeutlichen*	Explain the principle of waste separation in Germany.	give a clear, precise definition/explanation of a term/idea	• mediating (parts of) a text into another language in general requires you to consider the addressee(s), the meaning of the input text, as well as cultural and situational aspects • before writing, highlight/underline specific details in the text • you should refer to details but do not write wordy explanations – be as specific as possible • make references to lines in the text but do not quote – paraphrase instead → FoS, Mediation, p. 253
outline *darstellen* present *darstellen*	For an international school project in the EU, present the relevant information on the image of migrants in the German media in a formal email.	give a concise account of the main points or ideas of a text (clarifying culture-related aspects if necessary)	• focus on the structure of the text, e. g. how the author develops his/her line of argument, how a story develops, etc. • divide the text into paragraphs • refer to lines/arguments etc. in the text but do not quote – paraphrase instead → FoS, Mediation, p. 253
summarize, sum up *zusammenfassen*			• before writing a summary, underline the most relevant aspects in the text – leave out details • use your own words to paraphrase the main aspects: – do note quote from the text/do not use direct speech – do not refer to certain lines, etc. in the text • be factual and precise → FoS, Writing a Summary, p. 231 → FoS, Mediation, p. 253

Key word/terminology	Example	Definition	What you are expected to do
write (+ text type) *schreiben, verfassen, formulieren*	Using the information in the input article, write an article in English for your project website in which you inform your Polish partners how to get a sports scholarship at a German university.	produce a text with specific features	• be aware of the specific features of the literary genre and/or type of text you are working with • employ the formal characteristics of the text type or genre → FoS, Mediation, p. 253

Kompetenzbereich: Sprechen/an Gesprächen teilnehmen

<table>
<tr><th>Key word/terminology</th><th>Example</th><th>Definition</th><th>What you are expected to do</th></tr>
<tr><td>(try to) agree on, (try to) come to an agreement
sich einigen auf, eine Einigung/einen Kompromiss finden</td><td>Discuss which methods are best to prevent … Try to agree on two aspects …</td><td>to come to the same opinion or an understanding; try to reach a compromise</td><td rowspan="7">Oral examinations/presentations:
• read the tasks carefully
• underline/highlight relevant keywords and take notes on the most important aspects
• do not write down completely formulated answers and sentences – jot down the most relevant phrases and terms
• do not simply read out your notes/answers – paraphrase and explain them; speak as freely as possible
• make eye contact with your examiner

Discussions:
• interact with your partner(s) and respond to his/her/their remarks
• do not simply read out your notes on the topic – formulate your ideas as precisely as possible and avoid wordy explanations and empty phrases
• listen carefully to the questions and remarks of your partner(s)
• make sure you understand what is being discussed – if you do not understand, ask your partner(s) to reformulate or repeat remarks or questions

→ FoL, Conversation and Discussion, p. 254
→ FoS, Oral Examination, p. 257
→ FoS, Giving a Speech, p. 260
→ FoS, Presentation, p. 261</td></tr>
<tr><td>comment (on)
Stellung nehmen</td><td>Talk about photos in the media and their message. Comment on whether such photos are an effective way to make people aware of certain problems.</td><td>give your opinion and support your view with evidence or reasons</td></tr>
<tr><td>compare
vergleichen</td><td>Compare the … pictures and talk about the lives of the people you see.</td><td>show similarities and differences</td></tr>
<tr><td>discuss
diskutieren, erörtern</td><td>Discuss the advantages and risks of … Decide which aspects are most …
Agree on two things that you think should be organized … .</td><td>give arguments or reasons for or against and (try to) come to a conclusion</td></tr>
<tr><td>explain
erklären</td><td>Explain the message of the cartoon/quote/statement … and the means used to convey it.</td><td>make sth. clear</td></tr>
<tr><td>give reasons/justify
begründen</td><td>Which photo/picture would you choose to make people aware of certain problems? Justify your choice.</td><td>present reasons for decisions, positions or conclusions</td></tr>
<tr><td>talk about (the …)
sich äußern zu etw.</td><td>Talk about the photos. What do the photos suggest about …?</td><td>produce a text referring to certain aspects</td></tr>
</table>

Kompetenzbereich: Hör-/Hörsehverstehen

Key word/terminology	Example	What you are expected to do
answer *beantworten*	Answer the question in about 5 .../10 .../100 words.	• usually this kind of task requires you to fill in a prepared sheet of paper with different types of standardized tasks, e.g. multiple choice, matching, true-false, sentence completion, note-taking, etc. • before the first listening, read the tasks and explanations carefully • make sure you understand exactly what to do (e.g. tick one or more possible answers; tick only the answer that does not fit; use the exact number of words for your answer, etc.) • if you are not sure about the correct answer, take notes on a piece of paper and fill in or tick the answers after the second listening • while listening or viewing the first time, jot down notes and keywords and try to get a general understanding of the recording or scene • in a second listening, pay attention to details and complete your notes
complete *vervollständigen, komplettieren*	Complete the sentences below in 1 to 5 words. Complete the notes on the points listed below. Complete the table below.	
fill in *ausfüllen, ergänzen*	Fill in the missing information in 1 to 5 words.	
list/name *benennen, auflisten*	List/Name the most relevant aspects mentioned in the discussion.	
match *verknüpfen, etw. zuweisen, kombinieren*	Match each speaker with one of the statements.	
state *darstellen*	State the ideas supported by ...	
tick *ankreuzen*	Tick the correct answer.	

Abbreviations

abbr.	abbreviation	here:	special meaning in this context
arch.	archaic (not used anymore)	idm.	idiomatic expression
BE	British English	infml.	informal English
cf.	compare (confer)	joc.	jocular (meant as a joke)
coll.	colloquial	lit.	literary English
derog.	derogative (offensive)	poet.	poetic
e.g.	for example	phr. v.	phrasal verb (multi-word verb)
esp.	especially	sb.	somebody
euph.	euphemistic *(beschönigend)*	sl.	slang
fig.	figurative meaning *(metaphorisch)*	sth.	something
fml.	formal English	US	American English

Making a Difference: Generation Gaps and Gap Years

1

2

Tips on vocab

to have a cup of tea and a chat ■ to sit next to each other on the sofa ■ to communicate with sb. through social media ■ to have a stunned look on one's face

Tips on vocab

backpacker ■ to carry a backpack/rucksack ■ to wear a Chinese straw hat ■ Jesus sandals ■ sarong (Chinese skirt) ■ to be heavily packed ■ to be rosy-cheeked ■ to return from a trip to Asia

START-UP ACTIVITIES

1. Take a look at cartoon no. 1:
- How has 'grandma' spent her time?
- What digital tools does she use to communicate with her family?
- Speculate: Who might the lady be that she is talking to?

2. Discuss: Do you think that using (so many) digital tools is a good way for old people to keep in contact with their family? How do you stay in contact with your grandparents?

3. Spending a gap year abroad and doing humanitarian work has become very popular among young people after finishing school.
- What do you consider to be the benefits of volunteering abroad?
- Can you think of possible problems as well?

4. The article on the opposite page was written by a student and published in the student newspaper. Read the article and
a) point out the basic ideas behind volunteer programmes and humanitarian trips,
b) explain why these activities can be counter-productive and even harmful.

5. Describe the photo on the opposite page and cartoon no. 2.
a) What message do they convey?
b) Against the background of these visuals, explain the term "voluntourism".

Laurie-Anne Benoit

The Hidden Harm[1] of Voluntourism

Volunteering in Uganda, 2017

While the idea of going abroad to help impoverished[2] communities is commendable[3], volunteering abroad has several negative consequences that directly oppose the humanitarian intentions behind these trips. Many agencies that offer volunteer opportunities abroad sell the idea of 'contributing to a community,' whether by helping to build wells[4], schools, or even volunteering in an orphanage[5]. These actions, however, do not necessarily result in long-term positive effects for the people they intend to help. Often, the good intentions of travellers harm these communities.

The projects undertaken during these humanitarian trips, such as building schools or other infrastructures, are generally completed by unskilled, volunteer labourers. Academics[6] have pointed out that the lack of skills of the volunteers impedes[7] the genuine progress of the communities: Locals often have to rebuild what volunteers have worked on during their stay. Volunteers can also obstruct[8] opportunities for locals to have paid employment, since volunteers offer free, unpaid labour, and never work on a long-term basis. Unfortunately, these elements can lead host communities to become dependent on volunteer programs. Furthermore, some volunteer projects do not offer effective structures for communities to grow and develop by themselves – such as education or professional training – resulting in the stagnation[9] of their socio-economic situations. Travel organizations sell volunteers the idea that their actions – which are on a very short-term basis – can positively impact[10] a host community, without realizing that the volunteers' lack of expertise[11] ends up adversely[12] affecting[13] local communities.

Tourism has expanded in recent decades to include a different sector of voluntourism called 'orphanage tourism' as mentioned by UNICEF's 2011 report. Since international donors[14] are the main revenue source[15] for many orphanages, offering tourists the opportunity to come visit these orphanages in person enables them to receive more funding.

The consequences of orphanage tourism, however, go beyond the negative impact of unskilled volunteer labour. A supply of foreign volunteers encourages orphanages to remain dependent on charitable[16] labour rather than hiring the staff they need. This reliance[17] on international donors turns these orphanages into another element of the tourism industry. In most cases, volunteers go into this type of humanitarian trip with the good intention of providing emotional support and love to the orphans. But, it is important to keep in mind that these connections are short-lived and sporadic[18], and can be quite harmful for orphans.

UNICEF mentions that volunteering in orphanages "negatively impacts children in care, who must repeatedly try to form emotional connections with different adults." This constant cycle of connection and separation creates instability in the lives of orphaned children, who already suffer from separation anxiety[19] at a very young age.

In general, volunteers go abroad in hopes of effecting[20] positive changes; however, the romanticized notion[21] of being able to create a ripple effect[22] of positivity blinds[23] travellers from the issues with many humanitarian trip agencies. Many travellers are not aware of the impacts they are actually leaving behind. If one is set on embarking on[24] a volunteer trip, thorough research must be done beforehand on the purposes[25] behind and consequences of a given trip. Some organizations, for example, like Operation Groundswell, offer genuine help to host communities. The gesture of volunteering abroad is well-intentioned and admirable, but the execution of such trips remains harmful.

https://www.mcgilltribune.com/opinion/the-hidden-harm-of-voluntourism-392107/, 27 September 2016 [19.12.2020]

[1] **harm** injury or damage – [2] **impoverished** very poor – [3] **commendable** praiseworthy – [4] **well** *Brunnen* – [5] **orphanage** a home for children whose parents are dead – [6] **academic** a person who teaches at a college or university – [7] **to impede** (*fml.*) *verhindern, erschweren* – [8] **to obstruct** to stop sth. from happening or developing – [9] **stagnation** *Stillstand* – [10] **to impact** to have an influence on sb./sth. – [11] **expertise** [ekspɜːˈtiːz] a high level of knowledge or skill – [12] **adversely** in a way that has a negative or harmful effect – [13] **to affect** to have an influence on sb./sth. – [14] **donor** *Spender* – [15] **revenue source** *Einnahmequelle* – [16] **charitable** *gemeinnützig* – [17] **reliance** [rɪˈlaɪəns] the state of depending on or trusting in sb./sth. – [18] **sporadic** happening irregularly – [19] **anxiety** [æŋˈzaɪəti] a feeling of nervousness and worry – [20] **to effect** to achieve sth. – [21] **notion** a belief or idea – [22] **ripple effect** *sich allmählich ausbreitende Wirkung* – [23] **to blind sb. from sth.** to make sb. unable to see or understand sth. – [24] **to embark on sth.** (*phr. v.*) to start sth. new or important – [25] **purpose** *Absicht, Zweck*

Beyoncé

Commencement Address to the Class of 2020

AWARENESS

Beyoncé Giselle Knowles-Carter has been active as an artist since the age of eight, and has become world-famous and popular with *Destiny's Child*, one of the most successful girl groups of all time.

On 7 June 2020, during the first period of the coronavirus pandemic, many celebrities, political leaders and artists organized a virtual commencement celebration called *Dear Class of 2020*, in which they celebrated and encouraged the graduates, their parents and their communities.

The common question "What's next?" that graduates often ask themselves after graduating from school is even more challenging against the background of the coronavirus pandemic. Often, there are either too many interesting options to decide between or they simply do not have a clue about what to do next.

Step 1:

Team up with a partner and look at the cartoons below. Pay attention to visual and textual elements and state

- what plans the girl in cartoon no. 2 introduces to her stunned parents,
- what specific plans and ideas the boy in cartoon no. 1 has for his upcoming gap year, much to the parents' concern.

Step 2:

Discuss

a) what might have been the reasons for the girl/boy to plan a gap year like that,

b) whether you consider their ideas and plans to be promising.

1

"I'm worried – he says he's having a 'staycation' for his gap year."

2

COMPREHENSION

1. Listen to Beyoncé's commencement address and summarize her demands and recommendations.

Step 1:

Before listening to the speech, try to anticipate what Beyoncé might tell the students about

- her motivation to give the speech,
- her own experiences with and after school,
- what motivated her to become a successful artist,
- possible advice she might give to the students.

Take notes on the aspects listed above and exchange your ideas with a partner.

@ **Tip:** Do research on Beyoncé's life and (early) career for further ideas.

Step 2:

Divide the class into two groups, with one group working with the first part of Beyoncé's speech and the other group with the second part. Be prepared to listen to the speech at least twice, and access the web-code which provides you with the link to the speech.

WES-121500-001

Listen to your part of the speech for **a first time** and try to get a general understanding of the aspects Beyoncé mentions.

Tips on vocab – part 1

commencement (*US*) the ceremony at which students formally receive their degrees ■ **pandemic** a global potentially deadly disease affecting many people ■ **outrage** a feeling of anger and shock ■ **the killing of another unarmed black human being** reference to the killing of George Floyd by a white police officer on 25 May 2020 ■ **to step out** here: to lead an active social life ■ **to bet on yourself** to believe in yourself and your potential ■ **pivotal** central and important ■ **to chop down wood** here: to fight hard to achieve one's goals ■ **executive** sb. in a high position in business ■ **disparity** (*fml.*) the lack of equality in a way that is not fair ■ **to dedicate** to give all your time, energy, etc. ■ **profundity** (*fml.*) the quality of showing a deep and clear understanding of serious matters ■ **veil** *Schleier* ■ **appeasement** *Abwiegeln, Beschwichtigung*

Tips on vocab – part 2

to lean into sth. to try to accept ■ **vulnerability** *Verletzlichkeit* ■ **queerness** the personal state of being different or outside traditional norms ■ **compassion** a strong feeling of sympathy for the suffering and bad luck of others ■ **dumb** (*US, infml.*) stupid ■ **to deter sb. from sth.** *jdn. von etw. abhalten* ■ **fuel** power, activity ■ **blessed with** lucky to have a particular thing, quality, etc. ■ **rejection** *Zurückweisung* ■ **to surrender to sth.** here: to make do with what you have got ■ **to be dealt cards** here: to be born into certain circumstances ■ **to tear sb. down** (*phr. v.*) to intentionally destroy sb. ■ **in the last 14 days** here: since the killing of George Floyd on 25 May 2020 ■ **to foster sth.** to encourage the development or growth of developments or ideas ■ **to hold oneself accountable** *sich verantwortlich fühlen* ■ **to urge sb.** to strongly advise or persuade sb. ■ **to be about sth.** (*idm.*) to be ready ■ **distraction** *Ablenkung* ■ **to rip sth. off** (*phr. v.*) to remove sth. very quickly and care-lessly ■ **band-aid** *Pflaster* ■ **to acknowledge sb./sth.** to accept the truth or existence of sb./sth. ■ **to nurture sb./sth.** to take care of, feed and protect sb./sth. ■ **at the brink** at the point where a new and different situation is about to begin

Step 3:

Exchange your **general understanding** of the speech with your group and briefly summarize the gist of the speech to each other.

Step 4:
Now, listen to your part of Beyoncé's speech again, paying particular attention to these details:

1
- Beyoncé's welcoming remarks
- Beyoncé's references to Black Lives Matter
- Beyoncé's personal experiences with school and education
- the achievements and expectations of the students
- Beyoncé's development into becoming a successful businesswoman and artist
- the importance of black people and black lives

2
- Beyoncé's understanding of brilliance and excellence
- experiencing negativity and how to deal with it
- coping with surrender and loss
- investing in one's future and the future in general
- improving oneself and being a leader

WES-121500-001 Additionally, you can use worksheets 1.1 (part 1) and 1.2 (part 2) for a detailed listening comprehension.

Step 5:
Finally, the groups mix and share the information they have collected.

Step 6:
Now, write a summary of about 200 words, using your notes. Try to use your own words and follow the **introduction – main part – conclusion** pattern. First, write an introductory sentence that answers the w-questions.
Be careful to use the simple present and do not use any direct speech or quotations.

Begin like this: *In a virtual commencement address given to the class of 2020 on 7 June 2020, the famous singer Beyoncé expresses her thoughts on …*

Tips on vocab

to deliver a speech ■ to address an audience ■ to pay compliments to ■ to be critical about ■ to express concerns ■ to demand change ■ to motivate/encourage sb. ■ to set an example ■ to name and shame sb./sth.

ANALYSIS

2. Examine and analyse the relevant rhetorical devices* Beyoncé has employed in her speech and explain how they serve to appeal to the students and motivate them.

Step 1:
Beyoncé's speech is clearly argumentative and aims at motivating, encouraging and influencing the listeners.
Accordingly, it is important to have a look at the **train of thought*** and **line of argument*** to better understand the structure of the speech and intentions of the speaker.
a) Choose **one part of the speech** which you want to examine.
b) Following the order of topics, filter out essential aspects and arrange them in a flow chart that illustrates the logical order of arguments.

WES-121500-001 You can use worksheet 1.3 for your notes.

Step 2:

Beyoncé's core intention is to encourage and motivate students, and she has employed several rhetorical devices* to support her **message** and **appeal** to the audience.
Listen to the speech another time and take notes on the most relevant devices such as

- the use of positive emotive word fields,
- positive examples,
- personal experience,
- striking keywords and metaphors*,
- the use of personal pronouns (I, you, we, etc.).

Exchange your findings and results with a partner to clarify possible questions and make additions and/or corrections.

Step 3:

Finally, using your results, write an analysis of the speech in about 350 words.
Use the Tips on vocab boxes on p. 19 for further help and make sure to paraphrase the speaker's remarks, using indirect speech.
Remember to
a) use the simple present mainly for your analysis and
b) give evidence from the speech to support the accuracy of your analysis.

Example:
In 2020, the famous singer and artist Beyoncé gave a virtual commencement speech to the graduates of 2020 in which she encourages and motivates students to …
→ Focus on Skills, Analysis of a Political Speech, p. 242
→ Focus on Skills, Analysis of a Non-Fictional Text, p. 237
→ Focus on Language, Vocabulary for Text Analysis, p. 249

ACTIVITIES

3. In her speech, Beyoncé very much idealizes the idea of "becoming a leader", "stepping out" and improving oneself.
However, reality looks very different for millions of (African American) teenagers who are struggling to find their place in society and the world.
Write a letter to Beyoncé in which you refer to
a) those students who do not have a good education,
b) parts of society who struggle to make a living.

Tip: Remember that you are writing to a celebrity and renowned artist, and therefore, despite being critical, be polite and respectful.
→ Focus on Skills, Writing a Formal Letter, p. 267

GRAMMAR / LANGUAGE

4. Your school has a Nigerian partner school and you are doing an e-twinning project. Your Nigerian e-twinning partner is not really fluent in English and has difficulties in understanding the details of Beyoncé's speech. However, he or she is very interested in the empowerment of youth, and wants to know more about Beyoncé's speech.
Write an email to your friend in which you focus on essential parts of the speech. Use **reported speech** to transmit what Beyoncé says as precisely as possible. Remember to **backshift tenses** where necessary.

Tip: Think about appropriate introductory verbs, phrases and sentences and do not overuse the verbs "say" and "think". Use the verbs given in the Tips on vocab box on p. 20.

Examples:
- Beyoncé strongly appealed to the audience to be proud of their achievements.
- Beyoncé encouraged the listeners to take action and …

→ Indirect Speech, p. 293
→ Tenses, p. 300

5. You are a journalist for an international youth magazine and have listened to Beyoncé's speech. Your readers are particularly interested in her remarks on "being a leader" and improving oneself.
Write an article about the speech, using **reported speech** and paraphrasing (cf. Info box, p. 85) to report the essential parts.
Do not forget to formulate an introductory sentence.

Examples:
- Beyoncé explained her understanding of being yourself and …
- Additionally, she pointed out that …

→ Indirect Speech, p. 293
→ Tenses, p. 300
→ Focus on Skills, Writing a Newspaper Article, p. 270

Danielle DeSimone

Why Experiencing Culture Shock Is a Good Thing for Young Adults

AWARENESS

Doing a gap year abroad can be quite a challenge. Together with a partner, describe and explain the different stages in adjusting to a new culture and returning back home as depicted in the graphic below.

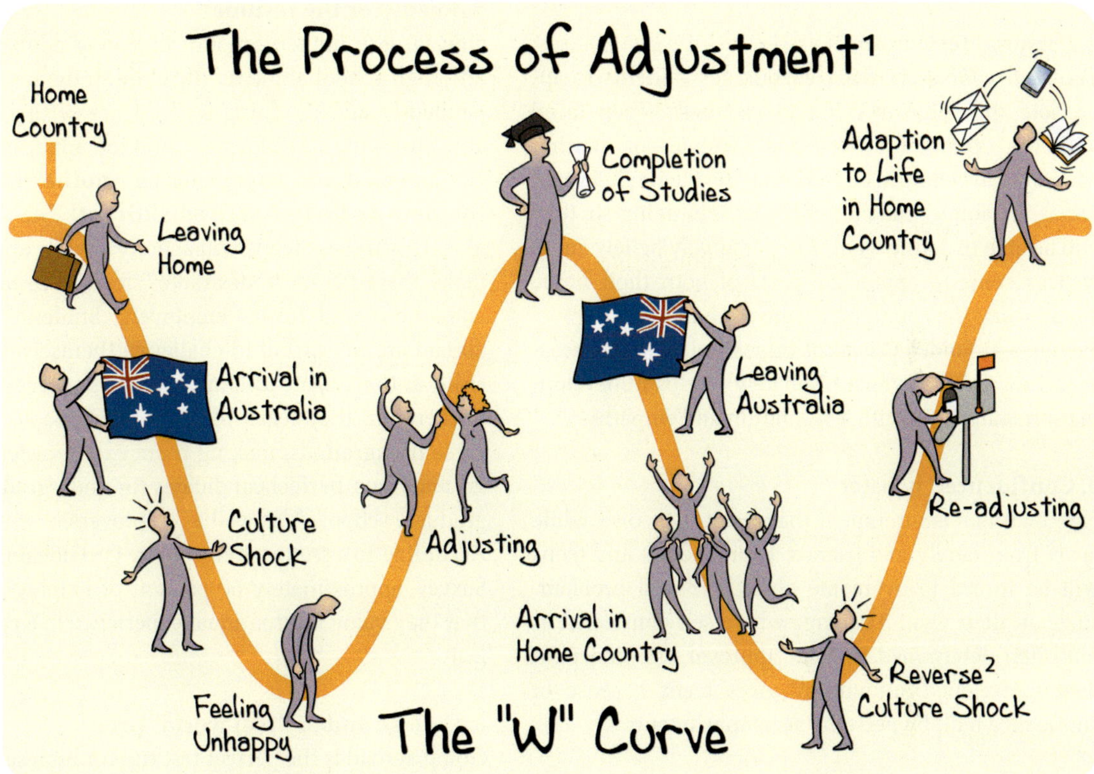

Sizing up[3] culture shock experiences

Your formative[4] years are the time that you start figuring out who you are and what you want out of life, which makes it the perfect time to participate in travel abroad programs for young adults. Traveling or studying in another country in your younger years (and well, anytime of life!) often has the side effect of Culture Shock: a feeling of disorientation that occurs when someone is immersed[5] in an unfamiliar culture, way of life, or set of attitudes. Experiencing culture shock as a teenager or young adult is a lot like growing pains[6] (but with less awkward[7] body hair or blue makeup phases). It's a little uncomfortable, but it will ultimately shape you into a much more interesting, well-rounded person, and goal-oriented individual – a perfect recruit[8] for your dream college or job.

9 benefits of experiencing culture shock

1. A new everyday routine

In a culture other than their own, almost anything in your day-to-day life can be different: how often people watch television, what time people wake up in the morning, or how much food is served at each meal. [...]

[1] **adjustment** the process of becoming familiar with a new situation – [2] **reverse** backwards – [3] **to size sb./sth. up** (*phr. v.*) to examine sb./sth. carefully and decide what to think about him/her; *jdn./etw. einschätzen* – [4] **formative** influencing future development – [5] **to be immersed** to be completely involved and active – [6] **growing pains** *Wachstumsschmerzen* – [7] **awkward** difficult to use, do or deal with – [8] **recruit** a new member of an organization

Although details such as when grocery stores[9] open, what hand you should eat with may seem insignificant at first, experiencing diverse cultural norms can open perspectives to a whole new way of life.
High schoolers and college students will learn to adapt quickly to new situations and environments both abroad and when they return home because of how they've had to acclimate to the challenges of living abroad. [...]

2. Personal reflection

Travel in your early years encourages students to appreciate the value in different cultures. When faced with the opinions, beliefs, and lifestyles of another country, travelers will be forced to reevaluate their own social, economic, and cultural values. In doing so, they will be able to define what *they* personally believe in, as well as come to appreciate parts of both their home country *and* the country they are studying in.
Having a grounded[10] sense of values and beliefs increases self-awareness, which ultimately[11] helps in developing soft skills like conflict resolution and empathy[12].

3. Confidence[13] booster

Faced with an environment that is not their own while apart from family and friends, young adults and teens will be forced to overcome obstacles[14] and problem-solve on their own. At an age where self-confidence is too often determined by peer approval, this independently-developed autonomy[15] gives teens a sense of confidence built by personal accomplishments[16].

4. Language learning op's[17] abound[18]

When traveling to another country, you'll typically find that your native language is not the predominant language spoken in the country you are studying in. Travel abroad programs often focus on language immersion[19]. This typically means that classes are taught in the language of the country that the teens are studying in; it also could involve homestay accommodations[20], with a local family, so that participants can practice their language skills outside of the classroom as well. [...] By fully immersing themselves in the country's native language, travelers not only learn a new language, but a new way of thinking and communicating. The effects of culture shock when navigating language barriers teaches young people crucial[21] lessons in communication and cultural sensitivity[22].

5. Ready for the resume[23]

Only a very limited amount of young adult travelers and high school students travel or study abroad independently and by doing so, you are setting yourself apart from the rest of college and job applicants. **Having traveled and experiencing another culture is the new de-facto[24] desired skill set!** The skills and global awareness teens will acquire[25] while abroad will make them far more desirable[26] for future university admissions and future employers. Students who go abroad are not afraid to challenge themselves, to take risks, or to navigate unfamiliar waters successfully, not to mention, they learn to work with people from diverse backgrounds, making them excellent team players and, thus, perfect candidates for undergraduate[27] or graduate schools[28], as well as employers.
According to a study conducted by QS Global Employer Survey, approximately 60 percent of employers stated that they value international experience in a candidate. [...]

6. College and/or "real world" prep

Going abroad is the perfect test run for high school students to experience life outside their often sheltered and comfortable bubble of home, so they can see what they want and what they are capable of when it is time to go to college. And for college students working closer to graduation, it can be a serious "reality pill" about the way the world works. By going so far from home, travelers experience much of the same disorienting loneliness and forced independence that freshmen[29] in college or new hires[30] go through, but on a much larger scale, as

[9] **grocery store** a store where food and small items for the household are sold – [10] **grounded** *fundiert* – [11] **ultimately** finally, after a series of things have happened – [12] **empathy** *Einfühlungsvermögen* – [13] **confidence** *Selbstvertrauen* – [14] **obstacle** *Hindernis* – [15] **autonomy** [ɔːˈtɒnəmi] being independent and organizing one's own activities– [16] **accomplishment** achievement; *Leistung, Errungenschaft* – [17] **op** (*abbr., infml.*) opportunity – [18] **to abound** to exist in large numbers – [19] **immersion** the act of becoming completely involved in sth. – [20] **accommodation** a place to live, work and stay – [21] **crucial** *entscheidend* – [22] **sensitivity** *Feingefühl, Einfühlungsvermögen* – [23] **resume** (pronounced résumé) a written overview of your personal details, education, skills, achievements and interests; *Lebenslauf* – [24] **de-facto** existing in fact – [25] **to acquire** to get sth. – [26] **desirable** worth having and wanted by most people – [27] **undergraduate school** a college or university which students attend after high school – [28] **graduate school** a college or university which awards advanced academic degrees, like a master or doctoral degree – [29] **freshman** a student in the first year of high school, college or university – [30] **hire** (*US*) a person to whom a company has given a job

the added cultural differences are even greater. […] Culture shock pushes everyone to their limits and teaches them what they're capable of handling and adapting to, making them far more ready for college or far-flung[31] employment in the future. Not to mention, going abroad makes for an incredible application essay or interview topic!

7. A whole new world

Disney jokes aside, going on a travel program for young adults gives students the invaluable realization of how much of a great, big world there is to explore out there. As this grand epiphany[32] usually takes place when older, you could almost say that by going abroad as a young pup[33], you're getting a head start[34] on a lifelong love and passion for travel and general curiosity[35] about the world.

8. Incomparable educational experiences

Learning abroad is entirely different from learning in a classroom at home, as students learn not only in class, but in their everyday interactions with the world around them. The beauty of studying abroad is that the subjects studied will be intrinsically[36] linked to the world around the students, the city, the country, and the culture teens have adopted during their time abroad. […] However, while the subjects that students learn in the classroom are important and crucial to the experience, culture shock is the true educator for students going abroad. Learning is not limited to the classroom. Students will learn on the streets, in taxi cabs, at the dinner table of their host family; each time they are interacting with a culture that is not their own, they are learning more about this new environment and about themselves.

9. Passion for very real social issues

Nothing can make a college or job app[37] sparkle[38] quite like community service. Volunteer abroad programs thrust students into environments that they could have never imagined. As most volunteer work abroad is either community-based, missionary work, or eco-conservation, many of the countries that students travel to are less-developed than their home country, or have drastically different lifestyles than what they are used to (or both).

Volunteering to help the less fortunate[39] can be truly shocking for teens who are used to a comfortable lifestyle, and can bring forth[40] deep reflection on their lives and the lives of others.

This reevaluation of how they live will ultimately help participants grow and make better, more people-oriented choices in the future. […]

Culture shock experiences shouldn't be avoided

You're about to embark[41] on one of the most incredible[42] and challenging experiences of your life.

Culture shock is something that affects almost everyone who travels in a country or culture that is different from his or her own, and its side-effects can definitely leave you spinning[43] and a bit confused. However, the difficult parts of culture shock are what make it so rewarding[44]; without it, there would be no personal growth. As clichéd as it might sound, some of the most important and exhilarating[45] parts of traveling and studying abroad is *not* seeing historical monuments, but getting to see yourself in relation to the diverse world around you.

Be willing to shock yourself – Go abroad and see where it takes you!

https://www.goabroad.com/articles/highschool-study-abroad/experiencing-culture-shock, 24 April 2018 [02.08.2020]

COMPREHENSION

1. Give an outline of Danielle DeSimone's article about culture shock and state the benefits she describes.

Step 1:

a) **Before reading** the article, team up with a partner and find reasons why a new or foreign culture can be "shocking".

b) Why are these shocks possibly "a good thing", as the author writes in the headline?

[31] **far-flung** very distant – [32] **epiphany** a powerful experience – [33] **pup** here: a young person – [34] **head start** a real advantage; *Vorsprung* – [35] **curiosity** *Neugier* – [36] **intrinsically** *wesentlich, wirklich* – [37] **job app** (*abbr., infml.*) job application; *Bewerbung* – [38] **to sparkle** to shine brightly – [39] **fortunate** lucky – [40] **to bring forth sth.** (*phr. v.*) to cause sth. to happen – [41] **to embark** (*fml.*) to go on a trip – [42] **incredible** impossible to believe – [43] **spinning** *drehend, taumelnd* – [44] **rewarding** satisfying and beneficial – [45] **exhilarating** making you feel very excited and happy

Step 2:
Read the first, introductory part of the text (ll. 1 – 16) and complete the sentences:
- Culture shock is …
- Culture shock makes young people …

Step 3:
a) Read paragraphs 1 – 9 of the text.
b) In order to get a **general understanding** of the article, do the comprehension tasks provided on worksheet 2.1.

WES-121500-002

Step 4:
In a second, **close reading**, identify relevant keywords and key phrases that help you to get a deeper understanding of the text and its details.
The Info box will give you some help in what to look for.

Info

Generally, **keywords** and **key phrases** are important when identifying the content and message of a text, and necessary for analysis of the text later on.
Keywords and **key phrases**
- are significant words which support details and messages of the text.
- are often repeated several times throughout the text.
- represent the main ideas of the author.
- can often be found in the headline/title of a text or at the beginning or conclusion of a paragraph.
- identify the topic of the text.
- are often descriptive (*beschreibend*) and/or illustrative (*veranschaulichend*).
- often occur in word fields or word groups.

Step 5:
After identifying and extracting the relevant keywords, it can be helpful to sort them in graphic organizers (e. g. a timeline, a flow chart, a mind map).

Tip: Include the statistical data given on p. 27.

Example:

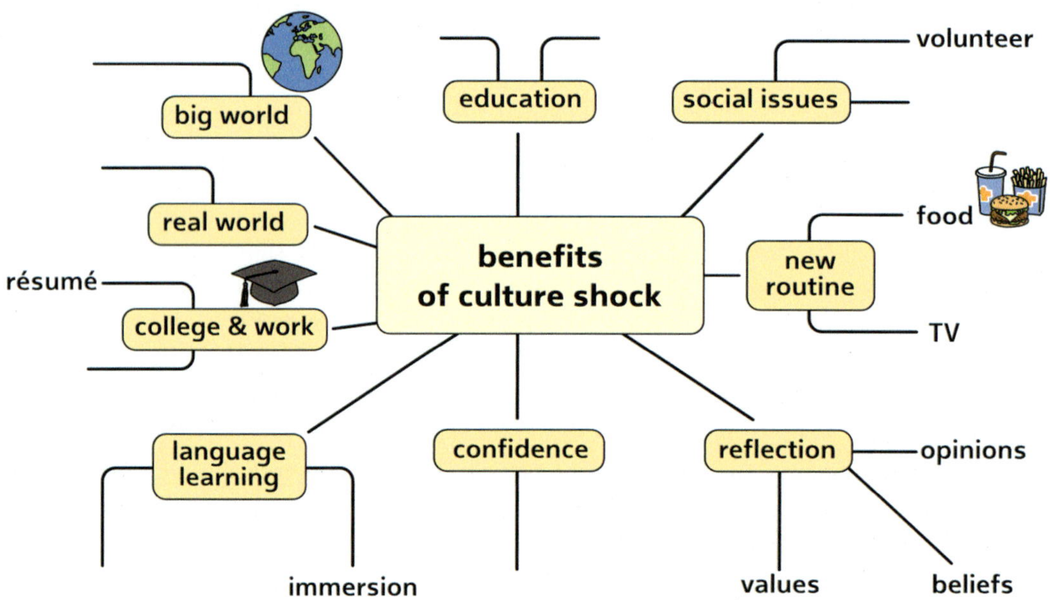

Step 6:
Using your results and findings, write an outline of the text.

Tip: Pay attention to the term 'outline' and keep in mind that it requires you to
- focus on the structure of the text,
- work out the main aspects, but leave out the more minor details.

→ Standardized Terminology for Tasks, pp. 10 ff.

ANALYSIS

2. Examine the infographic and relate the data to the text at hand.

3. Explain the author's concluding remarks on the most important side-effects of culture shock experiences (ll. 151 – 160):
What makes seeing yourself "in relation to the diverse world" more important than "seeing historical monuments", i. e. sightseeing?

seeing myself in relation to the diverse world	sightseeing, historical monuments
• immersing yourself in a new culture • …	• looking at culture (e. g. monuments) • …

Tip: Use the various aspects mentioned in the article on how travelling and studying abroad can help you to improve your personality and contrast them with the experiences you have when you simply do some sightseeing.

WES-121500-002

Use worksheet 2.2 to collect and juxtapose your ideas about these aspects.

4. Examine the specific style of the article and explain how the author conveys her positive message and tries to motivate young people.
Pay particular attention to these aspects:
• word fields, • positive emotive words, • superlatives.
→ Focus on Skills, Analysis of a Non-Fictional Text, p. 237

ACTIVITIES

5. Together with a friend, you have planned to go abroad on a gap year after finishing school. You have now read the article about culture shock and are not really convinced of Danielle DeSimone's enthusiasm. Write an email to your friend in which you state critically whether (or not) you agree with Danielle DeSimone's remarks and her advice.

GRAMMAR / LANGUAGE

6. Brush up and boost your vocabulary, finding **synonyms and antonyms** (= words that mean the opposite) to the words and phrases taken from the text.

WES-121500-002

Complete the grid provided on worksheet 2.3.

[1] **bias** ['baɪəs] *Voreingenommenheit, Vorliebe* – [2] **confident** *selbstbewusst* – [3] **maturity** the quality of behaving mentally and emotionally like an adult – [4] **sophisticated** *gebildet*

Volunteering Matters

AWARENESS

Volunteering Matters, founded in 1962, is the UK's leading volunteering charity organization, which also works overseas and runs many part-time and full-time projects involving tens of thousands of volunteers.

Step 1:
Take a look at the screenshot of the organization's homepage below and
a) state what impression the photo makes on you,
b) speculate about the intended effect on and message to the viewer.

Step 2:
@ WES-121500-003
Study the organization's website with a partner, and take notes on the various activities and projects that are offered and supported.

Tips on vocab

an aerial photo ■ a bird's eye view ■ a high-angle shot ■ a wide-angle shot ■ showing the Earth's curvature ■ a text overlay ■ a textual insert ■ motorways ■ patches of green ■ a built-up area

COMPREHENSION

1. Describe *Volunteering Matters'* promotional video clip and give an outline of the organization's activities and goals.

Step 1:
WES-121500-003
Use the link provided on the webcode and, in a **first viewing**, get a **general overview** and impression of the organization's work.

WES-121500-003

Step 2:
In a **second viewing**, get a more detailed understanding of the NGO's various projects and do the tasks provided on worksheet 3.1

Step 3:
Team up with a partner and exchange your findings and results, making additions and corrections where necessary.

Step 4:
In a (promotional) video clip, it is important to attract the viewers' interest and motivate them to take action. **Watch** the video clip **a third time** and focus on the cinematic devices that are used to create a particular atmosphere and convey a specific image to the viewers.

WES-121500-003

Use worksheet 3.2 for your notes and pay attention to these aspects:
- camera operations
- visual symbols
- the combination of text and images

→ Focus on Skills, Analysis of a Film Scene, p. 239
→ Focus on Facts, Camera Operations, p. 232

Step 5:
Using your previous notes and findings, write a coherent text of about 250 words which includes the design and composition of the video clip and the various projects of the NGO.

Tip: Do not forget to begin with an introductory sentence that answers the w-questions (who – what – where – when – why).

You can use the Tips on vocab for additional help to start off your text.

Tips on vocab

- The promotional video clip gives an overview of …
- Most of all, *Volunteering Matters* aims at helping and supporting …
- The video clip conveys the impression of …
- The video clip introduces the work of …
- The NGO offers a wide range of …
- The addressees of the video clip are …

ANALYSIS

2. The *Volunteering Matters* video clip basically has the functions to
a) introduce and promote the NGO's activities and projects and
b) appeal to the viewers and motivate them to participate.

Examine the rhetorical devices that are used in the video clip and explain how they support the message to and effect on the viewer. Pay particular attention to:
- the choice of (positive emotive) words, adjectives, etc.
- the use of pronouns/grammatical persons as patterns of solidarity and identification

WES-121500-003

Worksheet 3.3 provides you with a transcript of the video clip, which you can use for a close analysis of the text.

→ Focus on Skills, Analysis of a Non-Fictional Text, p. 237

3. Against the background of your findings and results from tasks 1 and 2, write a coherent text of about 250 – 300 words and explain why volunteering matters.

ACTIVITIES

4. Motivated by the work of *Volunteering Matters*, you want to initiate a volunteering project for your neighbourhood, town, school, etc. in which you and your team offer various projects:
- helping elderly people (e. g. shopping, cleaning, gardening)
- walking dogs
- helping out in an animal shelter
- a neighbourhood clean-up
- etc.

Team up in groups of four students and create short informational video clips in which you present your ideas and motivate people to participate.

5. You want to apply for a volunteering job in your hometown. Choose a job you like best and write a letter of application in which you
- introduce yourself,
- explain what motivates you to do the job,
- describe your qualifications for the job.

→ Focus on Skills, Writing a CV and a Letter of Application, p. 272

6. Following your application, you have been invited to an interview. Team up with a partner and act out job interviews with one of you playing the interviewee and the other playing the interviewer.
First, prepare role cards and take notes on the most relevant questions and aspects that have to be dealt with. Then, act out your interviews in class.

→ Focus on Skills, Job Interview, p. 256
→ Focus on Language, Conversation and Discussion, p. 254.

GRAMMAR / LANGUAGE

WES-121500-003

7. Practice your vocabulary skills and complete the grid provided on worksheet 3.4.

Erica Hill, Laura R. Hosid

Benefits of the College 'Gap Year'

AWARENESS

In contrast to the past, when young Americans tried to finish school/college and find a job as soon as possible, taking a gap year has become increasingly popular in the US.
A prominent example is the former US president Barack Obama's eldest daughter Malia, who took a gap year before going to university. She spent 12 months on an extended trip to Bolivia and Peru, which was organized by the company *Where There Be Dragons*, a company that promotes "immersive and responsible" travel aimed at enhancing social and environmental responsibility. Participants stay with local families and enjoy "cross-cultural and experiential education".
However, participating in these trips is pricey, and trips to Asia, Africa, Latin America or the USA cost between \$6,000 and \$19,000. The company's name derives from the Latin phrase *Hic sunt dracones*, a phrase used for maps in the 16th century to indicate the edges of the unknown.

Despite some young people's desire to travel, there might be other reasons for taking a gap year before going to college or university.
In groups of 3 – 4 students, collect ideas about possible reasons for taking a year off and their (assumed) benefits.

COMPREHENSION

1. Listen to the interview with the education expert Laura R. Hosid and summarize her remarks on the benefits of a college gap year.

WES-121500-004

Step 1:
Listen to the interview, which is provided on the webcode, and try to **understand the gist** (= general meaning) of what is said. Take notes on what the education expert Laura R. Hosid says about:
- Malia Obama,
- the general meaning of the term 'gap year',
- the most common reasons for taking a gap year in the US.

Tip: Do not try to understand every detail immediately. Listen for the main idea (key nouns, names, years, etc.), and do not bother about words or phrases you do not know. Focus on an overall understanding instead.
→ Focus on Skills, Listening Comprehension, p. 225

Tips on vocab

applicant *Bewerber* ■ **to opt** to make a choice ■ **increasingly** becoming larger in amount or size ■ **grad** (*US, infml.*) graduate; a person who has finished school, college, university ■ **mature** behaving like an adult ■ **pricey** (*infml.*) expensive ■ **misconception** *Irrglaube* ■ **to take time off** (*phr. v.*) to use a period of time for a purpose that is different from what a person usually does ■ **to gain** to get sth. useful or positive ■ **maturity** the quality of behaving mentally and emotionally like an adult ■ **pre-med** a student who is doing a course that prepares him or her for medical school ■ **to shadow sb.** to follow sb. while they are at work in order to learn about that person's job ■ **to be fried** (*US, infml.*) to be exhausted or worn out ■ **loan** *Darlehen, Kredit* ■ **major** the main subject that a college or university student is studying

WES-121500-004

Step 2:
Listen to the interview **a second time**, trying to understand the **details**, gather more information and do the tasks on worksheet 4.1.

WES-121500-004

Step 3:
Using your previous findings and results, sort the reasons for gap years as well as the concerns and benefits mentioned in the interview into the respective category. Use worksheet 4.2 for your notes.

reasons	concerns	benefits
• burnout • …	• pricey • …	• exploring … • …

Step 4:
Now, write a summary of the interview in about 200 words, using your notes. Try to use your own words and follow the **introduction – main part – conclusion** pattern. First, write an introductory sentence that answers the w-questions (who – what – where – when – why). Be careful to use the simple present and do not use any direct speech or quotations.

Begin like this: In an interview, given on the US TV channel MSNBC in 2016, the education expert Laura R. Hosid explains her understanding of the benefits of …

→ Focus on Skills, Writing a Summary, p. 231

Tips on vocab

to introduce a topic by … ■ to explain reasons for … ■ to refer to examples of … ■ to express concerns about … ■ to be critical of/about … ■ to highlight the benefits of … ■ to relativize the risks of … ■ to calm down concerned parents ■ to justify sth. ■ to explain the background of

ANALYSIS

2. An American pen pal of yours wants to convince his/her parents to allow him/her to take a break for a gap year. Although his/her parents have watched the TV interview, they are quite critical of and concerned about the idea. You have come across a German online article on stress and burnout symptoms of students and think it might be helpful for your friend.

M Mediate the article from *Euroakademie* (p. 33) and explain to your friend what the author thinks about
- the reasons for stress and burnout of students and children,
- overly ambitious parents,
- the impact of stress on students' health,
- the importance of leisure time.

→ Focus on Skills, Mediation, p. 253

3. Team up with a partner and
a) describe the cartoon,
b) explain the cartoon's message and relate it to the MSNBC interview.

→ Focus on Skills, Analysis of Cartoons, p. 244

"IF MY TEACHER CAN TAKE A SABBATICAL, WHY CAN'T I?"

ACTIVITIES

4. Comment critically on and evaluate the ideas presented in the interview as well as in the German online article. Against the background of rising numbers of students suffering from stress and burnout symptoms, are gap years a solution to coping with the pressure to perform (= *Leistungsdruck*) and over-extension (= *Überforderung*) in school?

→ Focus on Skills, Writing a Newspaper Commentary/an Editorial/a Blog Post, p. 266

GRAMMAR / LANGUAGE

5. Think about the pros and cons, possible benefits and risks of gap years given in the interview again and make if-sentences (types I, II, III).

Example:
- If Malia Obama didn't have wealthy parents, she couldn't afford to ... (type II)

→ Conditional Sentences (If-Clauses), p. 292

Anna Rüppel

Stress und Burnout: Kinder brauchen Freizeit[1]

Maja hat einen vollen Terminkalender[2]: montags Klavierunterricht, mittwochs Ballett, am Donnerstag geht sie zur Nachhilfe[3] und freitags zum Englischkurs. Natürlich muss sie auch zur Schule, Hausaufgaben machen, Klavier üben und Vokabeln lernen – viel Zeit zum Spielen, Toben[4], Entdecken und Nichtstun[5] bleibt da nicht. Maja ist nicht die jüngste Topmanagerin der Welt, sondern ein ganz normales siebenjähriges Mädchen. Trotzdem hat sie mehr zu tun als so manche*r Erwachsene. Welche Folgen hat das für ein Kind? Wirken sich die vielen Aktivitäten positiv auf die Entwicklung aus? Oder verursachen sie Stress und entgehen[6] den Kindern durch die verplante Freizeit am Ende sogar wichtige Lernerfahrungen?

Hobbys dürfen nicht überfordern7

Hobbys sind toll und wichtig. Sie machen Spaß und helfen, soziale Kontakte zu knüpfen[8]. Außerdem fördern sie die Entwicklung: Musikunterricht wirkt sich zum Beispiel positiv auf die emotionalen und kognitiven Fähigkeiten aus, Sport schult[9] die Motorik[10] und ist gesund. Aber Hobbys können auch überfordern, wenn sie keinen Spaß machen, mit großem Leistungsdruck[11] verbunden sind oder es einfach zu viele werden. Oft übertragen[12] Eltern ihre eigenen Wünsche auf ihre Kinder. Nur weil Mama früher so gerne Fußball gespielt hat, muss der Sohnemann[13] nicht dreimal pro Woche im Fußballverein lustlos[14] gegen die Bälle treten, wenn er doch eigentlich viel lieber Karate[15] lernen würde. Kinder entwickeln früh ihre eigenen Vorlieben[16]. Diese zu akzeptieren und zu unterstützen ist der beste Weg, das eigene Kind zu einem selbstständigen und glücklichen Menschen zu erziehen. [...]

Stress macht krank

Spielen ist also wichtig für die geistige und körperliche Entwicklung. Es gibt aber noch mehr Gründe, warum Eltern es mit den Freizeitaktivitäten und Fördermaßnahmen[17] nicht übertreiben sollten. Denn der durchgetaktete[18] Alltag kann die Kinder überfordern und im schlimmsten Fall sogar krank machen. Viele Termine – das kennen wir Erwachsene ja nur zu gut – bedeuten nämlich auch viel Stress, selbst, wenn die Aktivitäten an sich eigentlich angenehm sind. Bei Schüler*innen kommen noch die täglichen Hausaufgaben und der Notendruck[19] dazu. [...] Fast Hälfte der Schüler*innen fühlt sich gestresst. Bei einem Drittel äußert sich die Überforderung auch körperlich durch Kopfschmerzen, Schlafprobleme und Panikattacken. Diese klassischen Burnout-Symptome sind wichtige Warnsignale. Eltern, Erzieher*innen und Lehrer*innen, die diese Alarmzeichen bemerken, können den Kindern helfen, der Stressspirale zu entkommen – durch Ruhepausen, unverplante[20] Freizeit, gegebenenfalls mit therapeutischer[21] Unterstützung.

Ein Hoch auf die *Freizeit*

Freizeit bedeutet Freiheit. Ein Kind muss die Welt frei und spielerisch entdecken können, denn nur so kann es sich zu einem selbstständigen, erfolgreichen Erwachsenen entwickeln. Egal ob zu Hause, in der Kita[22] oder in der Schule, lassen wir die Kinder fantasievolle, kreative, nicht perfekte aber ganz wunderbare Kinder sein – erwachsen werden sie noch früh genug.

https://www.euroakademie.de/magazin/kinder-brauchen-freizeit/, 21 July 2020 [31.12.2020]

[1] leisure time – [2] agenda – [3] tutoring – [4] to cavort – [5] inaction – [6] to miss out – [7] to over-exert – [8] to socialize – [9] to train – [10] motor skills – [11] pressure to perform – [12] to project sth. onto sb. – [13] junior – [14] sluggish – [15] karate – [16] preference – [17] assistance measures – [18] to be jam-packed with appointments – [19] pressure to achieve grades – [20] not to have a heavy schedule – [21] therapeutic – [22] nursery

Osval

Migrant Youth

AWARENESS

In 2017, there were about 258 million migrants worldwide, of whom approximately 30 million were children and young people. The word migrant derives from the Latin verb 'migrare' which in fact has various meanings: to wander/to hike, to emigrate, to travel, to walk, etc. and generally refers to a person who moves from one place to another.

Do further research and try to find more precise definitions of the word 'migrant' and what groups of people it includes.

→ Focus on Skills, Doing Research and Citing Sources, p. 262

Migrant Youth by Osval, 15 April 2019

Tips on vocab

a backpacker ■ to carry a back-pack/rucksack ■ to wear a (blue) T-shirt/blue jeans ■ walking shoes/hiking boots ■ (to sit on) a suitcase/roller bag ■ to juggle with sth. ■ globe(s) ■ a white halo ■ a light grey background ■ to have an emotionless facial expression

COMPREHENSION

1. Describe the cartoon and identify the visual references and the allusions that are used.

WES-121500-005

Step 1:

In order to get an overview of the various elements the cartoon depicts, complete the labels in the margin of worksheet 5.1. Add further labels and take further notes on details of the cartoon.

The cartoon "Migrant Youth":

Step 2:
Describe the cartoon and, in a **first more general description**, focus on
a) the most relevant eye-catching components,
b) the use of colour, or the lack of it,
c) visual symbols,
d) your overall impression of the cartoon and the view it takes on migrant youth and travelling.

Step 3:
In the following, pay attention to **details** and describe the **different elements** of the cartoon:
- the arrangement of the different elements
- the combination of visual and textual elements (e. g. the title)
- allusions or references to political, social, economic or historical events

Tip: In order to avoid confusion or repetition, your description should follow a certain pattern, for example:
- Begin by describing the **foreground** of the cartoon.
- Continue by describing the people and objects in the **centre**.
- Complete your description by describing the **background** of the cartoon.

→ Focus on Skills, Analysis of Cartoons, p. 244

Step 4:
Using your notes and the Tips on vocab box, describe the cartoon in a coherent text of about 150 – 200 words.

Tip: Use the present progressive as the general tense to describe the cartoon.

The article "Addressing Rural Youth Distress Migration":

Step 5:
For the purpose of getting a deeper understanding of the symbolic elements of the cartoon, gather information on the thematic background the cartoon refers to.
Read the article on p. 38. Then, give an outline of it and state what it says about:
- the causes of migration
- the positive and negative impacts of migration on the areas of origin
- the problems rural areas have to face
- different kinds of migrants
- the development of global migration

Write a coherent text of about 150 words.

Step 6:
Using your previous results and findings, state what is implied by the cartoon's elements.

Tip: Do not interpret or analyse anything at this stage of your work. Just describe the cartoon and connect the description to the background information.

Step 7:
In a final step, use your notes and results and write a detailed description of the cartoon in about 250 words.

Tip: Remember to write an introductory sentence that briefly answers the w-questions and use the present progressive/simple present for your description.

Begin like this: The cartoon *Migration Youth* drawn by cartoonist Osval …, published on … illustrates …

ANALYSIS

2. Examine and explain the cartoon's main visual references, using your results from task 1 and complete the grid below.

elements/components	function	message
visual elements • young man/student • backpack • …	→ …	→ young people taking opportunities
allusions/references • going global • …	→ …	→ …

3. Commonly, a cartoon aims at criticizing a situation or person or wants to make people aware of a problem in a humorous way. Often, there is a discrepancy or contradiction between the association it evokes and what people think or hope to see as reality.
In this case, the cartoonist plays with people's general understanding of the expression 'migrant youth'.

Examine the contradiction/discrepancy between
a) the image presented in the cartoon and what it implies, and
b) the cartoon's title 'Migrant Youth' and its implied meanings and people's associations.
WES-121500-005 You can use worksheet 5.2 for your ideas and notes.

4. Examine the bar chart and explain the development of international migration.
→ Focus on Skills, Analysis of Statistical Data, p. 243

Number of International Migrants by Age

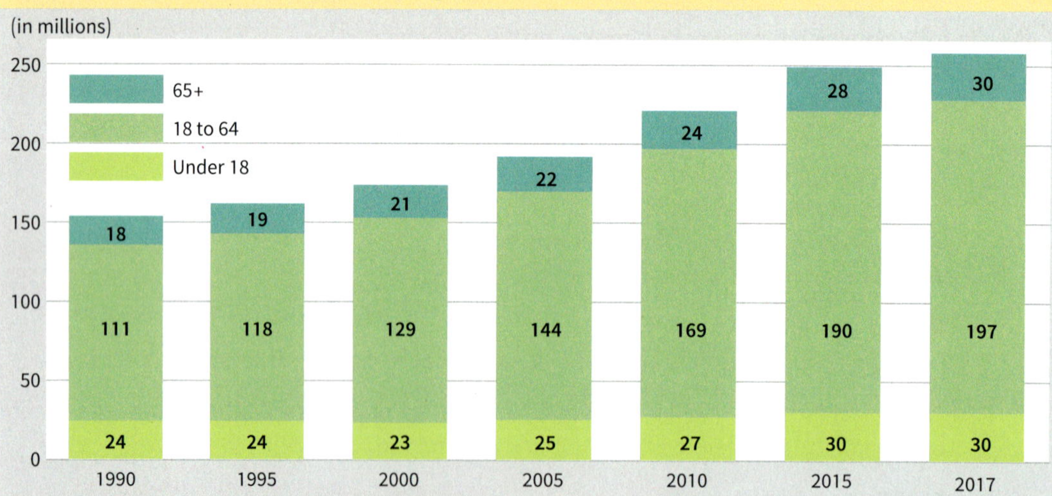

Data: United Nations, Department of Economic and Social Affairs, Population Divisions
Trends in International Migrant Stock: The 2017 Revision Migrants by Age and Sex. United Nations, New York, 2017

Tips on vocab

to compare sth. with/to … ■ to make/draw a comparison between … and … ■ to relate sth. to/with … ■ to establish a connection between … and … ■ to connect … to/with … ■ to contrast with … ■ to draw a distinction between … ■ to have a literal (*wörtlich*) and a figurative (*übertragen*) meaning

5. Using all your previous findings and results, relating to the cartoon, the bar chart and the UNICEF article, write an analysis of the cartoon in about 250 – 300 words.
Use the language help given in the Tips on vocab box on p. 36 to make your text flow better.
→ Focus on Skills, Analysis of Cartoons, p. 244

ACTIVITIES

6. Some people think that travelling, especially at a young age, broadens people's horizons and makes them more sensitive to global problems. Others, however, believe that 'travelling the world', especially in times of environmental and humanitarian crises is very foolish and a wasteful use of resources.
Write an essay for your school magazine in which you assess the possible positive and negative aspects.

Tips: Before writing your essay, make a grid in which you juxtapose the pros and cons.

Example:

pro	con
• studying abroad helps to … • a Work & Travel year can … • …	• gap years are the luxury of people from rich nations … • travelling to developing countries is … • the environmental impact …

Tip: In your essay, follow the **introduction – main part – conclusion** pattern to structure your text. Remember to use connectives to add to the fluency of your essay.

Tips on vocab

on the one hand … on the other (hand) ■ in contrast to ■ by contrast ■ although ■ in spite of/despite ■ instead of ■ except for ■ alternatively ■ but

GRAMMAR / LANGUAGE

WES-121500-005

7. Complete the table provided on worksheet 5.3 and collect vocabulary in connection with the topic of migration.

8. Find as many **synonyms** as possible for the words below, using your dictionary if necessary.

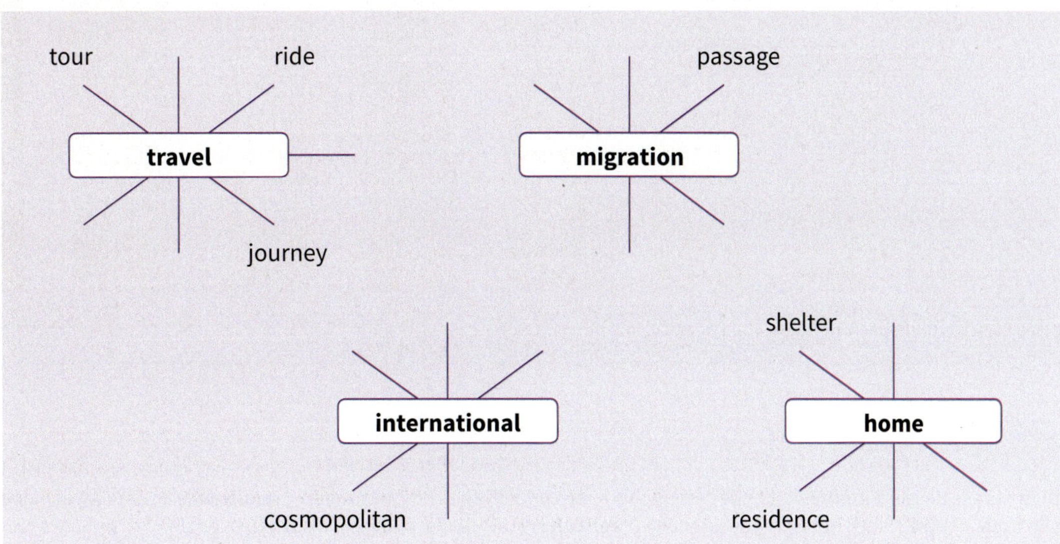

UNICEF

Addressing Rural Youth Distress[1] Migration

Migration out of rural areas is a complex issue, especially when caused by distress and lack of alternatives. The decision to migrate depends on a number of variables, including poverty, food insecurity, lack of employment opportunities, conflicts, natural disasters, poverty employment opportunities, and as well as household and individual characteristics. The impact of rural out-migration on the areas of origin can be positive or negative, or a combination of both: migrants and returnees can contribute[2] investments, remittances[3] and skills for rural development, but distress migration can also result in the loss of the most vital[4] and dynamic part of the workforce, with negative consequences on agricultural[5] productivity. For this reason, policies and actions addressing distress migration need to both target its root causes[6] and minimize negative consequences, while at the same time enhance[7] the positive contribution of migration to rural areas. [...]

In 2017, there were 258 million people worldwide living outside their country of birth; 30 million of them were children. Among the world's migrants are nearly 20 million refugees – some 10 million of whom are children – who have been forcibly[8] displaced[9] from their own countries. An additional 40 million people in 2017 were internally displaced due to conflict and violence, and an estimated 17 million of those were children.

Overview

Since 1990, the proportion of international child migrants as part of the world's child population has remained remarkably stable at just over 1 per cent, but a rising global population means that the absolute number of child migrants has increased in the past 27 years. The same is true for the overall international migrant population, which has remained at around 3 per cent of the total population. In 2017, there were 258 million international migrants, compared to 153 million just 27 years before.

In 2017, the number of international migrants reached 258 million; 30 million of them were children. [...]

Note: International migrants refers to people living in a country or area other than their country of birth.

https://data.unicef.org/topic/child-migration-and-displacement/migration, December 2018 [24.07.2019]

[1] **distress** a feeling of extreme worry, sadness or pain – [2] **to contribute** *zu etw. beitragen* – [3] **remittance** an amount of money that you send to sb. – [4] **vital** ['vaɪtl] necessary or essential – [5] **agricultural** *landwirtschaftlich* – [6] **root cause** origin – [7] **to enhance** to improve the quality, amount or strength of sth. – [8] **forcibly** *unter Zwang* – [9] **to displace** to force sb. out of his or her place of origin; *vertreiben*

John Lanchester
The Wall

AWARENESS

Step 1: Worldwide, about 258 million people – so-called migrants – have left their native countries because they want to start a better life somewhere else.
In class, collect ideas about the possible causes and people's reasons to migrate.

Tip: The Tips on vocab box on the right will help you to formulate your first ideas.

Tips on vocab

to seek refuge ■ to escape war/poverty/persecution ■ to seek a better life ■ political/religious persecution ■ torture ■ to improve your prospects ■ economic refugee ■ to participate in sth. ■ to suffer from ■ to be denied basic rights ■ to hope for

Step 2: Over the years, several hundred thousand migrants have tried to reach Europe's shores, crossing the Mediterranean and attempting to enter countries like Spain, Italy, Malta and Greece.
Team up with a partner and describe the cartoon below, paying attention to the visual and textual elements.

Klaus Stuttmann, 13 July 2019, in: Spiegel online

Tips on vocab

on the right: castle complex ■ fortress (*Festung*) ■ massive stone walls with battlements (*Zinnen*) ■ keep (*Burgfried*) ■ watchtowers ■ embrasure (*Schießscharte*) ■ shore with rocks ■ flag of the European Union ■ speech bubble

on the left: to capsize (*kentern*) ■ (rowing) boat ■ silhouettes of people ■ (yellow) life vests ■ to drown

Step 3: First, compare your findings in class. Then, try to explain the message of the cartoon. What attitude and behaviour does the German cartoonist Klaus Stuttmann describe and criticize?

In his 2019 novel, *The Wall*, the British author John Lanchester describes the life of the protagonist, Joseph Kavanagh, who begins his obligatory 2-year tour of duty on the Wall, a security system surrounding the British coastline. The novel is set in a near-future dystopian[1] British society.

1 Sometimes we would be told about a flotilla[2] of Others who had been spotted and attacked from the air, just in case some of them had survived and might still be coming in our direction. Occasionally there would be some big-picture news about crops[3] failing or countries breaking down or coordination between rich countries, or some other emerging[4] detail of the new world we were occupying since the Change. Sometimes there would be news of an attack in which Others had used new or unexpected tactics, or attacked in surprising strength. If Others ever got through, we were told about it. [...]

Although everybody always calls the Wall the Wall, that isn't its official name. Officially it is the National Coastal Defence Structure. On official documents it's abbreviated[5] to NCDS. [...]

2 Mornings on the Wall, dawn and dusk[6] and night, were times for poetry. Skyconcretewaterwind.

Afternoons were for prose[7]. Ten thousand kilometres of Wall. A Defender for every two hundred metres: fifty thousand Defenders on duty at any time. Another fifty thousand on the other shift, so a hundred thousand on duty, day in day out. Plus it's two weeks on, two weeks off. Half of the Defenders aren't on the Wall, they're on leave or on training or waiting for their two weeks' turn of duty[8]. So two hundred thousand active Defenders at any given moment. Add support and ancillary staff[9], officers and administrators, add the Coast Guard and the air force and the navy, people off[10] sick, whatever, and it's more than three hundred thousand people involved in defending the Wall. That's why everybody goes to the Wall, no exceptions. That's the rule.

3 Except for Breeders[11]. It's a paradox. Because the Wall needs so many people, we need people to Breed, so that there are enough people to man[12] the Wall. It's on a fine edge[13] as things currently stand, and there's talk of the tours having to be made longer, two and a half or three years, to make up[14] a shortfall[15]. But people don't want to Breed, because the world is such a horrible place. So as an incentive to get people to leave the Wall, if you reproduce, you can leave. You Breed to leave the Wall. Some people say that this isn't fair to the children, who are born into a world where they have to do time on the Wall in their turn. Maybe they won't, though. Maybe all the Others will have died off by then and we won't need the Wall. Who knows? And besides, the children can always Breed in their turn, and get off the Wall that way. Prolonging[16] the life of our species too, as a side effect. Breed to Leave, that's the slogan.

I should say that people don't despise[17] or look down on Breeders. They just think they're a bit weird. It's not so much, that's wrong, it's more, why would you? Why don't people want to Breed? It's an idea that caught on after the Change: that we shouldn't want to bring children into the world. We broke the world and have no right to keep populating it. We can't feed and look after all the humans there already are, here and now; the humans who are here and now, most of them, are starving and drowning[18], dying and desperate; so how dare we make more of them? They aren't drowning and starving[19] here, in this country, but they are almost everywhere else; so how dare we make more humans to come into this world? There are lots of different answers to that. Nobody can predict the future; that's one answer. God tells us to; that's an answer which works for some. Maybe the best answer, though, or maybe I'm just talking about the one that makes the most sense to me, is just, because. Because; the best/worst answer to most human questions. Why are we here? Because.

4 Back to the prose. Most Defenders stand on the Wall because that's where the manpower is needed, but the Wall isn't the only form of border and coastal protection. The Flight scans the sea for Others, locates them, sometimes 'takes them out' then and there. It's funny, only Defenders on the Wall talk about 'killing' Others: we're the ones who do it face to face, and we're the only

[1] **dystopian society** a society in which people do not work well with each other and are not happy – [2] **flotilla** a large group of boats or small ships – [3] **crop** *Ernte* – [4] **to emerge** *sich herausstellen* – [5] **to abbreviate** to make a word shorter by using the first letters of each word – [6] **dusk** the time before night when it is not yet dark – [7] **prose** written language in its ordinary form – [8] **one's turn of duty** *an der Reihe sein, Dienst zu tun* – [9] **ancillary staff** additional, supporting personnel – [10] **to be off** to be not at work – [11] **breeder** sb. who breeds (produces) animals; here: sb. who bears children – [12] **to man sth.** to operate sth. – [13] **to be on the edge** to be at a point where sth. unpleasant is likely to happen – [14] **to make up sth.** (*phr. v.*) *etw. ausgleichen* – [15] **shortfall** *Mangel* – [16] **to prolong sth.** to make sth. last longer – [17] **to despise sb./sth.** *jdn./etw. verachten* – [18] **to drown** *ertrinken* – [19] **to starve** to die from hunger

ones who don't use euphemisms[20] for it. The Flight consists of some people in planes and many more people operating drones. Sometimes the Flight marks their location for the Guards, full name Coast Guards but everyone calls them the Guards, who use ships of two main kinds, medium-range and short-range. They patrol the coast and the seas and their job is to sink the Others' boats. The Defenders are there for the rest of the Others: the ones who get through, which is a significant number, because there is a lot of sky and sea to watch, and because ten thousand kilometres of coast is a lot of coast. They come in rowing boats and rubber dinghies[21], on inflatable tubes[22], in groups and in swarms and in couples, in threes, in singles; the smaller the number, often, the harder to detect. They are clever, they are desperate, they are ruthless[23], they are fighting for their lives, so all of those things had to be true for us as well. We had to be clever and desperate and ruthless and fight for our lives, only more so, or we would switch places. I didn't want to die fighting on the Wall, but if it came to it, I would rather that than be put to sea. One in, one out: for every Other who got over the Wall, one Defender would be put to sea. A tribunal[24] of our fellow Defenders would convene[25] and decide who was most responsible, and those people, in that order of responsibility, would be put in a boat that same day. If five Others got over the Wall, five of us would be put to sea. It was easy to imagine being those people. Your old comrades pointing guns at you while you pushed you boat out into the water, the only time feeling colder and lonelier and more final than being on the Wall. […]

5 None of us could talk to our parents. By 'us' I mean my generation, people born after the Change. You know that thing where you break up with someone and say, It's not you, it's me? This is the opposite. It's not us, it's them. Everyone knows what the problem is. The diagnosis isn't hard – the diagnosis isn't even controversial. It's guilt, generational guilt. The olds feel they irretrievably[26] fucked up[27] the world, then allowed us to be born into it. You know what? It's true. That's exactly what they did. They know it, we know it. Everybody knows it. To make things worse, the olds didn't do time on the Wall, because there was no Wall, because there had been no Change so the Wall wasn't needed. This means that the single most important and formative[28] experience in the lives of my generations – the big thing we all have in common – is something about which they have exactly no clue. The life advice, the knowing-better, the back-in-our-day wisdom which, according to books and films, was a big part of the whole deal between parents and children, just didn't work. Want to put me straight about what I'm doing wrong in my life, Grandad? No thanks. Why don't you travel back in time and unfuck-up the world and then travel back here and maybe then we can talk.

There are admittedly some people my age who are curious about what things were like before, who like to hear about it, who love the stories and the amazing facts. Put it like this: there are some people my age who have a thing about beaches. They watch movies and TV programmes about beaches, they look at pictures of beaches, they ask the olds what it was like to go to a beach, what it felt like to lie on sand all day, and what was it like to build a sandcastle and watch the water come in and see the sandcastle fight off the water and then succumb to[29] it, a castle which once looked so big and invulnerable[30], just melting away, so that when the tide[31] goes out you can't see that there was ever anything there, and what was it like to have a picnic on the beach, didn't sand get in the food, and what was surfing like, what was it like to be carried towards a beach on a wave, with people standing on the beach watching you, and was it really true the water was sometimes warm, even here, even this far north? There are people who love all this shit. Not me. Show me an actual beach, and I'll express some interest in beaches. But you know what? The level of my interest exactly corresponds to the number of existing beaches. And there isn't a single beach left, anywhere in the world.

Not everyone agrees with me on this. Maybe most people don't. Lots of people like to watch old movies where everyone is on the beach all the time. My view? Stupid.

from *The Wall* by John Lanchester. Faber & Faber, London, 2019, pp. 9 ff.

[20] **euphemism** ['ju:fəmɪzm] *beschönigende Umschreibung* – [21] **dinghy** ['dɪŋgi] a small open (sailing) boat – [22] **inflatable tube** *aufblasbare Röhre* – [23] **ruthless** *cruel* – [24] **tribunal** [traɪ'bjunl] a special court chosen, esp. by a government, to examine a particular problem – [25] **to convene** to bring together a group of people for a meeting – [26] **irretrievably** in a way that is not possible to correct – [27] **to fuck sth. up** (*phr. v.; offensive*) to damage sth. or do sth. very badly – [28] **formative** (*fml.*) *prägend* – [29] **to succumb to** (*fml.*) here: to accept defeat – [30] **invulnerable** *unverwundbar* – [31] **tide** *Ebbe und Flut*

COMPREHENSION

1. Summarize the excerpt from the novel *The Wall* and point out how the protagonist describes
a) the country's system of protecting its borders,
b) the Others,
c) the societal and economic problems the country/the world is facing.

WES-121500-006

WES-121500-006

The material at hand can be dealt with in different ways:

- You can improve your **listening skills** by listening to the **audio version** of the excerpt from the novel first, and doing the respective tasks on the worksheet.
- Alternatively or additionally, you can **read the print version**, and do the **reading comprehension** tasks on the worksheet.
- Finally, you can **combine both text versions** and listen to the audio version while reading the print version in order to get a deeper understanding of details.

Step 1:
Read the first two paragraphs of the excerpt and find out what information is given about

- the narrator/the point of view,
- the setting (= time + place),
- the critical situation of the world,
- the Others,
- the Defenders,
- the Wall.

WES-121500-006

WES-121500-006

Step 2:
If you want to practice and improve your listening skills, listen to the audio version before reading the text and use worksheet 6.1 for your notes.

Tip: Listen to the audio text paragraph by paragraph and then do the respective tasks in the worksheet. Listen twice if necessary to complete your notes.

Info

Paragraphs subdivide a text into manageable portions and help to organize meaning. Often, each paragraph is organized around a central idea/keyword, which is usually made clear in the first sentence or phrase. However, paragraphs follow each other in a successive order and take the reader from a to b to c, usually linked by connectives or phrases. In a literary text, a new paragraph can indicate

- a change of place/time,
- the introduction of a new character,
- an interruption of the action,
- a change in the mode of presentation, e.g. descriptions/explanations given by the narrator (→ panoramic presentation*) and monologue/dialogue of the characters (→ scenic presentation*).

Step 3:
Now read the complete excerpt and subdivide it into paragraphs following the thematic units of the text.

Tip: Do not only follow the print pattern. If you have difficulties in paragraphing, pay attention to changes and breaks in the course of the narration as described in the Info box above.

WES-121500-006

Step 4:
With the help of worksheet 6.2, find a suitable heading for each paragraph, using your notes and your keywords.

WES-121500-006

Step 5:
In order to make sure that you have understood everything correctly, use worksheet 6.3 and do the reading comprehension tasks given there.

WES-121500-006

Step 6:
Collect relevant information given in the excerpt about these aspects and complete the grid. Use worksheet 6.2 for your notes.

the Change and its effects	the Others and their situation	the Wall	the Defenders	old vs. young
• crops failing • ...	• countries breaking down • ...	• ...	• ...	• none of us could talk • ...

Step 7:
After collecting the most relevant information, write a summary of about 250 words.

Tip: Brush up your knowledge of how to write a summary and read the respective skills page *Writing a Summary*, p. 231.
Most importantly, use the simple present as your basic tense. Remember to introduce and paraphrase what is said and not simply repeat the text.

Step 8:
Begin your summary with an introductory sentence that answers the w-questions (who – where – when – what – why) as well as the bibliographical information (author, title, place + time of publishing).

ANALYSIS

2. Examine how the author combines factual information and (personal) opinion and explain its intention and effect on the reader.

factual information	(personal) opinion	intention and effect
• ... the new world we were occupying since the Change (ll. 7 f.)		• a dramatic "change" has lead to "occupying" new areas → arousing suspense and curiosity in the reader
• ...	• Except for Breeders. It's a paradox. (l. 33)	• Expressing the (critical) view of the narrator on "breeding", i. e. "producing" people for the Wall.
	• ...	• ...

→ Focus on Skills, Analysis of a Fictional Text, p. 235

3. Throughout the whole text, the author creates a situation of 'them and us', referring either to Others vs. Defenders or young vs. old.
Give examples from the text that emphasize this contrast and explain them.

4. Analyse the author's choice of words* (word fields, positive/negative emotive words) and explain how they underline the particular situation and atmosphere.

ACTIVITIES

5. Imagine you are a reporter working for a national newspaper and your job is to boost morale among the frustrated younger generation.
Write a newspaper article that shines a positive light on the whole situation of having to serve on the Wall and protecting one's mother country.
→ Focus on Skills, Writing a Newspaper Article, p. 270

GRAMMAR / LANGUAGE

6. The future British society described by Kavanagh obviously has a lot of strict rules and regulations (*Anweisungen*).
Make a list of all the regulations mentioned in the excerpt, using **modal auxiliaries** and **if-clauses** (conditional sentences).

Example:
- If you belong to the generation born after the Change, you **have to** serve on the Wall for two years.

→ Modal Auxiliaries, p. 296
→ Conditional Sentences (If-Clauses), p. 292

7. As described by Kavanagh, most of the young people blame their parents/the older generation for having caused the Change.
Use different kinds of **if-clauses** (conditional sentences) and write down what the younger generation thinks about their parents and what they wish had not happened.

Examples:
- If they **hadn't caused** global warming, there **wouldn't have been** any rising sea levels. (type III)
- If the Others **didn't suffer** from hunger, they **wouldn't attack** us. (type II)

→ Conditional Sentences (If-Clauses), p. 292

Joe Pinsker

Oh, No, They've Come up with Another Generation Label

AWARENESS

Sociologists and demographers (= *Bevölkerungswissenschaftler*) have labelled generations with certain names in order to categorize or characterize them.

By definition, you and in general, people born between 1996 and 2010, belong to Generation Z. Your grandparents, for example, or in general, people born between 1946 and 1964, are called the baby boomers, because after World War II their parents were more confident about a better future and consequently, had many children.

Step 1:

In groups of 3 – 4 students, try to categorize or characterize *your* generation. What do you consider to be typical of your generation and how do you differ from your parents or grandparents?

Step 2:

Exchange and discuss your findings and views in class.

Step 3:

Take a look at the cartoon below, which categorizes different age groups and their assumed management performance at the workplace. Discuss whether (or not) you agree with these categories.

The cutoff[1] for being born into Generation X was about 1980, the cutoff for Generation Y (a.k.a.[2] the Millennials) was about 1996, and the cutoff for Generation Z was about 2010. What should the next batch[3] of babies be called – what comes after Z?

1 *Alpha*, apparently[4]. That's the (Greek) letter that the unofficial namers of generations – marketers, researchers, cultural commentators, and the like – have affixed[5] to Gen Z's successors[6], the oldest of whom are on the cusp[7] of turning 10.

[1] **cutoff** a fixed point at which you stop including people – [2] **a.k.a.** (*abbr.*) also known as – [3] **batch** a group of people considered similar in type – [4] **apparently** *offensichtlich* – [5] **to affix to** (*fml.*) to fasten one thing to another – [6] **successor** *Nachfolger* – [7] **cusp** *Scheitelpunkt*

The *Generation Alpha* label, if it lasts, follows the roughly 15-year cycle of generational delineations[8]. Those delineations keep coming, even as, because of a variety[9] of demographic factors, they seem to be getting less and less meaningful as a way of segmenting[10] the population; in recent decades, there hasn't been a clear-cut[11] demographic development, like the postwar baby boom, to define a generation around, so the dividing lines are pretty arbitrary[12]. How much do members of this new generation, or any generation, really have in common?
A picture of Generation Alpha, if a blurry[13] one, is starting to emerge[14]. In various articles about its members, analysts have stated that they are or will grow up to be the best-educated generation ever, the most technologically immersed[15], the wealthiest, and the generation more likely than any in the past century to spend some or all of their childhood in living arrangements without both of their biological parents. These are all notable[16] features[17], but some of them are broad and fairly low-stakes[18] observations, given that the global population has been getting richer, better educated, and more exposed[19] to digital technology for a while now.
Some marketers and consultants[20] who analyze generations have tried to get more specific. One suggested that Generation Alpha might be particularly impatient because they'll be used to technology fulfilling their desires from an early age. And a branding agency recently polled a bunch of 7-to-9-year-olds on a wide range of mostly nondivisive[21] issues[22] (such as the importance of "making sure everyone has enough food to eat") and arrived at the conclusion that Generation Alpha "cares more about all issues than their Millennial and Baby Boomer [predecessors[23]] did when they were kids, or even than they do now."
Many of these takeaways[24] seem premature[25], or at least overeager[26]. "They're still kids," says Dan Woodman, a sociology professor at the University of Melbourne who studies generational labels. "A lot of things we attach to a generation are around the way they start to think about politics, the way they engage with the culture, and [whether they] are a wellspring[27] of new social movements." The narrative[28] of a generation, he told me, "starts to get filled in with some meaningful – maybe not correct, but at least substantial[29] – content probably more when they start to enter their teens."
The term *Generation Alpha* is usually credited to[30] Mark McCrindle, a generational researcher in Australia who runs a consulting agency. McCrindle told me that the name originated from an online survey he ran in 2008 [...].
One popular option from the survey was "Generation A," but, McCrindle told me in an email, he thought the name for a cohort[31] that would shape the future shouldn't "be labelled by going back to the beginning." So once the Latin alphabet was exhausted[32], he hopped over to the Greek one – "the start of something new." [...]
2 For researchers and consultants[33], picking a winning name and becoming an authority on a particular generation can be highly lucrative[34]. [...]
Of course, the enthusiasm about naming generations isn't just among marketers and consultants. People "do love generations talk," Woodman said. They're "drawn to using these labels to pin down something they intuitively[35] feel about young or old people these days." He thinks that this desire is strong when the world is perceived[36] to be changing rapidly – people want to be able to identify their position amid the flux[37].
Unfortunately, though, "generations talk" can often devolve[38] into stereotyping, as generational labels necessarily lump[39] together people with a wide variety of experiences. [...]
"There's a continuous stream of people emerging in a population. How do we draw the line between the end of one cohort and the beginning of another?" said Rick Settersten, a professor of human development and family sciences at Oregon State University. "At some point, it's an arbitrary[40] game."
In some regards, the game is more arbitrary now than it used to be. [...] The age range of first-time mothers – whether they are 21, or 31, or 41 – "has widened dra-

[8] **delineation** *Abgrenzung* – [9] **variety** [və'raɪəti] *Vielzahl, Vielfalt* – [10] **to segment** to divide into different parts – [11] **clear-cut** distinct, easy to define – [12] **arbitrary** *willkürlich* – [13] **blurry** sth. that you cannot see clearly – [14] **to emerge** to appear by coming out of sth. – [15] **to immerse** to become completely involved in sth. – [16] **notable** *beachtlich* – [17] **feature** a typical quality of sth. – [18] **low-stakes** low-risk – [19] **to expose sb. to sth.** *jdn. etw. aussetzen* – [20] **consultant** specialist – [21] **nondivisive** sth. that cannot be separated – [22] **issue** a subject or problem that people are thinking and/or talking about - [23] **predecessor** *Vorgänger(in)* – [24] **takeaway** key point – [25] **premature** happening too soon – [26] **overeager** *übereifrig* – [27] **wellspring** source – [28] **narrative** description – [29] **substantial** important – [30] **to credit sth. to sb.** *jdm. etw. zuschreiben* – [31] **cohort** a group of people of the same age – [32] **exhausted** used up – [33] **consultant** *Berater, Gutachter* – [34] **lucrative** producing a lot of money – [35] **intuitively** instinctively – [36] **to perceive** to have a belief about sb./sth. – [37] **flux** continuous change – [38] **to devolve** to (cause power or responsibility to) be given to other people – [39] **to lump** (*phr. v.*; *infml.*) *über einen Kamm scheren* – [40] **arbitrary** *willkürlich*

matically," Settersten wrote in an email. "They share a life event – they all had first births at the same time – but they potentially come from different 'generations.'" (He put the term in scare quotes[41] to note that generations are essentially social constructs.) Woodman raised this point about other life milestones, such as leaving one's childhood home, starting a committed relationship[42], and purchasing[43] a house. "The life course isn't as synchronized as it once was, where everyone does stuff at the same time," he said.

That means that, from here on out, even more diversity[44] of human experience has to be crammed into[45] broad generational labels. Woodman said that "attach[ing] attributes to an entire group, like optimistic or pessimistic or entitled[46], snowflakey[47], resilient[48], or whatever, has always been a stretch[49], but it'll probably get even less helpful as time goes on."

Settersten made a similar point: "It probably has gotten more difficult to distinguish one generation from another, especially if you can't point to meaningful things that might define it, like a baby boom or bust[50]; or a historical event like the Great Recession[51]; or maybe the emergence[52] of some new technology, if we had reason to believe that it would mark [people] as a distinct group."

The march through the Greek alphabet may continue anyway. In 2024, by McCrindle's definition, the last of Generation Alpha will be born, making way for Generation Beta, whose birth years will span from 2025 to 2039. "If the nomenclature[53] sticks, then we will afterwards have Generation Gamma and Generation Delta," McCrindle said. Those placeholder names stand a good chance of catching on – so long as nothing important and generation-defining happens in the next half century, of course.

https://www.theatlantic.com/family/archive/2020/02/generation-after-gen-z-named-alpha/606862/, From The Atlantic. 21 Febuary 2020 [23.12.2020]

COMPREHENSION

1. Outline the author's
a) description of the emerging Generation Alpha and
b) views on categorizing and labelling generations.

Step 1:
Make sure that you have understood the complex task correctly and pay particular attention to the underlined keywords which indicate what to focus on. Additionally, (re-)read the definition of the task marked "outline" (p. 10) and what it requires you to do.

WES-121500-007

Step 2:
Read the **introductory sentences** and the **first part** of the text and do the comprehension tasks on worksheet 7.1.

WES-121500-007

Step 3:
Now, read the **second part** of the article and complete the assignments on worksheet 7.2.

Step 4:
Team up with a partner and compare your results from worksheets 7.1 and 7.2. Make corrections and additions if necessary.

Step 5:
In order to help you structure your outline,
a) subdivide the article into thematic units,
b) give each of the thematic units a suitable heading that captures its content.

[41] **scare quotes** *Anführungszeichen* – [42] **committed relationship** a relationship in which people spend time with and care about each other – [43] **to purchase** (*fml.*) to buy sth. – [44] **diversity** [daɪˈvɜːsəti] *Vielfalt* – [45] **to cram into** *vollstopfen* – [46] **entitled** *mit Anspruchsdenken* – [47] **snowflakey** *empfindlich, mimosenhaft* – [48] **resilient** *belastbar* – [49] **to be a stretch** *grenzwertig sein* – [50] **bust** (*infml.*) here: a total lack – [51] **Great Recession** the economic crisis between 2007 and 2009 – [52] **emergence** appearance – [53] **nomenclature** system of naming things

Step 6:
Use your previous notes and findings and write an outline of the article in about 250–300 words.

Tip: Follow the thematic structure of the text and focus on the most relevant aspects. Be careful not to repeat information.
Begin your outline with an introductory sentence that answers the w-questions (who – what – where – when – why).
→ Standardized Terminology of Tasks, pp. 10 ff.

Example:
The magazine article "Oh, No, They ..." by Joe Pinsker, published in ... on ... gives a rough outline of the characteristics of Generation Alpha ... and asks the question whether labelling ... .

ANALYSIS

2. The author of the article, Joe Pinsker, appears to be critical about labelling generations. Examine Pinsker's line of argument* and his choice of words, and explain how they emphasize his scepticism and the overall message of the text.
   → Focus on Skills, Analysis of a Non-Fictional Text, p. 237

3. Describe the cartoon on the right and explain what view the cartoonist takes on the generational divide.
   → Focus on Skills, Analysis of Cartoons, p. 244

"No, grandpa...LGBT is not a new kind of bacon, lettuce and tomato sandwich."

ACTIVITIES

4. The article seems to suggest that many of the generational labels are simply "placeholders" because nothing "generation-defining" happened to define a generation more specifically.
   Against the background of the coronavirus pandemic in 2020/2021, which had an enormous impact on people's lives globally, do you think that the emerging Generation Alpha might have to be renamed? Discuss your views in class.

5. As a member of Generation Z, write a letter to the editor in response to the article, in which you state your opinion on the labelling of whole generations.
   Do you think that there is some truth in the categories attached to a generation or do you agree with the author's view that these categories are insubstantial and not particularly helpful?
   → Focus on Skills, Writing a Letter to the Editor, p. 273

GRAMMAR / LANGUAGE

WES-121500-007

6. Throughout the article, the author has employed adjectives and phrases that describe characteristics or habits of a certain generation.
   Use a dictionary and look up further adjectives/phrases that describe the behaviour, attitude and living conditions of (past or future) generations. Worksheet 7.3 provides you with a grid and a choice of categories to begin with.

Charlotte Cowles

My Retirement Plan Is You

AWARENESS

Team up with a partner and look up the meaning of the terms below. What specific way of life do the terms describe? Explain.

blended family • close-knit family • extended family • nuclear family • patchwork family • single-parent family • multigenerational housing

Multigenerational housing was a common way of life in the past, particularly in rural areas. With more and more people living in urban environments and apartments, families have become smaller and more separated since the second half of the 20th century. However, along with economic crises and increasingly diverse and complicated work arrangements, the situation has changed again in the 21st century.

1 Americans without retirement savings are increasingly moving in with their millennial children.

Sian-Pierre Regis, 35, is used to living with roommates. For the past 10 years, he has split the rent on his apartment in the Chelsea neighborhood of Manhattan with two (in some cases, three) friends. But in June, he's getting a co-tenant[1] of a different sort: his 78-year-old mother, Rebecca Danigelis.

"I don't think either of us expected to be in this situation," said Mr. Regis, a freelance[2] filmmaker. His mother worked for over 40 years as a hotel housekeeper, rising to a management position, until her job was abruptly eliminated[3] three years ago.

Since then, she has lived off[4] her slim retirement savings (she liquidated most of her 401(k)[5] to pay Mr. Regis's college tuition[6] in 2002) and whatever part-time cleaning jobs she could find. When the coronavirus pandemic hit, she again was out of work, and at the end of May, the lease[7] on her subsidized housing[8] in Boston will expire[9]. She can't afford the rent.

"I don't know what she could have done better, or how she could have prevented this," Mr. Regis said. "She worked long hours, never called in sick and cleaned houses to make extra money when she wasn't at her hotel job. She had no vices[10]."

Still, as a single parent raising two children, she struggled to save. "When she lost her job, she had $600 in her savings account," he said. "She had nothing to fall back on."

2 Nothing except her son, that is. Which makes Mr. Regis one of the growing number of millennials who are supporting their parents financially and, in some cases, giving them a place to live. Known as the reverse[11]-boomerang effect, the phenomenon of parents moving in with their adult children, often for financial reasons, is on the rise. According to a Pew Research Center[12] analysis of population data, 14 percent of adults living in someone else's home in 2017 were a parent of the head of household, up from just 7 percent in 1995. And this trend is expected to balloon[13] in the coming decades as baby boomers leave the work force but can't afford to support themselves.

Expressed in starker[14] terms, the Center for Retirement Research at Boston College has predicted[15] that half of today's workers will not have enough savings to sustain[16] their standard of living when they retire. According to the AARP Public Policy Institute[17], one in five Americans will be over the age of 65 by 2030 (compared with one in seven in 2017), "and our nation will face a severe shortage in accessible[18] and affordable housing to meet their needs."

Enter the resurgence[19] of multigenerational housing, when adults from at least two generations share the same home. After declining[20] to its lowest point in 1980,

[1] **co-tenant** sb. who you rent an apartment or house with; *Mitbewohner(in)* – [2] **freelance** self-employed – [3] **to eliminate** to cut – [4] **to live off sth.** (*phr. v.*) to use sth. to pay for one's general needs – [5] **401(k)** an employer-sponsored retirement plan – [6] **tuition** university fees – [7] **lease** *Mietvertrag* – [8] **subsidized housing** *Sozialwohnung* – [9] **to expire** to come to an end – [10] **vice** costly habit like smoking or drinking; *Laster* – [11] **reverse** in the opposite direction – [12] **Pew Research Center** a US think tank based in Washington D.C. – [13] **to balloon** to quickly increase in size – [14] **stark** plain – [15] **to predict** *voraussagen* – [16] **to sustain** to allow sth. to continue – [17] **AARP Public Policy Institute** an independent think tank based in Washington D.C. – [18] **accessible** able to be reached and obtained easily – [19] **resurgence** (*fml.*) revival – [20] **to decline** to gradually become less

multigenerational housing is now close to its 1950 peak, representing 20 percent of the total American population in 2016, according to another Pew analysis.

While that trend is largely driven by 20-somethings living with their middle-aged parents, Pew researchers found that older adults were also significantly more likely to be living with their grown children in recent years than they were in the 1990s.

Younger Americans should take this pattern seriously, says Georgia Lee Hussey, a financial planner in Portland, Ore., who has clients across the country. "Most of my clients have at least one parent that needs to be factored into[21] their financial plan," she said. "What's tricky is that for some families, it can be unexpected. Especially in white American culture, people over 60 are often uncomfortable talking about their finances, and ashamed to ask their children for help."

And don't underestimate[22] the power of denial[23]. Ms. Hussey noted that many baby boomers watched their own parents enjoy an era of heartier pension plans and lower health care costs. Now, many Americans work hard all their lives but still don't have enough savings to retire. "Then, suddenly their child realizes, 'Oh, I'm going to have to take care of dad,'" she said. "It can lead to some incredibly difficult conversations." [...]

3 "At first, I felt really lost. My situation was foreign to my closest friends, the people I'd gone to college with," he [Sian-Pierre Regis] said. But when he made a documentary film about his mother's experience, "Duty Free," the response was huge. "When we released the trailer for the film, I heard from so many people, my own age and younger, who said, 'Thank you for making this. My mom just moved in with me, too, and I would do anything for her.'"

He also sees a silver lining[24]. "In our country, the elderly become invisible. We don't see them, and we don't feel like we need to help them," he said. "But they have so much to give, and maybe, if they live in our homes with us, people will realize that more."

https://www.nytimes.com/2020/05/02/business/Parents-retirement-moving-in-millennials.html, 2 May 2020 [06.12.2020]

COMPREHENSION

1. Describe the situation of Sian-Pierre Regis and his mother Rebecca Danigelis, and give an account of the "reverse-boomerang effect" and its causes.

Step 1:

In order to get an understanding of Mrs Danigelis's precarious financial situation and its causes,

a) read the **first part** of the article and

b) do the comprehension tasks provided on worksheet 8.1.

WES-121500-008

Step 2:

Now, read the **second part** of the newspaper article and collect information about the "reverse-boomerang effect" and the latest trends of "multigenerational housing".
Use worksheet 8.2 and do the reading comprehension tasks given there.

WES-121500-008

Step 3:

After reading the **third part** of the article, point out the benefits of making public his mother's experience for

a) Sian-Pierre Regis himself and

b) Rebecca and people like her.

Step 4:

Make sure that you understand correctly what the standardized term 'describe' requires you to do:

- refer to details given in the text
- give an accurate account of the matter
- make references to lines but do not quote
- do not write wordy explanations

→ Standardized Terminology for Tasks, pp. 10 ff.

[21] **to factor into** (*phr. v.*) to include in a calculation – [22] **to underestimate sth.** to judge sth. smaller than it is – [23] **denial** *Leugnung* – [24] **silver lining** an advantage that comes from a difficult or unpleasant situation

Step 5:
Finally, write a coherent text of about 250 – 300 words.
Tip: Use the simple present as your predominant tense and paraphrase what is said.

Step 6:
Begin your text with an introductory sentence that answers the w-questions and gives the bibliographical information (name of author and newspaper/magazine/book, date and place of publishing).

ANALYSIS

2. Examine how the author of the text combines factual information and personal experiences and explain the intended effect on the reader. Use the information given in the Info box.

Info

A **human interest story** is a feature story that presents people and their problems in an emotional way that attracts interest and evokes sympathy in the reader. It is often criticized as 'soft', sensationalist or manipulative news.

WES-121500-008

3. As referred to in the third part of the article (ll. 80 ff.), Sian-Pierre Regis has made a documentary film called *Duty Free* about his mother's experience. Access the webcode, watch the film trailer and explain
a) how Regis portrays his mother's life before and after her economic decline,
b) how Rebecca Danigelis copes with her situation,
c) what you consider to be the film's message.

4. Together with a partner,
a) describe the cartoon,
b) explain the message of the cartoon and
c) relate the cartoon to the newspaper article, stating similarities and differences.
→ Focus on Skills, Analysis of Cartoons, p. 244

"I know the younger generation are living at home longer these days, but you're not exactly the younger generation anymore son!"

ACTIVITIES

WES-121500-008

5. In the film trailer, Rebecca Danigelis says, "My new life's motto is, 'Rebecca, it's all about you now. It's always been about everybody else, but now it's survival.'"
In order to live her new life, she has made a bucket list of all the things she could not do while she was working and the things she wants to do before she dies.

1. Taking a hip-hop dance lesson
2. Skydiving in Hawaii
3. Milking a cow in Vermont
4. Joining Instagram
5. Flying a kite along John R and 8 Mile[1] in Detroit
6. Walking the Boston Marathon Route
7. Throwing a penny from London Bridge into the Thames

Step 1:
Discuss this wish list in class. Can you understand Rebecca's dreams?

Step 2:
Ask your grandparents or elderly friends or neighbours about their bucket list and all the things they were not able to do while they were working.

Step 3:
Do you think that postponing (= *zurückstellen, verschieben*) dreams or wishes until later in life, e. g. until retirement is a good idea, or do you think that people should fulfil their wishes when they are still young, active and working?
Discuss in class.

GRAMMAR / LANGUAGE

6. Put yourself in Rebecca Dangelis's shoes and think about what you should/should not have done earlier in your life. Use different **conditional sentences** (if-clauses) to express your thoughts.

Examples:
- If I hadn't lost my job, I would have been able to … (type III)
- If I didn't live with my son, I could not … (type II)

→ Conditional Sentences (If-Clauses), p. 292

[1] **John R and 8 Mile** major roads in a poor part of Detroit

Oma auf Zeit: Gut betreut dank Granny-Nanny

AWARENESS

a) What kind of job do you associate with the words 'au pair' and 'nanny'?

b) Team up with a partner and describe the cartoons below. What do the cartoons reveal about

- the parents,
- the children,
- the au pairs?

→ Focus on Skills, Analysis of Cartoons, p. 244

c) Do you think the cartoonists are (partly) right in mocking (= *verspotten*) and criticizing the fact that children are being taken care of by au pairs?
Discuss in class.

1

"Of course, we love you. Hasn't Maria told you?"

Tips on vocab

to have dinner ■ elegant dining room ■ to sit opposite each other ■ to look concerned ■ to have bulging eyes ■ to carry a tray with a soup tureen ■ to serve the food ■ housemaid ■ apron ■ to be emotionless

2

"Sweetie, when we leave you every day with Sarah, we're doing it for you. That way we can have successful careers and you can be proud of us."

Tips on vocab

to wear a business suit/a tie ■ to carry a briefcase ■ to look like a secretary ■ to pat sb. on the head ■ to encourage sb. ■ to wear a ponytail ■ to look grumpy ■ to clench one's fist

Am Sonntag geht's für Annegret wieder los. Ihr Ziel diesmal: die Schweiz. Es ist bereits das vierte Mal, dass sie als Au-pair ins Ausland reist – mit 71 Jahren. „Als Rentnerin[1] hatte ich plötzlich viel Zeit. Weil ich allein war, wurde mir das auf die Dauer zu langweilig", sagt die Granny-Nanny aus dem hessischen[2] Schlüchtern. „Gereist bin ich schon immer gerne, allerdings sind Reisen und Rente finanziell nicht gerade kompatibel."

Angetrieben[3] von der Frage, warum das Au-pair-Modell eigentlich nur für junge Leute angeboten wird, durchforstet[4] die 71-Jährige das Internet nach entsprechenden Angeboten für Ältere. Und stößt dabei auf die Hamburger Agentur „Granny Aupair", die lebenserfahrene[5] Frauen ins Ausland vermittelt[6].

Granny-Nanny statt Kita

„Wie auch ich hatten viele Frauen über 50 nicht die Gelegenheit, in jungen Jahren mal eine Zeit lang im Ausland zu leben", sagt Agentur-Gründerin und Vierfach-Oma Michaela Hansen. „Das habe ich für mich sehr

[1] pensioner – [2] Hessian – [3] driven by – [4] to trawl/comb through sth. – [5] worldly-wise – [6] to place sb.

bedauert[7], habe aber auch nicht eingesehen, warum man das nicht nachholen kann, wenn man älter ist. Ich möchte Frauen über 50, 60, 70 zeigen, dass da noch was geht!"

Inspiriert von der Sendung „Auf und davon" kam Michaela Hansen die Idee, ältere Frauen wie Annegret als Au-pair ins Ausland zu schicken. Ihr Konzept ging auf: Inzwischen hat die Hamburgerin rund 1 000 Frauen in über 40 Länder vermittelt – und: wurde mit zahlreichen Preisen ausgezeichnet.

Aber damit nicht genug. Nachdem Michaela Hansen Hilferufe von Vätern und Müttern erreicht haben, die sich eine Oma auf Zeit in ihrer Stadt wünschen, vermittelt die 54-Jährige nun auch Grannys in Deutschland (www.granny-als-nanny.de). Michaela Hansen: „Der Bedarf an Alternativen zu Kindergarten & Co. ist groß. Das hat zum Beispiel auch der Kita[8]-Streik gezeigt. Da sind wir eine gute Ergänzung." Vor allem, weil die Damen viel Lebenserfahrung[9] mitbringen.

Von Schlüchtern in die Welt

Annegret hat sich schon bei Michaela Hansens neuem Portal registriert[10]. [...]

Ihr erstes Mal als Granny-Au-pair führte sie nach Florida, wo sie spontan sechs Wochen als Ersatz für eine andere Leih-Oma[11] eingesprungen[12] ist. Anschließend ging's für ein halbes Jahr nach Katar, dann fünf Monate nach Belgien. [...]

„Wichtig ist, dass man sich als Granny-Nanny immer vor Augen hält, dass man Gast ist. Man kann einer Familie nicht seine persönlichen Lebensweisheiten[13] aufzwingen[14]. Wenn man sich daran hält, hat man's überall gut." Und die Familien? Hatten es bei Annegret offensichtlich auch gut – sie schicken der Ersatz-Oma regelmäßig kleine Videos von den Kids.

„Ich habe bloß Fernweh[15]!"

Annegret ist selbst übrigens keine Oma. „Die Frauen müssen selbst nicht Großmutter sein, um Granny-Au-pair zu werden", erklärt Michaela Hansen. „Wichtig ist, dass sie flexibel, einfühlsam[16], geduldig, tolerant und ein bisschen mutig sind. Aber vor allem sollten sie Lust haben, dieses kleine Abenteuer zu wagen."

Abenteuer – das ist es, was viele der Granny-Nannys in die weite Welt lockt. „Sie suchen noch einmal eine neue Herausforderung, möchten etwas Sinnvolles tun, ihre Zeit mit Kindern verbringen, sich einbringen und gebraucht werden, Fremdsprachenkenntnisse auffrischen, Länder und Menschen abseits der Touristenpfade kennenlernen", sagt Michaela Hansen über die Beweggründe ihrer Klientinnen, Oma auf Zeit zu werden.

Mehr als 30 Prozent sind wie Annegret Wiederholungstäterinnen. Heimweh? Das kennt die 71-Jährige nicht. „Ich habe bloß Fernweh!"

https://www.leben-und-erziehen.de/familie/familienleben/ granny-aupair.html [21.05.2021]

COMPREHENSION

M **1. Your American friend Sammy's grandmother has recently retired and now has more time than she knows what to do with. Her dream has always been to travel the world and get to know other people, but while she was working, she never had the time to do it. Mediate the German magazine article and write an email to your friend in which you describe Annegret's experiences as a granny-nanny.**

Tip: Before working with the German text, make sure you understand exactly what the term 'mediate' requires you to do. Here are some basics to pay attention to the following:

- Do not translate, but transform the text into another language.
- Focus on the essential, most relevant information and leave out irrelevant details.
- Paraphrase different passages or terms, using your own words (→ cf. Info box *Paraphrasing*, p. 85).
- Do not change the facts and do not interpret or evaluate the text.

→ Focus on Skills, Mediation, p. 253

Step 1:
In a **first reading** of the German text, find information on these aspects:

- Annegret's personal/family situation
- positive and negative work experiences
- Annegret's motivation to become a nanny
- looking into the future

[7] to regret – [8] day nursery – [9] life experience – [10] to sign up – [11] hired grandma – [12] to sub (substitute) – [13] worldly wisdoms – [14] to force sth. on sb. – [15] to have got the travel bug – [16] sensitive, empathetic

WES-121500-009

Step 2:
Use worksheet 9.1 to take notes in English and sort them into the respective categories.

Tip: Underline or highlight keywords and key phrases in the text and transform them into English.

Step 3:
Have in mind that the text is partly written from
a) Annegret's personal point of view and describes her personal hopes and experiences and
b) the agency owner Michaela Hansen's point of view.
Accordingly, be careful not to generalize the aspects mentioned in the text and use indirect speech for your formulations.

Example:
Annegret explains that she has always dreamt of living abroad. Michaela Hansen describes that ...
→ Indirect Speech, p. 293

Step 4:
Finally, using your notes, write an email to your friend Sammy, and mediate the German article into a coherent text of about 250–300 words.

Tip: Begin your email with some introductory remarks and end your email with a personal greeting.

Example:
Hi Sammy,
Great to hear from you again ... I was curious to learn about ... How cool that your grandma wants to ...

ANALYSIS

2. Compare Annegret's description of her hopes and dreams as well as Michaela Hansen's ideas and remarks to the cartoons on p. 53.
   What similarities and differences can you detect?

3. Examine the various offers made to seniors and retirees on how to work as a volunteer, a nanny, an au pair, etc.
   @ WES-121500-009
   Use the links provided on the webcode and take notes on
   - the design on the websites,
   - the opportunities offered,
   - financial aspects,
   - the duties and tasks mentioned.

   Present and discuss your findings in class.

4. Imagine you are a senior like Annegret and want to work as a nanny abroad. Write an application letter to an online agency and apply for a vacancy for a nanny in a country of your choice.

   Tip: Use the information Annegret and Michaela Hansen give in the text for your application.

GRAMMAR / LANGUAGE

5. Working as a nanny abroad can be wonderful but there are pitfalls and challenges as well.
   In groups of 3–4 students, use Annegret's dreams and Michaela Hansen's remarks and compile a small advisory folder. Think about useful tips and recommendations that would help seniors to avoid potential failures and disappointments.
   Use **modal auxiliaries** whenever possible, but be careful not to lecture (= *belehren*) or moralize.

   Example:
   You should be careful about the country you choose ... the climate can be ...
   → Modal Auxiliaries, p. 296

Identifying Personal Opinions and Bias

Whether it is political speeches, book or film reviews or commentaries written by journalists, the line between factual information and comment or personal opinion is often unclear. Although reviews in particular represent the writer's opinion of a certain publication, it is important to 'read between the lines' and find clues in the text that identify the writer's background and/or their attitude to certain topics.

Calvin Holbrook

The Power of Kindness: Why Being Nice Benefits Us All

Can you remember the last time when a stranger was kind to you? Maybe someone held a door open or offered you help with directions in the street? Or, perhaps you can recall the last time *you* helped somebody. After recently carrying out a few altruistic[1] acts myself, I wanted to find out more about the power and benefits of kindness.

Just before Christmas I passed a homeless man sitting outside a London Tube station. Coming out of a nearby coffee shop after paying almost £3 for a flat white[2], I couldn't justify spending that on a hot drink while he was sat with nothing. I started a conversation to find out how he was doing and he was thankful when I offered him some change and a banana. [...]

Later that week, I spotted an elderly lady hauling[3] a huge suitcase down some stairs – she was clearly struggling. Her face lit up with joy when I offered a hand. She was clearly touched someone had made the effort to assist, and I too walked away with a spring in my step and smile on my face.

In these examples the power of kindness is obvious for the recipient[4]: they were in a moment of need and received assistance. But the power of altruism also extended[5] to me – in fact, one major benefit of kindness is that the love spreads both ways; it's a win-win-situation.

After connecting with these people, I felt a sense of happiness and pride to know I'd made a small but meaningful impact on their day. [...]

In fact, it turns out that science backs up this kindness "ripple effect[6]".

A 2018 study focused on employees at a Spanish company. Workers were asked to either a) perform acts of kindness for colleagues, or b) count the number of kind acts they received from co-workers. The results showed that those who received acts of kindness became happier, demonstrating the value of benevolence[7] for the receiver.

However, those who delivered the acts of kindness benefited even more than the receivers. That's because not only did they show a similar trend towards increased happiness, but they also had a boost in life and job satisfaction, as well as a decrease in depression.

Furthermore, the effects of altruism were contagious[8]. Those colleagues on the receiving end of the acts of kindness ended up spontaneously paying it forward, themselves doing nice things for other colleagues. This study suggests the ripple effect really is one of the benefits of being nice. [...]

https://www.happiness.com/magazine/science-psychology/benefits-of-kindness/ [26.12.2020]

1. You have already dealt with various texts about being helpful and supportive in this unit.
   a) Read the text about the power of kindness above.
   b) Sort the keywords, phrases, adjectives and adverbials, which have already been highlighted, into the categories in the grid below.
   c) Finally, use the criteria given in the checklist on the opposite page and determine whether the text is positive or negative, biased or objective.

positive	negative	neutral/factual
• benefit • ...	• hauling (burden) • ...	• ...

2. Having practiced with the review on the opposite page, now team up with a partner and examine the review below about John Lanchester's novel *The Wall*, which you have dealt with in this unit. Use your previous findings as well as the aspects mentioned in the checklist.

[1] **altruistic** *selbstlos, uneigennützig* – [2] **a flat white** a coffee drink consisting of espresso and microfoam – [3] **to haul** to pull sth. heavy with difficulty – [4] **recipient** *Empfänger* – [5] **to extend to sb.** here: to reach sb.– [6] **ripple effect** *Welleneffekt* – [7] **benevolence** [bəˈnevələns] the quality of being kind and helpful – [8] **contagious** *ansteckend*

3. Against the background of your previous findings, write a review of a film, book or video game of your choice in which you include the aspects mentioned in the checklist.
Do not forget to flesh out your text with adjectives, adverbials and connectives.
→ Focus on Language, Connectives and Adverbs, p. 251

Johanna Thomas-Corr

The Wall by John Lanchester – Dystopian Fable for Our Time

The scene is Britain, the time the not-too-distant future. The air hangs heavy with metaphor. Ever since a climatic event known as the "Change", life has, well, changed. Movement between countries is outlawed. There isn't a single beach left anywhere in the world. Britain's coastline has been obliterated[1] by a National Coastal Defence Structure, known to everyone who serves on it as the Wall. Every British youngster is conscripted[2] to spend two years of their life as a "Defender", patrolling 10,000km of concrete walkways looking for "Others" who might appear at any moment from the sea. Life on the Wall is cold. It is boring. It is utterly[3] grim[4]. [...]

This is the dystopia that John Lanchester has created in his fifth novel, an environmental fable that manages to be both disquieting[5] and quite good fun at the same time. It's a calculated extrapolation[6] of our present anxieties[7] about rising sea levels, anti-refugee populism, post-Brexit scarcity[8] and intergenerational conflict, so the day after tomorrow it's all but guaranteed to be invoked[9] in newspaper columns and kitchen-table debates.

It's hardly a cakewalk[10] for young Defenders such as Kavanagh, whose conscription begins at a point of national crisis. Others are marauding[11] in "big numbers, dangerous numbers" (more than 94) according to a politician (known as "the blond baby") who visits the troops to deliver platitudinous[12] pep talks[13]. It comes as no surprise that the young are disgusted by "the olds". They are responsible for the Change but have never done time on the Wall, which is, as Kavanagh says, "the single most important and informative experience in the lives of my generation". When he visits his parents, they can't look him in the eye, ashamed that the world "broke on their watch". [...]

[...] Lanchester reveals with slow, steady control the cruelties of his strange new world. [...]

So why, then, is *The Wall* a little unsatisfying? One problem is that it's not nearly strange enough – the ambient[14] unease rarely trickles down[15] to a human level. [...]

Despite being very different to Lanchester's last novel, *Capital*, *The Wall* suffers from some of the same flaws[16]: underdeveloped characters, particularly the women, a lack of convincing detail and an overly schematic plot. [...]

The Wall feels a bit basic by comparison. But it's resolutely[17] British at least – and you can't help wondering if it's the dystopia our lonely, windswept[18] islands deserve.

https://www.theguardian.com/books/2019/jan/15/the-wall-by-john-lanchester-review, 15 January 2019 [01.08.2019]

The checklist below gives you some help with what to look at.

Checklist

Clues ...	... indicate ...
• the writer's (professional/personal) interest and neutrality	→ professionality and credibility
• background, medium and source where the text is published (public/private, NGO, political, etc.)	→ neutrality or personal/professional interest
• choice of words (positive/negative, emotive/neutral)	→ neutrality or bias
• supporting facts and references; quality of sources, e.g. cartoons, statistical data	→ reliability
• statements or conclusions (based on evidence or assumption)	→ neutrality, professionality
• use of language (formal, informal, disapproving)	→ neutrality or bias
• use of irony, exaggeration, superlatives	→ neutrality or bias
• clear distinction between fact and fiction	→ clarity and factuality
• use of (strong, judgmental) adjectives and adverbials	→ wielding influence and exerting emotion

[1] **to obliterate** (*fml.*) *auslöschen, ausradieren* – [2] **to conscript** to force sb. by law to serve in the armed forces – [3] **utterly** completely, totally – [4] **grim** worrying, without hope – [5] **disquieting** (*fml.*) causing worry – [6] **extrapolation** *Weiterführung* – [7] **anxiety** [æŋˈzaɪəti] fear, concern – [8] **scarcity** *Knappheit* – [9] **to invoke** (*fml.*) *anführen* – [10] **cakewalk** (*infml.*) *Kinderspiel* – [11] **to maraud** *plündern* – [12] **platitudinous** (*fml., disapproving*) boring and having no meaning – [13] **pep talk** *aufmunternde Worte* – [14] **ambient** completely surrounding – [15] **to trickle down** to gradually reach – [16] **flaw** weakness, fault – [17] **resolutely** (*fml.*) *entschlossen* – [18] **windswept** struck by strong winds

volunteering/going abroad		
to adapt to sth.	to change your behaviour to suit your environment	*sich anpassen*
altruism [ˈæltruɪzm]	the consideration for or devotion to the wellbeing of others without gaining anything for yourself	*Altruismus, Selbstlosigkeit*
autonomy [ɔːˈtɒnəmi]	the ability to act and live as you choose to	*Selbstständigkeit*
backpacker	sb. who is travelling whilst living out of a rucksack	*Rucksacktourist*
to broaden one's horizons	to increase the range of one's knowledge, understanding, or experience by doing sth. new	*seinen Horizont erweitern*
conflict resolution	bringing an end to an argument or disagreement	*Konfliktlösung*
culture shock	the feeling you have when you move somewhere completely different to what you are used to	*Kulturschock*
to embark on sth.	to start sth. new and important that usually involves a big change	*aufbrechen, sich aufmachen*
foreign aid	help that is given to poor or developing countries in the form of food, money, machinery or special skills	*Entwicklungshilfe*
homesickness	the feeling you experience when you are in a new place and missing home	*Heimweh*
humanitarian work	work that promotes social welfare and wellbeing	*humanitäre Arbeit*
to improve one's prospects	to do sth. specifically in order to stand a better chance of achieving sth.	*die eigenen Perspektiven verbessern*
life skills	the ability, often learned through experience, to adapt and remain resilient in overcoming life's challenges	*Lebenskompetenz*
to make a difference	to have a significant impact on sth. to change sth. for the better	*etw. bewegen*
maturity	the quality of thinking and behaving as an adult would	*Reife*
missionary work	work carried out by people of a certain religious group who are sent all over the world	*missionarische Arbeit*
Non-Governmental Organization (NGO)	a private organization, often not-for-profit, that carries out social and humanitarian work without government involvement or intervention	*Nichtregierungsorganisation*
to overcome sth.	to successfully get past a challenge or an obstacle	*überwinden*
voluntourism	the participation in foreign aid programmes that only benefits the volunteers and harms the local community	*Freiwilligentourismus*
education		
A levels	the final set of exams you take in school, aged 18	*Abitur*
A* – F	(from best to worst) the system used to grade A levels	*sehr gut – ungenügend*
apprenticeship	a course you take after leaving school to train for a specific job	*Ausbildung, Lehre*
bachelor's degree	the first degree you study at university as an undergraduate, usually a 3- or 4-year course and either of the Arts (BA) or the Sciences (BSc)	*Bachelor*
burnout	sth. you experience when you are overworked and stressed to the point you can no longer continue	*Burnout*
educational opportunities	the extent to which all children and young people have access to education irrespective of their social, ethnic or religious backgrounds	*Bildungschancen*
to fail an exam	not to pass an exam	*im Examen durchfallen*
first class	the highest level of achievement for a university degree	*mit Auszeichnung*
to flunk a course (*infml.*)	to fail a course	*in einem Kurs durchrasseln*
to graduate	to finish a stage of education, e. g. school or university	*graduieren*
high school dropout	sb. who did not finish secondary school	*Schulabbrecher*

master's degree	a more advanced degree you can study after a Bachelor's degree	*Magister*
	migration	
to deprive sb. of sth.	to prevent sb. from having access to sth., usually vital resources e. g. food, water	*jdm. etw. vorenthalten*
to displace sb.	to force sb. to leave the place where they normally live	*jdn. vertreiben*
distress migration	the movement of people due to miserable or dangerous circumstances beyond their control	*Elendsmigration*
food insecurity	a state of uncertainty about when you will next have food to eat and where it will come from	*Ernährungsunsicherheit*
international migrant	anyone who has left their country of birth to live elsewhere, not necessarily for negative reasons	*internationaler Migrant*
orphan	a child whose parents have both died	*Waisenkind*
people smuggler/human trafficker	sb. who takes refugees illegally from one country to another in exchange for money	*Schleuser*
to persecute sb.	to harm and cause suffering to sb., most likely because of their religious or political beliefs	*jdn. verfolgen*
(to seek/find) refuge	a place that provides protection or shelter from danger	*Zuflucht (suchen/finden)*
refugee	sb. who has been forced to leave their country for political, religious or social reasons, or during a war	*Flüchtling*
to seek asylum [ə'saɪləm]	to request a safe place to stay in a foreign country having been forcibly displaced from your home country	*Asyl suchen*
	generation gap	
baby boomers	the generation that grew up in the aftermath of WW2, so-called because there was a surge (or 'boom') in the number of babies born after the war	*Baby-Boomer*
to be estranged from sb.	to no longer be in touch with or receive support from a person you were formerly close to (e. g. parent, partner)	*von jdm. entfremdet sein*
blended family	a family that includes the children of one or both parents from a previous marriage	*Patchworkfamilie*
childcare	extra support for parents in looking after their children	*Kinderbetreuung*
close-knit family	a family that are very close to one another	*enge Familie*
Generation X (Gen X)	the generation born approximately between 1965 – 1980	*Generation X*
Generation Z (Gen Z)	born approximately between 1995 – 2005, the first generation to have grown up with the internet and smartphones	*Generation Z*
generational divide	the cultural differences between people of different ages, e. g. grandparents and their grandchildren	*Generationenkonflikt*
millennials	less commonly called Generation Y (Gen Y), the generation born between the 1980s – 1990s that then became adults around the turn of the millennium	*Millennials*
multigenerational household	a household with more than one generation of the same family under one roof	*Mehrgenerationenhaus*
nuclear family	a 'traditional' family structure with two parents and their child(ren)	*Kernfamilie*
to rebel against an authoritarian upbringing	to fight against too much control and the restrictions through parental principles and rules	*sich gegen autoritäre Erziehung auflehnen*
reverse-boomerang effect	here: the phenomenon of parents moving back in with their adult children and relying on them for support	
sense of entitlement	the feeling of having the right to do or have sth.	*Anspruchsdenken*
societal expectation [sə'saɪətl]	pressure placed on you by tradition and societal values to behave or live in a certain way	*gesellschaftliche Erwartungen*

Growing Up – No Longer Being a Child!

A Child No More by Christopher Weyant, 21 February 2018, in: The Boston Globe

Tips on vocab

to hide behind sth. ■ to tip over (*umkippen*) ■ things lying around ■ the Capitol building (Washington D.C.) ■ demonstrators ■ to protest/demonstrate against sb./sth. ■ to hold up placards ■ masses of people ■ backpackers

START-UP ACTIVITIES

"I can't see you, [therefore] you can't see me" expresses a typical way of thinking and behaviour of pre-school children – without eye contact, you are invisible. According to their understanding, it is impossible to see the other, unless two people make eye contact. In 2017, research by developmental psychologists of the University of Southern California revealed that children have a "we" perspective – they demand reciprocity and mental engagement between individuals. Thus, children feel unable to relate to a person unless the (non-verbal and verbal) communication flows both ways, because they cannot distinguish clearly between the "I" and "you" perspective yet.

Original contributuion

1. Team up with a partner and describe the two situations depicted in the cartoon above.
→ Focus on Skills, Analysis of Cartoons, p. 244

Miley Cyrus

Inspired

I'm writing down my dreams, all I'd like to see
Starting with the bees or else they're gonna die
There won't be no[1] trees or air for us to breathe
I'll start feeling mad, but then I feel inspired
Thinking about the days coming home with dirty feet
From playing with my dad all day in the creek[2]
He somehow has a way of knowing what to say
So when I'm feeling sad, he makes me feel inspired

We are meant for more
You're the handle on the door that opens up to change
I know that sounds so strange, to think
We are meant for more
Pull the handle on the door that opens up to change
I know that sounds so strange
'Cause you've always felt so small, but know you aren't at all
And I hope you feel inspired
Oh, I hope you feel inspired

How can we escape all the fear and all the hate?
Is anyone watching us down here?
Death is life, it's not a curse[3]
Reminds us of time and what it's worth
To make the most out of it while we're here

We are meant for more
Pull the handle on the door that opens up to change
I know it sounds so strange
We are meant for more
There's a lock[4] upon the door, but we hold the key to change

But how can we escape all the fear and all the hate?
Is anyone watching us down here?

2. Relate the statement "I put away childish things", made in the cartoon, to the short text underneath. What happens if there is no 'reciprocity' when you are a child – and later, when you are a teenager?

3. In a paired reading/listening activity, find examples in the song that reveal how the speaker overcomes fear, hate and sadness and finds inspiration and opportunities of change.
→ Focus on Skills, Analysis of Poetry and Lyrics, p. 241

[1] **there won't be no** (*infml.*) there won't be any – [2] **creek** a stream or narrow river; *Flüsschen* – [3] **curse** *Fluch* – [4] **lock** *(Tür-)Schloss*

Jennifer Clement
Gun Love

AWARENESS

The photograph below shows Slab City ("The Slabs") in the Sonoran Desert, the so-called California Badlands, approximately 170 miles southeast of Los Angeles. The Slabs is a compound owned by the state of California which is inhabited by approx. 150 permanent residents all year round. Many of them are homeless, dependent on social benefit and live in abandoned trailers or self-made shacks. The site has no electricity, running water, sanitary installations like sewers or toilets, or garbage removal services. The name Slabs derives from concrete slabs that were left behind after a WW II Marine Corps barracks was abandoned.
In a round-robin activity, describe the impression the community makes on you. What do you consider people's lives to be like?

In the 2018 novel *Gun Love*, the 14-year-old protagonist, Pearl, describes her and her mother's life in a trailer park in Florida that has gone to rack and ruin over time.

Me? I was raised in a car and, when you live in a car, you're not worried about storms and lightning, you're afraid of a tow truck[1].

My mother and I moved into the Mercury[2] when she was seventeen and I was newborn. So our car, at the edge[3] of a trailer park[4] in the middle of Florida, was the only home I ever knew. We lived a dot-to-dot life[5], never thinking too much about the future.

The old car had been bought for my mother on her sixteenth birthday.

The 1994 Mercury Topaz automatic had once been red but was now covered in several coats[6] of white from my

[1] **tow truck** *Abschleppwagen* – [2] **Mercury** an entry-level car brand, produced by the Ford Motor company; defunct in 2011 – [3] **at the edge** the outer point of sth. – [4] **trailer park** an area of ground where mobile homes can be parked, esp. by people using them as their homes – [5] **a dot-to-dot life** living just one day at a time – [6] **coat** here: a layer

mother painting the car every few years as if it were a house. The red paint still appeared under scratches and scrapes. Out the front window was a view of the trailer park and a large sign that read: WELCOME TO INDIAN WATERS TRAILER PARK.

Our car was turned off under a sign that said Visitors Parking. My mother thought we'd only be there for a month or two, but we stopped there for fourteen years.

Once in a while when people asked my mother what is was like to live in a car, she answered, You're always looking for a shower.

The only thing we ever really worried about was CPS, Child Protective Services[7], coming around. My mother was afraid that someone at my school or her job might think they should call the abuse hotline on her and take me off to a foster home[8].

She knew the acronyms that were like the rest-in-peace letters on tombstones: CPSL, Child Protective Services Law; FCP, Foster Care Plus; and FF, Family Finding[9].

We can't go around making too many friends, my mother said. There's always some person who wants to be a saint and sit on a chair in heaven. A friend can become Your Honor[10] in an instant.

Since when is living in a car something you can call abuse? she asked without expecting me to answer.

The park was located in Putnam County[11]. The land had been cleared to hold at least fifteen trailers, but there were only four trailers that were occupied. My friend April May lived in one with her parents, Rose and Sergeant Bob. Pastor Rex inhabited one all by himself while Mrs. Roberta Young and her adult daughter Noelle occupied one right next to the dilapidated[12] recreation area[13]. A Mexican couple, Corazón and Ray, lived in a trailer toward the back of the park, far from the entrance and our car.

We were not in the south of Florida near the warm beaches and the Gulf of Mexico. We were not near the orange groves[14] or too close to St. Augustine, the oldest city in America. We were not near the Everglades[15], where clouds of mosquitos and a thick canopy[16] of vines protected delicate orchids[17]. Miami, with its sounds of Cuban music and streets filled with convertibles, was a long drive. Animal Kingdom and the Magic Kingdom were miles away. We were nowhere.

Two highways and a creek, which we all called a river but was only a small stream off the St. John's, surrounded the trailer park. The town dump was at the back through some trees. We breathed in the garbage. We breathed in gas of rot and rust, corroded batteries, decomposing food, deadly hospital waste, odors of medicines and clouds of cleaning chemicals.

My mother said, Who would clear land for a trailer park and a garbage dump on a sacred Indian ground? This land belongs to the Timucua tribes and their spirits are everywhere. If you plant a seed, something else grows. If you plant a rose, a carnation[18] comes out of the ground. If you plant a lemon tree, this earth will give you a palm tree. If you plant a white oak, a tall man will grow. The ground here is puzzled.

My mother was right. In our part of Florida everything was puzzled. Life was always like shoes on the wrong foot.

When I read over the headlines on the newspapers that were lined up at the checkout counter at the local store beside the gum and candy, I knew Florida was asking for something. I read: DON'T CALL 911[19] BUY A GUN; BEAR RETURNS TO CITY AFTER BEING RELOCATED; DEADLY MEXICAN HEROIN KILLS FOUR; and HURRICANE BECOMES A CLOUDY DAY.

from *Gun Love* by Jennifer Clement. Hogarth Press, London, 2018, pp. 3 ff.

COMPREHENSION

1. In a paired reading activity,
- read the excerpt on your own first,
- then point out the overall situation that is depicted there to your partner.

Try to answer the w-questions (who – what – where – when – why) and clarify unknown vocabulary and further questions.

[7] **Child Protective Services** US governmental agency responsible for the protection and care of children – [8] **foster home** *Pflegefamilie* – [9] **Family Finding** national US organization helping to connect children with a family – [10] **Your Honor** (*fml.*) title of respect when speaking to a judge; *Euer Ehren!* – [11] **Putnam County** county in northeastern Florida – [12] **dilapidated** old and in poor condition – [13] **recreation area** area to relax and enjoy yourself – [14] **orange grove** *Orangenhain* – [15] **Everglades** US national park; a network of wetlands and forests – [16] **canopy** *Baldachin* – [17] **orchid** ['ɔːkɪd] *Orchidee* – [18] **carnation** *Nelke* – [19] **911** the phone number used in the US to call the emergency services; *110*

WES-121500-010

2. After reading the text a second time, do the reading comprehension tasks on worksheet 10.1 to get a more detailed understanding of the situation depicted in the excerpt.

3. Write a summary of about 150–200 words, pointing out briefly what the text is about.

Tip: Remember to begin your summary with an introductory sentence that answers the w-questions. Be careful to use the present tense in your text.

Example:
In the given excerpt from the novel *Gun Love*, published in 2018, the 14-year-old protagonist and the first-person narrator of the novel, Pearl, describes ...
→ Focus on Skills, Writing a Summary, p. 231

ANALYSIS

4. Examine the narrative and metaphorical devices* employed in the text and explain how they support
a) the message of the text,
b) the overall atmosphere,
c) the implicit (= not directly expressed) nightmare Pearl experiences.

Tip: Before you start working with the stylistic details in the text, make sure that you have understood the complex task. Pay attention to the **keywords in the assignment**, which show you what to focus on and what exactly you are expected to examine and explain. Pay particular attention to the standardized terminology (*Operatoren*).
→ Standardized Terminology for Tasks, pp. 10 ff.

Info

- **Imagery** words that appeal to the readers' senses, e.g. sights, sounds, etc.
- **Allusions** are indirect references to e.g. a famous event, a person or a well-known piece of literature.
- An **allegory** is a text that may be understood on a superficial or factual level and a deeper, more philosophical level that requires you to use your background knowledge and read between the lines.
- A **simile** is a comparison using *like* or *as*.
- A **metaphor** is a poetic comparison without using *like* or *as* (e.g. an ocean of tears).
- A **symbol** is sth. concrete that stands for sth. abstract (e.g. cross – Christianity)

Info

Narrative technique/narrative perspective:
- **point of view:** the perspective from which the characters or events are presented
- **unlimited point of view/omniscient narrator:** a narrator who knows everything, presents the action and the characters' thoughts, etc.
- **limited point of view:** e.g. a first-person narrator who only has limited insight
- **witness/observer narrator:** a narrator who is a character in the story (e.g. protagonist or minor character); usually has a limited perspective
- **stream of consciousness:** the presentation of experiences and thoughts through the mind (→ thoughts) of one character in a text (→ *erlebte Rede*); a special technique here is the interior monologue (a special kind of scenic presentation which is often not ordered or logical)
- **mode of presentation:**
  a) panoramic → the narrator tells the story
  b) scenic → the narrator shows an event in detail using dialogue and describing a scene, etc.

Step 1:

Using the clues given in the assignment and your notes from tasks 1 and 2, collect information about Pearl and the circumstances of her life.

Juxtapose (= *gegenüberstellen*) Pearl's remarks and descriptions with what you think is really meant and expressed.

Pearl's remarks/descriptions	implied meaning
• I was raised in a car … • My mother and I moved into the Mercury when she was seventeen and I was newborn. • …	→ Pearl has been homeless all her life → …

WES-121500-010

You can use worksheet 10.2 for your detailed notes.

→ Focus on Skills, Analysis of a Fictional Text, p. 235

Step 2:

Exchange and compare your findings in class and make additions and corrections to your notes if necessary.

Step 3:

In the given excerpt, the narrator particularly makes use of contrast (antithesis*) when talking about

- Florida,
- the 1994 Mercury Topaz automatic,
- the trailer park,
- the sacred Indian ground.

WES-121500-010

Use worksheet 10.3 and try to explain the function and meaning of these contrasts.

Step 4:

Brush up your knowledge of stylistic devices*, metaphors* and imagery using the info box on p. 64.

→ Literary Terms, pp. 274 ff.

Step 5:

Explain the function of the devices listed below using examples from the text.

- contrast (antithesis*)
- simile*
- allusion*
- rhetorical question*
- symbol*
- wordfield(s*)
- parallelism/anaphora*

WES-121500-010

You can use the grid provided on worksheet 10.4 for your notes.

Step 6:

Against the background of your findings and analysis results, draw conclusions about the message of the text.

Tip: Focus on relevant topics/aspects of the text and do not get sidetracked by too many details.

- What is (implicitly) said about homelessness?
- What is said about living in a trailer park (e.g. poverty, etc.)?
- What kind of people live in the trailer park?
- What overall atmosphere does the excerpt convey?

Step 7:

Finally, using all your notes and considerations, explain how the narrative perspective* and the stylistic devices* support the message of the text. Write a coherent text of about 350 words and use the **introduction – main part – conclusion** pattern for your text.

→ Focus on Skills, Writing an Analysis, p. 248

ACTIVITIES

5. The text at hand, taken from a novel, describes a serious topic through the eyes of a 14-year-old girl, who appears to be quite content and at ease with her situation. However, in real life, homelessness and particularly the homelessness of youth – or even worse, parenting youth (= teenage mothers/fathers) – has become a sad reality for many young people.
Take a look at the map and the tables below, which are taken from the *2018 Annual Homelessness Assessment Report to Congress*, and state the striking/peak numbers given there. What overall trends can you detect?
→ Focus on Skills, Analysis of Statistical Data, p. 243

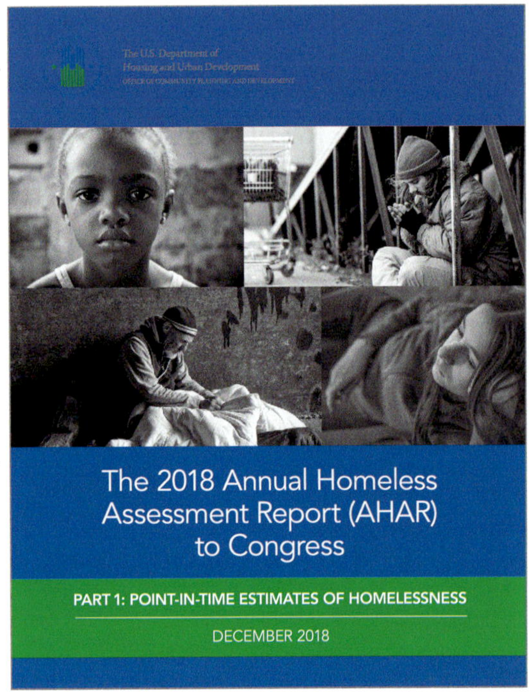

Estimates of Homeless People
By State, 2018

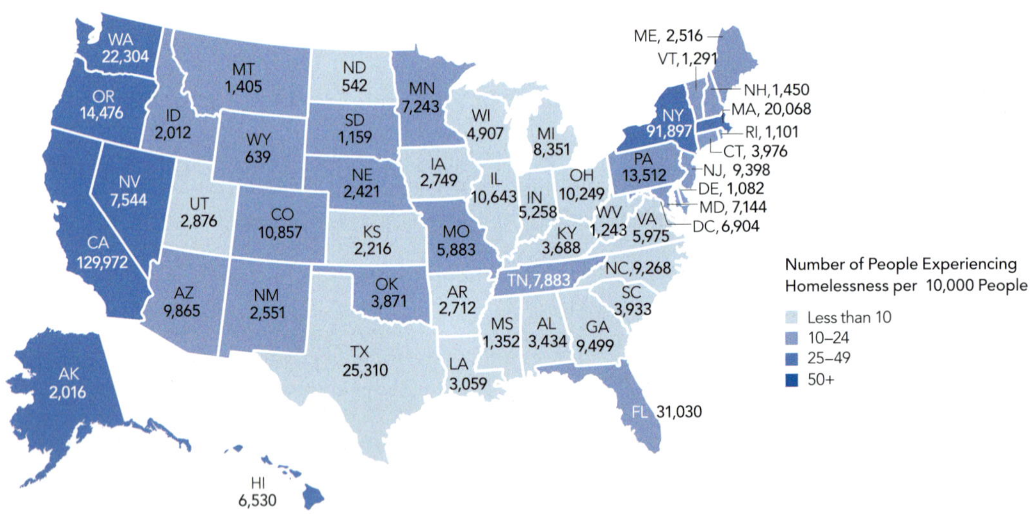

Parenting Youth
By Sheltered Status, 2018

	People in Parenting Youth Families		Sheltered People in Parenting Youth Families		Unsheltered People in Parenting Youth Families	
	Number	Percent	Number	Percent	Number	Percent
Total	8,724	100 %	88,249	100 %	475	100 %
Parenting Youth (Under 18)	87	1.0 %	77	0.9 %	10	2.1 %
Parenting Youth (18 to 24)	8,637	99.0 %	88,172	99.1 %	465	97.9 %
Children of Parenting Youth	11,319		10,791		528	

Demographic Characteristics of Homeless People in Families with Children
2018

Characteristics	All Homeless People in Families		Sheltered People in Families		Unsheltered People in Families	
	#	%	#	%	#	%
People in Families	180,413	100 %	164,023	100 %	16,390	100 %
Age						
Under 18	107,301	59.5 %	98,903	60.3 %	8,398	51.2 %
18 – 24	14,187	7.9 %	12,688	7.7 %	1,499	9.1 %
Over 24	58,925	32.7 %	52,432	32.0 %	6,493	39.6 %
Gender						
Female	109,340	60.6 %	100,842	61.5 %	8,498	51.8 %
Male	70,900	39.3 %	63,110	38.5 %	7,790	47.5 %
Transgender	75	0.0 %	44	0.0 %	31	0.2 %
Gender Non-conforming	98	0.1 %	27	0.0 %	71	0.4 %
Ethnicity						
Non-Hispanic/Latino	128,360	71.1 %	115,721	70.6 %	12,639	77.1 %
Hispanic/Latino	52,053	28.9 %	48,302	29.4 %	3,751	22.9 %
Race						
White	68,522	38.0 %	58,901	35.9 %	9,621	58.7 %
Black or African American	91,068	50.5 %	87,745	53.5 %	3,323	20.3 %
Asian	1,724	1.0 %	1,412	0.9 %	312	1.9 %
Native American	3,602	2.0 %	3,077	1.9 %	525	3.2 %
Pacific Islander	3,911	2.2 %	2,561	1.6 %	1,350	8.2 %
Multiple Races	11,586	6.4 %	10,327	6.3 %	1,259	7.7 %

HUD Exchange/The U.S. Department of Housing and Urban Development: The 2018 Annual Homeless Assessment Report (AHAR) to Congress

GRAMMAR / LANGUAGE

6. Imagine you work for an NGO that wants to help and support teenage mothers, runaway children and homeless youth. That means you have to **conduct interviews** with people like Pearl and her mother to get a full picture of their living conditions and needs.
Write down possible **questions** that encourage the interview partners to talk.

Info

1) **yes-no question** → Do you feel safe?
2) **open question** → What made you and your mom stay here?
3) **question after statement** → There has been a rumour about serious problems … what actually went wrong?
4) **question referring back** → The other inhabitants in the trailer park mentioned … How do you view …?
5) **confrontational question** → What do you tell people when they call you losers?
6) **indirectly expressed question** → Well, I thought you might be interested in giving us an overview of … .

Additionally, employ **modal auxiliaries** to phrase things politely and not offend or intimidate your interview partners.
→ Modal Auxiliaries, p. 296

Examples:

- You said, you and your mom live in a car … which is your home … could you tell us how it feels to live in a car?
- Without going into too much detail now, how would you describe your living conditions here in the trailer park?

Finally, act out the interviews in class and think about possible answers the interviewees might give.
→ Focus on Skills, Writing an Interview, p. 269

Sean Baker (dir.)

The Florida Project

AWARENESS

The Florida Project is a 2017 comedy-drama whose protagonists are 6-year-old Moonee and her 22-year-old mother Halley, who live in the Magic Castle Motel near Walt Disney World, Florida. Being dependent on social benefit, like most of the other inhabitants of the motel, Halley is working as an exotic dancer at a strip club to provide a minimum income, while trying to keep an eye on her daughter and avoiding homelessness. However, after refusing to have sex with the club's customers, Halley is fired, which causes the loss of TANF[1] money. Desperate to get some money for food and rent, she starts soliciting[2] for sex work online, and has clients in her motel apartment while keeping Moonee in the bathroom.

Step 1: In groups of 3 – 4 students, describe the film still below and discuss what it reveals about Halley and Moonee and their relationship.

Step 2: Do research on the different meanings of the film's title and find out what the word "project" implies.

Tips on vocab

in the foreground: (to push a) shopping cart ■ to stand in the middle of the street/a junction ■ pink plastic bags ■ a green backpack ■ to have a smile on one's face ■ to stick one's tongue out at sb. ■ to wear frayed shorts ■ to wear feathers in one's ear ■ to have tattoos on one's thighs and calves ■ to provoke ■ to look like siblings

in the background: a junction with traffic lights ■ palm trees ■ a nine-storey building ■ blue skies ■ a street sign for Vineland Road

[1] **TANF** (*abbr.*) Temporary Assistance for Needy Families; social benefits, welfare – [2] **to solicit** to offer sex for money

1 EXT.[3] MAGIC CASTLE – OUTSIDE ROOM 341 – DUSK

Halley and ten other residents of The Magic Castle are socializing[4], drinking and smoking on the balcony. Halley is hanging out with her best friend and Scooty's mom, ASHLEY (23) on the stairs outside Room 341 where music is blasting[5]. Some of the rooms' doors are open and some closed. GLORIA (60's) struts[6] over.

GLORIA Hey! Listen up, motherfuckers. You have one of two choices. You can all keep it down OR ... you can get a lady a beer.

Gloria sits down and joins the crowd and pops open a beer, which spills all over her.

ASHLEY I'm off tomorrow. Want me to take Moonee?

HALLEY No, it's cool, we got our appointment tomorrow. Now, what would happen if we smoke the fattest of blunts[7] right now?

We hear Bobby off-screen.

BOBBY (O.S.[8]) Ladies and gentlemen, let's wrap up[9]. We have over twenty guests this weekend and we're already having noise complaints.

A few residents can be heard protesting off-screen.

2 INT.[10] SOCIAL SERVICES – DAY

HALLEY is seated with a CASE WORKER (female, 30's). Moonee is messing around[11] with another LITTLE KID (4) while the adults talk.

HALLEY Most of those rachet-ass[12] bitches were doing extras ... ya know, in the back room. (gives a handjob[13] gesture) I'm not doin' extras. I'm fucking dancing for tips. That's what I do. I said no ... two days later with no warning Hector fires me ... after not letting me up on stage all fucking night. Fuckin' bullshit.

CASE WORKER Okay, well ... this will affect your TANF.

HALLEY No shit. That's why I'm here.

CASE WORKER Okay, you need to make a concerted effort[14] to find at least thirty hours.

HALLEY (frustrated) Yeah, well you find me thirty hours! I have applications[15] in at every shithole up and down Irlo Bronson and the parks ain't going to hire me.

CASE WORKER You can cover those up[16], Halley.

Halley is thrown off[17] for a second. She then realizes the case worker is referring to her tattoos.

HALLEY No, my record. And now that it's summer and I got her during the day ... C'mon.

CASE WORKER I get it. But you've got to give benefits three job contacts a week or you'll be considered non-compliant[18]. (reading file) And no child support[19].

Halley just shakes her head.

CASE WORKER (CONT'D[20]) When is he getting out?

Halley shakes her head again. [...]

3 EXT. MAGIC CASTLE – 2ND FLOOR WALKWAY – DAY

Moonee and Scooty continue to give Jancey[21] their tour into the grounds of The Magic Castle. They stop and point at every door. The sequence will play as if we are condensing[22] a documented tour with jump cuts[23] between every line of dialogue.

SCOOTY 216 is Abigail. She's a nice woman with lots of pillows. And sells drugs sometimes.

MOONEE And 217 is a family that has a brother who stabbed[24] someone on Valentine's Day.

The kids pass the elevator.

MOONEE (CONT'D) And nobody ever uses the elevator cause it smells like pee.

The kids round a corner.

SCOOTY And 222 is a family that fights like all day.

[3] **EXT.** (*abbr.*) exterior, outside – [4] **to socialize** to spend time when you are not working with friends or with other people in order to enjoy yourself – [5] **to blast** to make a very loud and unpleasant noise – [6] **to strut** *stolzieren* – [7] **blunt** (*sl.*) a large cigarette or cigar containing cannabis – [8] **O.S.** off-screen – [9] **to wrap up** (*infml.*) to be quiet – [10] **INT.** (*abbr.*) interior, inside – [11] **to mess around** (*phr. v.*) to do stupid and annoying things – [12] **rachet-ass bitch** (*sl.*) ignorant individual – [13] **handjob** (*sl.*) when one person stimulates another person's penis with their hand, usually resulting in ejaculation – [14] **concerted effort** *intensive Anstrengung* – [15] **application** *Bewerbung* – [16] **to cover sth. up** to hide sth. – [17] **to throw off sb.** (*phr. v.*) to cause a person to be confused – [18] **non-compliant** not obeying a rule or law – [19] **child support** *Kindergeld* – [20] **CONT'D** (*abbr.*) continued – [21] **Jancey** a new child living in the motel – [22] **to condense** to reduce sth. in length – [23] **jump cut** the connection of two scenes by omitting time; *Sprungschnitt* – [24] **to stab sb.** *jdn. erstechen*

MOONEE And the woman who lives in here thinks she's married to Jesus.

They approach the laundry room. Bertha is exiting the utility room[25] and enters the laundry room.

SCOOTY And that's Bertha. She smokes weeds[26]. [...]

4 EXT./INT. CALYPSO CAY – BUFFET ROOM – DAY

Halley takes Moonee to a much nicer hotel down Route 192 where they go in and partake in the free breakfast buffet. Moonee is most excited about how she can make her own waffles that are shaped as a famous mouse. Moonee is ecstatic about the delicious food she is eating. Halley tries her best to converse[27] with her daughter but spends most of the time holding back tears. (This scene will be shot holding on Moonee's face as she eats).

MOONEE I wish forks were made of candy. (beat) Then I could eat the forks after my meal. (beat) We gotta come here all the time. (beat) Mom, you look busted[28]. (beat) I'm going to put a strawberry, raspberry and bacon in my mouth at the same time.
Moonee continues to stuff her face. A HOTEL WORKER (female, 20's) walks over, eyeing them.

HOTEL WORKER Could I get your room number?

HALLEY 323.

HOTEL WORKER Thank you.

Halley winks[29] at Moonee. Moonee lets out a little smirk[30].
Moonee continues to eat as Halley sits in silence, her watery eyes watching her daughter at her happiest.

5 EXT. MAGIC CASTLE – ROOM 323 – DAY

Halley and Moonee come back from breakfast and walk by two police cars in the parking lot.
The Case Worker, DCF[31] Investigator, a DCF Worker and Bobby are accompanied by a DCF Supervisor and two Sheriffs.
Halley and Moonee make it to their room. Halley pushes past everyone and opens her room. She turns around and faces everyone.

HALLEY Can I help you? Because you'll need a court order to get me to take a drug test.

CASE WORKER Halley, these DCF officers are here in regards to Moonee.

HALLEY You wanna inspect my room? Be our guest.

The group follows Halley inside the room.

HALLEY (CONT'D) Wanna shake my cereal boxes to check for buried treasure? Look inside my fridge?

DCF INVESTIGATOR Halley?

HALLEY What? What do you want?

DCF INVESTIGATOR We have security footage[32] that shows nine different men entering and exiting your room over the last three weeks.

BOBBY Uh, why don't you take little Moonee outside so you can talk privately.

The case worker escorts Moonee outside the room.

DCF INVESTIGATOR We've also obtained[33] an online classified ad[34] soliciting customers for sexual activities with your phone number attached.

Halley takes a moment to make eye contact with each person. [...]

DCF INVESTIGATOR ... but luckily we have a family in Polk County that can take her for the entire course of the investigation.

Halley remains calm and collected. Bobby watches silently.

EXT. MAGIC CASTLE – ROOM 323 – DAY

MOONEE Can I say goodbye to my friend Scooty?

CASE WORKER We don't call it a goodbye but you can give your friend a hug. And you'll see them soon. I'll check to see if that's okay. [...]

Sean Baker, Chris Bergoch, https://www.dailyscript.com/scripts/The_Florida_Project_script.pdf, Final Production Draft, 31 July 2016, pp.10 ff. [24.07.2020]

[25] **utility room** a room in a house, where large items of useful equipment such as a washing machine can be kept and where things can be stored – [26] **weed** (*sl.*) cannabis; *Gras* – [27] **to converse** (*fml.*) to have a conversation with sb. – [28] **busted** pale and exhausted – [29] **to wink at sb.** *jdm. zuzwinkern* – [30] **smirk** *Grinsen* – [31] **DCF** (*abbr.*) Department of Children and Families – [32] **security footage** a film taped by a security camera in the building – [33] **to obtain** (*fml.*) to get – [34] **classified ad** a small advertisement that you put in a newspaper or a magazine, usually because you want to buy or sell sth. or to find or offer a job

COMPREHENSION

1. Together with a partner,
a) read the film script on your own first and try to get a general understanding of the events,
b) then summarize the excerpt to each other and clarify possible questions and misunderstandings.

WES-121500-011
2. While reading the excerpt a second time, do the tasks on worksheet 11.1 and get a detailed overview of 'who is who' in the film as well as the relationships of the characters to each other.

3. On their tour through the motel, Moonee and Scooty give further information about some of the residents. Describe what kind of people live in rooms 216, 217 and 222.

4. Write a summary of about 200 words, pointing out briefly what the excerpt is about.

Tip: Remember to begin your summary with an introductory sentence that answers the w-questions. Use the present tense in your text.

Example: The excerpt from the film script of *The Florida Project*, released in 2017, depicts the life of 6-year-old Moonee, who lives with her 22-year-old mother in …
→ Focus on Skills, Writing a Summary, p. 231

ANALYSIS

5. Examine the action, descriptions and dialogues in the film script and explain how they support
a) the message of the film,
b) the overall atmosphere,
c) the implicit (= not directly expressed) nightmare Moonee and her mother Halley experience.

Tip: Before you start working on the stylistic devices in the text, make sure that you have understood the complex task. Pay attention to the **keywords in the assignment**, which show you what to focus on and what exactly you are expected to examine and explain. Pay particular attention to the standardized terminology (*Operatoren*).
→ Standardized Terminology for Tasks, pp. 10 ff.

Tip: Use the information given on screenplays (film scripts) and their elements in Focus on Skills, Screenplays and Storyboards, p. 228.

Step 1:
WES-121500-011
Using the clues given in the assignment and your notes from the comprehension tasks, collect further information about the circumstances of people's lives in the Magic Castle Motel. Explain the deeper meaning behind people's actions and/or remarks and use worksheet 11.2 for your detailed notes.
→ Focus on Skills, Analysis of a Film Scene, p. 239
→ Focus on Skills, Analysis of a Fictional Text, p. 235

Step 2:
Exchange and compare your findings in class and make additions and corrections to your notes if necessary.

Step 3:
WES-121500-011
In order to get a better understanding of the characters and the atmosphere, watch the film trailer, which is provided on the webcode.
WES-121500-011
You can take notes on worksheet 11.3.

Step 4:

Against the background of your findings and analysis results, draw conclusions about the message of the text/film.

- What is (implicitly) said about being a single mom and poor/homeless?
- What is said about living in a motel (the residents, poverty, drugs, etc.)?
- What kind of people live in the motel?
- What overall atmosphere does the excerpt convey?

Step 5:

Finally, using all your notes and considerations, explain how the action, descriptions and dialogues support the message of the text. Write a coherent text of about 350 words and use the **introduction – main part – conclusion** pattern for your text.

→ Focus on Skills, Writing an Analysis, p. 248

ACTIVITIES

6. According to the non-profit organization Children of the Night, and UNICEF, there are about 300,000 – 600,000 juvenile prostitutes in the US under the age of 16, who are mostly runaways and who practice ‘survival sex’.

Although there are no credible data-supported facts about the size of this problem, the organizations fear that the real numbers might be even much higher. A 2016 report by the Urban Institute reveals that in the US, about 6.8 million people aged 10 – 17 are ‘food insecure’, and about 2.9 million people are <u>very</u> food insecure.

Teens in 13 of the 20 focus groups of the study talked about selling sex for money to pay for food. Teens in 18 of the 20 focused communities said that they engaged in criminal behaviour, from shoplifting food, selling drugs or stealing items to resell for cash (cf. https://childrenofthenight.org).

Step 1:

Against the background of this data and your results from the previous tasks, discuss this seemingly hopeless situation, and think about possible solutions and help for teenagers in need.

Step 2:

In groups of 3 – 4 students, sort your ideas and develop a programme that supports the homeless teens. Think about what needs to be done to

- provide them with a safe shelter/home, food,
- give them a perspective for the future, e.g. graduating from school, finding an apprenticeship, etc.,
- overcome drug addiction.

Step 3:

Prepare presentations in class and share and discuss your ideas.

GRAMMAR / LANGUAGE

7. Imagine you work for the DCF and want to help Halley and Moonee. **Conduct interviews** with Bobby and the residents of the Magic Castle Motel to get a full picture of the living conditions and needs from different perspectives. Write down possible **questions** that encourage the interview partners to talk. Use the tips given in the Info box on p. 67. Additionally, employ **modal auxiliaries** to phrase things politely and not offend or intimidate your interview partners.

Examples:

- You said that Halley has written countless applications … could you tell us …?
- Without going into too much detail now, could you describe your living conditions here in the motel?

Finally, act out the interview in class and think about possible answers the interviewees might give.

Tracy Geoghegan

Global Childhood Report 2019: Changing Lives in Our Lifetime

AWARENESS

The cover page of the 2019 *Global Childhood Report* shows 11-year-old Djeneba, a sixth-grade student from Mali, who appears to be a happy and healthy child. However, there are many more factors that determine childhood.

WES-121500-012

a) Team up with a partner and work with the various information given on worksheet 12.1.

b) Discuss in class: What do you consider to be the most/least relevant factors that determine a happy and healthy childhood? Make a ranking of these factors.

What has changed in 100 years?

Millions of children are alive and thriving today because of medical and technological advances[1] we tend to take for granted. Breakthrough discoveries of vaccines[2] to prevent childhood diseases, coupled with better care for mothers and babies, have saved countless lives and improved overall health. The world has also made good progress in building human and institutional capacity to deliver lifesaving solutions to the hardest to reach and most vulnerable[3] children.

But perhaps the most important change in the last 100 years is how we think about children. In 1919, when Eglantyne Jebb founded *Save the Children*, her conviction that children have a right to food, health care and education and protection from exploitation was not a mainstream idea. The *Declaration on the Rights of the Child*, drafted[4] by Jebb, was adopted by the League of Nations[5] in 1924. It asserted[6] these rights for all children and made it the duty of the international community to put children's rights in the forefront of planning. *The Convention on the Rights of the Child*, which was adopted in 1989 and has been ratified by all but one country, further changed the way children are viewed and treated – as human beings with a distinct[7] set of rights, instead of as passive objects of care and charity.

As these visionary frameworks[8] have gained acceptance, public opinion about children has been slowly but steadily shifting worldwide. For example, more people around the world now believe children belong in school, not toiling[9] in fields and factories. And more governments have enacted[10] laws to prevent child labour and child marriage, and make school free and mandatory[11] for all children, regardless of their gender, race, refugee status or special needs.

The world has come a long way in 100 years, but we still have a long way to go to ensure every child, everywhere grows up healthy, educated and protected from harm.

Fewer children are forced into work

Much of the decline in child labour in recent years has been credited to active policy efforts to extend and im-

[1] **advance** the forward moving or improvement of sth. – [2] **vaccine** *Impfstoff* – [3] **vulnerable** *verletzlich* – [4] **to draft sth.** to write a document for the first time, including the main points; *etw. entwerfen* – [5] **League of Nations** *Völkerbund*; an intergovernmental organization founded in 1920 as a result of the Paris Peace Conference that ended the First World War – [6] **to assert** (*fml.*) to say that sth. is certainly true – [7] **distinct** clearly noticeable – [8] **framework** a system of rules, ideas or beliefs that is used to plan or decide sth. – [9] **to toil** to work very hard – [10] **to enact** to make sth. law – [11] **mandatory** *verpflichtend*

prove schooling, extend social protection, expand basic services, and establish legal frameworks against child labour.

Globally, there has been better progress in reducing child labour among older children than among younger ones. The number of child labourers aged 12 to 17 has fallen 42 per cent, from 136 million in 2000 to 79 million today. During the same period, child labour among 5- to 11-year-olds fell by a third, from 110 million in 2000 to 73 million today. These young child labourers are of particular concern, as they are most vulnerable to workplace abuses and compromised education.

The most dramatic gains in ending child labour have been in eastern Europe and Central Asia. Uzbekistan cut[12] its child labour rate by an impressive 92 per cent [...]. Albania's child labour rate is down by as much as 79 per cent [...]. Azerbaijan, Belarus, Moldova and Ukraine each appear to have reduced their child labour rate among 5- to 14-year-olds by more than 60 per cent. Economic growth, poverty reduction and political commitments[13] have led to significant progress in this region. Each of the countries above has ratified[14] the International Labour Organization (ILO) child labour conventions. But while countries in this region have made progress in reducing child labour among 5- to 14-year-olds, almost all other child labourers in the region today are involved in hazardous[15] work.

HUNDREDS OF MILLIONS OF CHILDREN HAVE BEEN SAVED

Global progress has saved millions of childhoods since the year 2000. Now there are:

- 4.4 million fewer child deaths per year
- 49 million fewer stunted[19] children
- 115 million fewer children out of chool
- 94 million fewer child laborers
- 11 million fewer teen births per year
- 12,000 fewer child homicides[20] per year

Mexico has made impressive progress against child labour, cutting its rate by 80 per cent [...].

Vietnam's successful work to reduce poverty has improved living conditions for many families and reduced the need to send children to work. The country has invested heavily in education, ensuring high enrolment[16] rates, with a particular emphasis on ethnic minority children in remote mountainous areas. Mass media and international NGOs have helped to raise awareness of child rights and the harmful effects of child labour. Currently, Vietnam is implementing a national programme to prevent and minimize child labour from 2016 to 2020. [...]

Despite global progress, there are still 152 million children engaged in child labour – nearly 1 in 10 children worldwide – with almost half of them (73 million) in hazardous work that directly endangers their health, safety and emotional development. A hypothetical country made up only of these child labourers would rank as the world's ninth largest. Unless progress is accelerated[17], 121 million children will be engaged in child labour in 2025. Nearly half of the world's child labourers live in Africa (72 million). [...]

In contrast to all other regions, child labour has actually increased in sub-Saharan Africa. A breakthrough in this region will be critical[18] to ending child labour worldwide.

https://resourcentre.savethechildren.net/node/15264/pdf/global_childhood_report_2019_english.pdf, pp. 3, 23 f. [20.08.2019]

COMPREHENSION

1. Outline the excerpt from the ***Global Childhood Report*** and state which developments and improvements it highlights.

Step 1:

In order to get a general overview and understanding of the text,

WES-121500-012

a) read the text first. b) Then, do the comprehension task on worksheet 12.2.

Step 2:

In a second, **close reading**, identify relevant keywords and key phrases that help you to get a deeper understanding of the text and its details.

The Info box on p. 75 gives you some help in what to look for.

[12] **to cut sth.** to make sth. smaller; to reduce sth. – [13] **commitment** *Verpflichtungserklärung* – [14] **to ratify sth.** (*fml.*) to make an agreement official – [15] **hazardous** ['hæzərdəs] dangerous and likely to cause damage – [16] **enrolment** *Einschreibung (offizielle Anmeldung)* – [17] **to accelerate** to increase the speed of sth. – [18] **critical** here: of the greatest importance – [19] **stunted** prevented from growing or developing to the usual size; *körperlich zurückgeblieben* – [20] **homicide** (an) act of murder

Info

Generally, **keywords** and **key phrases** are important when identifying the content and message of a text, and necessary for analysis of the text later on.

Keywords and **key phrases**

- are significant words which support details and messages of the text.
- are often repeated several times throughout the text.
- represent the main ideas of the author.
- can often be found in the headline/title of a text or at the beginning or conclusion of a paragraph.
- identify the topic of the text.
- are often descriptive (*beschreibend*) and/or illustrative (*veranschaulichend*).
- often occur in word fields or word groups.

WES-121500-012

2. a) The text itself and the added statistics contain a lot of data and figures, some of which are rather general, others very precise. Use the grid provided on worksheet 12.3 to organize the statistical information.

b) Display your grids in class and discuss the developments and changes since 1919.

3. Using your results and findings, write an outline of the text.

Tip: Pay attention to the term 'outline' and keep in mind that it requires you to

- focus on the structure of the text,
- work out the main aspects, but leave out the more minor details.

→ Standardized Terminology for Tasks, pp. 10 ff.

ANALYSIS

4. The excerpt is taken from a report highlighting the 100th anniversary of the work of the NGO *Save the Children*. As can be expected, the report wants to acknowledge the NGO's work and praise the positive developments and changes their work has achieved.
Examine and analyse how the text highlights the NGO's work.

Step 1:

Use your results from task 1, step 2 and arrange the relevant keywords in a mind map.

Tip: Include the statistical data given on p. 74.

Example:

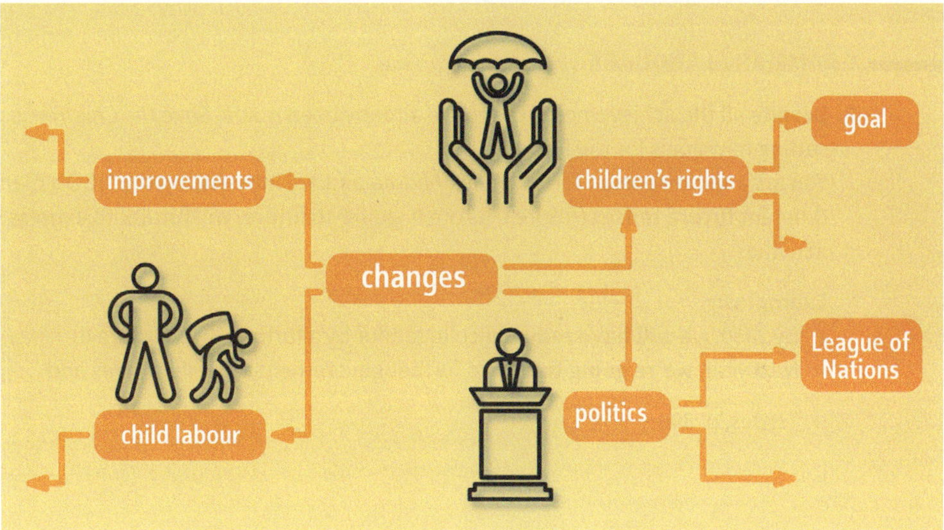

WES-121500-012

Step 2:
The examples given in the text are intended to praise the NGO's work. Use worksheet 12.4 and explain their function in detail.

Step 3:
In addition to the positive examples mentioned above, the text contains numerous stylistic devices which emphasize the NGO's work and success.

WES-121500-012

Use worksheet 12.5 for your notes and pay particular attention to these devices:
- superlatives
- positive emotive words
- adjectives/adverbs
- numbers

Tip: Remember to refer to the lines in the text where you found the devices.

Step 4:
Write an analysis of the text in about 300 words in which you explain the means the author uses to praise *Save the Childen's* work.
→ Focus on Skills, Analysis of a Non-Fictional Text, p. 237

Tip: Use the *Vocabulary for Text Analysis* pages (pp. 249 f.) to make your text more fluent. Additionally, follow the **introduction – main part – conclusion** pattern and remember to quote from the text to underline the accuracy of your work.

ACTIVITIES

5. As the report points out, there have been fundamental changes in the lives of children worldwide in the past decades.
Do a project in class on the topic and interview your older relatives (parents, grandparents, etc.) about
a) what their childhood was like,
b) what they hoped for and dreamed of,
c) what changes concerning children's rights, etc. they have experienced in their lives.

@

6. Do research on Eglantyne Jebb (1876 – 1926), the founder of *Save the Children*.
Prepare 5-minute presentations and share your findings in class.
→ Focus on Skills, Doing Research and Citing Sources, p. 262
→ Focus on Skills, Presentation, p. 261

GRAMMAR / LANGUAGE

7. Despite all the achievements that have already been made, *Save the Children* is planning ahead and setting new goals for the future.
You are a spokesperson for *Save the Children* and are introducing the NGO's plans to the public. Use different **future tenses** (future I, future II, going-to future, will future) to express your plans and future activities.

Examples:
- By 2030, we **will have reduced** child labour by a further 30 %. (future II)
- Next year, **we're going to talk** to further government representatives and … (going-to future)

→ Tenses, p. 300

Nosheen Iqbal

Generation Z: 'We Have More to Do than Drink and Take Drugs'

AWARENESS

Demographers[1] and researchers usually use birth years, ranging from the early 20th century until today, to identify and categorize generational characteristics and developments/trends.
Do research and find information about these major generations:

- Lost Generation
- Greatest Generation
- Silent Generation
- Baby Boomers
- Generation X
- Millennials
- Generation Z

→ Focus on Skills, Doing Research and Citing Sources, p. 262

1 They drink less, take far fewer drugs and have made teenage pregnancy a near anomaly[2]. Generation Z – one of several terms used to describe post-millennial youth born after 1996 – prefer juice bars to pub crawls[3], rank quality family time ahead of sex and prioritise good grades before friendship, at least according to a report published by the British Pregnancy Advisory Service last week.

An onslaught[4] of sneering[5] headlines followed, characterising today's youth as boring, sensible and hopelessly screen-addicted.

So, are the kids all right?

"We have so much more to do than [just] drink and take drugs," says Demi Babalola, a 19-year-old philosophy and sociology student. "I'm not surprised those [statistics] show that's the case: it makes sense. We have a lot more to distract[6] us now."

What's her biggest time stealer? "Social media." Babalola toggles between[7] Snapchat, Twitter and Instagram, although she rolls her eyes at the mention of Facebook, full as it is of "older people".

But it's not just the breadth[8] of entertainment and culture that is so instantly available – and disposable[9] – to Babalola and her peers. There is also a growing feeling that the preoccupations[10] of her parents' generation seem, well, a bit lame.

"Going out takes a lot of effort: it's boring, repetitive and expensive," she says. "Obviously, I used to go out a lot in my first year [at university], but now we do more kickbacks[11]." [...]

2 The cliché that many young people spend far too much time online, instead of indulging in[12] a romanticised form of rebellion, may have some truth, but as futurologist Rhiannon McGregor points out, Gen Z-ers are more cautious[13] and risk-averse[14] than their parents, partly because that technology exists.

"They're aware from an early age of how they're portrayed online and offline, so they curate[15] themselves in a more conservative way," she says. (In other words, no one wants to be publicly shamed getting messy or being recklessly[16] daft[17].)

"But they're also more socially aware and see themselves as part of a global community. It's easier to get and feel connected to someone in Africa or Asia and share concerns about climate change, for instance."

3 Clara Finnigan, 22, who grew up in Devon and is in her final year at the University of the Arts London, points out that one size doesn't fit all. She still goes out, "often to gay clubs".

She believes her generation is unfairly judged and that it reports levels of stress and depression that are higher than ever because of the economic and political state of the world it has inherited[18].

"The whole anxiety[19] of not having stability in your future is something that is definitely very present. I won't probably ever own my own house, unless I get really lucky."

She slumps[20] in her seat at the pretentiously[21] swanky[22] bar we meet in. "I just want what previous generations have had: you work hard, you reap the rewards[23] of that.

[1] **demographer** [dɪˈmɒɡrəfər] *Bevölkerungskundler/-in, Demograf* – [2] **anomaly** (*fml.*) sth. that is different from what is usual – [3] **pub crawl** *Kneipentour* – [4] **onslaught** very powerful attack – [5] **to sneer** *spöttisch grinsen* – [6] **to distract** *ablenken* – [7] **to toggle between** to switch a feature on a tablet or mobile phone on and off by pressing the same button – [8] **breadth** [bredθ] *Breite* – [9] **disposable** intended to be thrown away after use – [10] **preoccupation** the thing you think about most – [11] **kickback** small gathering of a group of friends – [12] **to indulge in** *jdm./etw. nachgeben* – [13] **cautious** avoiding risks, careful – [14] **risk-averse** unwilling to take risks – [15] **to curate** to select things such as documents, music, products or internet content to be included as part of a list or collection, or on a website – [16] **reckless** *leichtsinnig* – [17] **daft** stupid – [18] **to inherit** *erben* – [19] **anxiety** [æŋˈzaɪəti] fear, worry – [20] **to slump** to sit or fall heavily and suddenly – [21] **pretentious** trying to give the appearance of great importance – [22] **swanky** (*infml.*) very expensive and stylish – [23] **to reap the rewards of sth.** *den Erfolg von etw. ernten*

Sometimes I feel a bit hopeless because [my degree and hard work] won't make a difference.

"I don't expect to have one full-time gig[24]; my career won't be defined by one job. I know I'll have to do stuff I don't enjoy to be able to do passion projects that I do."

4 Amelia Colthart, a 22-year-old graduate from Leicester, and Myesha Owen Munro, a 17-year-old A-level student from north London, both agree.

"At my age, my parents and my grandparents owned their own home," says Colthart. "I don't go out clubbing[25] – I know my limits. I go to friends' houses [for kickbacks], but I have to prioritise my career goals because it's a lot harder to achieve what I want."

Owen Munro adds: "My generation feels bitter about all the things we won't be able to do because of what the older generation chose."

The subjects of Brexit and of dropping out of university to pursue[26] less mind-bogglingly[27] expensive apprenticeships[28] come up a lot. As does a consistent refusal[29] to accept that anyone should be defined by traditional markers of identity.

"We're more inclusive[30]," says Babalola. "You can do what you want as long as you don't harm anyone and stay safe. It's about freedom. Previous generations always made distinct[31] separations between being gay or straight. [...]

While statistics show that smoking, drinking and clubbing may be in decline for today's young people, the health and wellness industry is booming with the same demographic – in part, because these young people have had so much information at their disposal[32].

"The risks and downsides of doing all of those things have been drummed into[33] us at school from an early age," says Colthart. "Self-care is a much bigger deal for us."

5 Generation Z-ers will, after all, be living longer and more healthily, and looking better for it.

A report (pdf) from the Institute of Alcohol Studies suggests that changing demographics also play a part, reporting that "ethnic minority children ... are less likely to drink, [which] can directly explain a small proportion of the fall in underage drinking" but also that there is evidence these same minority students can also influence their peers. [...]

So what is the new going out? The Generation Z idea of fun that is inexplicable[34] to older adults? Owen Munro, Allely and Babalola instantly refer me to Snapchat, where they communicate in a constant group feed with their friends. Broadcasting the minutiae[35] of her day – a good outfit, a trip to Westfield[36] – is as second nature[37] as breathing to Babalola.

"It's kind of documenting your life, but you have an audience and you immediately know who's interacting. I enjoy it – it makes me feel important that 100 people are watching what I'm eating."

"It's easier than Instagram," agrees Owen Munro. "I hate putting up a picture and waiting to see if anyone likes it. It's scary."

And what are Babalola's plans for today? "My friends and I go out to London, or cycling. We might go to a cute cafe and take pictures."

https://www.theguardian.com/society/2018/jul/21/generation-z-has-different-attitudes-says-a-new-report, 21 July 2018 [22.08.2019]

COMPREHENSION

1. Give an outline of the article and say what it writes about
   - the general attitude of Generation Z.
   - Generation Z's
     a) likes and dislikes, b) concerns and anxieties, c) plans for the future, d) handling of social media.

   Write a coherent text of about 200–250 words.

2. Team up with a partner, and mediate and describe the bar charts on pp. 80 f. depicting
   - Generation Z's attitude toward social responsibility and the protection of the environment,
   - Generation Z's criteria for shopping textiles.

   → Focus on Skills, Analysis of Statistical Data, p. 243

[24] **gig** (*infml.*) a job – [25] **to go out clubbing** to go out dancing in clubs – [26] **to pursue** to try to achieve a plan over a long period of time – [27] **mind-boggling** (*infml.*) extremely surprising and difficult to understand or imagine – [28] **apprenticeship** *Ausbildung, Lehre* – [29] **refusal** *Weigerung* – [30] **inclusive** determined to include many different types of people and treat them all fairly and equally – [31] **distinct** clearly noticeable – [32] **at sb.'s disposal** (*fml.*) available to be used by sb. – [33] **to drum sth. into sb.** *etw. in jdn. hineinhämmern* – [34] **inexplicable** [ˌɪnˌɪkˈsplɪkəbəl] unable to be explained or understood – [35] **minutiae** [mɪˈnuːʃiaɪ] small and often unimportant details – [36] **Westfield** large shopping mall in London – [37] **second nature** sth. that is so familiar that it is done without having to think about it, natural

ANALYSIS

3. Analyse the structural and stylistic devices* of the article and determine its credibility.

Step 1:
Identify the train of thought/line of argument in the article as well as its compositional patterns. Draw a flowchart to visualize your findings.

Example:

Introduction of report/ general characteristics …	… reaction to …	… question: …
	Example: Demi Babalola …	
Report …		**Conclusion:** …

Info

Structural devices are used to organize and structure a text and guide the reader through it. Here are some commonly used structural devices:
- **column** (*Textspalte*)
- a **heading/headline** used to arouse the reader's interest
- a **conclusion** often re-states the main idea and summarizes the main aspects of the text
- the **introduction** leads into the topic, attracts the reader's interest and draws him/her into the story
- **main part:** the topic/problem is demonstrated and the intention/problem is discussed
- **paragraph:** a division of text dealing with a particular idea
- **subheading:** a caption that divides the text into logical sections
- **line of argument(ation):** the way different reasons are gradually developed to convince a reader of a particular point of view
- **train of thought:** the way a series of ideas is gradually developed and structured

Step 2:
In a further step, focus on stylistic devices* the author employs in order to emphasize the line of argument*. Pay particular attention to these devices, sort them in a grid and explain their function. Use worksheet 13.1 for detailed notes.

WES-121500-013

device	example from the text	function	message
enumeration	… drink less, take fewer drugs and have made …	→ emphasis on correctness → anti-climax (fewer, less …)	→ this generation is very different → they behave very correctly
positive vs. negative emotive words	…	→ …	→ …
keywords	…	→ …	→ …

→ Focus on Skills, Analysis of a Non-Fictional Text, p. 237
→ Literary Terms, pp. 274 ff.

Step 3:
After completing the grid, write a coherent text of about 300 words in which you explain the author's line of argument* and the message of the text. Be careful to quote from the article to prove the accuracy and correctness of your analysis.
→ Focus on Skills, Analysis of a Non-Fictional Text, p. 237

Tip: Make sure to employ connectives and linkers to make your text flow better.
→ Focus on Language, Connectives and Adverbs, p. 251

Tips on vocab

- The author describes the characteristics of …
- The writer makes an allusion to …
- The author's train of thought is underlined by …
- The intention of the author is to …
- At the beginning of the article …
- The main/principal idea is that …
- In the main/final part, the author …
- The author raises the question about …
- The author/article relates to …

Tips on vocab

to begin with ■ to start with ■ furthermore/moreover ■ generally speaking ■ in comparison to ■ in contrast ■ therefore ■ as a matter of fact ■ according to ■ seemingly

ACTIVITIES

4. Your American friend Jasmine is doing a project on 'Generation Z' in her social sciences class. In an email, she asks you if you can help her with further material on the matter.
You have come across the bar charts below/on page 81 in the online version of the German newspaper *Die Welt*, which show the contradictory shopping habits of Generation Z.
In an email, tell your friend about the bar charts and give her the most relevant information in English about the core aspects regarding Generation Z's attitude towards:
- the environment and sustainability
- social values
- fashion and shopping

→ Focus on Skills, Mediation, p. 253

Das widersprüchliche Kaufverhalten der Generation Z

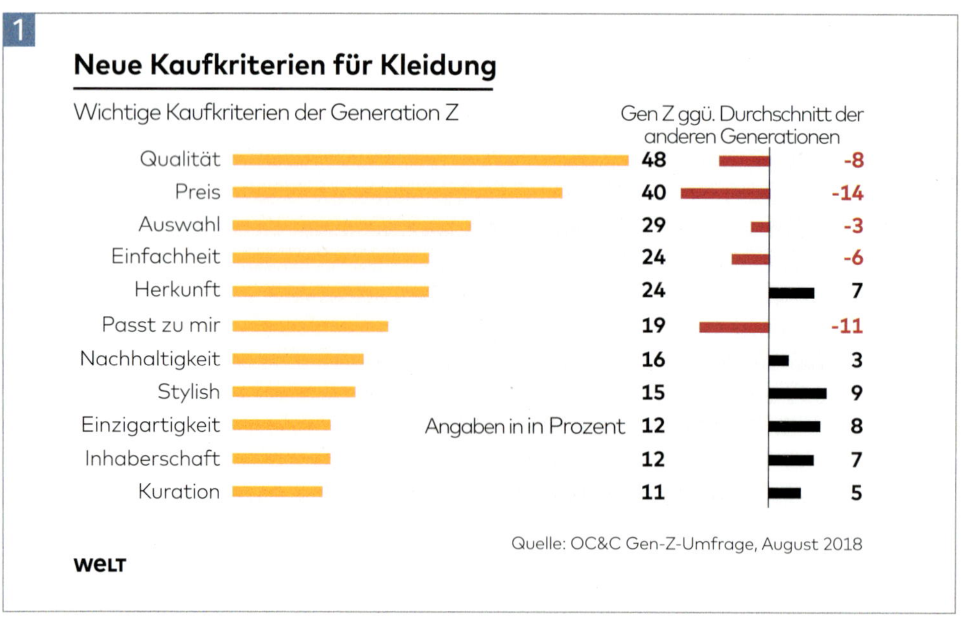

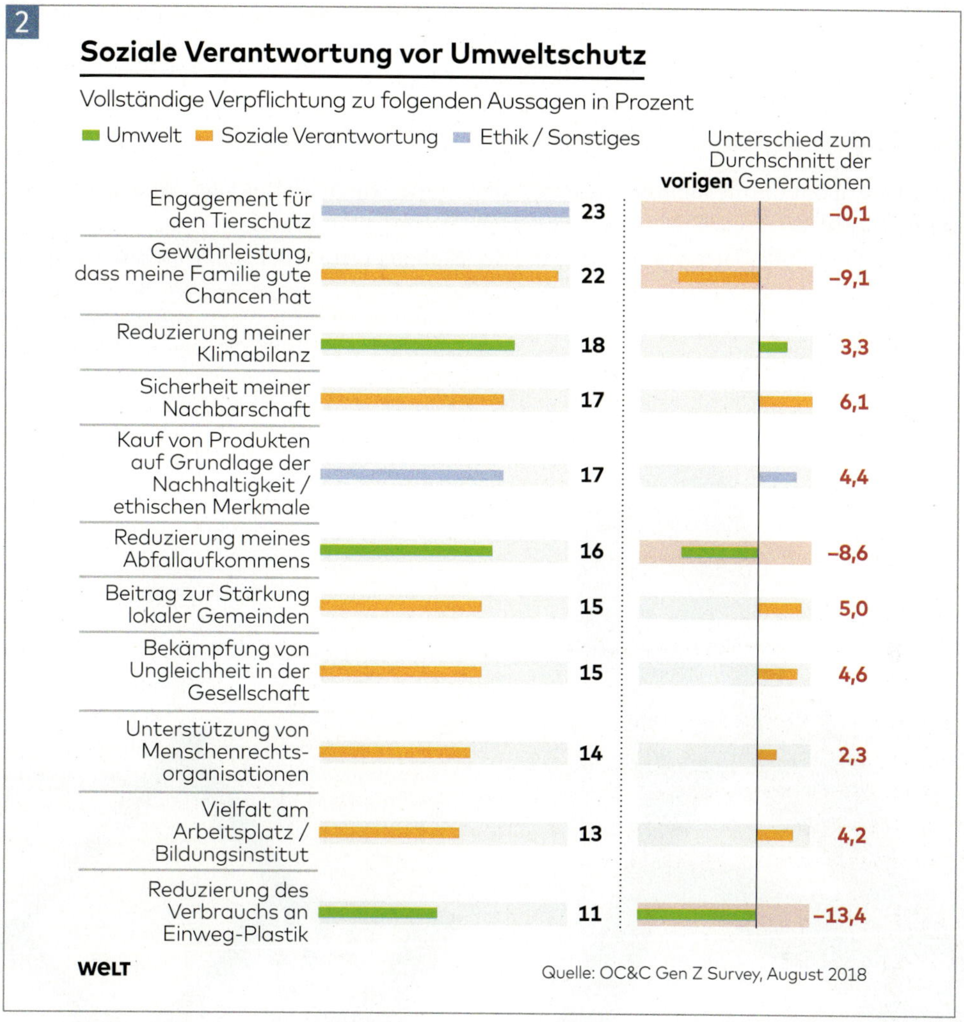

GRAMMAR / LANGUAGE

5. Write a letter to the editor in which you state your view on the matter. Employ **gerund and participle constructions** to vary your style and way of expressing your ideas.

Examples:
- Feeling bitter about what the older generation was able to do … widens the gap …
- Instead of openly rebelling against injustices, Gen Z prefers to …

→ Focus on Skills, Writing a Letter to the Editor, p. 273

6. Turn the language and phrases in the box below into everyday English.

Example:
- post-millennial youth → sb. born after the year 2000

screen-addicted • peers • global community • markers of identity • wellness industry • to prioritize • demographic • WhatsApp • face-to-face interaction

Max Schroth

Endstation Offline

AWARENESS

a) Speculate about the meaning of the term "FOMO – The Fear of Missing Out". What kind of state does the word describe?

b) Describe the painting below. What does the way Steffen portrays himself reveal about his situation?

Self-portrait: While in therapy, Steffen painted himself. The portrait shows him sitting in front of his laptop. The red strokes represent the pain he suffered from sitting all day.

Tips on vocab

(to be at) the end of the line ■ a yellow halo ■ security ■ vicious circle ■ bent (*gebeugt*) ■ to bend (bent, bent) over sth. ■ backache ■ to have problems with your back ■ to have an aching behind (*Hintern*)

Tagelang verließ er die Wohnung nicht. Aß kaum, duschte unregelmäßig. Sogar den Gang zur Toilette schaffte er nur noch unter größten Anstrengungen[1]. Das alles erschien ihm unnötig. Steffen schaute sich im Netz eine Serie nach der anderen an. Ob „Game of Thrones", „The Walking Dead" oder irgendwelche YouTube-Videos, er starrte pausenlos auf seinen Laptop. Bis zu 15 Stunden täglich. Steffen ist süchtig. Seine Droge: das Internet. Doch anders als Haschisch[2] oder Heroin[3] ist sein Stoff jederzeit in unbegrenzter Menge frei verfügbar[4].
Online-Süchtige nutzen das Internet so exzessiv[5], dass sie andere Lebensbereiche vernachlässigen. Freunde

[1] effort – [2] hash/cannabis – [3] heroin – [4] available – [5] excessive(ly)

und Familien werden ihnen gleichgültig. Sie schwänzen[6] die Schule. Pinkeln in Flaschen, um sich nicht vom Bildschirm entfernen zu müssen. Bei Entzug werden sie aggressiv. Nur eine neue Dosis kann sie beruhigen. Die Symptome ähneln denen eines Drogenabhängigen oder Alkoholkranken.

Nach Schätzungen von Experten sind in Deutschland über 700000 Menschen von Online-Sucht betroffen. Zweieinhalb Millionen gelten als problematische Internetnutzer. Und mit voranschreitender[7] Digitalisierung werden es immer mehr: 99 Prozent der jungen Menschen in Deutschland sind online, 27 Prozent sagen sogar, dass sie praktisch nie offline sind. Dessen ist sich Bert te Wildt, Chefarzt[8] an der Psychosomatischen[9] Klinik Kloster Dießen, sicher. Junge Menschen seien besonders gefährdet. „In dieser Gruppe geht man von drei bis vier Prozent aus, was als Indiz[10] dafür zu werten[11] ist, dass die Zahlen weiter steigen werden."

Fast jeder Mensch besitzt ein Smartphone und ist so rund um die Uhr online. Doch für Chefarzt te Wildt ist die Internet-Nutzungsdauer[12] lediglich ein Richtwert und nicht maßgeblich[13] für eine Diagnose. „Wer beispielsweise beruflich viel online ist, ist nicht gleich auch süchtig", erklärt der 49-Jährige.

Die Verführung, der sich vor allem junge Menschen immer häufiger nicht entziehen können, entsteht eher in der Freizeit[14]. Die Sehnsucht[15], 24/7 am Leben einer virtuellen Gemeinschaft teilnehmen zu wollen, bloß nichts zu verpassen. Der Psychologe[16] Dan Ariely von der renommierten[17] Duke University nannte diese Sorge „Fear of Missing Out" (kurz: FOMO). Und im Zeitalter der ständig verfügbaren[18] sozialen Medien eskaliert[19] diese Angst. Es gehört eine gewisse Routine dazu, bis wir realisieren, dass Facebook-Fotos von Mittagsmahl oder Alpenglühen[20] kein Erlebnis reproduzieren, sondern synthetische Gefühle darstellen. Wer es mit der Achtsamkeit[21] und also auch mit sich selbst ernst nimmt, gönnt sich digitale Auszeiten. So wird aus FOMO die JOMO: „Joy of Missing Out". Die Freude an der Ruhe. [...]

Steffen ist von schmächtiger[22] Statur. Er hat kurze braune Haare und einen Dreitagebart[23]. In seinem blau-weißen Karohemd sitzt er am Tisch im Konferenzsaal. Er nippt an seinem Kaffee und hält kurz inne. Dann beginnt er seinen Weg in die Sucht zu erzählen: „Angefangen hat alles im Grundschulalter." Er wuchs in schwierigen Familienverhältnissen auf, war zu Hause oft allein. Beide Elternteile arbeiteten viel und hatten für ihren Sohn keine Zeit. Es kam oft zu Streit. Er fühlte sich einsam.

Aus Langeweile verbrachte er viel Zeit am Computer. „Das war damals zwar noch nicht pathologisch[24] oder problematisch, aber ich hatte schon relativ früh einen Zugang dazu und habe das auch viel zur Stressregulation verwendet." In der digitalen Welt fand er endlich die Geborgenheit[25], nach der er zu Hause vergeblich gesucht hat. Sie wurde sein Ruhepol[26]. „Ich konnte mich da einfach reinbeamen und musste dann nicht mehr meine Umgebung[27] wahrnehmen oder an Probleme denken, die ich irgendwie nicht lösen konnte." [...]

Im schlimmsten Fall kann die Online-Sucht sogar tödlich sein. Menschen, die sich ums Leben zocken[28], sind mittlerweile keine Seltenheit mehr. Te Wildt verweist auf einen besonders tragischen Fall in einem taiwanischen Internet-Café aus dem Jahr 2015. Ein 32-jähriger Mann starb nach einem dreitägigen Computerspiel-Marathon an Herzversagen[29]. Sein Ableben wurde zunächst noch nicht einmal bemerkt. Die anderen Computerspieler wähnten ihn schlafend. „Bei ihm hatte bereits die Leichenstarre[30] eingesetzt, als die Rettungskräfte[31] eintrafen." [...]

Für Steffen hat die Sucht zwar noch keine lebensbedrohlichen Ausmaße angenommen. Allerdings spürt er erste Anzeichen dafür, dass Komaglotzen[32] ihn physisch krank[33] macht. [...]

In seinem Zimmer kann Steffen sich entspannen. Überall liegen Bücher, Zeitungen und selbst gemalte Bilder herum. Er hat diese Beschäftigungsmöglichkeiten[34] neu für sich entdeckt. Es gibt aber auch kaum Alternativen. Das einzige technische Gerät, auf das er Zugriff hat, ist ein kleines Radio. Sein Handy hat er nach drei Wochen abgegeben. „Das hat mir am Anfang als Methadon[35] genützt." Für ihn ein erster Sieg.

FOCUS, 18/2019, 27 April 2019, pp. 70 ff.

[6] to play truant – [7] to progress – [8] chief physician – [9] psychosomatic – [10] indicator – [11] to assess sth. as – [12] period of use – [13] relevant – [14] leisure time – [15] desire – [16] psychologist – [17] renowned – [18] available – [19] to escalate – [20] alpenglow – [21] mindfulness – [22] wispy – [23] three-day beard – [24] pathological – [25] feeling of security – [26] haven of tranquility – [27] surroundings/environment – [28] to gamble – [29] cardiac arrest – [30] rigor mortis – [31] paramedics – [32] binge watching – [33] physically ill – [34] offer of (various) activities – [35] methadone

1

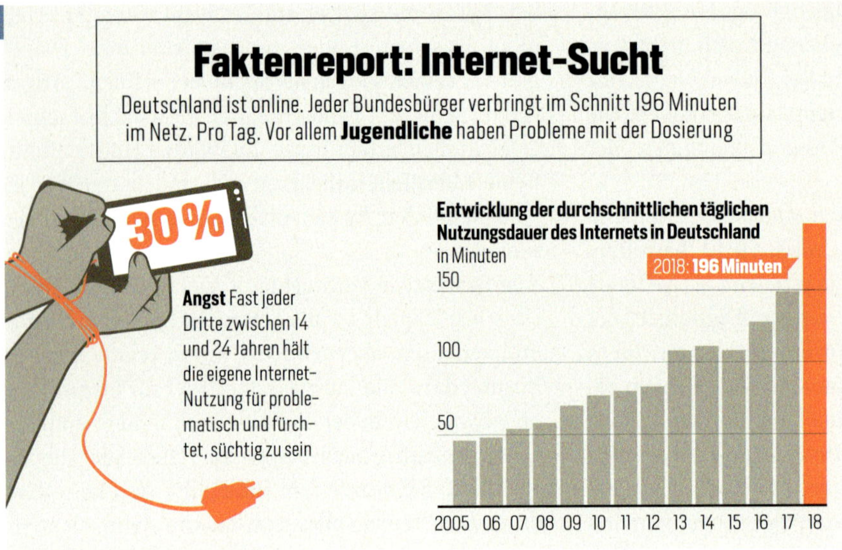

Tips on vocab

bar chart ■ to rank first … second … last ■ the highest/lowest figure ■ no/a little/a big difference between ■ the figures are similar to/different from ■ to experience a sudden rise in ■ a striking/slow rise in

2

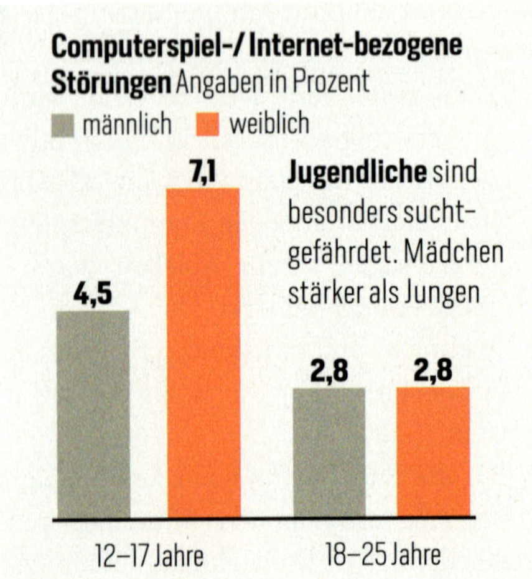

Tips on vocab

bar chart ■ in comparison with ■ in contrast to ■ a striking difference between ■ comparable figures ■ the age group of …

3

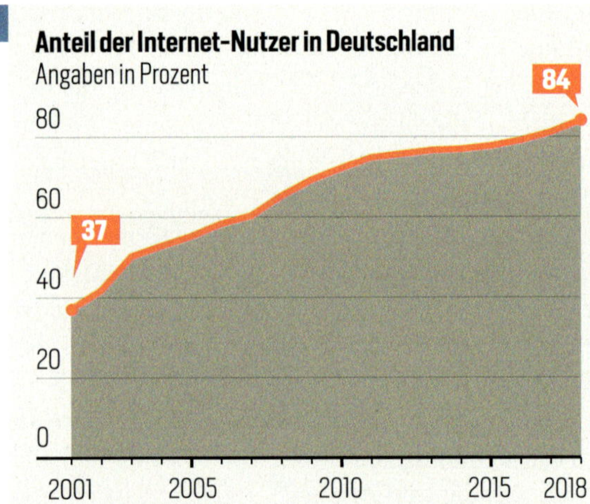

Tips on vocab

line graph ■ to reach a peak/to increase/rise/go up ■ a gradual/steady/continual line ■ continually rising ■ a significant rise

4

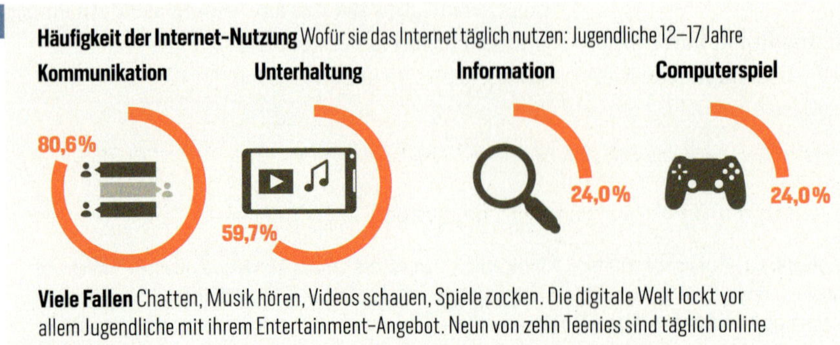

Tips on vocab

pie chart ■ a share of … % ■ the circle stands for ■ percentage-wise ■ the chart reveals a percentage of …

5

Viele Fallen Chatten, Musik hören, Videos schauen, Spiele zocken. Die digitale Welt lockt vor allem Jugendliche mit ihrem Entertainment-Angebot. Neun von zehn Teenies sind täglich online

Von der Gruppe der Abhängigen angegebene Hauptaktivität, Pinta-Studie 2013

Suchtpotenzial Die meisten Betroffenen sind süchtig nach sozialen Medien oder Online-Spielen wie „World of Warcraft". Aber auch Pornos, Shoppen oder Filmeschauen können süchtig machen

FOCUS, 18/2019, 27 April 2019, p. 76

Tips on vocab

a horizontal bar ■ to be divided into thirds ■ the figures are (almost) identical ■ a similar number of people ■ the figures show an identical number of users

COMPREHENSION

Against the background of a growing number of internet-addicted people, you have done some research and found an international online forum that discusses the issue and offers help. They are always looking for further information and institutions or people that offer (professional) help.

The magazine article:

Tip: Although you are given quite a number of annotations, be careful not to translate the magazine article word for word. Use the annotations to get **a general idea** of how to **mediate** and **contextualize** the article with regard to the content.

1. Read the article and look out for relevant information and keywords on these topics:
- Steffen's life before the therapy
- online addiction – facts and data
- dangers for young people
- turning FOMO into JOMO
- Steffen's therapy
- an example from Taiwan

2. a) Now sort your findings and mediate them into English. Fill in the respective English words, phrases and expressions and complete the grid below.

Steffen's life before the therapy	online addiction – facts and data	dangers for young people
• Watching video clips 15 hours a day • …	• 700 000 people … • …	• …
turning FOMO into JOMO	**Steffen's therapy**	**an example from Taiwan**
• 24/7 … • …	• …	• …

Tip: You can use the annotations and a dictionary for specific technical terms – but try to formulate and paraphrase difficult expressions and passages in your own words as much as possible. The Info box below will give you additional help.

→ Focus on Skills, Mediation, p. 253

Info

Paraphrasing means rewriting somebody else's thoughts or formulations in your own words. This often requires you to
- use simpler language and less complex sentences and formulations.
- transform technical terms into everyday language.
- convey a message to non-experts.
- use synonyms of certain ideas or concepts.
- refer to examples to illustrate a complicated or complex matter.

b) Subdivide the article into thematic units and find a suitable headline for each paragraph, using your own words.

3. Using your notes and answers, write an email about online addiction and Steffen's situation, mediating the German magazine article into a coherent text of about 250 – 300 words.

Tip: Begin your email with a few introductory words and remember to include the source where you found the information (i. e. name of the magazine, name of the author, title of the article, publication date, etc.).

Example:
Dear …,
Only recently I found a most interesting magazine article about how to treat the internet addiction of young people. The article, entitled …, was published in the German … on …

The infographics:

M **4.** a) Team up with a partner and mediate the data presented in the different illustrations and graphics on pp. 84 f. using the Tips on vocab boxes.
→ Focus on Skills, Mediation, p. 253

WES-121500-014 b) In order to check your overall understanding of the infographic do the tasks provided on worksheet 14.1.

ANALYSIS

M **5. Taking into consideration the information given in the magazine article *Endstation Offline*, analyse the presented data on the content and different forms of internet addiction in Germany and try to explain the correlated causes for this development as well as the possible consequences for the people.**

Step 1:
Study **illustration no. 1** and explain the increase of time spent on the internet as well as the increase in the number of users in Germany.

Tip: In addition to the information given in the infographic, use further aspects given in the Info box to find possible causes for the depicted development.

Step 2:
Try to find reasons for the data given in **illustration no. 2**.

Step 3:
Explain the rise in the overall number of internet users depicted in **illustration no. 3**.

Step 4:
Explain the information given in **illustration no. 4**. What makes online
- chatting,
- entertainment,
- research,
- gaming

particularly interesting for 12 – 17-year-olds?

Step 5:
"World of Warcraft", porn movies, shopping, watching videos … What actually made internet users addicted? Try to find answers in **illustration no. 5** and the Info box.

Step 6:
Examine how the German magazine article reports on the matter and pay attention to specific formulations and their effect and message.

Examples:
- „Tagelang verließ er … Aß kaum … den Gang zur Toilette …"
  → emotional impact; human interest; disgust and pity are evoked in the reader
- „Aß kaum, duschte unregelmäßig … Bis zu 15 Stunden täglich …"
  → short, elliptical* sentences, paratactic*; easy to understand
- „Fast jeder Mensch … rund um die Uhr …"
  → generalization; (indirect) appeal to the reader

Info

The development and release of digital media and gadgets

1993	portable MP3 players
1997	Google is registered
2000	USB flash drives
2001	Wikipedia
2003	Skype
2005	YouTube
2006	Facebook
2007	Dropbox – Apple TV – iPhone – mobile GPS – Netflix
2009	WhatsApp
2010	iPad – Instagram
2011	Facebook has 550 million users
2014	Google Glass – Amazon Alexa
2015	Apple Watch – Amazon Echo
2016	Tesla Powerwall – Amazon Echo Dot – Pokemon Go
2017	Surface laptop
2018	Google Pay

Step 7:
Finally, write a coherent analysis of the infographic and various data and explain the interdependencies and correlations.

Tip: Use this structure for your analysis:
- **introduction** (title, author, topic, time of publication)
- **main part**
  a) identifying and describing the data
  b) comparing the relevant data
  c) relating the data to other data/information available (→ contextualization)
  d) drawing conclusions and explaining the facts and data
- **conclusion** (summing up the main/most relevant aspects in one to two sentences)

→ Focus on Skills, Writing an Analysis, p. 248
→ Focus on Skills, Analysis of Statistical Data, p. 243

Example:
The infographic, published by the German magazine *Focus* on …, presents and illustrates data on the state of … The five different sections of the infographic present = focus on …

ACTIVITIES

6. Being an online and digital device user yourself, take the opportunity to respond to the information and warnings given in the article. Write a letter to the editor in which you
   a) state your opinion on the topic,
   b) respond to specific statements made in the article, commenting on and/or evaluating them from your point of view,
   c) suggest possible alternatives or solutions.

→ Focus on Skills, Writing a Letter to the Editor, p. 273

WES-121500-014

7. Compare the article at hand to the online article by Elizabeth Hartney which is provided on worksheet 14.2.
- What further details on internet addiction and its impact does the article provide?
- Who do you think are the potential addressees of these articles? Discuss in class.

→ Focus on Language, Conversation and Discussion, p. 254

8. Critically evaluate and comment on the infographic.
- To what extent are the statistics informative and differentiated?
- In what way does the presented data match your own experiences with the use of internet services?

Present your results in class and discuss whether (or not) they match the view conveyed by the magazine *Focus*.

→ Focus on Language, Conversation and Discussion, p. 254

GRAMMAR / LANGUAGE

WES-121500-014

9. Read the online article about internet addiction provided on worksheet 14.2 again. Think about whether to use the **adjective or adverb** and cross out the incorrect alternative.

→ Adjectives and Adverbs, p. 289

M **10.** Mediate the sentences below, which are taken from the omitted parts of the magazine article, into English. Use the **passive voice** whenever possible to make your formulations less personal.

→ Passive, p. 298

- In seinem Buch „Digital Junkies" warnt te Wildt vor der Suchtgefahr durch das World Wide Web.
- Viele Videospiele generieren durch das Zufallsprinzip Erfolge und stimulieren das Belohnungssystem im Gehirn.
- Die Weltgesundheitsorganisation (WHO) plant Internetsucht als „Gaming Disorder" in ihren Krankheitskatalog aufzunehmen.
- Bisher tragen die Krankenkassen Kosten von 250 Euro pro Tag.
- Die Sucht zerstört soziale Kompetenzen und macht Menschen unsicher.

11. Imagine Steffen writes a diary and asks himself what would have happened if he had not …
Write that diary entry, using **conditional III** sentences and reflect on what would or could have been different.

Examples:
- If I hadn't been alone that often, I wouldn't have felt lonely.
- If I had begun the therapy earlier, I could have …

→ Conditional Sentences (If-Clauses), p. 292

12. Compare the words and phrases from the box below and form **collocations** (= a combination of related words). Some words can be used more than once.

Example: to surf the net

to go on • online shopping • a website • to access • the internet • social networks • ~~the net~~ • to use • to download sth. from • images • to maintain • to navigate • a file • to do • information • to browse • online • to delete • to attach • ~~to surf~~ • to display

WES-121500-014

13. Find further **collocations** and do the tasks on worksheet 14.3.

John Moore

2-Year-Old Yanela Sanchez and Her Mother, Sandra Sanchez

AWARENESS

On 12 June 2018, photographer John Moore took the now-famous photo of a crying two-year-old girl from Honduras, Yanela Sanchez, while her mother, Sandra, was being checked by a border control agent prior to both mother and child being taken to a processing centre for migrants. Yanela and her mother had just crossed the Rio Grande, hoping to request asylum. In Apríl 2019, John Moore's photo was named the World Press Photo of the Year by an independent jury.

In a round-robin activity, express your first impression of the photo and what it means.

Yanela and her mother at the Mexican border, 12 June 2018; photo by John Moore

Tips on vocab

background: night – dark surrounding background ■ gravel road

left side: huge police car/tyre ■ an inscription and the police logo is partly visible ("US")

centre: small/fragile child ■ pink shirt and pink shoes (eye-catcher) ■ crying/sobbing ■ desperate facial expression ■ tousled hair ■ woman leaning on to police vehicle ■ arms and legs spread

right side: tall police officer ■ carrying a gun ■ handcuffs (*Handschellen*) ■ wearing blue plastic gloves ■ checking the woman's belt

COMPREHENSION

1. Describe the photograph in detail, paying attention to:
- the overall atmosphere it conveys
- the people, their actions, body language and facial expressions
- the surroundings
- striking eye-catchers and visual symbols

WES-121500-015

Tip: Use worksheet 15.1 for a precise labelling of details.

Tip: Use the Tips on vocab box on p. 89 and, in a final description of the photo, answer the w-questions (who – what – where – when – why?).
Additionally, think about a particular structure for your description, e. g. from left to right, from background to foreground, etc.

ANALYSIS

2. Analyse the emotional impact as well as the intended message of the photo by examining its various visual elements and symbols.

Step 1:

@ WES-121500-015

The photo was chosen the World Press Photo of the Year 2019. In order to gain a deeper understanding of the background of the photo, access the webcode and research the various links given there.
- What features/categories did the jury select from?
- Why might the jury have selected this particular photograph from the many taken by professional photographers?

Step 2:

WES-121500-015

Against your findings and results from worksheet 15.1 and taking your research results into consideration, examine the **function** of the photo's elements. Use the grid provided on worksheet 15.2 for your notes.

Step 3:

WES-121500-015

Using your previous findings and results, reflect on the intended **message** of the photo's various elements, and complete the grid provided on worksheet 15.2.

Step 4:

Finally, connecting your results from the previous steps as well as the comprehension task, write an analysis of about 250 – 300 words.
→ Focus on Skills, Analysis of Photos, p. 246

Tip: Use the help given in the vocab box for your formulations.

Tips on vocab

to reveal a strong contrast between … ■ to have an emotional impact on the viewer ■ to be in contrast with … ■ to expose the helplessness of … ■ to emphasize the brutality of …

ACTIVITIES

3. You are a journalist writing for either a quality or a popular newspaper and are asked to write a story about the photo taken at the Mexican border.
Write an article/a cover story for a newspaper of your choice that captures the situation and employs additional information on the people and the political background.

Step 1:

Team up with a partner and
a) decide on the type of newspaper you want to write for,
b) brush up your knowledge of the specific features and characteristics of your chosen newspaper (cf. → Focus on Facts, The Press, p. 229),
c) think about the characteristic features and elements your article should include and complete the grid provided on worksheet 15.3.

WES-121500-015

	quality newspaper	popular newspaper
characteristics	• informative • critical • …	• sensationalist • emotional • …
elements/components	• research data • …	• banner headlines in bold type • human interest story • …
language	• formal • …	• superlatives • …
photos/visuals	• …	• …

Step 2:

Use a dictionary to find the respective formal and informal synonyms of adjectives, nouns and phrases you want to use in your article. Usually, the more formal words have more syllables and derive (*abstammen*) from Latin or French. In contrast, many of the everyday words are short.
You can use the grid provided on worksheet 15.3 for your notes as well.

WES-121500-015

Examples:

adjectives/nouns/phrases	everyday/informal English	formal English
ängstlich	scared, frightened	
hilflos	helpless	
auf. jdn. zugehen		to approach sb.
helfen	to help	
Hilfe	help	
etc.		

Step 3:

a) Using a computer, design and type-set the newspaper page on-screen. Think about a layout that matches your chosen newspaper and arrange the necessary elements (e.g. columns of text, photos, an interview, banner headline, etc.) accordingly.
b) Finally, write the textual elements of your newspaper article, proofread it and make sure to cross-check the factual information, figures, etc. in order to have valid and correct information. Remember to cite the sources you have used.

→ Focus on Skills, Writing a Newspaper Article, p. 270

Tip: In order to flesh out your story with more details and background information on Yanela and her mother, and the reasons for their immigration to the USA and their arrest at the border:

- conduct an interview with Yanela's mother
- conduct an interview with the police officer
- write a human interest story about people who have suffered from crossing the border, being arrested, parents separated from their children, etc.
- appeal to the readers to stand up for migrant rights, human rights, etc.

GRAMMAR / LANGUAGE

4. Replace some of the (overused) **verbs, adjectives and nouns** in the sentences below in order to formulate them more clearly and specifically.
   - Many people from Mexico think that everything is better in America than at home.
   - Sometimes, the police officers are angry and not nice to the refugees.
   - Human rights activists say that the places where Mexicans are taken to are dangerous and dirty.
   - Often, parents and children cannot stay together.
   - Yanela's mother thinks that the police officer is not a good man.

Ben Smith

Doggerland

AWARENESS

Step 1:

Wind farms and turbines have become a common sight in many regions, whether they are on land or offshore. Although they have been built to generate 'green', sustainable energy, they are highly controversial and debated in public.

In class, collect the possible advantages and disadvantages of wind farms and turbines.

Step 2:

As a result of climate change and rising sea levels, many (coastal) areas worldwide are facing the danger of flooding in the future.

Together with a partner, describe and mediate the cartoon below, paying attention to the visual and textual elements.

Tip: The Tips on vocab box will help you to formulate your ideas.

Tips on vocab

1st image:

wind turbines ■ coastal area ■ trees and bushes ■ rocks ■ silhouettes of two people ■ in the longer term ■ to produce wind power ■ a peaceful place

2nd image:

two silhouettes in a rowing boat ■ the coastline has disappeared ■ the water level has risen ■ to be under water ■ to be flooded ■ offshore wind farm

Ben Smith's 2019 novel *Doggerland*[1], set on a vast offshore coastal wind farm in the North Sea in the near future, deals with a young man, called "the boy", whose job is to repair turbines. "The boy" is looking for his father, who disappeared while working on the rig some years before. An "old man" is the boy's only companion and human contact on the rig.

Nothing. Nothing. Nothing. Something. Fourth hook[2] down on the drop-line[3] there was a dark shape. The boy stopped pulling and sat back on his heels. The swell[4] was small that day and it was more than three metres from the platform down to the sea. The boy watched as the shape stretched and buckled[5] beneath the grey water.

"Strange fish," he said to no one.

The wind was blowing in from the west – consistent, ten or eleven metres per second by the feel of it – droning[6] through the platform's pipes and grilles[7] and pushing the sea into hard ridges[8]. The North Sea shifted from horizon to horizon, like a tarpaulin[9] being dragged over rough ground. It looked sluggish[10] but, under the surface, currents[11] ripped[12] and surged[13]. It was hard to imagine the sheer tonnages[14] hauling[15] past every minute, every second.

The boy wound the line around the railing until it was secure, then took hold of the hanging length, lifted it a few inches[16] and let it fall. He moved it from side to side, but the hook was lodged[17]. He'd have to pull it up. He moved the line again. It was heavy, whatever it was. He hoped his line wouldn't break. It had taken him a long time to get that length of cord[18]. How long? Months? Years? He looked out at the horizon as if it would give him an answer, but couldn't even pick out where the grey of the sea became the grey of the sky. It was good cord. That was all that mattered. And a hundred miles offshore[19] it wasn't easy to get hold of good cord. Could you even get proper fishing line any more? The wind squalled[20] and worked itself through the seams[21] of his overalls. Who could he ask? The old man wouldn't know. He didn't know. And there was no one else out there.

He stood up, set his feet shoulder-width apart and pulled his sleeves down over his hands. He moved his hands slowly and kept the rest of the body very still, as if trying to steady himself[22] against the motion of sea and sky. His legs were planted almost a metre apart and his sleeves barely covered his wide, calloused[23] palms[24]. Of course, the boy was not really a boy, any more than the old man was all that old; but names are relative, and out in the grey some kind of distinction[25] was necessary.

He took hold of the line and, using the rail as a fulcrum[26], began to haul it up out of the water. As soon as the load broke the surface, the line tightened and rasped[27] through his sleeves. He stopped for a moment and let the wind smooth the edges[28] of the pain, then carried on pulling until the fourth hook was level with the platform. He looked down over the rail.

It was a load of junk as usual – a greasy mass of netting and plastic, streaming[29] and reeking[30]. The whole thing was tangled[31] into a dense[32] lump[33], along with an oil-can, some polystyrene[34], and what looked like a burnt-out panel from a door.

The boy tied off the line, straightened his back and blew lightly into his palms. "Good catch," he said.

Beside him, the thick steel support rose twenty metres to the rig. Above the rig's squat[35] rectangular housing, the blades[36] of the nearest turbine turned slowly in the washed-out sky. All around, to every horizon, the blades of the wind farm turned.

The line spun slowly – ten turns one way, then a pause, then ten turns back. The boy lay down on his stomach, reached out and held the netting until it stilled[37].

The fields stretched out around him – row after row of turbines, like strange crops[38]. From a distance, they all looked identical, but up close each tower was marked with dark blooms[39] and scabs[40] of rust. There were seepages[41] of oil and grease creeping downward, streaks of salt corrosion reaching up, forming intricate[42] patterns

[1] **Doggerland** a possible reference to Dogger Bank, a fishing ground in the North Sea – [2] **hook** *Fischhaken* – [3] **drop-line** a line which is set vertically in the water to catch fish – [4] **swell** a slow up-and-down movement of the sea – [5] **to buckle** *sich wölben* – [6] **to drone** *brummen* – [7] **grille** *Gitter* – [8] **ridge** *Meeresrücken* – [9] **tarpaulin** *Plane* – [10] **sluggish** operating more slowly than usual – [11] **current** *Strömung* – [12] **to rip** to tear violently and quickly – [13] **to surge** to increase suddenly and strongly – [14] **tonnage** here: volume of water – [15] **to haul** to pull sth. heavy slowly and with difficulty – [16] **inch** 2.54 cm – [17] **to lodge** to become stuck in a place – [18] **cord** rope; *Seil* – [19] **offshore** at a distance from the coast – [20] **to squall** to make a loud sharp noise – [21] **seam** *Saum* – [22] **to steady o. s.** to make o. s. stop moving – [23] **calloused** *schwielig* – [24] **palm** *Handballen* – [25] **distinction** a difference between two similar things – [26] **fulcrum** *Stützpunkt* – [27] **to rasp** *raspeln* – [28] **edge** here: *Schärfe* – [29] **to stream** *triefen* – [30] **to reek** to have a strong unpleasant smell – [31] **to tangle** to become an untidy mass – [32] **dense** *dicht* – [33] **lump** *Klumpen* – [34] **polystyrene** a kind of plastic – [35] **squat** short and thick – [36] **blade** *Propellerflügel* – [37] **to still** to stop moving – [38] **crops** plants like grain, fruit or vegetables – [39] **bloom** a flower or a plant – [40] **scab** *Kruste* – [41] **seepage** *Durchsickern* – [42] **intricate** *verschachtelt*

of stalactites and stalagmites. Some of the turbines had slumped down[43] at an angle, their foundations crumbling like silt[44]. Some had damaged blades and threw their remaining limbs[45] around in jolting[46] arcs[47]. Others were missing their blades and nacelle[48] entirely, leaving only the towers standing, like fingerposts marking the steady progression of malfunction and storm.

He tried to feel his way down to where his hook was caught. The net had floats[49] and some kind of weights threaded through[50] it, and it was twisted up with what could have been strips of weed[51] but the boy knew were actually sheets of black plastic – he'd been finding them all over the farm recently. He worked his hand in and found the hook, then took a knife out of his pocket and began to cut away at the netting, strand[52] by strand, until it slumped down into the water, leaving just the hook and the object it was stuck in.

It was a boot – black, company issue, the same as the boy's, except, where his were dark and supple[53] from regular cleaning and waterproofing, this one was salt-stiffened, bleached and cracked, making it look like it was cut from some kind of rough stone.

He reached out slowly, tilted[54] it and looked inside. The laces had come undone and it was empty, which was a relief. He'd found a boot once before, floating through the farm, still laced up tight. When was that? It had been down in the south fields. That boot had been brown, pointed at the toe. The leather and its contents had been scratched and picked apart. There must have been birds around then. And fish.

The boy put the knife away in his pocket and took out a battered digital watch. It was missing its strap[55] and one button, and when he touched the display, bubbles of moisture spread inside the casing[56]. It read quarter past five. He looked up at the sky and saw, perhaps, a paler patch of cloud in the west. When he closed his eyes, the same patch appeared on the backs of his eyelids.

The wind dragged across the rig. Sometimes it sounded thin and hollow, sometimes it thudded[57] as if it were a solid wall, impossible to move past. The line rocked. The turbines groaned and thrummed[58]. The boy held the boot still. The sole was smooth and washed clean: the sea already cleaning things up, making things anonymous.

"Where have you come from?" he said. His voice was barely audible above the wind and the blades. Which was probably for the best, because it was a stupid question. And he was talking to a boot.

The currents that came through the farm swept in from the oceans and cycled round the whole North Sea, hauling waste and cast-offs[59] out from every coastline. Some days there would be swathes[60] of shining fluid that coated the surface of the water. Other days, shoals[61] of plastic bags and bottles would rise from the depths like bulbous[62] light-seeking creatures. The boy would find tidal[63] barrages[64] of bleached clothing, the brittle[65] shells of electrical appliances[66]. He'd seen furniture and timbers[67] tangled together so they looked like makeshift[68] rafts[69]; and once, a whole house torn loose from its moorings[70], drifting through the farm, slumped and tilting on its flotation tanks[71].

Days, months and seasons passed through untethered[72] and indistinct among the flotsam[73]. Sometimes it felt colder and there were more storms, and sometimes a big spring tide would raise the water level up closer to the platform. But it was always cold, and there were always storms. It was spring now, according to the rig's computer. He looked down at his watch – it still read quarter past five.

He put it away and unhooked the boot carefully from his line. Then he got up off his stomach and sat on the platform, drawing his knees up against the wind and holding the boot in front of him. It could have come from anywhere. It could even have come from the farm. It could have been lost and then got stuck in one of the gyres[74] that looped through the fields, catching everything that was adrift[75] inside and not letting go. It could have been cycling around the turbines, round the edge of the rig, for years.

The boot was the same size as his own. Whoever it had belonged to would have been about his height, his build. The wind pressed in and the skin on his back tightened. What if …? But he didn't let himself finish

[43] **to slump down** to lean to one side – [44] **silt** *Schlick* – [45] **limb** *Körperglied* – [46] **jolting** *ruckartig* – [47] **arc** a curved line – [48] **nacelle** *Machinenhaus* – [49] **float** *Schwimmkörper* – [50] **to thread** [θred] **through** *durchziehen* – [51] **weed** *Seegras* – [52] **strand** *Strang* – [53] **supple** *biegsam, geschmeidig* – [54] **to tilt** to hold at an angle – [55] **strap** *Armband* – [56] **casing** a covering that protects sth.; *Gehäuse* – [57] **to thud** to hit sth. with a heavy sound – [58] **to thrum** to make a rhythmic humming sound – [59] **cast-offs** clothes that you no longer want – [60] **swathe** [sweɪð] a large area – [61] **shoal** normally, a large number of fish swimming together – [62] **bulbous** fat and round – [63] **tidal** [ˈtaɪdəl] *Gezeiten-* – [64] **barrage** huge amount – [65] **brittle** delicate and easily broken – [66] **appliance** household equipment – [67] **timber** *Holzbalken* – [68] **makeshift** sth. improvised – [69] **raft** *Floß* – [70] **mooring** *Anlegeplatz* – [71] **flotation tank** *Wasserausgleichstank* – [72] **untethered** [ʌnˈteðəd] not fastened to sth. – [73] **flotsam** *Treibgut* – [74] **gyre** *Wirbel* – [75] **adrift** unmoored

the thought. There was no point going over all that. [...]

"Ahoy there, Cap'n Cod[76]." The old man, Greil, spoke from where he was slumped in his chair. He had his feet up next to the bank of monitors and didn't bother turning round. The boy had been trying to walk quietly past the control room, but now stopped in the doorway.

"Why are you sneaking[77] about?" the old man said.

The boy didn't answer.

"I saw you." The old man inclined[78] a foot towards one of the monitors. "I see all from my eyrie[79]. I am omniscient[80]." A hand appeared in emphasis, holding an enamel[81] mug, in which sloshed[82] a brutal-smelling ichor[83]. [...]

"What are you going to do with your bootlace?" The old man spoke quietly. His eyes reflected the pale light of the monitors.

"Put another hook on my line."

The old man raised his mug. "Then we shall feast like kings on the fruits of the sea." He drank, shuddered[84].

The boy waited in the doorway. "Do you reckon[85] there's anything down there?"

The old man leaned back and cradled[86] his mug in both hands. "There's plenty down there."

"I meant ..." But it was too late. Soon the old man would say "a whole country, a whole continent."

"A whole country, a whole continent."

The boy pressed his forehead against the doorframe. "Yeah, I know."

"Right here, just below us. Thousands of years ago, all this was land."

"I know."

The old man closed his eyes. "Riverbeds, forests, open plains. Villages, fire-pits ..."

The boy walked down the corridor until the old man's voice was swallowed by the rig's own creaks and mutterings.

Doggerland by Ben Smith. 4th Estate, London 2019, pp. 1 ff.

COMPREHENSION

WES-121500-016 **Tip:** In addition to reading the excerpt, you can also listen to it and **improve** your **listening skills**. Moreover, you can **combine both text versions** to get a deeper understanding of details.

1. Sum up the excerpt from the novel *Doggerland* and point out how the narrator describes
   a) the situation and the atmosphere on the rig/the wind farm in the North Sea.
   b) the boy's attempt to catch or find something.
   c) the relationship between the boy and the old man.

2. **Step 1:** Read the introductory part of the excerpt to l. 79 and extract information given about
   - the narrative point of view,
   - the setting (= time + place),
   - the situation on the rig,
   - the boy.

   Step 2: Now read the complete excerpt and, while reading, subdivide it into paragraphs, following the thematic units of the text.

   WES-121500-016 a) With the help of worksheet 16.1, find a suitable heading for each paragraph, using your notes and your own words.

   WES-121500-016 b) In order to make sure you have understood everything correctly, use worksheet 16.2 and do the reading comprehension tasks given there.

   Tip: Do not only follow the print pattern. If you have difficulties in paragraphing, pay attention to changes and breaks in the course of narration as described in the Info box on page 42.

   → Focus on Skills, Understanding Complex Texts, p. 230

   Step 3: After collecting the most relevant information, write a summary of about 250 words.

   Tip: Brush up your knowledge of how to write a summary and read the respective Skills page (→ Focus on Skills, Writing a Summary, p. 231). Most importantly, use the simple present as your basic tense. Remember to introduce and paraphrase what is said and not simply repeat the text.

[76] **Cap'n Cod** (*joc.*) *Kapitän Kabeljau* – [77] **to sneak** to go somewhere secretly – [78] **to incline** to move downwards – [79] **eyrie** normally, an eagle's nest; here: a lookout – [80] **omniscient** all-knowing – [81] **enamel** *Emaille* – [82] **to slosh** *schwappen* – [83] **ichor** ['aɪkər] (*archaic*) *eitriges Sekret* – [84] **to shudder** *schaudern* – [85] **to reckon** (*infml.*) to think or believe – [86] **to cradle** to hold sth. gently

Use the phrases given on the page *Vocabulary for Text Analysis*, p. 249.
Begin your summary with an introductory sentence that answers the w-questions (who – where – when – what – why) as well as the bibliographical information (author, title, place + year of publication).

ANALYSIS

3. Analyse the author's way of directly and indirectly characterizing the boy and the old man.

Step 1:
Find out about the narrative perspective and technique used to characterize the boy and the old man.

Tip: Use the information given on direct/indirect characterization on the Focus on Skills page "Characterization of a Figure in Literature", p. 247.

Examples:

- ll. 1 ff.: *Nothing. Nothing. Nothing. Something. Fourth hook … etc.*
  → interior monologue; the boy reflects about his possible catch
- ll. 5 f.: *The boy watched as the shape stretched …*
  → third-person perspective is used to describe what the boy is doing

Step 2:
Find references given in the text about the two characters
a) in an indirect way or b) in a direct way.
Use the grid provided on worksheet 16.3 for your findings.

WES-121500-016

Tip: Do not forget to provide examples from the text.

Tips on vocab

- The text deals with/is about …
- The text is composed of/consists of …
- The story is told from the perspective of …
- The narrator expresses his thoughts on …
- The text conveys the impression that …
- The narrator takes a negative/positive/neutral view of …

Step 3:
Taking your notes into consideration, draw conclusions about the boy's/old man's character and nature. Use your dictionary and collect appropriate words to describe and characterize them.

Tips on vocab

the boy keeps dropping the line ■ he is persistent in … ■ he has been trying for months to … ■ the boy is lonely and does not know … ■ the boy and the old man are anonymous ■ the boy is anxious to find out about … ■ he speculates about … ■ the old man teases and provokes the boy ■ he refers to the past and …

Step 4:
Examine how the author creates the specific atmosphere and collect examples from the text of how the narrator describes a) the weather (seasons, temperature, etc.) and b) the North Sea.
How are the weather and the North Sea connected to the characters and their behaviour?

Step 5:
Finally, write a literary characterization of the boy and the old man, paying attention to

- their outward appearance,
- their behaviour/attitude and
- their relationship to each other.

Tip: Use the **introduction – main part – conclusion** pattern for your text and use quotations to back up your results and findings. Remember to use the simple present as the predominant tense for your analysis.
→ Focus on Language, Vocabulary for Text Analysis, p. 249

ACTIVITIES

4. Team up with a partner and
   a) describe the cartoon below,
   b) examine what the cartoonist criticizes and explain the message of the cartoon.

Tips on vocab

on the left side:
a seabird covered in oil ■ oil spill/oil pollution ■ an offshore oil rig ■ to leak (oil) ■ bands of clouds above the sea ■ to look dangerous and threatening

on the right side:
the rotating blades of a turbine ■ razor-sharp ■ to decapitate sb. ■ a seagull ■ bulging eyes ■ to look horrified ■ to appear clean ■ to shred tens of thousands of seabirds

5. In ll. 68 – 79, the narrator describes the wind farm as a malfunctioning and dilapidated location. Together with a partner, speculate on what might have happened to the wind farm and the possible reasons for everything falling apart.
   Write an additional paragraph in which you imagine what happened.

6. In ll. 184 – 188 the old man says that "thousands of years ago, all this was land … Riverbeds, forests, open plains. Villages …".
   Imagine what might have happened in the past when this "land" was flooded and write a short story of about 300 – 400 words that describes the apocalyptic scenario.

GRAMMAR / LANGUAGE

7. "What if …?" – The boy, who is trying to trace his disappeared father, asks himself if he can find any sign of him.
   Use **if-clauses (conditional sentences)** and the references in the excerpt and write down sentences that reflect the boy's hopes and concerns.

   Examples:
   - If the boot came from one of the platforms, it could belong to … (type II)
   - If I could find any sign, it could indicate that … (type II)

   → Conditional Sentences (If-Clauses), p. 292

WES-121500-016
8. Brush up your vocabulary for characterizing a person and collect adjectives and adverbs. Use worksheet 16.1 for your notes.

The Nearer the Friends, the Stronger the Regional Identity

AWARENESS

Travelling, going abroad, learning about new people and countries …
What do you think about it? Are you a homebody or have you caught the travel bug? Discuss in class.

A new job, an academic career or a romantic relationship – there are many reasons for young people to move. But this does not necessarily lead to happiness. Satisfaction increases when people can identify with the region in which they live. The proximity of people who are emotionally important to them, however, is essential for creating this feeling of commitment[1]. Psychologists at Friedrich Schiller University, Jena, have now identified and described these factors and their effects in a longitudinal study[2]. They have reported their research findings in the toptier[3] journal *Developmental Psychology*. "As well as professional and personal success, it is mostly a person's commitment to his place of residence that is decisive for a truly successful life," explains Dr Elisabeth Borschel, who carried out the study as part of her doctoral research. "However, young adults in particular are under enormous pressure to be mobile, as they are expected to move frequently in order to make a start in life. We have studied the resulting tensions[4] more closely in a longitudinal study. The study was funded by the Free State of Thuringia[5]."

Skyping is no substitute for personal proximity[6]

The Jena psychologists studied more than 1,000 students throughout Germany shortly before they graduated and then on two more occasions within the next year. Five hundred of them left the place where they had studied, while a second group did not move. The researchers also recorded the places of residence[7] of the people named by the students as being important to them – family members, friends or partners. The panel study[8] showed that the proximity of such key social contacts was of great influence on the way people identified with the region they lived in. "This is a surprising and therefore very enlightening result for us, as it contradicts[9] a major promise of post-modern society and capitalism, which is that in our era of high mobility and modern means of communication, we can also maintain relationships independently of time and space," says Prof. Franz J. Neyer of the University of Jena, who also worked on the study. "It would seem that Skype or emails cannot compensate for the loss of personal – and thus geographical – proximity." This means that the greater the distance, the greater the dissatisfaction.

Moving away also has an impact on those who remain

Admittedly, there are also interactions between the emergence[10] of a regional identity and the creation of a social network. "It really is a two-edged sword," says Elisabeth Borschel, "because someone who identifies with his geographical surroundings also finds it easier to establish important social contacts. For this reason, mobility cannot be condemned[11] in principle[12], but the new location has to meet the right basic conditions for a person to find new people he or she can relate to." Employers, for example, should take this into account[13] and support it when they advertise for new recruits nationwide. "In addition, we can identify what is called passive mobility," says Neyer. "This means that if a person moves away, it also affects the significant people who stay behind – the identification with their surroundings also fades[14]." Therefore, the research results should be taken into account in political decisions, because the spatial[15] proximity between significant contacts also has effects on the state of a society. Appropriate[16] measures which do not force young people to move to a new location to find a job – economic structural support[17], for example – could be a means of significantly[18] boosting[19] the satisfaction of people living in this region.

Friedrich-Schiller-Universität Jena, https://www.sciencedaily.com/releases/2019/03/190312103705.htm, 12 March 2019 [20.07.2019]

[1] **commitment** *Bindung* – [2] **longitudinal study** longitudinal research is done on people or groups over a period of time – [3] **toptier** here: very influential; **tier** [tɪər] one of several layers or levels – [4] **tension** a feeling of nervousness or anger – [5] **Free State of Thuringia** *Freistaat Thüringen* – [6] **proximity** (*fml.*) closeness – [7] **place of residence** *Wohnort* – [8] **panel study** *Längsschnittuntersuchung* – [9] **to contradict** *widersprechen* – [10] **emergence** the fact of sth. becoming known or starting to exist – [11] **to condemn** *verdammen* – [12] **in principle** *grundsätzlich* – [13] **to take sth. into account** (*idm.*) *etw. in Betracht ziehen* – [14] **to fade** to lose strength gradually – [15] **spatial** *räumlich* – [16] **appropriate** *angemessen* – [17] **economic structural support** money given by the government – [18] **significant** important or noticeable – [19] **to boost** to improve or increase sth.

COMPREHENSION

1. After reading the text, complete the following sentence with evidence from the text:
Skyping is no substitute for personal proximity because …

WES-121500-017 **2.** Get a more detailed understanding of the academic findings and do the tasks provided on worksheet 17.1.

ANALYSIS

3. The authors make a specific assertion (= *eine Behauptung aufstellen*) in the heading of the text. Examine the Thuringian scientists' line of argument* and explain how it supports and verifies the assertion made in the heading.

Step 1:
Juxtapose (*gegenüberstellen*) and contrast the results of the study in the categories 'happiness/satisfaction' and 'unhappiness/dissatisfaction'.
Team up with a partner and complete the grid below.

happiness/satisfaction	unhappiness/dissatisfaction
• identification with the region • …	• being expected to move frequently • …

→ Focus on Skills, Analysis of a Non-Fictional Text, p. 237

Step 2:
Read the article a second time and, using your results from worksheet 17.1, identify the various examples and arguments given in the text. Additionally, take notes on the conclusions the scientists have drawn.
WES-121500-017 Use worksheet 17.2 for your notes.

Tip: Remember to note the lines where you found the information in the text.

Info

A **line of argument** is the way different reasons are gradually developed and structured to convince a reader of a particular point of view.

There are different ways of structuring an argumentation, e. g.
- Listing structure → enumerating facts, ideas, aspects
- Progressive structure → developing a cause-to-effect or problem-solution arrangement
- Antithetical structure → contrasting and juxtaposing facts, ideas and arguments

→ Focus on Facts, Basic Types of Non-Fictional Texts, p. 227

Step 3:

a) The Nearer the Friends, the Stronger the Regional Identity (heading)
b) The proximity of people […] is essential for […] this feeling of commitment. (ll. 5 ff.)
c) … the proximity of […] key social contacts was of great influence … (ll. 31 ff.)
d) … Skype or emails cannot compensate for the loss of personal […] proximity. (ll. 39 ff.)
e) … the […] proximity has effects on the state of a society. (ll. 63 ff.)

Explain the function and effect of the (very similar) statements listed above, which are made throughout the whole text.

Step 4:
Finally, write a coherent text of about 250 – 300 words in which you explain the scientists' line of argument*.
→ Focus on Skills, Analysis of a Non-Fictional Text, p. 237

Tip: Remember to quote from the text to prove the accuracy of your text and use the simple present.

ACTIVITIES

4. Write a comment in response to the article in which you critically state whether (or not) you agree with the Thuringian academic study results and the conclusions drawn from them.

Step 1:
Think about a concise and strong introduction, in which you raise a controversial question or refer to a disputed example or event. You can also make an (provocative) introductory remark or statement on a disputed matter.

Step 2:
In the main part of your comment, state and describe the pros and cons of your topic.

Tip: Use the general pattern of **introduction – main part – conclusion** for your comment.
- **introduction** (answering the w-questions who – what – where – when – why? and attracting the reader's attention)
- **main part** (presenting arguments)
- **conclusion** (briefly summarizing the main ideas)

Tips on vocab

I consider that ■ I believe that ■ I hold the view that ■ To my mind ■ I have the impression that ■ As far as I know ■ I am sure about/of ■ I have doubts about ■ I doubt that ■ It seems possible that ■ It's rather unlikely ■ The author seems to ■ I (dis-)agree with ■ The author has reason to believe ■ I share/don't share the author's view on ■ I consider it to be right/wrong to say ■ I would like to clarify ■ The author's opinion/statement contrasts with/contradicts

Tip: Use connectives and linking phrases to make your text more fluent.

Tips on vocab

furthermore ■ for example ■ yet ■ however ■ as well as ■ perhaps ■ because of this ■ having said that ■ on the contrary ■ beyond that ■ moreover ■ in order to ■ despite ■ bearing in mind ■ on the other hand

Step 3:
Write the comment in a coherent text of about 300 words, and express your views on the matter.

Tip: Remember to refer to the text and employ quotes to substantiate your arguments.
→ Focus on Skills, Writing a Newspaper Commentary/an Editorial/a Blog Post, p. 266

GRAMMAR / LANGUAGE

5. Brush up your vocabulary, finding **synonyms and/or antonyms** (= words that mean the opposite) to the words and phrases taken from the text.
Complete the grid provided on worksheet 17.3.

WES-121500-017

Wenn Kinder von Helikoptereltern erwachsen werden

AWARENESS

Divide the class into groups of 3–4 students. Each group can choose the cartoon they like best, but all of the cartoons should be dealt with.

a) Describe the cartoon, paying attention to details.
b) Explain the cartoon's message: What specifically does the cartoonist want to mock and/or criticize?
c) What is your experience with and opinion of helicopter parents? Discuss.

1

Tips on vocab

to give an experience report ■ to stand in front of the class ■ to play on words ■ to welcome the class/parents after the summer holidays ■ to look bored ■ to be ashamed of sb./sth. ■ the silhouettes of students ■ to sit at the desk

2

"Don't mind them. I've got a helicopter mom and a drone dad."

3

YOU DON'T THINK YOU'RE JUST A TAD OVERPROTECTIVE?

Tips on vocab

to splash around (*plantschen*) ■ inflatable swimming pool ■ a wooden garden fence ■ to peep over sth. ■ to watch secretly ■ to monitor sb.

Tips on vocab

toddlers ■ to splash around ■ to be sitting in the bathtub ■ towels on a towel rack ■ to hire a life guard ■ to be overprotective ■ to drop by (*vorbeischauen*) ■ high seat ■ to sit with one's legs crossed

1 An Weihnachten fallen selbst viele Erwachsene plötzlich wieder in die Kinderrolle, heißt es. Was für einige Stunden im Jahr okay sein mag, geht erwachsenen Kindern von Helikoptereltern ständig so: Mama und Papa können einfach nicht loslassen[1]. Bewerbung, Ausbildung[2], Studium, Job, Partnerwahl: Bei allem wollen sie mitmischen[3] – und tun das auch, völlig ungeniert[4].

„Das Schärfste[5], was ich einmal erlebt habe", erzählt der Geschäftsführer eines IT- und EDV-Unternehmens, „waren Eltern, die ihren 21-jährigen Sohn zu seinem ersten Ausbildungstag bei uns begleitet[6] haben." Nachdem er den jungen Mann begrüßt hatte, habe es geklingelt und die Mutter habe vor der Tür gestanden mit der Bitte, eintreten zu dürfen. „Ich war so perplex[7], dass ich sie hereingelassen habe. Sie hatte kaum Platz genommen, da klingelte es wieder, diesmal war es der Vater. Er entschuldigte sich wegen der Verspätung[8] – die Parkplätze – und drängte[9] auch ins Büro. Auf meine völlig hilflose Frage, was sie denn hier wollten, erklärten die beiden: ihren Sohn am ersten Arbeitstag unterstützen."

Selbst Unis und Unternehmen sprechen[10] längst die Eltern an, um ihre Studiengänge[11] und Ausbildungsmöglichkeiten anzupreisen[12]: „Eltern haben bei der Studien- und Berufswahl[13] ihrer Kinder eine wichtige Funktion. Wir sprechen deshalb auch Eltern von Studieninteressierten an und ermöglichen ihnen, eigene Fragen in Bezug auf ein Studium ihres Kindes zu klären", teilt die Uni Göttingen mit – und verschickt sogar eine Pressemeldung[14] zum Informationsabend[15] für Eltern von Studieninteressierten.

Auch auf der Website der Deutschen Bahn heißt es: „Hier findet Ihr Kind eine Übersicht der Dualen Studiengänge[16]" und „Egal ob Onlinebewerbung, Lebenslauf oder das Vorstellungsgespräch: Wir erklären Ihnen Schritt für Schritt, wie die Bewerbung Ihres Kindes aussehen sollte".

Und was machen echte Helikoptereltern, wenn es bei der 24-jährigen Tochter offenbar nicht so recht klappt bei der Partnersuche? Dann schalten sie in einer großen Tageszeitung eine Anzeige[17], wie die „tz" berichtete:

„Liebe Eltern! Echter Münchner mit Familienunternehmen / Immob. möchte dem Glück seiner Tochter, 24 J., hübsch, 1,70 m, studiert, sportlich, unternehmungsfreudig, vielseitig interessiert, auf die Sprünge helfen[18]. Gesucht wird: junger Mann bis 35 J., ab 1,78 m groß, gutaussehend, charmant, strebsam, NR[19], aus guter Familie / gerne Unternehmer / Handwerker / Akademiker. Bitte Bildzuschrift[20]."

Auch eine deutsche Mutter, die mit ihrer Familie in den USA lebt, bevormundete[21] ihre Tochter jahrelang, optimierte[22] deren Leben und half überall, noch bevor sie darum gebeten wurde.

2 Erst als die Tochter für ein Praktikum das Land verließ, schaffte es die damals 22-Jährige, ihre Mutter in einer E-Mail darum zu bitten, sie selbstständiger werden zu lassen. [...] Hier ist ein Auszug:

„Mama,
bitte hör mir gut zu, denn ich werde noch verrückt, weil ich nicht weiß, wie ich es Dir sagen soll, ohne gemein zu klingen oder Deine Gefühle zu verletzen. Das ist nicht meine Absicht, aber ich möchte auch nichts beschönigen[23], also sag ich es jetzt: Hör auf, mir zu helfen.
Ich frage Dich fast nie um Hilfe, aber Du machst es einfach. Mein ganzes Leben lang hast Du Dinge für mich getan, bevor ich sie selbst probieren konnte. Als ich hier ans College kam, musste mir meine Mitbewohnerin[24] erst einmal zeigen, wie man Wäsche wäscht. [...]
Bitte denk nicht, Du wärst eine schlechte Mutter. Du bist eine tolle Mutter und ziemlich cool und ich liebe Dich, aber ich wünsche mir, dass Du mit dem Helfen aufhörst. Es reicht, wenn Du einfach da bist, und ich werde kommen und um Hilfe bitten, wenn ich sie brauche, aber zuerst muss ich Dinge allein versuchen. Wenn ich jetzt wie ein schlechter Mensch wirke, tut es mir leid, aber das bin einfach ich, wie ich erwachsen werde, und das ist doch etwas Gutes!"

Sie habe sich erst kurz erschrocken[25] über den Brief, sagte die Mutter, dann sei sie aber erleichtert[26] gewesen. „Ich bin jetzt frei", habe sie gedacht. Und sie weiß heute: „Das Leben meiner Tochter ist nicht perfekt durch meine Hilfe. Wie auch?" [...]

3 So berichten auch im dritten Band der lustigsten Anekdoten[27] über Helikoptereltern wieder Erzieher, Lehrerinnen, Ärztinnen und Supermarktmitarbeiter von kuriosen Begegnungen[28] und Erlebnissen.

So wie die Hebamme[29], die angerufen wurde, weil ein Baby Schluckauf[30] hatte, und die Erzieherin, die in der

[1] to let go of sb./sth. – [2] apprenticeship – [3] to interfere with sth. – [4] blithely – [5] the weirdest – [6] to accompany sb. – [7] dumbfounded – [8] delay – [9] to push/shove – [10] to address sb. – [11] academic course – [12] to advertise – [13] studies and career choice – [14] press release – [15] information evening – [16] integrated degree programme – [17] to run an advertisement – [18] to give sb. a leg up – [19] non-smoker – [20] attached photograph – [21] to patronize sb. – [22] to optimize – [23] to gloss over sth.– [24] roommate – [25] startled – [26] relieved – [27] anecdote – [28] odd encounter – [29] midwife – [30] hiccup

Kita[31] die Klobrille[32] vorwärmen sollte. Oder die Lehrerin, die beobachtet, wie Mütter dem Schulbus hinterherfahren oder auf dem Schulhof herumlungern[33] und dass Väter die Hausaufgaben für ihre Kinder machen. Auch vor Fake-WhatsApp-Accounts schrecken Eltern nicht zurück, damit sie – als Jugendliche getarnt – heimlich mit ihren Kindern chatten, um zu sehen, „wie unsere Töchter reagieren".

„Bitte denk nicht, du wärst eine schlechte Mutter. Aber hör auf, mir zu helfen!" Der Spiegel, 18.12.2020 https://www.spiegel.de/familie/helikopter-eltern-wenn-selbst-erwachsene-kinder-uebermuttert-werden-a-993dfc82-1ce1-4e78-b327-69e49ee8a529 [18.12.2020]

COMPREHENSION

1. a) Read the German magazine article and get an overview of the aspects mentioned.

M b) The article has already been subdivided into three thematic parts. Find an appropriate heading in English for each part that reflects its relevant contents.

2. Together with a partner, take notes in English on the examples and explanations given in the article. Use worksheet 18.1 for your notes.

WES-121500-018

ANALYSIS

M **3. Mediate the German magazine article and explain how helicopter parents patronize their children.**

Tip: Be careful not to translate the article. Extract the most relevant information and transform it into English, using the annotations given and adding further explanations where necessary.

Step 1:
Read the **first part** of the text a second time and explain the effect and impact that helicopter parents have on the lives of their children.

Step 2:
Study the **second part** of the article and explain what the daughter wants her mother (not) to do.

Step 3:
Explain the examples given of overly protective parents in the **third part** of the text.

Step 4:
Finally, sort all your results and write a coherent analysis of the controversial topic of helicopter parents in about 250 words.

Tip: Use this structure for your analysis:
- **introduction** (title, author, topic, time of publication)
- **main part**
  a) identifying and describing the information given
  b) relating the information to other information available
  c) drawing conclusions and explaining the facts and information
- **conclusion** (summing up the main aspects in one or two sentences)

→ Focus on Skills, Mediation, p. 253
→ Focus on Skills, Writing an Analysis, p. 248

Example:
The magazine article … published on … by *Der Spiegel* … illustrates the controversial and problematic situation of …

[31] nursery – [32] toilet seat – [33] to hang around

ACTIVITIES

4. A growing number of students and young people in general are suffering from their overly protective or even intrusive helicopter parents. Therefore, you and your team have decided to initiate an online self-help group which
a) offers help and support;
b) gives advice on how to emancipate oneself and
c) answers questions.

Step 1:

@ WES-121500-018

In groups of 3 – 4 students, compile a website for students/teenagers/young people seeking help. Use your results from the previous tasks for your website and additionally, do further research on helicopter parents using the links provided on the webcode.

→ Focus on Skills, Doing Research and Citing Sources, p. 262

Step 2:

Present your various homepages in class and discuss the information given and support offered there.

GRAMMAR / LANGUAGE

5. Put yourself either in the helicopter mother's/parents' or the teenager's position and reflect on what you could or should have done better or differently to improve the situation. Use **conditional sentences** and **modal auxiliaries** for your formulations.

Examples:

- If I had told Mom earlier, we **could have** avoided so much trouble. (type III)
- I used to have a bad conscience because I thought I **should have**/I had to … (type II)

→ Modal Auxiliaries, p. 296
→ Conditional Sentences (If-Clauses), p. 292

Identifying Visual and Textual Symbols

Imagery consists of descriptive language that produces images (pictures), evokes associations in the reader's mind and adds symbolism. It includes figurative (*bildlich*) and metaphorical language and appeals to the five senses – taste, touch, sight, smell and sound. **Visual/graphic symbols** are used to represent forms, which allows for an interpretation beyond the literal (*wörtlich*) definition. Often, they illustrate unspoken feelings. There are simple graphic symbols (e.g. traffic signs, emojis) and more complex ones (e. g. butterfly → metamorphosis; owl → wisdom, etc.).

Jennifer Clement

Gun Love

My mother was a cup of sugar. You could borrow[1] her anytime.

My mother was so sweet, her hands were always birth-day-party sticky[2]. Her breath held the five flavors of Life Savers[3] candy.

And she knew all the love songs that are a university[4] for love. She knew "Slowly Walk Close to Me," Where Did You Sleep Last Night?," "Born Under A Bad Sign," and all the I'll-kill-you-if-you-leave-me songs.

But sweetness is always looking for Mr. Bad and Mr. Bad can pick out Miss Sweet in any crowd.

My mother opened her mouth in a great wide O and breathed him right into her body.

I couldn't understand. She knew all the songs, so why would she get messed and stirred up with this man?

When he said his name was Eli she was down on her knees. [...]

My mother named me Pearl because, she said, You were so white. You came from a place that is far away from any normal birthplace like a hospital or clinic.

She said, Nobody knew, and I gave you your birthday, to you all alone, by myself, in silence. I did not cry and you did not cry. [...]

She said, You were so small. You fit inside a hand towel. You were so white. More like a pearl than skin. You were like ice or cloud, like a meringue[5]. I could almost see inside your body. I looked at your pale-blue stone eyes and named you. Just that, she said.

I was a pearl. People stared at me. I didn't know a different life. I didn't know what it was like to walk around and not be noticed. They could think I was beautiful or ugly but, no matter what, everyone stared. Hands were always reaching out to touch my silver hair or the white glaze[6] of my cheek.

You're all luster[7], my mother said. Being with you is like wearing pretty earrings and a new dress.

My mother lived in her father's house for two months after my birth without anyone knowing I was there.

She said, When I had to go to school or leave to do something, I placed you in the closet[8] in my room, all in the dark, all wrapped up[9]. I made a bed for you on the shoe rack[10] with towels and my sweaters. I nested you there like a kitten. I used paper towels from the kitchen as diapers[11]. The house was so big, no one ever heard you cry.

You were born in a fairy tale, my mother said.

from *Gun Love* by Jennifer Clement. Hogarth Press, London, 2018, pp. 5 ff.

1. You have already read and dealt with another excerpt from the novel *Gun Love* in Skill 5.
   a) Read the excerpt from the novel.
   b) Some of the imagery employed in the text has already been highlighted.
   c) Use the checklist on the opposite page and first, determine the respective device; second, explain its function and effect.
   d) Detect and explain further imagery in the excerpt.

2. Using the criteria given in the checklist about visual and graphic symbols, work with the two visuals on the opposite page:
   a) How do they appeal to the reader's emotion?
   b) What is the message the cartoonist/photographer wants to convey?

[1] **to borrow** *etw. ausleihen* – [2] **sticky** *klebrig* – [3] **Life Savers** peppermint ring-shaped candy – [4] **university** here: a source of information (about love) – [5] **meringue** [məˈræŋ] *Baiser, Schaumgebäck* – [6] **glaze** here: shiny softness – [7] **luster** brightness – [8] **closet** a small cupboard or room used to store things – [9] **to wrap sth. up** *einwickeln* – [10] **shoe rack** *Schuhregal* – [11] **diaper** [ˈdaɪəpə(r)] *Babywindel*

Banksy street art, *Slave Labour*, London 2012

A homeless mother and her children in Paris, France

Tips on vocab

1 a boy of pre-school age ■ to squat/to crouch (*hocken*) ■ sewing machine ['səʊɪŋ məʃiːn] ■ old-fashioned ■ to have a distressed (*bekümmert*) facial expression ■ to sew [səʊ] sth. ■ bunting (*Wimpelgirlande*) ■ Union Jack/British national flag ■ dungarees (*Latzhose*)

2 to be huddled up ■ to sit on sb.'s lap ■ to huddle together (*zusammenkauern*) ■ huge plastic bags ■ one's belongings (*die Habe*) ■ to live from hand to mouth ■ to sit on a (dirty) pavement

3. The title of this unit is "Growing Up – No Longer Being a Child!"
Collect photographs, cartoons, graffiti and snippets from newspapers/magazines that reflect
a) the implications of this title.
b) the various aspects that come to your mind when thinking about 'growing up'.
Present/display your wallpapers in class and discuss their implied messages.

Checklist

imagery	meaning/function/effect
metaphor	→ poetic comparison without 'like' or 'as'
simile	→ comparison using 'like' or 'as'
personification	→ objects/ideas/animals are given human characteristics (a smiling moon)
onomatopoeia	→ words that imitate a sound associated with a thing that is named (e.g. hum, cuckoo)
visual/graphic symbols	**meaning/function/effect**
items in focus/ visually dominant elements	→ guiding the viewer → eye-catcher
reduction to essentials/ simplification	→ focusing on the problem
snapshot character	→ emotional appeal to the viewer
colour(s)/lack of colour	→ focus on contrast → emotional appeal
caption	→ eyecatcher, evoking interest and curiosity

teenage life		
(to have an) abortion	a medical operation to end a pregnancy	*eine Abtreibung vornehmen lassen*
adolescence	the period during which a young person develops into an adult	*Jugend*
adolescent	a young person between the ages of 12 – 18	*Jugendliche(r)*
the age of majority	the age at which sb. becomes an adult in the eyes of the law	*Volljährigkeit*
anxiety [æŋ'zaɪətɪ]	a feeling of intense nervousness or panic	*Angst*
to be attracted to sb.	to like sb., esp. sexually	*sich zu jdm, (sexuell) hingezogen fühlen*
birth control	the practice of controlling when you do or do not fall pregnant, usually involving contraception	*Geburtenkontrolle, -regelung*
to (not) conform to sth.	to (not) follow what is generally accepted and considered 'the norm' by society	*sich (nicht) an etw. anpassen*
to find one's feet (e. g. at a new school)	to become used to new or unfamiliar surroundings, to settle in	*sich zurechtfinden (z. B. an einer neuen Schule)*
to grow up	to transition physically and psychologically from a child into an adult (a 'grown up')	*erwachsen, groß werden*
to have a crush on sb.	to experience strong, one-sided affection for sb.	*in jdn. verknallt sein*
identity	the values/qualities/attributes a person has that define them and their sense of self	*Identität*
hormones	chemical substances in the body that contribute to sb.'s physical and psychological development	*Hormone*
to learn life lessons	to learn what (not) to do in life through experiencing things for yourself	*lebensdienliche Erfahrungen machen*
mature	fully grown and developed; sensible and reasonable	*reif/erwachsen*
(a) minor	sb. who is legally considered underage or under the age of majority, and so is not yet an adult	*Minderjährige(r)*
peer group	a group of people of the same age or social status	*Altersgruppe*
peer pressure	a strong feeling that you must do the same things as other people of your age, even if you do not want to	*Gruppenzwang*
to practice contraception, to be on/take the pill	to prevent sex from resulting in pregnancy, by means of condoms or medicine	*Verhütung praktizieren, die Pille nehmen*
pregnancy test	a medical test to show if you are pregnant or not	*Schwangerschaftstest*
puberty	the stage of adolescence where sexual organs develop and a person is now able to have children	*Pubertät*
pubescent [pjuː'bɛsnt]	currently going through puberty	*pubertierend*
to rebel [rɪ'bel] **against sb./sth.**	to oppose or to fight against sb. in authority/an idea/a situation you do not agree with	*rebellieren (gegen jdn./etw.)*
to search for one's own identity	to try and find out what you do/do not like, what your abilities/values are, who you are as a person etc.	*seine Identität suchen; herausfinden, wer man ist*
to seek fun/entertainment	to look for amusement, enjoyment, pleasure at parties, with friends, on holiday	*Spaß/Unterhaltung haben*
(to show) disregard (for) traditional values	to pay a lack of proper attention to or respect for	*Missachtung von traditionellen Werten (zeigen)*
to stand one's ground	to refuse to accept defeat in an argument, etc.	*sich nicht unterkriegen lassen*
to suffer from (loneliness, frustration, a lack of drive)	to experience pain, loss, difficulty, etc.	*leiden an (Einsamkeit, Enttäuschung, Antriebslosigkeit)*
teenage pregnancy	the state of being pregnant whilst still a teenager	*Teenage-Schwangerschaft*

truancy	the act of deliberately skipping school	*Schwänzen*
underage	sb. who is legally considered too young to do sth.	*minderjährig*
youth culture	the behaviour patterns and trends among young people	*Jugendkultur*
	addictions/habits/temptations	
addiction (to)	the condition of being unable to stop doing sth. e. g. taking harmful drugs, drinking alcohol	*Abhängigkeit (von)*
alcoholic	sb. who regularly drinks too much and has no control over their alcohol intake	*Alkoholiker(in)*
ASBO (= anti-social behaviour disorder)	an official order in GB to restrict the behaviour of a person likely to cause harm or misery to other people	*eine öffentliche Verwarnung mit Auflagen*
to be addicted to sth.	to be unable to stop using or doing sth. as a negative habit	*süchtig sein nach etw.*
binge drinking	drinking a large amount of alcohol very quickly to get drunk, lacking self-control	*‚Komasaufen'*
to break the cycle of sth.	to stop doing sth. you do constantly and find hard to stop	*den Kreislauf von etw. durchbrechen*
coping mechanism	sth. that you rely on to help deal with difficulties or problems in your life	*Bewältigungsmechanismus*
counselling	professional psychological guidance that helps sb. cope better with difficulty and struggle	*Beratung, Seelsorge*
to deal drugs	to sell drugs illegally to other people	*mit Drogen dealen*
to display self-harming tendencies	to physically hurt oneself	*selbstverletzendes Verhalten zeigen*
drug abuse	the practice of taking illegal drugs	*Drogenmissbrauch*
to feed one's addiction through crime	to satisfy one's addiction by committing crimes	*seine Sucht durch Verbrechen finanzieren*
to give vent to one's anger	to express a strong feeling of annoyance or displeasure freely, sometimes violently	*seinem Ärger Luft machen*
to go cold turkey	to suddenly stop doing sth. you are addicted to, e. g. taking illegal drugs, drinking alcohol	*einen abrupten Entzug machen*
habit	sth. that you do regularly, often without thinking	*Gewohnheit*
helpline	a telephone number you can ring when you need (often urgent) help or support	*Notrufnummer, Telefonseelsorge*
hooligan	usually, a young man who causes trouble by fighting, often football-related	*Randalierer, Rowdy, Hooligan*
juvenile prostitute	an underage person who sells their body for sex	*minderjährige Prostituierte*
to lose one's temper	to have no control over one's feelings, esp. anger	*die Beherrschung verlieren*
misfit	a person unfit or unable to live together with others	*unsozialer Eigenbrötler, Außenseiter*
out of/under control	(not) held in check, manageable, restrained	*außer/unter Kontrolle*
(to engage in) prostitution	to be paid to have sex with people	*sich prostituieren*
rehabilitation centre (rehab)	somewhere you can go for assistance in recovering from an addiction	*Rehabilitationszentrum*
to smoke a blunt/joint	to smoke a rolled cigarette or cigar filled with cannabis	*Cannabis rauchen*
solvent abuse	the habit of inhaling dangerous chemicals, usually found in glue, to achieve a state of intense relaxation	*Lösungsmittelmissbrauch*
survival sex	the act of engaging in prostitution because you have no other chance to make money and survive	
therapy	professional treatment of a mental or physical illness	*Therapie*
vandalism	intentional or needless damage to or destruction of public or private property	*Vandalismus, Zerstörungswut*

violence	the (often harmful) use of physical or emotional force	*Gewalt*
withdrawal symptoms	the body's physical and mental response when an addict stops taking drugs, sometimes very severe	*Entzugssymptome, -erscheinungen*
	friendship	
to be (non-) judgmental	to listen with(out) the intention to criticize and quickly form judgments on what you hear	*(nicht) wertend sein*
to be there for sb.	to offer your support to sb. when they need it	*für jdn. da sein*
a call or cry for help	desperate request for support and assistance	*Hilferuf*
to care about sb.	to feel affection towards sb.	*sich um jdn. Gedanken machen*
empathy	ability to share and understand another person's feelings	*Einfühlungsvermögen*
a feeling of togetherness	feeling of being close to other people	*Zusammengehörigkeitsgefühl*
to feel valued by sb.	to know that sb. appreciates you	*sich von jdm. geschätzt fühlen*
free of prejudice	not showing any unfair thoughts or feelings about sb./sth.	*ohne Vorurteile, vorurteilsfrei*
friendship group	a circle of friends that spend time together	*Freundeskreis*
to give sb. a helping hand	to help sb.	*jdm. Helfen*
loyalty	the quality of being loyal, committed to sb./sth.	*Loyalität*
mutual respect	respect that is shared between two or more people	*gegenseitiger Respekt*
partner-in-crime	a light-hearted term used to describe a close, long-term friend who you have shared lots of experiences with (nothing to do with crime!)	*Komplize, Partner*
platonic (love)	the affection you feel for a friend who is not a romantic partner	*platonisch(e Liebe)*
reliable	the quality of being sb. others can depend on or trust	*zuverlässig*
to rely on sb.	to trust sb. to help you when you need help	*sich auf jdn. verlassen*
sense of belonging	the feeling that you are loved and appreciated where you currently are	*Zugehörigkeitsgefühl*
to support sb.	to encourage sb. in a positive, helpful way	*jdn. unterstützen*
to take responsibility for sb.	to accept the duty of supporting sb. And keeping them away from harm	*Verantwortung übernehmen*
toxic	used to describe a negative dynamic in a friendship or relationship, often involving jealousy or controlling behaviour	*toxisch*
to trust sb.	to believe that sb. is reliable, honest and of good character	*jdm. vertrauen*
trustworthy	the quality of being dependable, able to be trusted with anything	*vertrauenswürdig, zuverlässig*
	children's rights	
ban on corporal punishment	the act of forbidding physical punishment	*Verbot körperlicher Züchtigung*
child labour	often harmful/dangerous/illegal work that damages a child's development, education and livelihood	*Kinderarbeit*
child protection	the act of ensuring all children are safe from exploitation, abuse and negligent treatment	*Kinderschutz*
child trafficking	the act of recruiting, smuggling or keeping children for the purpose of exploitation	*Kinderhandel*
to detain sb.	to hold sb. back, keep sb. in custody or confinement	*jdn. festhalten*
to do sth. in sb.'s best interest	to act in a way that you think will be most helpful or useful for sb. else	*etw. im besten Interesse von jdm. machen*
domestic violence	any form of physical, emotional, verbal or sexual abuse that takes place at home	*häusliche Gewalt*

to exploit sb./sth.	to take advantage of or control sb. in an unfair, harmful way, usually involves a power imbalance	*jdn. ausbeuten*
exploitation	the act of taking advantage of sb. or violating their rights	*Ausbeutung*
juvenile delinquent	a youth offender; sb. under the age of majority who has behaved illegally or committed a crime	*jugendlicher Straftäter*
mental/physical/sexual abuse	the act of causing violent or sexual harm or lack of attention which could be damaging to a child's psyche	*seelischer/körperlicher/ sexueller Missbrauch*
non-discrimination	the basic principle that ensures all children have equal access to their rights and effective protection	*Antidiskriminierung*
personal development	the process of growing more confident in your identity	*Persönlichkeitsentwicklung*
Save the Children	a non-governmental organization (NGO) that works to protect children's rights around the world	
security	protection from anything or anyone harmful	*Sicherheit*
social services	either public or private services that ensure the welfare and security of vulnerable or at-risk groups	*Sozialeinrichtungen*
to take advantage of sb./ sth.	to exploit your power over sb. more vulnerable to get what you want, even if it harms them	*jdn./etw. ausnutzen*
The 1989 Convention on the Rights of the Child (CRC)	the first legally binding document for child protection signed by all Member States of the UN in 1989 that outlines the rights of children around the world	*Das Übereinkommen über die Rechte des Kindes*
a victim of child abuse	a child that has suffered harm	*Opfer von Kindesmissbrauch*
to violate sth.	to disregard or break sth. important, e. g. the law, sexual consent, a person's rights	*etw. verletzen*
violation	the act of violating or the state of being violated	*Verletzung, Verstoß*
vulnerable	the state of being susceptible to physical or emotional harm, influence or attack	*verwundbar, ungeschützt*
youth/juvenile detention centre	the place where juvenile delinquents stay, sometimes temporarily but often to serve the full punishment for their crime	*Jugendstrafanstalt*

The Blue Planet – Consumption and Environment

Ed Hawkins

Warming Stripes

In May 2018, Ed Hawkins, a climate scientist and professor at the University of Reading, England, published a chronologically ordered series of coloured vertical stripes aimed at visualizing global warming on the website www.ShowYourStripes.info.

> "I wanted to communicate temperature changes in a way that was simple and intuitive, removing all the distractions of standard climate graphics so that the long-term trends and variations in temperature are crystal clear. Our visual system will do the interpretation of the stripes without us even thinking about it."
>
> https://earther.gizmodo.com/this-climate-visualization-belongs-in-a-damn-museum-1826307536, 25 May 2018 [20.09.2019]

Annual global temperatures from 1850 – 2018, with each stripe representing one year. The colour scale represents the change in global temperatures covering 1.35°C.

Annual temperatures in Germany from 1881 – 2018, with each stripe representing one year. The colour scale goes from 6.6°C (dark blue) to 10.3°C (dark red).

Tips on vocab

a dolphin with its jaws wide open ■ looking directly into the viewer's eye ■ different kinds of plastic trash ■ disposable packaging ■ disposable plastic cups/bottles/plates/straws ■ aluminium/tin/plastic foil ■ to suffocate from sth. ■ to digest sth. ■ to get sth. into one's system ■ WWF logo ■ panda bear ■ banner headline/caption ■ to be fed up (to the back teeth) with sb./sth. (*infml.*) ■ appeal to the viewer to stop the flood of plastic ■ appeal to donate money ■ to launch a campaign

START-UP ACTIVITIES

1. Take a close look at the warming stripes and
   a) describe the (obvious) trends in temperature in Germany and globally,
   b) exchange your opinion of the graphics and what they represent and reveal.

2. Do further research on the matter and prepare short presentations. Here are some helpful websites:
- https://en.wikipedia.org/wiki/warming_stripes
- https://www.climate-lap-book.ac.uk/2018/warming-stripes

→ Focus on Skills, Doing Research and Citing Sources, p. 262

3. The third visual depicts another alarming global development: the thoughtless and irresponsible use and waste of plastic.
   Team up with a partner and
   a) describe the various visual and textual elements of the poster,
   b) explain the poster's symbolic meaning and intended message.

→ Focus on Skills, Analysis of Photos, p. 246

Jason Momoa

Address to the United Nations on Climate Crisis

AWARENESS

From 21 – 23 September 2019, the UN Climate Summit was held in New York City. It was accompanied by a *Global Week for Future*, a series of international strikes between 20 – 27 September demanding immediate action against climate change. While 65 countries pledged to intensify their efforts to reduce greenhouse gas emissions to zero by 2050, China and India refused to increase their commitments, and the US did not even speak at the conference.

In order to get an overview and first understanding of some of the effects of climate change,

- team up with a partner and read Katharina Buchholz's short informative text and the attached info-graphic,
- get an overview of the people and countries most affected by rising sea levels and list them in a ranking.

Katharina Buchholz

Rising Sea Levels Will Threaten 200 Million People by 2100

According to new research published by scientific magazine Nature Communications, 200 million people in the world will live below the sea level line by 2100. An additional 160 million will be affected by higher annual flooding due to rising ocean levels. These numbers are much higher than those published in previous studies, which used different coastal elevation[1] models and assumed that only 250 million people in total would be affected by these adverse[2] events.

Out of the 200 million directly affected by rising sea levels, researchers estimate that 70 percent will live in just eight countries in Asia. Most people affected would live in China: 43 million or around 20 percent. At 32 million and 27 million affected people, Bangladesh and India would also be hit hard, as would Vietnam, Indonesia, Thailand, the Philippines and Japan.

In Europe, the Netherlands would theoretically be the most affected. Here, more than 4 million people are expected to live below sea level in 2100. Yet, the country has one of the most effective flood control networks in the world (not taken into account by the study's modelling), which is expected to keep citizens safe. Other countries in Europe where rising sea levels could be a problem are the UK (1.5 million people at risk), Germany (1 million people), Turkey, France and Italy (500,000 people each).

The model used in the study assumes a global average temperature increase of 2°C and does not take into account the possibility of accelerated[3] ice sheet[4] melting.

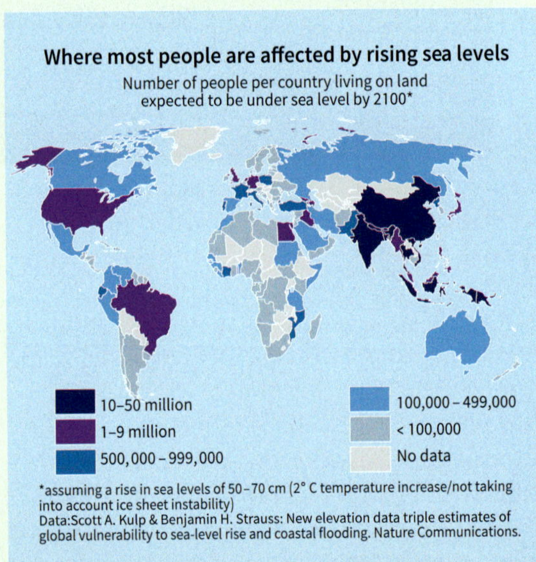

https://www.statista.com/chart/19884/number-of-people-affected-by-rising-sea-levels-per-country/, 11 February 2020 [23.07.2020]

[1] **elevation** the height of a place above the level of the sea – [2] **adverse** having a negative or harmful effect on sth. – [3] **to accelerate** to go faster – [4] **ice sheet** a thick layer of ice that permanently covers an area of land

As a representative of the *Small Island Developing States* (SIDS), American actor and model Jason Momoa delivered an emphatic (*eindringlich*) speech, calling on the world to take immediate action and help fight climate change.

Aloha, your excellencies, distinguished[1] delegates, ladies and gentlemen.

Today, I stand before you as a singular representative of all island nations. I am honoured to represent those who continue to fight as stewards[2] of this planet. As a native Hawaiian, born to a mother from Iowa, I have seen how one place can be oblivious[3] to another. The issues facing an island can feel so far removed from that place that is landlocked[4] in the middle of our country.

However, with a foothold[5] in two worlds, I quickly began to see how a problem for one will soon become a problem for all. As a human family, through innovation and creativity, we have elevated[6] ourselves and perceivably[7] stand as the most powerful beings on Earth. Yet our ego, our fear and our relentless[8] drive for profits have made us the only species willing to force disharmony with the natural balance of our world.

We are the living consequence of forgotten traditions. We suffer a collective amnesia[9] of a truth that was once understood; the truth that to cause irreversible[10] damage to the Earth is to bring the same unto ourselves.

We, the island nations, and all coastal communities, are the frontlines in this environmental crisis. The oceans are in a state of emergency. Entire marine ecosystems are vanishing with the warming of the seas and as the waste of the world empties into our waters, we face the devastating[11] crisis of plastic pollution.

We are a disease that is infecting our planet.

From the atmosphere to the abyssal zone[12] we are polluted.

It is a known fact that the Great Garbage Patch floating in the Pacific is larger than the country of France. Even at the depth of the Mariana Trench[13] we are discovering nanoplastics.

And shockingly, there are more plastic particles in the ocean than stars in the Milky Way. It is shameful.

Yet the greatest threat to small island developing states is the fact that entire islands are drowning[14] into the sea due to the enormous volume of emissions generated by the first world countries.

Island nations contribute the least to this disaster but are made to suffer the weight of the consequences.

Our governments and corporate entities[15] have known for decades the immediate changes needed, yet change still has not come.

And when the frontline is gone, we are doomed[16]. There is no undoing.

If you continue to watch, unsympathetic to the issues of island nations, this realization will soon come: that you stood by and witnessed the world cross the critical tipping point[17], watching the death of our planet.

69 of the 100 richest entities in the world are corporations, they are not governments. Obviously, it is naïve to believe that one does not influence the other.

But we are watching, and the people will hold our governments and corporate powers accountable[18] for the destruction you are allowing to our environment.

Three years ago, in Paris, the world stood united and vowed[19] to keep the Earth below 1.5 degrees of warming. We pledged[20] to hold ourselves to a higher standard and to do what is right.

I'm standing here today because I am ashamed that not all of our leaders have honoured this agreement.

Delegates, I ask you now: do we still stand in unity for this cause? Do you intend to honour the commitments for the betterment of mankind? Or will you continue to chase[21] short-term profits above our children's basic human rights to live on this Earth?

Change cannot come in 2050, or 2030, or even 2025, the change must come today.

[1] **distinguished** used to describe a respected person; *ehrenwert* – [2] **steward** a person whose job it is to take care of a particular place – [3] **oblivious** not conscious of what is happening around you; *achtlos* – [4] **landlocked** surrounded by land and having no coast – [5] **to have a foothold** *ein Standbein haben, verankert sein* – [6] **to elevate** to make more important – [7] **perceivably** clearly – [8] **relentless** *schonungslos* – [9] **amnesia** [æmˈniːziə] a medical condition that makes you unable to remember things – [10] **irreversible** impossible to change back to a previous condition – [11] **devastating** causing a lot of damage and destruction – [12] **abyssal zone** *Tiefsee* – [13] **Mariana Trench** located in the western Pacific Ocean; the deepest oceanic trench (*Graben*), approx. 11 km depth – [14] **to drown** *ertrinken, versinken* – [15] **entity** *Körperschaft, Gebilde* – [16] **doomed** certain to die or be destroyed – [17] **tipping point** a time at which a change cannot be stopped – [18] **to hold sb. accountable** *jdn. zur Rechenschaft ziehen* – [19] **to vow** to promise to do sth. – [20] **to pledge** to make a serious formal promise – [21] **to chase** *jagen, verfolgen*

We can no longer afford the luxury of half-assing[22] it as we willingly force ourselves beyond the threshold[23] of no return.

As a human species we need the Earth to survive, but make no mistake, the Earth doesn't need us.

We are demanding global unity for a global crisis to once again bring harmony between mankind and the natural balance of our world.

We must right the wrongs we have done against our children and grandchildren because we are gifting[24] them with a world that suffers from our irresponsible stewardship[25].

I leave you with an island proverb that states: He wa'a he moku, he moku he wa'a. [The canoe is an island; the island is a canoe.] These words teach us that all land, no matter how big or small, floats on the ocean like a canoe in the middle of the sea – and that our planet is nothing more than an island floating amongst an ocean of stars. Life on a floating vessel[26] has limited resources. It requires strict conservation practices and carefully planned navigation to ensure survival.

We must work together as a global community to best steer our canoe in the right direction, the direction of a healthy and abundant[37] future on Earth that we call home.

Mahalo nui loa [Thank you very much]. Please join us, the Samoa Pathway[28], in unified commitment to protect and heal the planet.

This is for all of us. Aloha.

Ku kia'i mauna! [Guardians of the mountain]

https://www.youtube.com/watch?v=tloVBA4pxxY, 27 September 2019 [23.07.2020]

COMPREHENSION

Tip: This speech offers you a choice of how to work with it. You can
a) improve your **listening skills** and just listen to the audio text,
b) read the speech to improve your **reading skills**,
c) **read and listen** to the speech at the same time.

WES-121500-019

1. In a paired listening/reading activity, read/listen to/watch Jason Momoa's speech, which is provided on the webcode, on your own and try to understand the **gist** (= general meaning) of what he says.
Take short notes on what Jason Momoa says about:

- his motivation to give the speech
- the difficult situation of island nations
- the world's responsibility

→ Focus on Skills, Listening Comprehension, p. 225

Tip: Do not try to understand every detail at first. Listen for the main idea (key nouns, names, years, etc.). Jot down words which you understand, and do not bother about words or phrases you do not understand.

WES-121500-019

2. In order to practice your **listening skills, listen to or watch** the speech **a second time**, trying to understand the details and get more information. Then, do the tasks on worksheet 19.1.

WES-121500-019

3. If you want to practice your **reading skills, read** the speech (again), do the tasks provided on worksheet 19.2 and take notes on the deeper meaning of some of Jason Momoa's statements.

4. Now, write a summary of the speech in about 150 – 200 words, using your notes. Try to use your own words and follow the **introduction – main part – conclusion** pattern.
First, write an introductory sentence that answers the w-questions. Use the simple present and do not use any direct speech or quotations.

→ Focus on Skills, Writing a Summary, p. 231

[22] **half-assing** (*sl., disapproving*) *halbherzig* – [23] **threshold** *Schwelle* – [24] **to gift sb. with sth.** to give sb. sth. in an official way – [25] **stewardship** care or management – [26] **vessel** (*fml.*) a large boat or ship – [27] **abundant** more than enough – [28] **Samoa Pathway** an intergovernmental framework which supports SIDS

Begin like this: In a speech, given to the 2019 United Nations Climate Change Summit in New York City, American actor Jason Momoa, calls on the delegates to …

Tip: Leave out metaphorical or emotional language, and try to be as factual as possible.

ANALYSIS

5. Examine Jason Momoa's abilities as a speaker and explain how his use of stylistic devices emphasizes his concerns and conveys his message to the listeners.

WES-121500-019

Tip: Use the transcript of Momoa's speech, which is provided on worksheet 19.3, for your analysis.

Step 1:
Brush up your knowledge of rhetorical devices and read the Focus on Skills page Analysis of a Political Speech on page 242.

WES-121500-019

Step 2:
Use the transcript provided on worksheet 19.3 and highlight/underline words/phrases/lines in the text where you can detect these devices:
- personal/possessive pronouns (I – you – we – us – our, etc.),
- positive and negative emotive words and word fields,
- repetition (anaphora*, parallelism*),
- references to the island nations and their cultures and cultural specifics.

WES-121500-019

Step 3:
Team up with a partner and explain the function and effect of the stylistic devices employed in the speech. Use worksheet 19.4 for your notes.

Tip: Remember that stylistic devices are like sound or colour devices in a film. Their function is to emphasize the meaning of what is said, thus serving to convey a specific message to the listener. Accordingly, alliteration, anaphora or repetition help to stress certain words that are important. Many positive and negative emotive words create a certain mood and atmosphere (hopeful, depressing, friendly, scary) aimed at influencing the listener.

Step 4:
Now, after connecting and sorting your findings from the previous tasks, write an analysis of Jason Momoa's speech in about 300 words.
→ Focus on Skills, Analysis of a Political Speech, p. 242
→ Focus on Language, Vocabulary for Text Analysis, p. 249

Tip: In order to prove the quality and accuracy of your work, follow these steps:
1) Identify the device in the text.
2) Use the correct technical term.
3) Refer to the line and/or quote.
→ Focus on Skills, Analysis of a Non-Fictional Text, Step 2b, p. 237
4) Explain the function and effect of the device.
5) Relate your findings to the intended message of the text.

Tip: Speakers sometimes use a lot of stylistic devices in their speech, and usually you do not have the time to explain or analyse all of them. Therefore, choose the ones which are a) used frequently throughout the text, b) most striking and effective.

Begin like this: In his speech, Jason Momoa speaks as a representative of the island nations. His intention is to make people aware of … Doing so, he employs several stylistic devices to highlight and dramatize …

6. In June 2019, in preparation for the Climate Summit, the United Nations organized an international competition called "I am a Youth of a Small Island", which was open to young people from SIDS ages 15 – 24. The submissions (*Einreichungen*) had to be creative and reflect the reality of young SIDS inhabitants and include economic, social, cultural and/or environmental issues.
The poem on pp. 119 f. was written by a 17-year-old young woman from the Caribbean island of Saint Lucia, and focuses on the peculiarities (*Besonderheiten*) of living on an island.

I am a Youth of a Small Island – International Competition

a) Together with a partner, first read the poem, then extract information that characterizes the life on the speaker's island. Pay attention to the three different 'categories' of people the speaker talks about and complete the grid provided on worksheet 19.5. (WES-121500-019)

b) Explain why – according to the speaker – "my island" is not little but great. Give evidence from the poem to support your explanation.

c) Collect further information about the various creative works of young islanders and research the website which is accessible via the webcode. (@ WES-121500-019)

ACTIVITIES

7. Prepare and organize a public hearing in which you collect information and exchange your views on the danger of rising sea levels for the world in general and the small islands in particular.

Step 1:
Collect information about the immediate dangers of rising sea levels caused by global climate change and research the weblinks provided on the webcode. Take notes on the relevant aspects with regard to the public hearing. (@ WES-121500-019)

→ Focus on Skills, Doing Research and Citing Sources, p. 262

Step 2:
Divide the class into different groups, which take on different roles, e. g.

- concerned citizens,
- environmental activists,
- etc.
- politicians,
- scientists,

Step 3:
Each group prepares a short presentation (e. g. using PowerPoint) to introduce and explain their position in class.

Info

Public Hearing

In law, a hearing is a proceeding before a court or a decision-making body such as a government agency. It is conducted as an oral argument in order to decide issues of law, and many also include the cross-examination of witnesses or representatives of organizations.

- Form groups in class and decide who will be interviewed or questioned on a certain matter.
- One or two students should function as moderator(s) and conduct the discussion.
- One or two students should keep the minutes (*Protokoll führen*) and take short notes on the results of the hearing and the answers given.
- Do research on the matter and prepare role cards on which you take notes on the issue.
- Formulate critical questions that you want to ask.
- Do not just ask question after question but listen and respond to the answers given.

Tip: Try to be as objective as possible and do not evaluate rashly by employing judgmental adjectives like shocking, inhuman, appalling, etc.

→ Focus on Skills, Presentation, p. 261

Step 4:

Based on research results and notes from step 1, prepare role cards and take notes on the possible pros and cons, causes and effects as well as possible solutions to the matter.
Additionally, select and write down phrases that you will need for the discussion (→ Focus on Language, Conversation and Discussion, p. 254).

Step 5:

Finally, act out the public hearing and exchange your views and arguments.

GRAMMAR / LANGUAGE

8. You are a journalist for an international youth magazine and have attended the conference. Your readers are particularly interested in Jason Momoa's speech.
Write an article about the UN climate summit and Momoa's speech in particular, using **reported speech** and **paraphrasing** (cf. Skill 14, p. 85) to report the essential parts of the speech.
Remember to backshift tenses where necessary and to formulate an introductory sentence.

Examples:

- Jason Momoa explained that – although being half American and half Hawaiian himself – he spoke on behalf of …
- He explained that living on an island could feel very different from …

→ Indirect Speech, p. 293
→ Tenses, p. 300

Khadijah Ashanna Halliday (17), Saint Lucia

To Those Who Haven't Visited My Island

Those who haven't visited my island ... paint postcard coloured beaches and Pixar[1] blue skies with the brushes[2] of their imagination.

Those who haven't visited my island ... expect beaming, bubbly heads atop painted bodies kissing the island's head at night and day.

Those who haven't visited my island ... imagine that my island offers them an escape from harsh reality as a night of sleep offers from a long day of work.

Those who haven't *lived* on my island don't think that "little" islands like mine can have big problems like theirs.

Somewhere between the anticipation[3] of cerulean blue[4] waters making love to sandy white shores ... the people who haven't lived on my island forget that where people exist, problems do as well and that the allure[5] of the aqua skies is not enough to erase this reality.

Those who've never been to my island ask
"What's so great about my "little" island?"

And of course, anyone could pour oceans of answers.

One could say it is our colorful culture;
One could say it is our dance and dress and delicacies;
One could say it is the bouquet of our boisterous[6] laughs and our beckoning[7] grins which are benevolent[8] gifts of unblemished[9] bliss[10] ...

These are all beautifully scripted answers, each deserving to swim to the end of the question.

But the funny thing about me living on an island is that I never learned to swim ...
So, as everyone makes these beautiful but prescripted[11] strokes[12] to the horizon ...
With one dive[13], I immediately touch the ocean bed.

[1] **Pixar** the shortened name of Pixar Animation Studios, a computer-generated imagery (CGI) animation company that created hit movies like *Toy Story*, *A Bug's Life* and *The Incredibles* – [2] **brush** *Pinsel* – [3] **anticipation** *Vorfreude* – [4] **cerulean blue** (*lit.*) deep blue – [5] **allure** the quality of being attractive, interesting or exciting – [6] **boisterous** noisy, energetic and rough – [7] **to beckon** to attract people – [8] **benevolent** [bəˈnevələnt] kind and helpful – [9] **unblemished** without faults and not spoilt in any way – [10] **bliss** perfect happiness – [11] **prescripted** given as a rule – [12] **stroke** *Pinselstrich* – [13] **dive** *Sprung*

With only one dive, I reach the ocean bed.

The people who've never heard of my island ... ask me what's so great about my "little" island.

I answer from the ocean's bed.

The greatness of my island is its littleness.
Or rather, its perceived littleness.

I call it ...
The paradox of the "little" island.

It giggles[14] me to see the raised eyebrows I get with this answer.
But once you've touched the ocean bed, swimming in line with everyone else becomes less about distance and more about depth.

And my little island, though it floats on the irises[15] of the waters, is made deeper by its paradox: The paradox of the "little" island.

For both the people who live and don't live on my island ...
Mere[16] mention of an island regardless of true denotation[17],
Is a piece of land embraced gently by the welcoming waves of the ocean

But detached[18] from this fairytale description,

Those who live on my island firsthand know the dangers posed to the reefs[19] of our economy and society and country.

We are an island but we are a country. And Derek Walcott[20] from my country said 'We are either a nobody or a nation'. And like me, nations too sometimes don't take easily to swimming. So sometimes my nation ... my country ... my island thrashes[21] in the waters.

Those who live on my island
Have watched young fish like me either been disowned[22] from homes or abandon homes disheartened[23] by our economic restraints[24] ... And these young fish have been devoured[25] by the ravenous[26] sharks of the bigger seas.

Those who live on my island
Have watched young fish like me become hypnotized by the glimmering glow of the foreign TV ... And these young fish have chosen to be young Columbuses and, in his imitation, have lost themselves.

Those who live on my island
Have watched young talented fish like me swim, swim, swim till caught in a net because of lack of opportunity ... And because of lack of opportunity, few of these young fish are able to make it free from the net so so much talent is caught in a net of unfair reality.

However,

I who live on my island
Know that the littleness of my island is its greatness because although we thrash, we never drown.

I who live on my island
Understand that we fight together bonded[27] by the shallows[28] we've all witnessed that has generated[29] the desire to swim by both depth and horizons.

I who live on my island
Love my island because there is so much more talent within one polyp[30] square inch[31] than there could be within one state square inch of larger 'unislands'.

I who live on my island
Understand that because we are so small, we are so big.

I who live on my island
Realize that the smallest gets amplified[32] not merely by its achievements but by its effort and tenacity[33] and perseverance[34].

Therefore,
Those who do not live on my island
Need to stop inserting the word 'little' before island.

https://sustainabledevelopment.un.org/content/documents/samoawin/to_those_who_have_not_visited_my_island.pdf [02.09.2020]

[14] **to giggle** *jdn. zum Kichern bringen* – [15] **iris** the coloured circular part of the eye that surrounds the black pupil (= central part) – [16] **mere** *bloß* – [17] **denotation** the main, factual meaning of a word – [18] **detached** separated – [19] **reef** *Riff* – [20] **Derek Walcott** (1930–2017) a Saint Lucian poet and playwright who received the 1992 Nobel Prize in Literature – [21] **to thrash** to move from side to side in an uncontrolled way – [22] **to disown** *enteignen* – [23] **to dishearten** *entmutigen* – [24] **restraint** sth. that limits or controls what people can do; *Einschränkung* – [25] **to devour** to eat up, to destroy sth. completely – [26] **ravenous** extremely hungry; *gierig, gefräßig* – [27] **to bond** to develop a close connection – [28] **shallow** *Untiefe* – [29] **to generate** to produce – [30] **polyp** here: tiny, simple sea creature – [31] **square inch** 2.54 cm^2 – [32] **to amplify** to make sth. stronger – [33] **tenacity** *Zähigkeit* – [34] **perseverance** *Beharrlichkeit*

John Chester
The Biggest Little Farm

AWARENESS

The Biggest Little Farm is a 2018 American environmental documentary film which deals with John Chester's and his wife Molly's realization of their dream. They purchase Apricot Lane Farms in California and leave Los Angeles to re-establish a perfect eco-system in which animals and plants of every kind can co-exist.
Besides John and Molly, the film stars Emma, the pig, and her best friend Mr Greasy, the rooster, along with many other loveable animals.

a) Take a look at the two photos and read the quotations below them.
b) Choose one photo and the quotation that matches your photo best.
c) Team up in groups of four and discuss your choices. Discuss how you understand the quotation and whether you agree or disagree with the understanding of farming given in the quotation and the photo.

Organically raised pig and hen

Piglets playing with each other

The ultimate goal of farming is not the growing of crops[1], but the cultivation and perfection of human beings. *Masanobu Fukunoka*

Farming is a profession of hope. *Brian Brett*

There are two spiritual dangers in not owning a farm. One is the danger of supposing that breakfast comes from the grocery, and the other is that heat comes from the furnace[2]. *Aldo Leopold*

Many years from now, our descendants will look back on the use of animals for food – particularly the intense animal suffering in factory farms – as a moral atrocity[3]. *Jacy Reese*

[1] **crops** grain, fruit or vegetables grown in large amounts – [2] **furnace** *Ofenanlage, Heizkessel* – [3] **atrocity** an extremely cruel, violent and shocking act; *Gräueltat*

COMPREHENSION

WES-121500-020
WES-121500-020

1. In order to get an overall understanding of the film and the Chesters' project and intention watch the trailer of the documentary using the link provided on the webcode and do the tasks given on worksheet 20.1.

2. Watch the trailer **a second time** and answer the questions below in your own words:
- What is John's and Molly's vision of the farm?
- What unexpected challenges and problems do they have to deal with?
- What different kinds of animals and plants are raised and grown on the farm?

3. A film scene always works on two different levels:
- **the narrative level**, i. e. the story that is told to the viewer
- **the cinematic level**, i. e. the devices that are used to tell the story and turn it into pictures

WES-121500-020

Watch the trailer **a third time** and focus on the cinematic devices that are used to convey the particular atmosphere and message of the story. Use worksheet 20.2 and focus on these aspects:
- camera operations
- visual symbols
- film music and sound
- (special) effects

→ Focus on Skills, Analysis of a Film Scene, p. 239
→ Focus on Facts, Camera Operations, p. 232

4. Write a coherent text (about 200 – 250 words) that includes the narrative and cinematic levels of the trailer.

Example:
The emotionally gripping trailer of the 2018 documentary *The Biggest Little Farm*, released on YouTube …, deals with …

Tip: Use your notes for your description and use connectives to make your writing flow better.
→ Focus on Language, Connectives and Adverbs, p. 251

Tips on vocab
- The film depicts the setting of …
- In the first/second … part of the trailer …
- In the introductory/main/concluding part …
- Despite all the problems …
- Eventually, the Chesters have to cope with …
- The film stars animals like … and presents them as …
- Finally, …

ANALYSIS

5. In addition to releasing the trailer, Molly and John Chester gave a lot of interviews to promote not only their film, but also their understanding of sustainable living and farming.
Read the interview with Dave Davies, which focuses particularly on the Chesters' problem with coyotes on the farm.
Illustrate John Chester's solution to the problem by visualizing the vicious circle he was caught in at first – and how he breaks it at last.

Example:

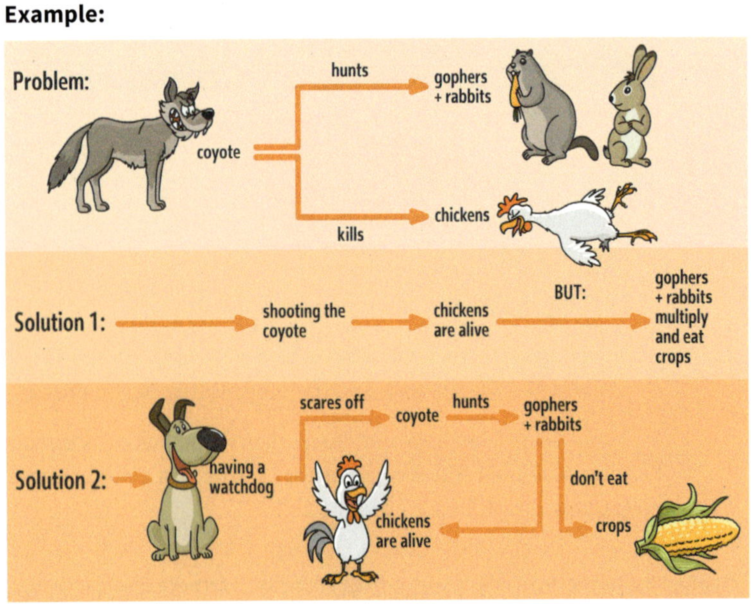

6. Explain John Chester's understanding of the 'job' a farm has to do.

7. Against the background of your results and findings, work creatively and compile your own trailer for a documentary on farming the way you understand it.
WES-121500-020 Use worksheet 20.3 and work out a storyboard* in which you plan and visualize your film clip.
→ Focus on Facts, Screenplays and Storyboards, p. 228

Tip: Either use snippets from newspapers or magazines to illustrate your ideas or make rough sketches to visualize characters, setting, visual symbols, etc.

ACTIVITIES

8. The Chesters' (successful) experiment has triggered a controversial debate about the necessity of organic farming, the pollution of the environment through mass animal farming, animal rights, etc. Put yourself in the position of a (local) politician and prepare a short speech to your constituency (*Wählerschaft*) in which you explain a) your view of the problem and b) possible solutions to the problem.

→ Focus on Skills, Writing a Speech Script, p. 271

Step 1:
In preparation of your speech, first get an overview of the various aspects connected with the main topics of your speech.
@ Do research, draw a mind map and reflect on what you are going to talk about.
→ Focus on Skills, Doing Research and Citing Sources, p. 262

Example:

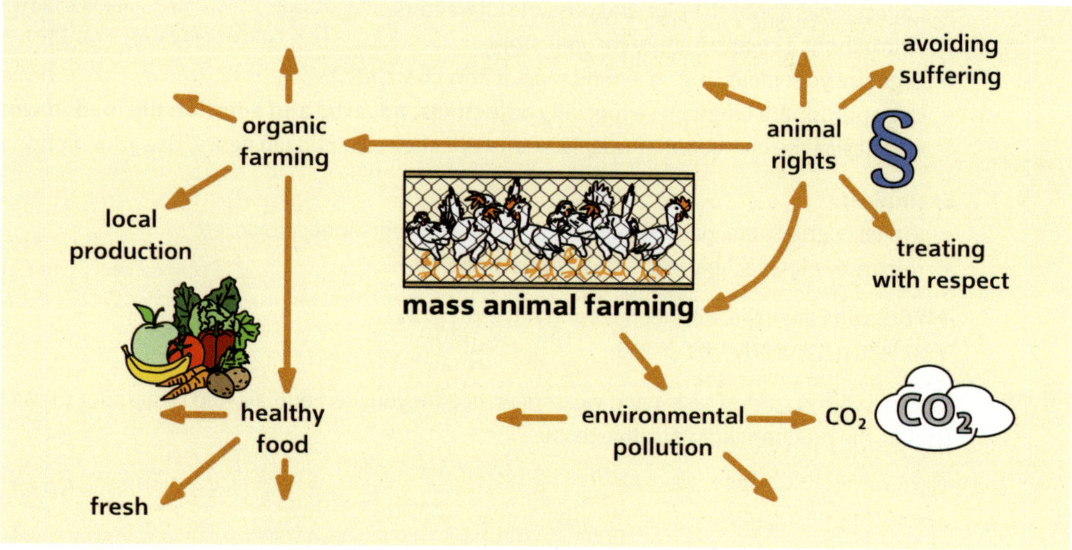

Tip: Concerning possible solutions to the problems, think about
a) what politics and politicians can/should/have to do,
b) what consumers can/should/have to do.

Step 2:
Sort your findings and give your ideas a logical train of thought.

Tip: Follow the **introduction – main part – conclusion** pattern for your speech.

Step 3:

Use the **postcard technique**:

a) Divide up your speech into thematic sections.
b) Give each section a heading.
c) Write one heading and a few easily-read prompt words on each postcard.
d) Number the postcards in the order that you want to talk about these points.

Tip: You might want to prepare an additional PowerPoint presentation in which you illustrate your speech with some visuals and/or statistics.
Be careful not to overdo things. You and your speech should be centre stage, not the PowerPoint presentation.

Step 4:

a) Think about a pithy (*prägnant*) statement and/or opening remark to greet the audience, grab their attention and start off your speech.
b) Think about vivid (*anschaulich*) examples to illustrate your point of view.
c) End your speech with a concluding remark, and thank your audience for listening.

→ Focus on Skills, Giving a Speech, p. 260
→ Focus on Language, Conversation and Discussion, p. 254

GRAMMAR / LANGUAGE

9. Based on the trailer of *The Biggest Little Farm*, compile a short screenplay* for a documentary about the difference between organic and traditional farming and their environmental impacts. Choose a different genre from the one given, e. g. an eco drama, a sci-fi story, a (tragic/romantic) love story, a thriller, etc.
Before you start:

- Find out about the characteristics of your chosen genre.
- Collect ideas about the plot and possible characters.
- Think about a clear structure for your story.
- Organize your ideas (e. g. in a mind map, a flow chart, etc.).
- Use appropriate language, especially **adjectives, adverbs and emotionally loaded words** to emphasize the character, atmosphere and effect of your chosen genre. Use your dictionary for help.

Examples:

- thriller → gruesome, painful, blood-thirsty, deadly, poisonous, toxic, etc.
- romance → loving, heart-breaking, empathetic, etc.

→ Focus on Language, Connectives and Adverbs, p. 251
→ Adjectives and Adverbs, p. 289

WES-121500-020

Tip: Use your results of task 4 and worksheet 20.3 for your screenplay. And remember to use the **simple past** as the predominant narrative tense.

Dave Davies

"Biggest Little Farm" Chronicles One Couple's Effort to "Jump-Start the Soil"

Molly and John Chester took a massive leap[1] when they decided to leave Los Angeles to start an organic farm[2]. John's new documentary tells the story of their struggles and successes. [...]

The Chesters tried to turn a dry and soil-depleted[3] 200-acre parcel[4] into a lush[5], organic farm. They were determined to tend[6] fruit orchards[7] and raise cows, pigs and chickens in harmony with nature.

Drought[8], pests[9], windstorms and fire threatened to end the venture, but after eight years, their farm, Apricot Lane Farms, is thriving[10]. John Chester, who was a filmmaker before he tried farming, directed a new documentary called "The Biggest Little Farm," about the obstacles[11] he and Molly, a former private chef[12], faced and overcame and what their experiences can tell us about the relationship between humans and our environment. "The Biggest Little Farm" has won several awards at film festivals and will be in theaters this Friday. Molly and John Chester spoke with FRESH AIR's Dave Davies. [...]

DAVIES: This is FRESH AIR. And we're speaking with John and Molly Chester, whose remarkable effort[13] to create a 200-acre biodynamic farm battling[14] droughts, pests and fire is the subject of the new documentary directed by John called "The Biggest Little Farm."

While you were still struggling to get the fruit crops going, you were – you had a lot of chickens. And they laid a lot of eggs, and you were able to sell those. So that was really working. But there was a problem with coyotes[15] eating the chickens. How did you try and address that?

J CHESTER: Well, the coyotes ate about 350 of our chickens.

DAVIES: Wow.

J CHESTER: And, you know, we refused to shoot the coyote because we wanted to find a way to collaborate[16]. But, you know, ultimately[17], I succumb[18] to it, and I kill a coyote. And I think it's a really important moment in the film because there's something that happens after that that has a profound[19] effect on the way I look at the coyote's role.

The coyote also happens to eat gophers[20] and rabbits, another pest on the farm. If we kill all the coyotes, we're going to make that problem worse. And that forced us to find a solution.

DAVIES: It is quite a moment in the film when you shoot the coyote. He's trapped trying to get through a fence, and we can see you level the – looks like a shotgun. What were you thinking then? What were you feeling emotionally?

J CHESTER: In shooting the one coyote, the thing that was weighing on me the most was that I knew this wasn't the only coyote. I was going to have to obliterate[21] every coyote that crossed our path. And we were the farm that had animals, like, that they were eating. You know, we were creating a food system for coyotes. So it was going to be an endless battle of constantly killing coyotes, and I think that's the thing that scared me the most – was that it felt like an incredibly[22] slippery slope[23]. [...]

DAVIES: And then you found a way that the coyotes became helpful. How did that happen?

J CHESTER: Well, after we had shot the one coyote, there was a coyote that ran into the fence of the garden, and it had paralyzed[24] itself. And I had to actually now, you know, euthanize[25] this coyote. It was still alive, but it couldn't move. But when I asked, why is this coyote in the garden? I looked around and it had been digging holes in the garden. It was eating gophers. It was chasing rabbits. It was actually helping to balance another problem. And so I thought, there's got to be another way. And we finally found one of our guardian dogs didn't eat chickens.

DAVIES: (Laughter).

J CHESTER: The only one. Her name was Rosie, and Rosie became the guardian dog of our flock[26]. And,

[1] **leap** a big change, increase, improvement – [2] **organic farm** *Bio-Bauernhof* – [3] **soil-depleted** having lost much of its soil – [4] **parcel** (*US*) an area of land – [5] **lush** with lots of green, healthy plants, grass, etc. – [6] **to tend** (*fml.*) to care for – [7] **fruit orchard** [ˈɔːtʃəd] *Obstgarten* – [8] **drought** [draʊt] *Dürre* – [9] **pest** *Schädling, Plage* – [10] **to thrive** to grow, develop, be successful – [11] **obstacle** *Hindernis* – [12] **chef** *Koch, Köchin* – [13] **effort** *Mühe* – [14] **to battle** to fight – [15] **coyote** [kaɪˈəʊti] – [16] **to collaborate** to work with sb. – [17] **ultimately** finally – [18] **to succumb to** (*fml.*) to accept defeat – [19] **profound** *tiefgreifend* – [20] **gopher** *Erdhörnchen, Nagetier* – [21] **to obliterate** (*fml.*) to make sth. disappear completely – [22] **incredibly** extremely – [23] **slippery slope** a bad situation that is likely to get much worse – [24] **to paralyze** *lähmen* – [25] **to euthanize** [ˈjuːθənaɪz] here: *einen Gnadenschuss geben* – [26] **flock** a group of birds

knock on wood[27], we've not lost any chickens since then. So, you know, the coyotes are busy eating, you know, gophers and rabbits.

DAVIES: So the gophers were eating the roots of the fruit trees. That was the problem. And now ...

J CHESTER: Right.

DAVIES: ... That the coyotes can't get the chickens, it goes for the gophers, which is a big help to you.

J CHESTER: Yeah. Nature is – they're simple opportunists[28], and you just need to make it slightly harder on one side so that they go the other direction. It sometimes doesn't require as much effort as you think. [...]

DAVIES: You know, to kind of see the process unfold in the movie is really beautiful. You know, we've had a couple of interviews on the show lately about climate change. [...] And I think this film is as inspirational as it can be discouraging, in a way. And it almost makes it hard for me to ask kind of the hard questions, which I do wonder about. Like, can this scale – I mean, can farming this way feed a planet? You know, because we had the Green Revolution in the '60s with all the hybrid seeds[29] and then the monoculture agriculture that does a lot of harm but produces an awful lot of cheap food. I mean, I don't know if you think about it on these terms, but is this a way to feed the planet and change the way we grow food and eat it?

J CHESTER: I think the other way to ask that question is, if we don't start working with our land in a more regenerative[30] way, can the planet feed us? You know, just in the last 260 years, we've destroyed more than a third of the topsoil[31]. We've deforested 46% of the trees. We've doubled CO_2 from 260 to 400 parts per million. We are an incredible force of nature, humans. And we've done all of that unconsciously[32]. And just imagine with consciousness[33] for the infinite possibilities of collaboration with nature. Imagine what we could do with that.
I think that charge[34] of a farm to feed the world, you know, comes, like, from post-World War II. It's not the job of a farm to feed the world. It's the job of a farm to feed its community, and the loss of just that understanding is how we got here. Our goal is to feed, you know, the area around us. And yes, is it economically possible? Sure. I mean, not – our way specifically is not the way for every farm, but there's farms that are working in a regenerative way that are economically sustainable[35] – absolutely. And it's just a decision, you know, an act and an understanding of the kinds of farms you're going to support, you know? That's probably going to give us the best chance at a change.

DAVIES: Molly Chester, John Chester, thank you so much for spending some time with us. Good luck with the farm, and congratulations on the film.

J CHESTER: Thank you so much.

M CHESTER: Thank you very much.

https://www.npr.org/2019/05/06/720697998/biggest-little-farm-chronicles-one-couple-s-effort-to-jump-start-the-soil?t=1563702092029, 6 May 2019 [21.07.2019]

[27] **knock on wood** *toi toi toi!* – [28] **opportunist** sb. that makes the most of a situation; *Opportunist* – [29] **hybrid seeds** *Hybridsaatgut* – [30] **regenerative** making sth. grow again; *sich erneuernd* – [31] **topsoil** *Mutterboden* – [32] **unconsciously** *unbewusst* – [33] **consciousness** *Bewusstsein* – [34] **charge** responsibility – [35] **sustainable** *nachhaltig*

Tamara Kolevska, Ljubo Stefanov

Honeyland

AWARENESS

Honeyland is a 2019 Macedonian documentary film which portrays the humble (*bescheiden*) life of one of Europe's last wild bee keepers, Hatidže Muratova, who lives in a remote mountain village in Northern Macedonia, together with her 83-year-old mother. The village has no electricity or running water, and her only source of income is the honey she sells at a market, a four-hour walk from her home. When Hatidže harvests (*ernten*) the honey, she follows the golden rule of 'half for me, half for you', and leaves enough honey to the bees to make sure they survive.

The documentary received numerous awards, including two Oscar nominations in 2019.

a) Take a look at the two film stills below and describe what they reveal about Hatidže's way of life.

b) Read the quotations on the following page and choose the one you like best.

c) Team up in a group of four and discuss

- your impressions of the film stills and what they reveal,
- how you understand the quotation and whether you agree or disagree with its message.

Northern Macedonia

Hatidže taking care of her old mother

Hatidže with a bee hive

Tips on vocab

1 a landlocked country in South-east Europe ■ bordering on … ■ the capital: Skopje ■ Hatidže's home village: Bekirlija

2 a dark and very simple room ■ to wash one's hands over a bucket ■ to wear a head-scarf ■ to have a hunchback ■ an iron oven

3 golden and muted light ■ buzzing/whirring bees ■ a cap-shaped bee hive (*Bienenkorb*) ■ to wear protective headgear ■ an idyllic atmosphere

> Sharing is multiplying. *Jan Jansen*
>
> When we share, we open doors to a new beginning. *Paul Bradley Smith*
>
> People that have problems with sharing usually don't accomplish much. *J. A. Perez*
>
> We make a living by what we get; we make a life by what we give. *Winston Churchill*

COMPREHENSION

WES-121500-021

1. Naturally, the trailer of the film only provides the viewer with fragments and a scattering of impressions. Here, the viewer is given a glimpse into Hatidže's life, the nature and landscape of Northern Macedonia, Hatidže's new neighbours as well as contrasting views of untouched nature and people's way of handling it.

WES-121500-021

With this in mind, **in a first viewing**, watch the trailer and do the tasks given on worksheet 21.1.

WES-121500-021

2. Watch the trailer **a second time** and take notes on the aspects and questions below:
- Give examples from the trailer that serve as markers of social and cultural identity.
- How does the film present the contrast between nature and civilization?
- How does the film trailer present (and contrast) the life of
  - Hatidže and her mother,
  - the family moving in next to her?

3. A film scene always works on two levels:
- **the narrative level**, i. e. the story that is told to the viewer
- **the cinematic level**, i. e. the devices that are used to tell the story and turn it into pictures.

WES-121500-021

Watch the trailer **a third time** and focus on the cinematic devices that are used to convey the particular atmosphere and message of the story. Use worksheet 21.2 and focus on the following aspects:
- camera operations
- visual symbols
- film music and sound
- (special) effects

→ Focus on Skills, Analysis of a Film Scene, p. 239

4. In order to get a more complex understanding of the film *Honeyland* and its background, read the BBC article on pp. 131 ff.

WES-121500-021

The while-reading tasks on worksheet 21.3 will help you to focus on relevant details and background information.

5. Write a coherent text of about 200 – 250 words that includes the narrative and cinematic levels of the trailer.

Tip: Remember to write an introductory sentence that contains:
- the title, the type of film and the running time of the film/video clip
- the director's name
- the year of release
- the topic the film deals with
- the main protagonists

Tips on vocab

- The film depicts the setting of …
- In the first/second … part of the trailer …
- In the introductory/main/concluding part …
- The protagonist, Hatidže, has to cope with … she makes a living …
- Eventually, Hatidže's new neighbours …
- The film presents Hatidže's philosophy of life by …
- Finally, …

Example: The trailer of the 2019 documentary *Honeyland*, which is available on YouTube, portrays the humble life of … in … who has to cope with …

ANALYSIS

6. Hatidže's willingness to share her wisdom and teach the Sam family how to keep bees and harvest and produce honey, finally leads to utter disaster.
In order to fully understand what went wrong, visualize
a) the scientific background of Hatidže's ancient wisdom of sharing with the bees, using the information given in the Info box below,
b) the vicious circle that Hussein's greed triggered.

Example:

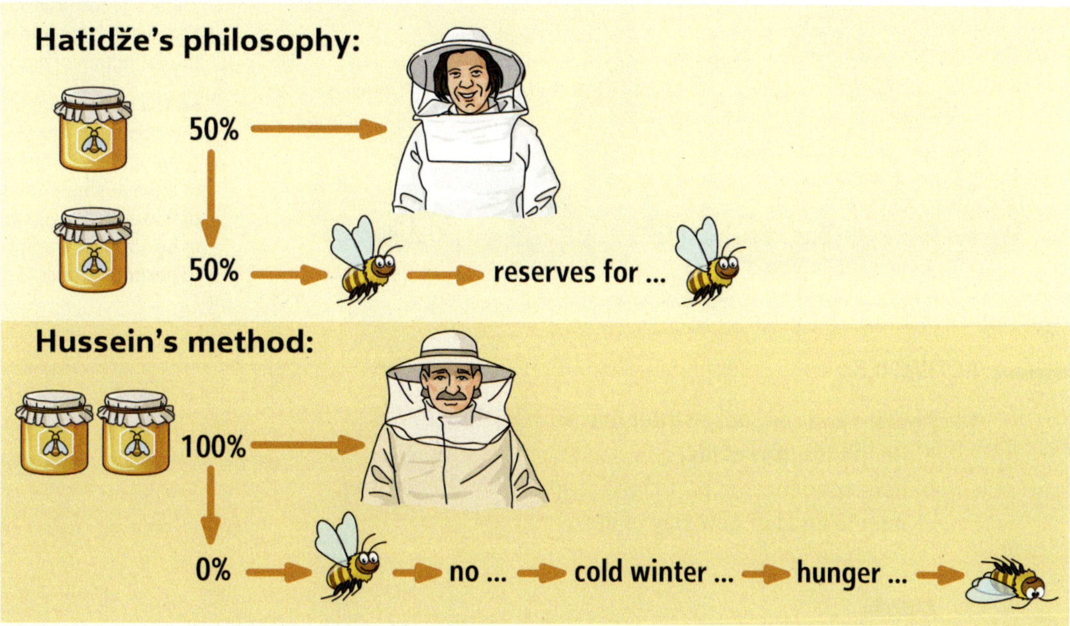

Info

Bees harvest nectar and convert the sugary liquid into honey. In turn, the honey becomes the primary source of carbohydrates (*Kohlenhydrate*), providing the bees with energy for flight and colony maintenance.
In order to store honey, bees place it in cells and cap them off with beeswax; this is called a honeycomb (*Bienenwabe*). Stored honey becomes food for winter and other hard times. When there is not enough honey to make it through these nectar-poor times, two things can happen: the colony will starve, or they will attack and raid other, weaker colonies looking for honey.
The 'half for me, half for you' rule is important to fend off starvation and leave something for tomorrow and those who are providing for you.

7. Explain why *Honeyland* can teach people living in industrialized countries a lesson about 'making bad decisions' and sharing with others/the wrong people.

8. Team up with a partner and read the text *Last Year, 40 % of the Honey-Bee Colonies in the U. S. Died* about the loss of honey-bee colonies in the US (pp. 133 f.). Take notes on these aspects:
- the decrease of bees in particular and the extinction of insects in general
- the role of insects in nature
- the cause of the dramatic decline
- the threat to humankind's survival

9. After describing the cartoon below, explain its message and relate it to the documentary *Honeyland*.
→ Focus on Skills, Analysis of Cartoons, p. 244

AUSGESTORBEN

Tips on vocab

on the left: dinosaurs ■ to have a bemused facial expression ■ to be frightened or concerned ■ a pterosaur (*Flugsaurier*) flying through the air ■ a field of flowers ■ an approaching ball of fire ■ reference to the Triassic and Jurassic periods about 230 million years ago ■ reference to the asteroid impact hypothesis 66 million years ago, which triggered the ice age and the extinction of dinosaurs

on the right: orangutan ■ bee ■ rhinoceros ■ lizard ■ butterfly ■ to buzz and whirr around ■ to stare at sth. ■ an idyllic field of flowers ■ a gigantic shoe ■ to be about to trample on sth. ■ to become extinct

ACTIVITIES

10. Prepare and conduct an interview with Hatidže about
a) her philosophy of life,
b) her experiences in participating in the film *Honeyland*,
c) her old and her new way of life.

@ WES-121500-021

Step 1:
Learn more about Hatidže's life and the making of the documentary *Honeyland* and watch the video clips provided on the webcode.

Tip: Take notes on the aspects listed in task 7 while watching.

Step 2:
Team up with a partner, with one of you being the interviewer and the other one being Hatidže.

Step 3:
Now, formulate your questions.

Tip: Remember not to ask yes/no questions but open-ended questions, which allow your interview partner to give fuller answers.

Info

1) **yes-no question** → Do you feel lonely?
2) **open question** → What made you and your mother stay here?
3) **question after statement** → At first sight, your new neighbours seemed to be nice … what actually went wrong?
4) **question referring back** → Your neighbour said that … How do you view …?
5) **confrontational question** → What do you tell people when they call your life old-fashioned?
6) **indirectly expressed question** → Well, I thought you might be interested in giving us an overview of …

Step 4:

The student taking Hatidže's role should answer the questions against the background given in the film trailer and the video clips you watched in step 1.

Step 5:

Finally, act out your interviews in class.

→ Focus on Skills, Writing an Interview, p. 269
→ Focus on Language, Conversation and Discussion, p. 254

GRAMMAR / LANGUAGE

WES-121500-021

11. In order to improve your vocabulary, read the text by Aylin Woodward (pp. 133 f.) and do the tasks provided on worksheet 21.4.

Tamara Kovacevic

Honeyland: Life Lessons from Europe's Last Wild Beekeeper

One of the more unlikely[1] films competing in this weekend's Oscars is a fascinating story about a wild beekeeper in the Balkans. *Honeyland* has a strong ecological message, but it's the life story of the woman at the centre of the film that has struck a chord[2] around the world. *Honeyland* is the first film to compete for both the best documentary award and best international feature film. The documentary's success is even more remarkable because it started almost accidentally[3].

Macedonian directors Tamara Kotevska and Ljubo Stefanov were researching in a remote[4] mountainous area of the country for a short nature documentary. They noticed beehives[5] behind a rock on the mountain where they were filming. This led them to Hatidže Muratova, one of Europe's last wild beekeepers, who uses ancient methods passed down through the generations for harvesting wild honey.

This was the beginning of a "crazy adventure" of three years, filming through scorching[6] summers and freezing winters. After another year editing[7], their first feature film was born.

Honeyland chronicles a period of Hatidže's life when her ancient methods of beekeeping came up against[8], and conflicted with, those of a newcomer to her remote home region.

The directors say the film profoundly[9] changed their lives. *Honeyland* has much to say about conserving nature, but its lessons are also about human life and relationships.

Sharing to survive

"Half for me and half for you" is Hatidže's mantra, which she repeats as she tends[10] to tame[11] the bees on the mountain. But it's a message which is in danger of being lost in the modern world.

Hatidže lives in Bekirlija, an abandoned[12] village with no electricity, running water or roads, where she looks after her ailing[13] mother.

The honey she sells at the market in the capital of North Macedonia, Skopje, is her sole[14] source of income. She takes only half of the honey, leaving the rest for the bees.

She lives by that simple principle "sharing with bees and with nature is the key to her survival," says Stefanov.

But her quiet existence is fundamentally changed when the nomadic Sam family, consisting of parents with seven unruly[15] children, a noisy vehicle and a large herd of cattle, moves into the village.

When the Sam family arrives, she welcomes them with an open heart, and teaches them how to harvest the wild honey.

However, Hussein, the father of the family, wants to harvest honey on a larger scale and for more profit. He

[1] **unlikely** surprising – [2] **to strike (struck, struck) a chord** to make people feel sympathy or enthusiasm – [3] **accidentally** by chance; *zufällig* – [4] **remote** a long way from any towns or cities – [5] **beehive** *Bienenkorb* – [6] **scorching** very hot – [7] **to edit** to make changes to a text or film, deciding what will be removed and what will be kept in, in order to prepare it for being printed or shown – [8] **to come up against sth.** (*phr. v.*) to have to deal with a problem – [9] **profoundly** in a way that has a very great effect – [10] **to tend to do sb./sth.** (*phr. v.*) to like or prefer to do sth. – [11] **to tame sb./sth.** *jdn./etw. zähmen* – [12] **abandoned** *verlassen* – [13] **ailing** ill and not getting better – [14] **sole** only – [15] **unruly** difficult to control and often not obeying rules

takes all the honey from his own hives, but his bees respond to this by attacking Hatidže's hives, leading to their destruction, and a conflict between the human neighbours.
Kotevska says that the directors do not want to portray the Sam family as symbols of destruction, but merely as "the mirror to all of us who make bad decisions", based on the need to survive and provide.

Wisdom can be more powerful than force

"To be able to communicate with bees you need to have a personal strength to approach them, patience to learn how to tame them, and this way of life requires not force but wisdom," says Kotevska.
She says that beekeeping has made Hatidže such a remarkable person.
Hatidže gets very close to the bees, often using no protection. She does not get stung, the bees seem to trust her.
"Everything we've heard from Hatidže refers to bees. She has been working with the bees all her life and everything she has learned, she learned from them."
The directors say that wild beekeeping was something that only a few people in the region learned how to do. It was never the main source of income for the villagers, but the families passed it down through generations.
In Hatidže's family, learning the skill skipped[16] a generation – she learned it as a girl from her grandfather, rather than her parents.

You can be alone but not lonely

"Hatidže acts with the bees as if they were her family and she takes care of them as if they were her children," says Kotevska. "And through that, even though her life is very harsh[17], Hatidže doesn't feel lonely."
In one scene of the film, Hatidže asks her mother why she turned down offers of marriage that were brought for Hatidže. Nazife says she did not turn them down, but Hatidže's late[18] father did.
Stefanov says that in the traditional communities in that part of the world, regardless of the religion or ethnicity, "there is an unwritten rule that the last-born female child stays with the parents until their death".
"So, Hatidže's destiny was to stay and take care of her parents."
But Hatidže was longing for[19] her own family. In the film, she develops a special bond with one of the Sam boys.
"The love that she was keeping for a family of her own, that never came true, eventually went to the bees," says Kotevska.
"She finds happiness and companionship in every living creature around her. She will continue to find happiness again and again as long as she lives."

Pictures can speak more loudly than words

Honeyland is a film set in a remote land, where the people live in ways unfamiliar[20] in the West. But it has still connected with a worldwide audience through the protagonists' body language, relationships and emotions.
Both the Sams and Hatidže's family are ethnic Turks[21] and they speak in Turkish dialect throughout the film. In the past, there were about 10 Turkish villages in the area, Stefanov says, but most villagers left for Turkey after World War Two.
Today, about 78,000 ethnic Turks still live in North Macedonia, making up just under 4 % of the country's population of 2.1 million.
"Not understanding Turkish was a problem during the shooting, but we decided to let them speak as they naturally would," says Kotevska.
"When we came to editing, we spent a week or more just being completely stuck[22]. We spent hours just thinking what to do with this material. In the end, we came up with the best possible solution and that's to edit on mute[23]. This gave us the power of the visual story that we made.
"This was the most valuable lesson for us as the authors of the future films. We are now very trained to see the stories that are created visually."
Kotevska says there were many other disadvantages from the beginning of the shooting but most of them ended up working out well.
"They make you extremely creative, we thought of the solutions that turned out to be quite unique[24]."

Bees and humans are similar

Hatidže says her bees are uniquely resilient[25] and can survive very high and very low temperatures, unlike many other species. The film shows that to be true of the people living in the region too.

[16] **to skip** to leave out, to miss out – [17] **harsh** unpleasant, difficult – [18] **late** no longer alive – [19] **to long for** *sich sehnen nach* – [20] **unfamiliar** not known – [21] **ethnic Turk** a native speaker of the Turkish language – [22] **to be stuck** to be unable to continue working – [23] **on mute** without sound – [24] **unique** special – [25] **resilient** *widerstandsfähig*

But the similarities between people and bees do not stop there.

What caught the directors' interest early on was observing Hatidže's life and her relationship with her mother. Kotevska says they were struck by how similar Hatidže was to a worker bee[26] and how her mother resembled the queen bee[27]. In the film, Nazife never leaves the house, but her wisdom guides her daughter at the time of crisis.

A conflict played out between human neighbours is also mirrored by the bees.

"The Sam family that comes later are the other group of bees who are attacking the previous group of bees, which is Hatidže and her family. We really enjoyed making this comparison during the shooting."

It is well known that male and female bees fill very different roles, but the film shows everybody doing the same jobs.

Hussein, his wife and the children all share the roles around the cattle. In one scene, one of the young sons is shown helping a cow give birth, while another boy attempts milking with his father nearby.

Kotevska and Stefanov say that, like beekeeping, all the other jobs in this harsh environment have been done equally by men and women.

"Everyone has to do the same work to survive. You can see this in our film – in both families, it doesn't make a difference what gender they are, they all do the same things."

And, like the jobs in the village of Bekirlija, the making of the film was shared between Stefanov and Kotevska, who is one of only a handful of female directors to be nominated for an Oscar this year.

Kotevska says that many people assume that she, as a woman, was the one who was closer to Hatidže, and Stefanov with the boys from the other family. In fact, it was the other way round.

"It's important who we were as people, our personalities, this was crucial[28]. Gender shouldn't be the topic of discussion."

Neon lights cannot match North Macedonia stars

Hatidže has travelled to Hollywood for the Oscars ceremony, and she has also been to several other film festivals, in places as far apart as New York, Switzerland, Sarajevo and Turkey. But Kotevska's main impression of Los Angeles is: "From the tall buildings, I cannot see the stars."

The film has already enabled Kotevska and Stefanov to buy Hatidže a house in another village, close to her brother's family. Nevertheless, she still spends the bee season in her old village.

The untouched nature of Hatidže's home couldn't be further away from the glitz and glamour of film festivals. After Hollywood, she will head[29] there again in the spring and watch the stars from her little stone hut.

https://www.bbc.com/news/entertainment-arts-51401315, 9 February 2020 [20.07.2020]

Aylin Woodward

Last Year, 40 % of Honey-Bee Colonies in the US Died

- During the winter, about 40% of honey-bee colonies in the US perished[1].
- Honey bees pollinate[2] $15 billion worth of US crops every year. Their decline[3] has a major impact on our food production and supply.
- But the honey bee is just one of many insects in decline – 40% of the world's insect species[4] are in decline, according to a February 2019 study.
- The die-offs[5] are happening primarily because insects are losing their habitats[6] to farming and urbanization. The use of pesticides[7] and fertilizers[8] is also to blame, and so is climate change.
- The rapid shrinking of insect populations is a sign that the planet is in the midst of a sixth mass extinction.

[26] **worker bee** a female bee that cannot produce any young but collects food for the other bees that it lives with – [27] **queen bee** in a group of bees, a single large female that produces eggs – [28] **crucial** extremely important – [29] **to head** to go in a particular direction

[1] **to perish** to die – [2] **to pollinate** to put pollen into a flower or plant – [3] **decline** reduction; *Niedergang* – [4] **species** [ˈspiːʃiːz] – [5] **die-off** *(phr. v.) Aussterben* – [6] **habitat** the natural environment in which a plant or animal lives – [7] **pesticide** [ˈpestɪsaɪd] *Unkraut-/Ungeziefervernichtungsmittel* – [8] **fertilizer** *Dünger*

It may feel more natural to fret about[9] wolves, sea turtles, and white rhinos dying off than it is to feel remorse[10] about vanishing bugs[11].

But the loss of insects is a dire[12] threat – one that could trigger a "catastrophic collapse of Earth's ecosystems," according to a February 2019 study.

The research, the first global review of its kind, looked at 73 historical reports on insect declines around the world and found the total mass of all insects on the planets is decreasing[13] by 2.5 % per year.

If this trend continues unabated[14], the Earth may not have any insects at all by 2119.

"In 10 years you will have a quarter less, in 50 years only half left and in 100 years you will have none," Francisco Sanchez-Bayo, a study coauthor and researcher at the University of Sydney, told The Guardian.

The latest evidence of this trend's progression comes from honey-bees: Researchers from the University of Maryland reported this week that about 40 % of the US honey bee colonies died between October 2018 and April 2019 – the highest winter loss in 13 years.

A recent study published in the journal Nature Communications found similar problems in the UK; one-third of 353 wild bee and hoverfly[15] species there experienced declines between 1980 and 2013.

The loss of bees and other bugs is scary, since insects are food sources for countless bird, fish, and mammal[16] species. Pollinators[17] like bees and hoverflies also perform a crucial role in fruit, vegetable, and nut production. [...]

'Catastrophic consequences for ... the survival of mankind'

The study emphasized that insects are "essential for the proper functioning of all ecosystems" as food sources, crop pollinators, pest[18] controllers, and nutrient[19] recyclers in soil.

"If insect species losses cannot be halted[20], this will have catastrophic consequences for both the planet's ecosystems and for the survival of mankind," Sanchez-Bayo told The Guardian.

Timothy Schowalter, a professor of entomology[21] at Louisiana State University, told Business Insider that

substantial[22] declines in insect populations threaten the food, timber, and fiber[23] production that humanity's survival depends on.

"The pollinator declines jeopardize[24] 35 % of our global food supply, which is why European countries are mandating[25] protection and restoration of pollinator habitats," he said.

The authors of the UK study noted that the geographic range of bee and hoverfly species there declined by 25 % – that's a net loss of about 11 species per square kilometer, primarily due to a reduction in the pollinators' habitats. Only one in ten surveyed species had a wider range.

"The declines in Britain can be viewed as a warning about the health of our countryside," the UK study's lead author Gary Powney told The Guardian.

Schowalter added that the many birds, fish, and other vertebrates[26] that rely on insects for food would disappear if their prey[27] does.

"Insects are often maligned[28], or at least their significant contributions to ecosystem productivity and delivery of ecosystem services are underappreciated," Schowalter said. "In short, if insects and other arthropods[29] do decline, our survival would be threatened." [...]

https://www.businessinsider.com/insects-dying-off-sign-of-6th-mass-extinction-2019-2?r=DE&IR=T, 21 June 2019 [27.07.2020]

[9] **to fret about** to be nervous or worried about sth. – [10] **remorse** the feeling of sadness and being sorry for sth. you have done – [11] **bug** a very small insect – [12] **dire** very serious – [13] **to decrease** to become less – [14] **unabated** (*fml.*) without becoming weaker in strength or force; *unvermindert* – [15] **hoverfly** *Schwebfliege* – [16] **mammal** *Säugetier* – [17] **pollinator** an insect that carries pollen from one plant to another – [18] **pest** *Ungeziefer* – [19] **nutrient** any substance that plants or animals need in order to live and grow – [20] **to halt** to stop – [21] **entomology** the scientific study of insects – [22] **substantial** considerable – [23] **fiber** *Ballaststoff, Naturfasern* – [24] **to jeopardize** [ˈdʒepədaɪz] to endanger, to threaten – [25] **to mandate** to demand – [26] **vertebrate** an animal with a backbone; *Wirbeltier* – [27] **prey** *Beute* – [28] **to malign sb./sth.** to say false and unpleasant things about sb./sth. – [29] **arthropod** *Gliederfüßler*

George Monbiot

Too Right It's Black Friday[1]: Our Relentless[2] Consumption Is Trashing the Planet

AWARENESS

Back in the day, people were used to sorting (*reparieren*) things, e. g. socks with holes or stockings with runs (*Laufmaschen*) were not thrown away but darned (*stopfen*) and mended.

Step 1:
Interview your parents or grandparents about which household items or textiles they (had) repaired and why they (or their parents) did not throw them away.

Step 2:
Team up with a partner and describe the cartoon below. What does it reveal or criticize about the 'throwaway mentality' of people today?

Step 3:
Discuss in class: What makes people today not repair most of the household items or textiles but buy new ones instead?

Tips on vocab

then: a single-family house behind a wooden fence ■ to pass sth. over to sb. ■ an electric iron ■ a mechanic in a repair shop ■ to repair/to mend sth.

now: a hand/arm reaching out of the window ■ to dispose of sth./to throw sth. away ■ a heap of rubbish ■ household items ■ washing machine, refrigerator, electric iron, monitor ■ to board sth. up ■ spiderweb ■ to shut down a business

The Throw-Away Society by Popa Matumula, 17 May 2012

[1] **Black Friday** the Friday after Thanksgiving when stores in the US reduce the price of goods in order to attract customers who want to start their Christmas shopping – [2] **relentless** continuing in a severe and extreme way

COMPREHENSION

1. **While reading** the text, finish the following statements using evidence and information from the text.
   a) (Economic) growth is …
   b) Rising consumption is destroying the planet because …
   c) Politics and marketing tell us that …
   d) People are ending their own options of survival by …
   e) Green consumption is a false promise because …
   f) Many people want to be 'green' and recycle but …
   g) The belief that economic growth is essential for humankind's survival is wrong because …
   h) Our current system is based on …
   i) A different system would include …

Growth must go on – it's the political imperative everywhere, and it's destroying the Earth. But there's no way of greening it, so we need a new system

Everyone wants everything – how is that going to work? The promise of economic growth is that the poor can live like the rich and the rich can live like the oligarchs[1]. But already we are bursting[2] through the physical limits of the planet that sustains[3] us. Climate breakdown, soil[4] loss, the collapse of habitats[5] and species, the sea of plastic, insectageddon[6]: all are driven by rising consumption. The promise of private luxury for everyone cannot be met: neither the physical nor the ecological space exists.

But growth must go on: this is everywhere the political imperative. And we must adjust our tastes accordingly. In the name of autonomy[7] and choice, marketing uses the latest findings in neuroscience[8] to break down our defences[9]. Those who seek to resist must, like the Simple Lifers in *Brave New World*[10], be silenced – in this case by the media. With every generation, the baseline of normalised consumption shifts. Thirty years ago, it was ridiculous to buy bottled water, where tap water[11] is clean and abundant[12]. Today, worldwide, we use a million plastic bottles a minute.

Every Friday is a Black Friday, every Christmas a more garish[13] festival of destruction. Among the snow saunas, portable watermelon coolers and smartphones for dogs with which we are urged[14] to fill our lives, my #extremecivilisation prize now goes to the PancakeBot: a 3D batter[15] printer that allows you to eat the Mona Lisa, the Taj Mahal, or your dog's bottom every morning. In practice, it will clog up[16] your kitchen for a week until you decide you don't have room for it. For junk like this, we're trashing the living planet, and our own prospects of survival. Everything must go.

The ancillary[17] promise is that, through green consumerism, we can reconcile[18] perpetual[19] growth with planetary survival. But a series of research papers reveal that there is no significant difference between the ecological footprints of people who care and people who don't. One recent article, published in the journal Environment and Behaviour, finds that those who identify themselves as conscious consumers use more energy and carbon than those who do not.

Why? Because environmental awareness tends to be higher among wealthy people. It is not attitudes that govern our impact on the planet but income. The richer we are, the bigger our footprint, regardless of our good intentions. Those who see themselves as green consumers, the research found, "mainly focused on behaviours that had relatively small benefits".

I know people who recycle meticulously[20], save their plastic bags, carefully measure the water in their kettles, then take their holidays in the Caribbean, cancelling any environmental savings a hundredfold[21]. I've come

[1] **oligarch** one of a small group of powerful and wealthy people who control a country or an industry – [2] **to burst** to break open suddenly – [3] **to sustain** to keep alive – [4] **soil** *Mutterboden* – [5] **habitat** the natural environment in which plants or animals usually live – [6] **insectageddon** neologism which means the mass extinction of insects – [7] **autonomy** [ɔːˈtɒnəmi] the right to be independent and govern oneself – [8] **neuroscience** [ˌnjʊərəʊˈsaɪəns] the scientific study of the nervous system and the brain – [9] **defence** protection against attack or infection – [10] **Simple Lifers in *Brave New World*** people designed in laboratories and living a careless life without worries and dangers; reference to Aldous Huxley's 1932 dystopian novel *Brave New World* – [11] **tap water** *Leitungswasser* – [12] **abundant** more than enough – [13] **garish** unpleasantly bright – [14] **to urge sb.** *jdn. drängen* – [15] **batter** *Teig* – [16] **to clog up** *vollstopfen* – [17] **ancillary** providing support or help – [18] **to reconcile** *in Übereinstimmung bringen* – [19] **perpetual** continuing for ever – [20] **meticulously** *akribisch* – [21] **a hundredfold** a hundred times as much

to believe that the recycling licences[22] their long-haul[23] flights. It persuades people they've gone green, enabling them to overlook their greater impacts.

None of this means that we should not try to reduce our footprint, but we should be aware of the limits of the exercise. Our behaviour within the system cannot change the outcomes of the system. It is the system itself that needs to change. [...]

A global growth rate of 3% means that the size of the world economy doubles every 24 years. This is why environmental crises are accelerating[24] at such a rate. Yet the plan is to ensure that it doubles and doubles again, and keeps doubling in perpetuity[25]. In seeking to defend the living world from the maelstrom[26] of destruction, we might believe we are fighting corporations and governments and the general foolishness of humankind. But they are all proxies[27] for the real issue: perpetual growth on a planet that is not growing.

Those who justify this system insist that economic growth is essential for the relief of poverty. But a paper in the World Economic Review finds that the poorest 60% of the world's people receive only 5% of the additional income generated by rising GDP[28]. As a result, $111 of growth is required for every $1 reduction in poverty. This is why, on current trends, it would take 200 years to ensure that everyone receives $5 a day. By this point, average[29] per capita income will have reached $1m a year, and the economy will be 175 times bigger than it is today. This is not a formula for poverty relief. It is a formula for the destruction of everything and everyone. [...]

Green consumerism, material decoupling[30], sustainable growth: all are illusions, designed to justify an economic model that is driving us to catastrophe[31]. The current system, based on private luxury and public squalor[32], will immiserate[33] us all: under this model, luxury and deprivation[34] are one beast with two heads.

We need a different system, rooted[35] not in economic abstractions but in physical realities, that establish the parameters[36] by which we judge its health. We need to build a world in which growth is unnecessary, a world of private sufficiency[37] and public luxury. And we must do it before catastrophe forces our hand[38].

https://www.theguardian.com/commentisfree/2017/nov/22/black-friday-consumption-killing-planet-growth, 22 November 2017 [04.05.2019]

Jeff Koterba, 20 November 2018

COMPREHENSION

2. **After a second reading**, subdivide the text into paragraphs, following the thematic units of the text. Find a suitable headline for each paragraph using your own words.

WES-121500-022

3. The article contains a lot of formal or idiomatic and specialized vocabulary that you might not know. In order to get a better understanding of the details do the exercise provided on worksheet 22.1.

[22] **to licence sth.** *etw. erlauben, genehmigen* – [23] **long-haul** travelling a long distance – [24] **to accelerate** to go faster – [25] **in perpetuity** (*fml.*) forever – [26] **maelstrom** *Sog* – [27] **proxy** *Stellvertreter* – [28] **GDP** (*abbr.*) Gross Domestic Product; the total value of goods and services produced in a country in one year – [29] **average** *durchschnittlich* – [30] **to decouple** *etw. entkoppeln* – [31] **catastrophe** [kəˈtæstrəfi] – [32] **squalor** *Elend* – [33] **to immiserate** (*fml.*) to make sth. miserable – [34] **deprivation** *Ent-behrung, Mangel* – [35] **to root in sth.** *in etw. wurzeln* – [36] **parameter** *Faktor* – [37] **sufficiency** (*fml.*) *hinreichendes Auskommen* – [38] **to force sb.'s hand** *jdm. zum Handeln zwingen*

ANALYSIS

4. Examine and analyse the author's stance on (green) consumption, taking into consideration
a) the line of argument, b) the type of text, c) relevant stylistic devices.
→ Focus on Skills, Analysis of a Non-Fictional Text, p. 237
→ Focus on Skills, Basic Types of Non-Fictional Texts, p. 227

5. With a partner, describe and explain the cartoon on page 137. How does the message of the cartoon support Monbiot's harsh criticism of mankind's behaviour?
→ Focus on Skills, Analysis of Cartoons, p. 244

ACTIVITIES

6. Are humans really polluting and destroying the whole planet without considering the consequences? What about the Green Party movement and the millions of people who support organic food and textiles and try to live sustainably?
Compile and present information and graphics that visualize an alternative version to Monbiot's gloomy perspective of humanity's doom.

Tip: A good and convincing presentation should consist of several elements:
- a short speech
- audio-visual material
- a concise handout for each listener that provides the relevant information graphics, etc.

Step 1:
@ Do research on ecological and 'green' trends, organizations, activist groups, etc. and collect information to flesh out and visualize your presentation.
→ Focus on Skills, Doing Research and Citing Sources, p. 262

Step 2:
Sort the information and your research results in a mind map to get a better overview.

Tip: Contrast your examples with the negative examples given in the text to show that solutions are possible.

Example:

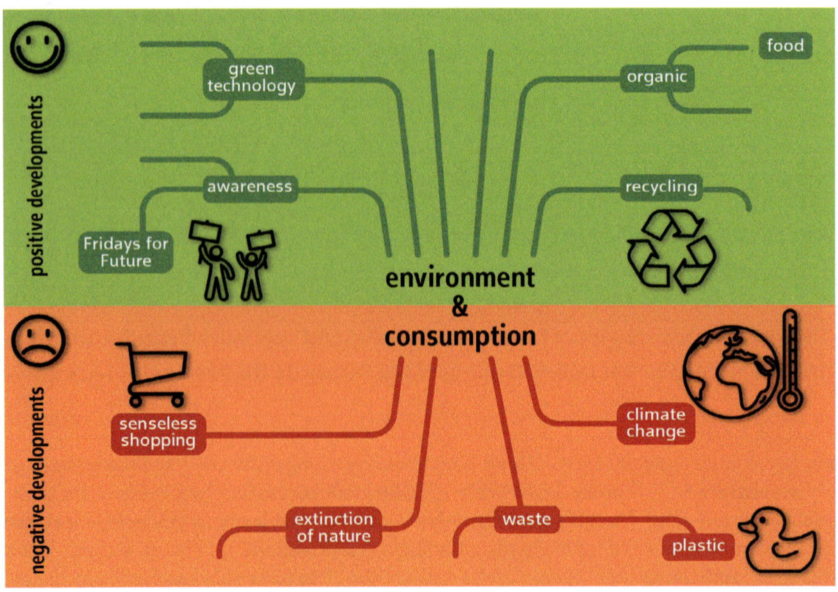

Step 3:
After sorting your ideas, make notes on cards to structure the information and divide your presentation into thematic units.

Tip: Study the respective skills pages in the Appendix.
→ Focus on Skills, Presentation, p. 261
→ Focus on Skills, Giving a Speech, p. 260

Step 4:
Finally, give your presentation, informing the audience about 'green' trends.

Tip: Start your presentation with an 'ice-breaker', an introductory friendly remark that grabs the attention of the audience.
The Tips on vocab box below will give you some ideas.

Tips on vocab

- Do we really think of ourselves as 'fools' that do not care about anything?
- Let's use our imagination and think about …
- Human spirit was never limited to …
- Man's intellectual capacity has never shrunk back from … or was limited by …
- Even in the darkest hours of crises human beings were able to …
- People's capacity to adapt to extreme situations … changes … has made them …
- In nature, nothing is perfect and everything is perfect. Trees can be contorted (*verkrüppelt*), bent in weird ways, and they're still beautiful. (*Alice Walker*)
- Some people walk in the rain, others just get wet. (*Roger Miller*)
- Nature does not need people – people need nature; nature would survive the extinction of the human being and go on just fine, but human culture, human beings, cannot survive without nature. (*Harrison Ford*)

GRAMMAR / LANGUAGE

7. Extract Monbiot's most relevant arguments and statements from the text. Use **defining and non-defining relative clauses or participle constructions** to give an account of his ideas and thoughts.

Examples:
- The promise of economic growth, which is false, is based on …
- The simple-minded people (who are) depicted in the novel *Brave New World*, are silenced by …
- It is unbelievable, the global growth rate reached every year, means that …

→ Relative Clauses, p. 299
→ Participles, p. 297

Simon Hage et al.

Living Sustainably: Can We Save the Planet Without Having to Do Without?

AWARENESS

Step 1: Look at the cover of the 2019 July issue of the German magazine *Der Spiegel*, which was published at the beginning of the German summer vacation season. What image of the 'average German' does the cover convey?

Step 2: Discuss the question asked in the caption.
- Is living 'right' and 'well' (= pleasantly, satisfactorily) morally and ethically (still) possible?
- What is your understanding of a 'good' life?

Step 3: The headline of the article poses the controversial question as to whether (or not) living sustainably and saving the world and living one's life to the fullest is possible.
Try to anticipate what the article's answers might be. What aspects/problems/trends do you expect the authors will focus on? Discuss.

1 **Many in Germany are trying to do their part to slow climate change. They are conscientious[1] about the purchases[2] they make, they ride bikes and they try to reduce their trash and carbon footprint. They can't solve the problem on their own, but they could force politicians and businesses to act.**

Saving the planet isn't going to be easy. It'll take effort[3]. Like packing children's lunches into recycled glass jars[4] and wrapping them in wool socks to prevent them from shattering in kids' backpacks. Or making homemade detergent[5] out of curd soap[6], soda and water. Whatever it takes to avoid plastic packaging. The Meuser family has been living this way for half a year.

"We're only taking small steps, but that alone feels so liberating," says Maik Meuser, 42. "But we also have to invest time and energy," says Nicole Kallwies-Meuser, 41.

Both work full-time. He's a TV host and she's a project manager. They have three children. Their day-to-day family commitments[7] are challenging enough as it is, but at the beginning of the year, the parents asked themselves: How can we leave behind a world for our children that is worth living in and beautiful? Because if something doesn't change soon, the Meusers thought, it's over. And not only for them, but all of humanity.

Surveys show that nearly three-quarters of all Germans are worried about their planet's future. It's no wonder then, that the secretary general of the United Nations

hardly misses an opportunity to call climate change the "greatest systematic threat to humanity."

What's new is this: There is an increasing amount of people like the Meusers who are not only worried but

[1] **conscientious** thoughtful; *gewissenhaft* – [2] **purchase** (*fml.*) the act of buying sth. – [3] **effort** *Mühe* – [4] **jar** *Einmachglas, Konservenglas* – [5] **detergent** *Waschmittel* – [6] **curd soap** *Kernseife* – [7] **commitment** *Verpflichtung*

are seriously looking for ways to change the way they live. These are people who have decided that saving the environment isn't merely[8] the purview[9] of the hippy-dippy-granola crowd[10], but for everyone.

[...]

2 A new dynamic has emerged, primarily because the climate issue is largely perceived[11] as a question of justice – intergenerational justice. Millions of young people have understood that their future is at stake[12] and that one day they'll pay the price if something doesn't change soon.

"'Fridays for Future' has developed more political power than Greenpeace on its best day," Welzer says. "The process of cultural change that has begun is palpable[13]."

On the other hand, this will to change isn't reflected in figures everywhere. Meat consumption in Germany, for one, hasn't declined[14] at all, even though many people now express a wish to live vegan[15]. And despite the fact that sustainable tourism is en vogue at the moment, just as many Germans fly to their vacation destinations as ever before.

How does this all fit together?

The Germans, it seems, were long a people of "climate-concerned climate sinners," the German Federal Environment Agency states. They buy organic sausages, put them in their reusable jute[16] bags and drive home in their SUVs. [...]

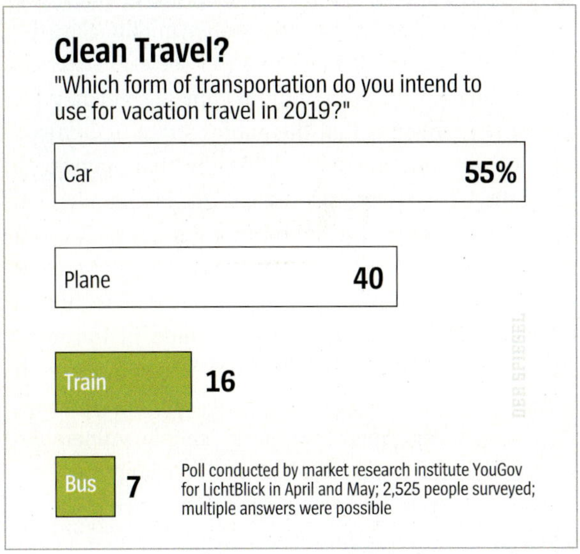

Companies are struggling with similar issues in other industries as well. They want to – and have to – offer more environmentally friendly products. But so far, most of them remain niche[17] offerings. As great as consumer pressure is on the one hand, on the other, it's hard to change consumers' behavior. Everything is supposed to become more sustainable and more ecological – but please, don't let it become at all uncomfortable or unaffordable[18].

The coffee chain Starbucks declared nearly a decade ago that it wanted to replace all of its disposable paper cardboard cups with reusable ones. Then in 2015, its goal was to have at least a quarter of all Starbucks cups used in the United States be reusable. In 2018, only 1.8 percent were. This begs the question: If consumers won't voluntarily forgo[19] cardboard cups, why not slap[20] them with a mandatory[21] surcharge[22]? [...]

3 In no other industry, however, does sustainability appear to be as big a deal as in the textile industry. One reason is because there are few industries that are dirtier. Textile manufacturers emitted more than 1.2 billion tons of greenhouse gases in 2015 – more than all international flights and global shipping combined. What's more: 63 percent of all materials used in clothing production are plastic.

According to a recent study by the management consulting firm McKinsey, nearly 80 percent of buyers of fashion chains are now operating under the assumption that sustainability will have a major influence on consumer purchasing decisions in the coming years, especially in mass fashion. McKinsey predicts that sustainability will be at "the center of innovation in the fashion industry." [...]

4 The Highest Hurdles Are Psychological

This means that the highest hurdles today are psychological rather than ideological. "People change their behavior when the effort requires the least psychologically and financially," says Renn. Swapping[23] plastic bags for cloth bags, for example. [...]

When it comes to sustainable behavior, Grünewald says the average German shows a very clear tendency. "People are conflicted: They want to protect the environment, but plastic bags are just so convenient[24]." The

[8] **merely** only; and nothing more – [9] **purview** (*fml.*) *Zuständigkeitsbereich* – [10] **hippy-dippy-granola crowd** (*infml.*) *durchgeknallte Müsli essende Leute* – [11] **to perceive** to understand or think of sb./sth. in a particular way – [12] **at stake** in danger of being lost – [13] **palpable** so obvious that can be easily seen or known – [14] **to decline** to gradually become less – [15] **vegan** a person who does not eat or use any animal products, such as meat, fish, eggs, cheese or leather – [16] **jute** [dʒuːt] – [17] **niche** [niːʃ] affecting only a small number of people – [18] **unaffordable** *unerschwinglich* – [19] **to forgo** (*fml.*) to do without sth. – [20] **to slap sb.** here: to punish – [21] **mandatory** *verpflichtend* – [22] **surcharge** an extra amount of money – [23] **to swap** to exchange – [24] **convenient** *praktisch, bequem*

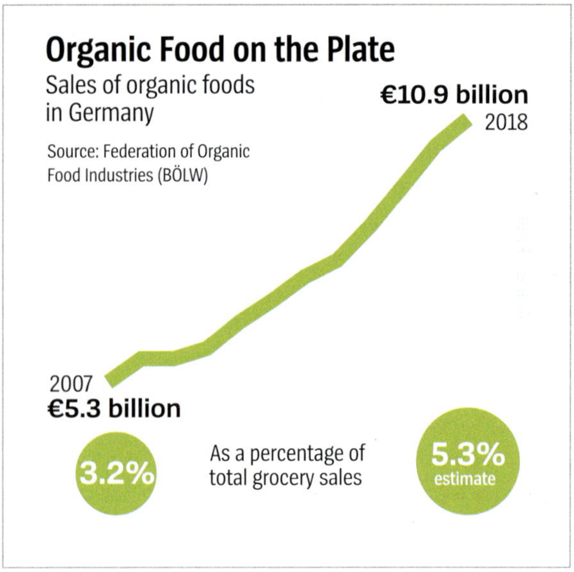

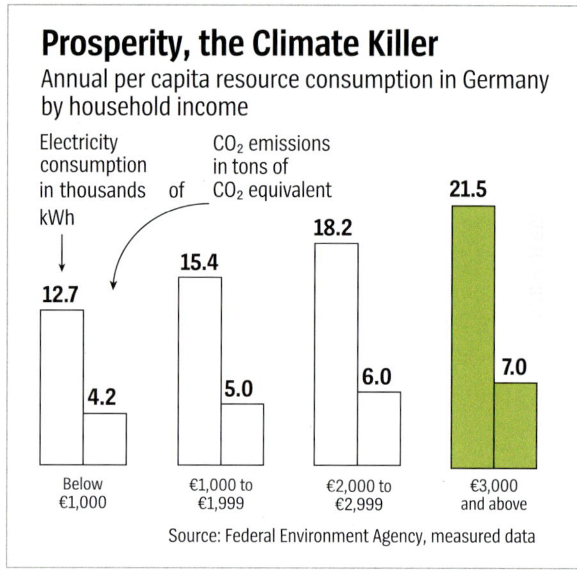

easiest way to resolve[25] this inner strife[26] would be to force them to change their behavior. "That's why people want bans – so they don't have to rely on self-discipline."

In other words: Consumers do best when they have no other choice but the alternative. "Germans have the habit of following these kinds of rules particularly conscientiously – you can already see that with recycling," says Grünewald. [...]

5 Does Climate Protection Have to Remain a Luxury Good?

It's actually pretty simple: Things that damage the climate should be expensive. There are plenty of scientific studies available on how to get people to change their behavior. One thing pops up again and again: As soon as it hits their pocketbooks[27], even people with the most entrenched[28] behaviors are willing to change. If the holiday flight to Thailand no longer costs 800 euros, but 5,000 euros, then people would probably prefer to take a train to the Alps in Bavaria. So, what are we waiting for? Politicians should simply impose[29] proper[30] eco-taxes on everything that harms the environment so that companies make their products more sustainable. If they cost more, then we, as consumers, will just all have to pay more. It would be reasonable to demand that in order to save the planet. [...]

6 Sustainability Needs to Be Fair

That's why the first and most important hurdle that needs to be cleared if we are really serious about finding the path to a more sustainable society is to make sure that it is fair – not only for moral reasons, but also for purely practical ones. "People with lower incomes will only join in if they feel that poor and rich are equally burdened," says Renn. He says this has been a repeat finding in numerous studies he has conducted. In other words: Nothing will come of saving the planet if sustainability is affordable for the upper middle class, but not for those in the lower strata[31] of society. There can be no climate protection without climate solidarity. [...]

The only problem is that the poorer strata in Germany already consume much less than the rich, anyway. In 2016, the UBA[32] prepared a study on "Per Capita Consumption of Natural Resources in Germany." It essentially states that, "the higher the education and income, the greater the consumption of resources." The highest total energy consumption is also found in the upper strata, "since they generally have above-average incomes and a lifestyle geared toward[33] status and ownership." On average, members of the "simple, vulnerable[34] strata" have the lowest total energy consumption.

In short: If there's a certain group destroying the climate, it's the high-earning, college-educated people who are fond of[35] showing the world to their children

[25] **to resolve** to end a problem or difficulty – [26] **strife** (*fml.*) conflict – [27] **pocketbook** *Geldbeutel* – [28] **entrenched** established firmly so that it cannot be changed – [29] **to impose** *etw. erheben (Steuern, Gebühren)* – [30] **proper** real, suitable – [31] **stratum** *Gesellschaftsschicht* – [32] **UBA** (*abbr.*) *Umweltbundesamt* – [33] **to gear sth. toward** *etw. ausrichten auf* – [34] **vulnerable** *verletzlich* – [35] **to be fond of sb./sth.** to like sb./sth. very much

during summer vacation, own two cars as well as a Vespa for the summer and have to heat a 200-square meter [...] apartment in the winter.

7 Ultimately[36], the question is this: How can the poor and the rich live more sustainably, without a reduction in their current quality of life? And how can we maintain our system of economic growth without being so destructive? It's a bit like the Meusers, the family from Dormagen trying to eliminate plastic from their lives. Their children are still allowed to eat ice cream, even if it comes packed in plastic. Otherwise, their enthusiasm would dissipate[37] rapidly. Or like the Henkes in Giessen: As long they can't afford an electric car, they will likely keep driving one with a combustion engine[38].

It's a complicated way of life, and there will be fierce[39] debate about many things on the path to sustainability. But the first step is simple, as Welzer, the expert on society with a special feel for Germans' nature, emphasizes. "Just stop whining[40] and start doing something."

Living Sustainably: Can We Save the Planet Without Having to Do Without? [...] Der Spiegel, Simon Hage, Anton Rainer, Thomas Schulz, Gerald Traufetter, 18.07.2019
https://www.spiegel.de/international/sustainability-can-we-save-the-planet-without-having-to-do-without-a-1277789.html [19.07.2019]

COMPREHENSION

1. The article has already been subdivided into seven parts for you. Divide your class into seven groups/teams, each one dealing with one of the parts.
Take notes on your respective part of the text and clarify the questions below in your group.

1
- Present how many Germans have changed their lives so far.
- Describe how the Meuser family is trying to live sustainably.

2
- State what is meant by "the new dynamic".
- Outline the problem that Germans are "climate-concerned climate sinners" and how companies deal with the situation.

3
- Specify the problem posed by the textile industry.
- Point out which future trends are to be expected concerning customers of fashion chains.

4
- Point out the "psychological dilemma" many people are in.
- Present what needs to be done to persuade consumers to change their habits.

5
- Describe the author's idea about "expensive things".
- Point out the consequences that environmentally harmful behaviour should have.

6
- State the author's demand for fairness.
- Specify the reasons why "the rich" are destroying the climate.

7
- Point out the essential questions the author asks regarding the gap between rich and poor.
- State what – according to the author – should be done to make Germans live more sustainably.

Next, change groups, with each group consisting of one member of the former group. In this new group, each member informs the others about the results from their first group.

ANALYSIS

2. Each new group chooses one of the paragraphs, analyses the stylistic and rhetorical devices* and explains how they help to depict the controversial issue. Focus particularly on:
- the line of argument*
- the use of (rhetorical) questions*
- the use of references and examples
- the use of contrast/antithesis*

→ Focus on Skills, Analysis of a Non-Fictional Text, p. 237

36 **ultimately** in the end – 37 **to dissipate** (*fml.*) to gradually disappear – 38 **combustion engine** *Verbrennungsmotor* – 39 **fierce** powerful, frightening – 40 **to whine** *jammern*

3. Analyse the graph and the bar charts (pp. 141 and 142) and relate them to the article:
a) What do the Germans' choices of transportation reveal about their eco-friendliness?
b) Describe the pattern of Germans' grocery purchases?
c) Explain the connection between resource consumption and income in Germany.
→ Focus on Skills, Analysis of Statistical Data, p. 243

ACTIVITIES

4. At least since the record heat wave in the summer of 2018 and the emerging *Fridays for Future* initiative, more and more people are concerned about climate change and its impact.
Faced with the new developments, you and your friends have organized a youth conference and invited various experts and people with experience on the matter.
You have been asked to give the introductory speech to the conference, in which you describe the situation, outline the controversy about how to react and motivate those attending the youth conference to take action.

Step 1:
@ You can use the information given in the article (and the attached statistics), but you should also do further research on
- climate change/global warming,
- the impact of climate change on flora and fauna,
- statements and assessments from experts.

→ Focus on Skills, Doing Research and Citing Sources, p. 262
Sort your findings in the following categories, which you can use for your speech later on.

information/facts	impact of climate change	action taken so far
• 75 % of Germans are worried about … • 1.2 billion tons of …	• carbon footprint … • …	• avoiding packaging … • …

Step 2:
Prepare your speech and select the aspects and information you want to talk about. As you are expected to speak in favour of environmental protection and against using plastic, too much waste, etc. your speech should have a clear line of argument in which you present the problems, the pros and cons as well as possible solutions – but finally come to the conclusion that the disadvantages of plastics, etc. outweigh the possible benefits.

Tip: Outline your argumentative strategy in an overview and collect and sort your arguments like this:

Topic/starting point: ____________________

arguments/examples: ← arguments: → counter-arguments/ counter-examples:

____________ ←→ ____________
____________ ←→ ____________
____________ ←→ ____________
____________ ←→ ____________

→ conclusion: ←

____

→ Focus on Skills, Basic Types of Non-Fictional Texts, p. 227

Step 3:

Bear in mind that your speech introduces the conference. So you should make some welcoming remarks first:

a) introducing the invited guests and experts to the participants/audience

b) thanking your guests/experts for coming and sharing their knowledge with you

Additionally, think of a good introduction to the subject of the conference to make your listeners aware of the problem and arouse their interest.

You can, for example, use the *Spiegel* front cover (p. 140) or the cartoon (below) to illustrate the controversy.

Tips on vocab

- Dear friends, ladies and gentlemen, distinguished guests and experts …
- Let me say how grateful I am to …
- We are so grateful to have you here …
- There is no denying that the situation has become alarming …
- Do we really know what problems our relentless consumption and careless wastefulness is causing?
- Can we really risk …?
- Why are we naive enough to believe that …?

Extinction Cruise by Steve Sack, 7 May 2019, in: The Minneapolis Star-Tribune

Tips on vocab

Noah's Ark ■ a pirate impersonating/symbolizing fossil fuels ■ sabre (*Säbel*) ■ animals crammed into the ark ■ penguin ■ chimpanzees ■ giraffes ■ tortoises ■ elephants ■ chamois (*Gämse*) ■ rabbits ■ rhino ■ flamingo ■ ostriches (*Strauße*) ■ tiger ■ to look scared ■ to pull the corners of one's mouth ■ to have worry lines on one's forehead

Step 4:

Make use of the **postcard technique**.

a) Structure your speech by breaking it into sections (sense units),

b) give each section a heading,

c) write one heading and a few easily-read prompt words or some data on each card,

d) think about a logical structure for your speech that makes it easily comprehensible for your listeners,
→ Focus on Skills, Basic Types of Non-Fictional Texts, p. 227

e) decide on certain formal and stylistic devices that you will employ in your speech in order to make it more appealing and interesting for the audience,
→ Focus on Skills, Analysis of a Political Speech, p. 242

f) number the cards in the order in which you want to present these points.

Step 5:

Finally, give your speech and convey your point of view to the listeners, according to the following structure:

- Greet the audience and introduce yourself.
- Rather than simply reading out what is on your cards, your transparency, PowerPoint, etc., paraphrase and explain it.
- Speak more slowly and loudly than usual.
- Make eye contact.
- Pause and take a break after each point.
- If you feel comfortable and confident enough, you can ask your audience whether they have any questions.
- At the end, conclude with a concise summary of your topic and a meaningful (= *prägnant*) final sentence or remark.

→ Focus on Skills, Giving a Speech, p. 260
→ Focus on Skills, Presentation, p. 261
→ Focus on Language, Connectives and Adverbs, p. 251

Tip: Additionally, prepare a handout for your listeners that contains the relevant information and gives them an overview of the issue.

WES-121500-023 Worksheet 23.1 provides you with a sample for you to use.

Tips on vocab

- to face reality
- to gain a deeper insight of
- to stop ignoring
- to quit glossing over
- an irresponsible denial of risk and reality
- to ignore potential dangers and risks
- to turn a blind eye to sth.

GRAMMAR / LANGUAGE

WES-121500-023

5. Brush up your **vocabulary** in connection with the topic of the environment and sustainability. Complete the vocabulary list provided on worksheet 23.2 and fill in the empty boxes. Use a dictionary for help if necessary.

Emma Bryce

What Really Happens to the Plastic You Throw Away

AWARENESS

Garbage in general and plastic debris (*Abfall*) in particular that gets washed up onto beaches has become a global problem. Manila Bay is a natural harbour in the port of Manila in the Philippines. It covers an area of about 2,000km^2 and consists of coral reefs, mangroves and wetlands, which are home to around 200,000 birds in excess of 90 species.

With a partner, look at the photograph below and

a) describe the polluted environment,

b) speculate about possible consequences of this amount of plastic pollution,

c) speculate about why the children might be collecting the rubbish.

Children collect plastic bottles among garbage washed ashore in Manila Bay

Tips on vocab

in the background:
wooden shacks on stilts ■ corrugated-iron huts ■ crowded together ■ a dark, cloudy sky ■ a dark, depressing mood

in the foreground:
children collecting plastic debris ■ poorly dressed ■ plastic debris and driftwood everywhere ■ plastic bags ■ flip flops ■ plastic containers

COMPREHENSION

WES-121500-024

1. Watch the animated video clip about three discarded plastic bottles, which is provided on the webcode, and get a **general understanding** of the plot.

Tips on vocab

to discard to throw sth. away ■ **to diverge** to follow a different direction ■ **to conceive** to cause a baby to begin to form ■ **oil refinery** a factory where oil in its natural state is cleared ■ **to bond** to stick materials together ■ **monomer** a chemical substance whose basic molecules can join together to form polymers ■ **polymer** a chemical substance consisting of large molecules ■ **pellet** a small hard ball of any substance ■ **mold** *(Gieß-)Form* ■ **resilient** *widerstandsfähig* ■ **triplets** *Drillinge* ■ **unceremoniously** rude, sudden, informal ■ **poised** ready to be moved at any moment ■ **edge** the furthest point of sth. ■ **brethren** (*old use*) brothers ■ **dump** a place where people are allowed to leave their rubbish ■ **to compress** to press sth. into a smaller space ■ **compound** *Bestand-teil* ■ **stew** here: *breiige Masse* ■ **leachate** *Deponiesickerwasser* ■ **soil** *(Mutter-)Boden* ■ **agonizing** causing extreme physical or mental pain ■ **to decompose** to decay; *kompostieren* ■ **trickle** *Rinnsal* ■ **vortex** *Strudel* ■ **to accumulate** to gradually increase in amount ■ **current** *Strömung* ■ **debris** *Abfall, Schutt* ■ **gyre** *Wirbel* ■ **pollutant** a harmful substance that causes pollution; *Schadstoff* ■ **entangled** *verwickelt, verwoben* ■ **to starve** to die of hunger ■ **lanternfish** *Laternenfisch* ■ **squid** *Tintenfisch* ■ **tuna** *Thunfisch* ■ **destined** *vorherbestimmt* ■ **eternally** forever ■ **to spare** to prevent sb. from having an unpleasant experience; *jdm. etw. ersparen* ■ **purgatory** *Fegefeuer* ■ **humble** ordinary, not very important

WES-121500-024

2. Watch the video clip a second time and do the comprehension tasks provided on worksheet 24.1.

3. Summarize the different biographies of the three 'plastic brothers' in about 200 – 250 words.

Tip: Keep in mind that the verb 'summarize' requires you to
- leave out details,
- avoid wordy explanations,
- use predominantly the simple present.
- be as precise and specific as possible,
- use direct (reported) speech and/or paraphrase,

Tip: Remember to write an introductory sentence that contains
- the title, the type of text and the running time of the film/video clip,
- the author's/director's name,
- the year of publication/release,
- the problem/topic the text/film deals with,
- important characters/features.

Use the help given in the Tips on vocab box above.

Example:
The animated video clip *What Really Happens to the Plastic You Throw Away* released on TED-Ed … in … deals with the fictitious biographies of …

→ Focus on Skills, Writing a Summary, p. 231

ANALYSIS

4. Examine the style of the animated video clip and explain its function and effect. Pay attention to the narrative devices that have been employed, e. g.
- the animated elements,
- the use of irony* and exaggeration*,
- the visualization of scientific information.

→ Focus on Skills, Analysis of a Film Scene, p. 239

ACTIVITIES

5. Prepare and act out a panel discussion in which you exchange your views and opinions about the use of plastic in general and the use of plastic bottles in particular, and how to cope with and solve the problem of plastic waste.

Step 1:

@ Do further research on:

a) the Great Pacific Garbage Patch,
b) the impact of plastic waste on the environment and marine animals,
c) the dangers of (micro)plastics for the food chain,
d) facts and data concerning the production of plastics,
e) facts and data concerning the reuse and recycling of plastics.

→ Focus on Skills, Doing Research and Citing Sources, p. 262

Step 2:

Divide the class into six groups, each group representing one particular view on plastics:

- representatives of a recycling plant
- representatives of a marine animal rescue station
- producers of plastic bottles
- customers
- environmentalists
- owners of a landfill
- politicians

Step 3:

Each group prepares a short presentation and explains their position to the class.

Tip: Remember to provide additional visuals, samples and/or a handout for the listeners. Try to be as objective as possible and do not evaluate by employing judgmental adjectives like 'shocking', 'inhuman', 'appalling', etc.

Step 4:

Before starting the discussion, prepare role cards and take notes on the possible pros and cons of the matter. Additionally, select and note down phrases that you will need for the discussion.

WES-121500-024 Worksheet 24.2 provides you with a set of role cards and the first ideas for your argumentation.

Step 5:

Act out the panel discussion and exchange your views and arguments.

GRAMMAR / LANGUAGE

6. Following the panel discussion, write a newspaper article of about 250 words which contains the different views and opinions expressed in the discussion.
Choose **adverbs** from the grid on page 154 and add them to your formulations. Be careful to put them in the right position.

Examples:

- A few days ago, we had the opportunity to watch a heated discussion about …
- Representatives of recycling plants repeatedly explained how they successfully managed …

→ Focus on Language, Connectives and Adverbs, p. 251

Noah Haidle

Everything Beautiful

AWARENESS

The protagonist of Noah Haidle's play, Cookie Close, is an aging, once successful door-to-door saleswoman who works for the American cosmetics company *Mary Kay*. Mary Kay's business strategy is direct sales, i.e. salespeople ("beauty consultants") selling the products directly to customers and getting a commission for what and how much they sell. In the company's strict hierarchy, beauty consultants are on the lowest level but can work their way up the company ladder, depending on how successful they are. Based on their respective position within the company, they must wear certain uniforms and colours (e. g. beauty consultants → pink; sales directors → royal blue).

The scene at hand depicts Cookie Close coincidentally meeting Vera, an old friend of hers, who has just returned from her husband's funeral service and is understandably distressed.

a) What impression does the photo convey of Cookie and her "customer", Vera?

b) What do the colours reveal about the overall atmosphere during this scene?

COOKIE
Have you ever thought about trying a new look?

VERA
What's wrong with my look?

COOKIE
Nothing!
Oh, God, I didn't mean to say it like that, I meant to say it like, taking agency[1], being in charge of[2] circumstance, seeing yourself for what you are.

VERA
And what is that?

COOKIE
Another iteration[3] of God's masterpiece.

VERA
What would you suggest I change?

COOKIE
Well.

She opens her rolly bag.
Lots of cosmetics.

COOKIE
I might suggest beginning with age fighting moisturizer[4].
Oh certainly foundation primer[5].
Perhaps the ultimate Mascara.
Wow, I can't believe I still have the Luminosity[6] Luminizing[7] Set, an impossibly popular item, definitely that.
Wrinkle-be-gone[8], who can live without it, am I wrong?
And Lovestruck Cranberry Lipstick.
And the Bedroom Eyes[9] Eyebrow definer pencil.
And the Understated Mask.
And exfoliant[10], pumice stones[11], moisturizer, and finally the Standard Bromwich Nail File, the gold standard of nail files.

Cookie Close (right) selling cosmetics to Vera (left); photo taken during a theatrical production at the Theater Krefeld-Mönchengladbach

[1] **to take agency** to be in charge of sth. – [2] **to be in charge of sb./sth.** to be responsible for sb./sth. – [3] **iteration** (*fml.*) the process of doing sth. again and again, usually to improve it – [4] **moisturizer** *Feuchtigkeitscreme* – [5] **foundation primer** *Grundierung* – [6] **luminosity** *Brillanz, Leuchtkraft* – [7] **to luminize** to light up – [8] **wrinkle** *Falte, Runzel* – [9] **bedroom eyes** the sensual/seductive look you have when you are in the mood for a romantic and/or sexual experience – [10] **exfoliant** *Peeling* – [11] **pumice stone** *Bimsstein*

VERA
Wow.
That's a lot.

COOKIE
Hey sister, tell me about it.
But looking good outside makes you look good inside.
I'm proof!
Look at me.
Do you think this amount of togetherness comes easy?
No way, Josie.
Hours every day.
Upkeep[12]!
It's endless.
But!
The results, if I might say so myself, are worth the effort.
Michelangelo said that his sculptures were waiting for him, inside the marble[13], calling to him to let them out.
God made us in His own image.
I say let the image out!
So that we might be reminded that we are all His beautiful creatures.
Will these products heal you?
No, I'm not promising that, nothing can except time, but by God you can look good while you're waiting.

VERA
What do I owe you for all these?

COOKIE
I can't accept money from you, Vera.
This is on the house.
You're grieving[14].

VERA
Cookie.

COOKIE
This is to help you feel beautiful again!
In this time of dire[15] need for it.

VERA
But this inventory[16], it comes out of your pocket.
I know how direct sales[17] works.
I insist.

Cookie sighs.

COOKIE
The Ultimate Mascara, Wrinkle Be Gone, the moisturizer, eyebrow pencil, and sleep mask are all $39.99, the lipstick usually goes for $27.99 but I can knock it down to $23 even, friend prices, the Luminizing set, which I can't believe I still have in stock, is $179.99, the exfoliant and pumice stones are $18 each, and I'll throw in[18] the Standard Bromwich Nail File for free, so, with 8% sales tax brings the grand total to $474.05, but for efficiency[19] and to honor our shared history, let's just say $474.

VERA
Wow.

COOKIE
That's the price of beauty!

VERA
Let me just go inside and get my purse.

COOKIE
I'll wait!!

Everything Beautiful by Noah Haidle. Bildungshaus Schulbuchverlage, Braunschweig, 2019, pp. 23 ff. © Noah Haidle, 2018

COMPREHENSION

1. After reading the scene, find evidence from the text that supports the statement: "Cookie: I don't sell cosmetics, I sell beauty!"

2. **While reading** the scene **a second time**, find sentences that match the following statements.
   Note: There are more aspects listed than can be found in the text.
   a) Vera's looks do not reveal her inner self.
   b) Cosmetics highlight God's masterpiece.
   c) Vera appears to be relatively old.

[12] **upkeep** the cost or process of keeping sb./sth. in good condition – [13] **marble** *Marmor* – [14] **to grieve** to feel or express great sadness, esp. when sb. dies – [15] **dire** very serious or extreme – [16] **inventory** the total amount of goods in stock – [17] **direct sales** a sale that is made directly to the customer and not through a store; *Direktverkauf* – [18] **to throw in** to include sth. with what you are selling, without increasing the price – [19] **efficiency** *Effizienz*; here: *Zeitersparnis*

d) Luminizers help to brighten up faces.
e) Vera's skin reveals that she is old and tired.
f) You can only feel good if you look good.
g) Women are like Michelangelo's statues.
h) Cookie spends a lot of time putting on her makeup.
i) Cookie wants to emotionally support Vera.
j) Makeup helps to bring out women's true image.
k) Vera knows how poor Cookie is.
l) Cookie helps Vera because they are old friends.
m) Cookie offers Vera a special discount.
n) Vera is ashamed by Cookie's generous offer.

ANALYSIS

WES-121500-025

3. Examine Cookie's sales strategy and how she praises and promotes her products. Use worksheet 25.1 for your analysis.

WES-121500-025

4. Analyse the course of the dialogue: How does Cookie lure (*locken*) Vera into buying her cosmetic products? Worksheet 25.2 provides you with the respective material.
→ Focus on Skills, Analysis of a Fictional Text, p. 235

5. Characterize Cookie's behaviour – is she the good friend she pretends to be? How does she treat Vera?
→ Focus on Skills, Characterization of a Figure in Literature, p. 247

6. Compare Cookie's behaviour to advertising (strategies) in real life.
- How does advertising use or abuse the emotional condition of people?
- Have you ever been lured into buying sth. because you were sad/frustrated/happy?

7. Examine and explain the statistical data on the best-selling cosmetic products and the top cosmetic companies worldwide (below and on p. 153).
- What are the sales and product strategies?
- Who are the global leaders in beauty sales?

→ Focus on Skills, Analysis of Statistical Data, p. 243

1 **Top Winning Strategies in World Cosmetics Market**

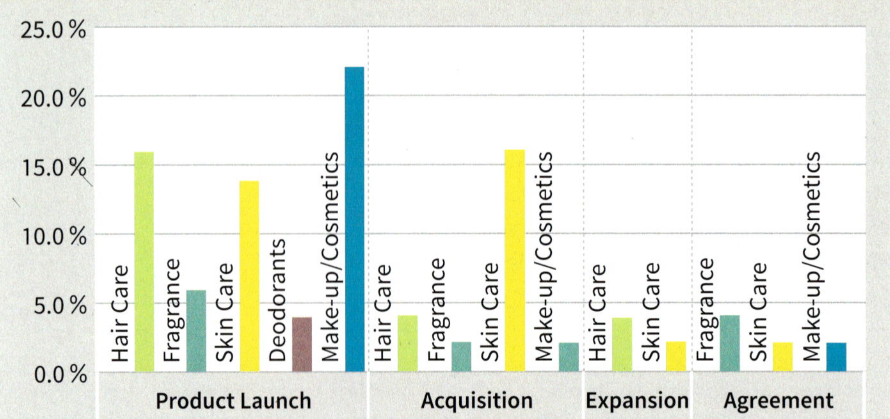

Data: Allied Market Research, 2016

2 **Company Beauty Sales/Top 10 Players**

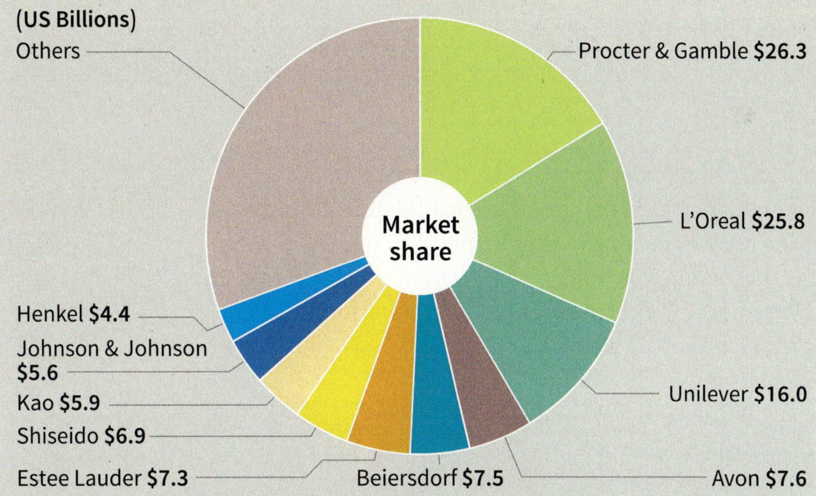

Data: Economic analysis of Cosmetic Industry, Lovneet Singh, 2010

ACTIVITIES

8. Environmental activists in cooperation with the Green Party have launched a campaign addressed particularly to young people which wants to inform them about and warn them against the enormous increase of cosmetics products and their environmental and health risks.
They conduct interviews with teenagers from different backgrounds to find out more about their
a) shopping habits and preferences for particular cosmetic products,
b) willingness to buy less,
c) economic/financial background and how much they spend on cosmetics,
d) interest and knowledge of the harmful environmental impact of cosmetics,
e) knowledge of animal experiments to develop and test cosmetic products.

Tip: Use the information given in the statistics for more specific and investigative questions.

Step 1:
Make some notes on topics and background information you would like to interview the respective person about, e.g.
- what (further) information and personal experiences they can add to the matter,
- what specific experiences they have made with certain cosmetics,
- their personal view of (certain) cosmetic products,
- etc.

Step 2:
Now, formulate your questions.

Tip: Use the information given on how to formulate questions in the info box in Skill 10, p. 67.

Examples:
- Which cosmetic products do you use?
- What do you like or dislike about cosmetics?
- What makes you buy or want to buy certain products?
- How environmentally-friendly are the products you buy?

Step 3:

After having written down a number of questions, put yourself in the position of the respondent and think about possible answers that might reflect the person's situation and position.

Tip: In order to make the interview more realistic, employ linguistic devices and communicative strategies such as

- 'fillers',
- feedback phrases to emphasize that you are listening closely,
- friendly comments to create a good and conciliatory atmosphere,
- turn-taking phrases to bring in another person,
- avoiding judgmental comments,
- expressing yourself indirectly by using conditional forms,
- making a pause after a statement,
- using question tags,
- making suggestions.

→ Focus on Language, Conversation and Discussion, p. 254
→ Focus on Language, Connectives and Adverbs, p. 251

Tips on vocab – fillers

last but not least ■ in answer to that point ■ in general ■ to put it more clearly ■ it seems obvious to me that ■ it appears to be evident ■ what I'd like to say is

Tip: Be careful not to overdo it and use too many fillers – you do not want to produce empty phrases.

GRAMMAR / LANGUAGE

9. A major cosmetics company wants to know about the satisfaction of their customers with their products. Therefore, they send out interviewers to personally ask customers about their opinion.
Team up with a partner and act out these interviews about the specific likes and dislikes concerning cosmetic products you use.
Use **adverbial clauses of time, reason, result, purpose, conclusion and contrast** for your questions and answers. Choose adverbs from the grid below and add them to your formulations. Be careful to put them in the right position.

Examples:

- Even though the lotion was expensive, it didn't have any effect on my skin.
- Have you ever bought a cosmetic product because it was advertised?

adverbs of time	adverbs of reason	adverbs of result	adverbs of purpose	adverbs of conclusion	adverbs of contrast
now then today tomorrow annually daily nightly weekly yearly before meanwhile	hence therefore	such so … that so much that in order that such that	since so thus therefore	definitely once and for all positively finally decisively	although though even though even if while whereas however despite in spite of on the other hand rather but nevertheless

→ Adjectives and Adverbs, p. 289

Claire Charters

Are Cosmetics Bad for the Environment?

AWARENESS

Step 1:
Take a look at the two photographs below, which show 'two sides of the same coin': the mass production and consumption of cosmetics and personal care products and the slashing and burning of the Amazon rainforest.

Shelves with cosmetic and personal care products in a supermarket

The slash-and-burn method used for land clearance in the Amazon rainforest

Step 2:
After reflecting on the connection between the photographs, complete the sentences below:
- The production of cosmetics is/should be …
- Cosmetics are …
- The Amazon rainforest is/should be …
- The deforestation of rainforests is/causes …

Tip: Write your statements on slips of paper which you can then attach to different sides of the blackboard.

Step 3:
Discuss your statements in class and explain your respective views.

COMPREHENSION

1. **Before reading** the blog about the use of cosmetics,
   a) team up with a partner,
   b) take a look at the six sub-headings above the paragraphs,
   c) speculate on what each paragraph might be about,
   d) take notes on your ideas from b) and develop further ideas about the respective topic/danger the sub-heading refers to.

WES-121500-026

Use worksheet 26.1 for your notes.

2. **While reading** the complete blog, find sentences that match the following statements.

Note: There are more aspects listed than can be found in the text.
a) Plastic and personal care products produce toxins.
b) Cosmetics destroy wildlife and marine animals and their habitats.
c) Palm oil causes the extinction of rainforests.
d) Microbeads end up in the human food chain.
e) The attributes 'natural' and 'organic' cover up the use of pesticides and the violation of human rights.
f) Sustainable farming and mining exclude mass production and mass quantities.
g) The mass production of palm oil causes the extinction of wild animals.
h) The production of palm oil leads to the deforestation of rainforests.
i) Palm oil is used for shampoos and soaps.
j) Corporations and even non-governmental organizations (NGOs) are ignoring the fact that palm oil destroys nature and wildlife.
k) Sunscreens contain dangerous chemicals that kill coral reefs.
l) Wet wipes kill marine animals.
m) Plastic packaging is deadly.
n) Plastic trash turns into toxic waste that poisons the oceans.
o) Microbeads/microplastics threaten aquatic life.
p) Cosmetic chemicals can be found all over the planet and in all the oceans.
q) Consumers have a responsibility to put pressure on corporations.

Ever stopped to wonder what environmental impact all your cosmetics, beauty products and personal care items are having on the planet? Truth is – cosmetics are affecting our environment in a negative way. Whether the product is washed down the sink[1] or disposed of[2] in the bin, all the chemicals, toxins and plastics are poisoning our waters and planet, which then results in killing coral reefs, turtles, rainforests, wildlife habitat[3] and more.

The packaging of cosmetic products can take hundreds of years to break down in landfill whilst leaching[4] toxins into the soil and waterways.

Most mainstream cosmetics are filled with toxic chemicals, these chemicals eventually make their way into our soil and oceans, destroying natural habitat and wildlife.

Pesticides[5] sprayed on the raw ingredients[6] whilst being farmed poison our planet as they seep into[7] the soil and make their way to bodies of water[8].

Many products contain palm oil, one of the number one contributors to rapid deforestation[9], wildlife extinction[10] and climate change.

Turtles and marine animals are ingesting[11] microbeads, wet wipes[12] and plastic packaging, which eventually block their digestive tract[13] and cause them to die.

The toxic ingredients found in mainstream sunscreens[14] is killing corals and marine ecosystems at an alarming rate.

As consumers, we are becoming more and more educated on the health dangers posed by cosmetics and per-

[1] **sink** *Spüle* – [2] **to dispose of sb./sth.** (*phr. v., fml.*) to get rid of sb./sth. – [3] **habitat** the natural environment in which a plant/an animal normally lives – [4] **to leach** *auswaschen, durchsickern lassen* – [5] **pesticide** *Unkraut-/Insektenvernichtungsmittel* – [6] **raw ingredient** natural substance – [7] **to seep into** *versickern* – [8] **body of water** *Gewässer* – [9] **deforestation** the destruction of forests by people, the cutting down of woods in a large area – [10] **extinction** *Aussterben* – [11] **to ingest** to swallow – [12] **wet wipe** *Feuchttuch* – [13] **digestive tract** *Verdauungstrakt* – [14] **sunscreen** a substance that protects your skin against the sun

sonal care products thanks to all the not-for-profit agencies working so hard to raise consumer awareness in the hope that it forces brands to do better. [...]

So what effect are all the trillions of beauty products having on the planet? Here's a look at how cosmetics are damaging our environment and how they are affecting the natural world around us.

1. 'Natural' Is Destroying Our Planet

Companies are cashing in[15] on the word 'natural', they seem to think by putting a few natural ingredients in their product it makes their product natural – even though it is overflowing with other chemical and toxic ingredients.

Here's where it gets interesting. Because more companies are seeking out natural ingredients (so they can put 'natural' on their bottle) the demand for natural ingredients has increased at an unsustainable[16] level. In order to supply the rising demand means that more farming and mining needs to occur[17]. Now; this would be a wonderful thing if it was done sustainably. However, big companies want to buy it in mass quantities and they want it cheap and fast.

So, forget about sustainable farming and mining – more pesticides are being sprayed on the earth and more human rights are being exploited[18]. When done mindlessly, the mining of minerals and oils for natural ingredients disrupts[19] ecosystems and depletes[20] non-renewable natural resources.

The environment friendly solution:

Choose beauty companies and beauty products that use a high amount of either organic ingredients or wild-crafted[21] ingredients in their product. Also, if you choose to buy a product that doesn't contain organic ingredients, do a little research on how the company sources[22] its ingredients – look for Fair Trade Practices and give back initiatives. Look for sustainable ingredients such as coconut oil, hemp[23] oil and aloe vera, for they are easily renewable and therefore make a great eco-friendly option.

2. Palm Oil Can Never Be Sustainable

So, what's the deal with palm oil? And is there a sustainable way to farm it. The answer is kinda[24] "no".

Firstly, most of us are aware of the destructive deforestation that happens with the majority of palm oil production. To keep up with the incredibly high demand for the cheaply produced oil, acres of rainforest are being cut down at alarming rates – leading to a loss of animal habitat for endangered species.

In the past 16 years, the quest[25] for palm oil has led to the death of an estimated 100,000 orangutans[26], according to research.

Other animals such as elephants, rhinos and tigers are also at risk.

Over the years, we have seen the introduction of sustainable palm oil. However, there is no such thing as sustainable palm oil.

And the reasoning is: to produce palm oil, the fruit is collected from the trees, which can live an average of 28 to 30 years. However, once the trees grow too high, making it difficult to reach the fruit, they are cut down and the forest is set alight[27] to make room for new trees – which still contributes to deforestation of the rainforest. This process happens no matter if it is sustainable palm oil or not.

Bottom line is that there is no way to produce sustainable palm oil that did not come from deforestation, and those sustainable claims[28] by corporations, certification schemes and non-government organizations are simply 'green-washing'. If a company uses palm oil, certified or not, they are most definitely destroying tropical forests.

Today, almost all chocolate, shampoo, chips, household cleaning products, cosmetics, and even pet foods use palm oil – many of them claiming they use "sustainable palm oil". [...]

The environment friendly solution:

This one is simple – don't buy products that contain palm oil or vegetable oil

3. Your Sunscreen Could Be Damaging Coral Reefs

A common chemical ingredient used in almost every sunscreen is 'oxybenzone' also known as 'benzophenone-3'. This is an active chemical[29] that absorbs UVA[30] and UVB[31] rays, therefore protecting the skin from the

[15] **to cash in** (*phr. v., infml.*) to make money from a situation in a dishonest way – [16] **unsustainable** *nicht nachhaltig* – [17] **to occur** to happen – [18] **to exploit** *ausbeuten* – [19] **to disrupt** to prevent a system to run as usual – [20] **to deplete** to reduce sth. – [21] **wild-crafted** made by nature – [22] **to source** to get from a particular place or person – [23] **hemp** *Hanf* – [24] **kinda** (*infml.*) kind of – [25] **quest** *Nachfrage* – [26] **orangutan** [əˈræŋuːtæn] – [27] **alight** on fire – [28] **claim** *Behauptung* – [29] **active chemical** a substance that produces a chemical or biological effect – [30] **UVA** (*abbr.*) ultraviolet A; radiation from the sun with long wavelengths – [31] **UVB** (*abbr.*) ultraviolet B; radiation from the sun with short wavelengths

sun. Whilst this ingredient does a very effective job at protecting your skin, it is also having a very negative impact on the world's coral reefs. Research has shown that sunscreens that contain oxybenzone have been contributing to the bleaching[32] of the coral reefs.
Every time we apply sunscreen, we are killing the coral reef – it will either wash off in the ocean, river or lake when we go swimming or it will trickle down[33] the drain[34] when we take a shower. All bodies of water eventually make their way to the ocean.
The studies show that oxybenzone damages the coral's DNA and interferes with the reproduction and growth of young coral. Coral reefs house diverse ecosystems that provide habitat and food for many marine organisms, they also generate[35] billions of tourist dollars to local economies. It is important we keep them alive.

The environment friendly solution:
When buying sunscreen, look for ingredients that contain titanium dioxide and zinc oxide instead. These compounds act like a mirror, reflecting the sun's rays. They are not only better for our health but also much less damaging for the environment.

4. Are You Feeding the Turtles Your Wet Wipes?
Most of us at some point have used wet wipes, whether it is to clean our face, remove make-up or clean up a baby's bum[36]. At some point we have all probably flushed one down the loo[37] – after all they do say flushable[38].
Today I am here to tell you that wet wipes are anything but flushable. Even the ones that say they are bio-degradable[39] still wreak havoc[40] with our sewage[41] systems, oceans and marine life. They clog up[42] sewage systems, don't bio-degrade and by the time they make their way into the ocean, they get ingested[43] by sea creatures, such as turtles, who mistake them for jellyfish and eventually die. Even if you don't flush your wet wipes, they end up in landfill where the toxic chemicals used to make the wet wipe seep into the soil and poison our earth.

The environment friendly solution:
Avoid using wet wipes in the first place – and if you really feel like you can't live without them, then choose a non-toxic one and dispose of it in the bin.

5. Deadly Plastics Are Behind All That Beautiful Packaging
The packaging of cosmetics and personal care products also has damaging effects on the environment. All those plastic bottles and tubes that hold shampoo, moisturizers[44], our favourite shade of lipstick and an array[45] of other products, these all end up in either our oceans or landfills where they leach toxins into the environment and can take hundreds of years to break down.
Then there are all the microbeads – the tiny balls of plastic used in body scrubs[46], toothpastes and body exfoliators[47]. Some products can contain over 300,000 microbeads – per tube. These microbeads get washed down our drains and make their way into the ocean where marine animals ingest them, this then blocks the marine animals' digestion tract and causes them to die.
The beauty industry has come under fire in recent years for its use of microbeads, and as a result of consumer demand several companies are opting[48] to slowly phase them out[49].

The environment friendly solution:
When buying products, choose to go plastic free and opt for product packaging made with glass and recycled paper. Even better – many companies are dropping the packaging and are up-cycling bottles or using little to no packaging. Also check all labels on toothpastes, exfoliators and body/face scrubs, if they contain plastic microbeads, then seek out an alternative brand[50]/product.

6. The Chemical Ingredients Are Slowly Poisoning Our Planet
The chemical components of many products don't break down and instead accumulate[51] in our ecosystems. Cosmetics and personal care products do most damage to the environment after they are washed down our sinks. The chemicals are recycled into our lakes, streams, rivers and public water systems. [...] Cosmetic chemicals are not just hazardous[52] to aquatic life. All life on Earth is dependent on the water cycle. Water vaporizes[53] into the atmosphere, re-accumulates into clouds, then re-liquifies[54] and returns to the Earth as rain. The chemicals that have been introduced into aquatic ecosystems evaporate[55] along with the water and are then

[32] **bleaching** *Bleichen* – [33] **to trickle down** *durchsickern* – [34] **drain** *Abfluss* – [35] **to generate** to produce – [36] **bum** (*infml.*) behind; *Po* – [37] **loo** (*infml.*) toilet – [38] **flushable** that can be flushed down the toilet – [39] **bio-degradable** *biologisch abbaubar* – [40] **to wreak havoc** (*fml.*) to cause immense damage or destruction – [41] **sewage** *Abwasser* – [42] **to clog up** to block – [43] **to ingest** to eat or drink sth. – [44] **moisturizer** *Feuchtigkeitscreme* – [45] **array** *Ansammlung* – [46] **body scrub** *Körperpeeling* – [47] **exfoliator** *Peeling* – [48] **to opt** to make a choice – [49] **to phase sth. out** (*phr. v.*) to stop using sth. gradually – [50] **brand** a type of product made by a particular company – [51] **to accumulate** to gradually increase – [52] **hazardous** dangerous and likely to cause damage – [53] **to vaporize** *verdampfen* – [54] **to re-liquify** *sich verflüssigen* – [55] **to evaporate** *verdunsten*

transferred to other areas through rain. Cosmetic-related chemicals have been found in rivers, oceans, streams, lakes, public water supply, agricultural soil and even household dust particles.

The environmental damage caused by cosmetics are far-reaching; however, consumers have the power to keep these toxins out of the environment by choosing not to support any products or brands that are not environmentally minded. Consumer demand has already inspired many companies to "green" their products. This progressive behaviour reinforces[56] that at the end of the day we, the consumers, have the power to put pressure on companies to adopt greener, safer and sustainable practices. With education and responsible purchasing[57] practices, consumers have the power to stop the pollution caused by cosmetics and their toxic chemicals.

https://botanicaltrader.com/blogs/news/how-your-beauty-products-are-killing-coral-reefs-turtles-rainforests-more, 20 January 2019 [02.08.2020]

ANALYSIS

3. Critically examine and evaluate the various pieces of advice and "environment friendly solutions" that are given in the blog.
- Are these solutions helpful and realistic?
- How can a consumer identify all the (toxic) ingredients and substances mentioned in the blog?

4. Analyse the author's strategy to appeal to and address her readership. Pay particular attention to the author's
- use of (personal) pronouns,
- use of informal English,
- use of technical terms/expert language,
- use of positive and negative emotive words and word fields.

→ Focus on Skills, Analysis of a Non-Fictional Text, p. 237

5. Describe the cartoon below and
a) explain the cartoonist's intention and the cartoon's message.
b) relate the message of the cartoon to the appeals and accusations (*Anschuldigungen*) in the blog.

→ Focus on Skills, Analysis of Cartoons, p. 244

[56] **to reinforce** to make sth. stronger – [57] **to purchase** to buy

ACTIVITIES

6. **After reading and discussing the blog, your school's environmental club has decided to invite the author and conduct an interview with her which will also be broadcast on your town's local radio station.**
Team up in a group and prepare an interview with Claire.

Tip: Use the information given in the blog as well as the statistical data provided on pp. 152 f.

Step 1:
Make some short notes on topics and background information you would like to interview Claire about, e. g.

- which sources of information she has used for her blog,
- what specific experiences she has made with certain cosmetics and personal care products,
- etc.

Step 2:
Now formulate your questions.

Tip: Use the information given on how to formulate questions in the Info box (material no. 10, p. 67).

Step 3:
After having written down a number of questions, put yourself in the position of the respondent and think about possible answers that Claire might give.

Additionally, use the Tips and the Tips on vocab boxes on fillers and communicative strategies on page 154.

GRAMMAR / LANGUAGE

7. A major cosmetics company has taken notice of the blog and the radio interview and now wants to refute (*entkräften*) the harsh criticism of their practices and products and, of course, wants to reassure its customers.
Team up with a partner and work out a coherent counter statement which can be written or read out in a radio broadcast.
Use **adverbial clauses of time, reason, result, purpose, conclusion and contrast** for your statements. Choose adverbs from the grid on page 154 and add them to your formulations. Be careful to put them in the right position.

Examples:

- Our company has a long tradition of high-quality cosmetics. Since … we have been …
- We definitely do not use any harmful substances, but there might be …

→ Adjectives and Adverbs, p. 289

Ricarda Richter

Nicht von Pappe[1]

AWARENESS

Step 1:

Although people know that plastic has a bad impact on the environment, the volume of plastic items that are bought and sold is growing rapidly. Possibly, many people do not really know how dangerous plastic items are.

WES-121500-027

Watch the short video clip published by the World Wildlife Fund (WWF) Germany, which is provided on the webcode.

- What overall impression does the video clip convey?
- What specific dangers of plastic pollution does the video clip present?

Step 2:

a) Together with a partner, read the transcript of the WWF video clip below.

b) Working creatively with the text, turn the statements into English first.

c) Arrange the English statements in verses like in a poem and display your poems on sheets of paper in class.

Tip: Remember not to translate the statements word by word but transform them into English. Additionally, you can further illustrate your poems, add photos, snippets from magazines, etc.

d) In a gallery walk, read your poems first, then discuss your results and ideas.

Leicht bin ich. Schnell und stark. Ich bin deine Lust[2]. Dein Vergnügen[3]. Ich versüße[4] dein Leben. Mache es bunt und hell, bequem und leicht. Bin ich einmal da, gehe ich nicht mehr weg. Ich bin überall. Auf der ganzen Welt, denn du lässt es geschehen. Aber gib acht[5]: Ich töte gerne. Und morde. Ohne Skrupel[6], ohne Rast[7]. Ich vergifte. Ich quäle[8] und mache vor nichts halt[9]. Die Meere mach ich mir zu Eigen[10]. Dort fühle ich mich wohl[11]. Verpeste[12] und verschmutze. Vergifte und quäle, ohne Rücksicht auf Verluste[13]. Ich bin überall. Und bin ich einmal da, gehe ich nicht mehr weg. Das ist mein wahres Gesicht. Ich bin dein Plastikmüll.

Anne Thoma: Ich bin dein Plastikmüll, WWF Deutschland, https://www.youtube.com/watch?v=Cl3iLzOVEFI, 6 February 2019 [29.01.2021]

COMPREHENSION

The author of the German newspaper article *Nicht von Pappe* describes the highly controversial (global) debate about how to deal with the enormous amounts of plastic (trash).

1. After a **first reading**,
   a) divide the text into thematic units and
   b) give each unit a suitable English heading.

2. Complete the statements below using information given in the article.
   a) The coronavirus pandemic triggered the popularity of plastic because …
   b) The bad image of plastic changed during the coronavirus pandemic, and people thought …
   c) Germany and the EU have passed a law which …

[1] nothing to sneeze at – [2] desire – [3] pleasure – [4] to sweeten – [5] beware – [6] unscrupulously – [7] rest – [8] to torture – [9] to stop at nothing – [10] to take possession of sth. – [11] to feel comfortable – [12] to poison, to contaminate – [13] regardless of the consequences, at all costs

d) In the 1950s, plastic was popular because …
e) Plastic poses a danger to the climate because …
f) Only selected plastic items are prohibited, which …
g) The most important advantage of plastic-free products is …
h) The problem of many paper cups and paper straws is that …
i) The recycling of plastic is environmentally friendly because …
k) Start-ups are looking for innovative products, e. g. …

→ Focus on Skills, Mediation, p. 253

Besteck, Teller und Trinkhalme aus Einwegplastik[14] sind ab Sommer 2021 verboten. Das schont nicht unbedingt[15] die Umwelt, glauben Experten

Als die Corona-Pandemie ausbrach[16], erlebte Einwegplastik einen zweiten Frühling[17]. Laut dem größten deutschen Recyclingunternehmen Remondis wuchs die Menge des Plastikmülls aus deutschen Haushalten um 5 bis 14 Prozent. Die Deutschen saßen im Homeoffice und hamsterten[18] Lebensmittel, Lieferdienste boomten und mit ihnen Essensbehälter aus aufgeschäumten Polystyrol[19].

Das merkte auch Katja Kantelberg. Sie führt den Online-Shop von Papstar, das Einmalprodukte des täglichen Bedarfs an Großkunden[20] vertreibt: Geschirr[21], Essensboxen, Partyartikel. „In den vergangenen Monaten haben wir so viele Plastikprodukte verkauft wie seit Jahren nicht", berichtet sie. Besonders beliebt sei das Set aus Löffel, Gabel, Messer und Serviette, in durchsichtige Folie[22] verpackt, das in vielen Krankenhäusern ausgegeben werde. Plötzlich galt Kunststoff wieder als besonders hygienisch, wenngleich Studien zeigen, dass sich das Virus auf Kunststoffoberflächen deutlich länger hält[23] als auf Pappe und Papier.

Der Boom der vergangenen Monate könnte das letzte Aufbäumen[24] des Plastiks gewesen sein. Vom 3. Juli 2021 an ist es der gesamten Europäischen Union verboten, Besteck, Teller, Trinkhalme[25], Rührstäbchen[26] sowie Luftballonstäbe, Wattestäbchen[27] und bestimmte Lebensmittel- und Getränkebehälter aus Einwegplastik zu produzieren und zu verkaufen. Ende Juli [2020] brachte die Bundesregierung eine entsprechende Verordnung[28] auf den Weg, um die EU-Richtlinie in Deutschland umzusetzen. Der Bundesrat[29] muss noch zustimmen, pro forma[30].

Deutsche Verbraucher[31] müssen wohl künftig auf Alternativen zum Kunststoff umsteigen. Auf Holzbesteck, Pappboxen und Strohhalme aus Papier. Wie sinnvoll ist das? […]

Das Ende des Einwegplastiks wäre das Ende einer Ära. Sie begann in den 1950er-Jahren, als die Menschen anfingen, mehr und mehr zu konsumieren. Verpackungen[32], die man nach dem Essen einfach wegwerfen konnte, waren praktisch und günstig, für Unternehmen vereinfachten sie die Lieferketten[33]. Kunststoff galt zudem als modern, elegant und sauber. Seit 1950 wurden amerikanischen Forschern zufolge mehr als neun Milliarden Tonnen Plastik produziert, ein Großteil in Form von Einwegprodukten und Verpackungen.

Die Wegwerfmentalität[34] wurde zum Problem der Ökosysteme. Neun der zehn vom Verbot betroffenen Gegenstände zählen zu den am häufigsten gefundenen Einwegplastikprodukten an europäischen Stränden. […]

Plastik verursacht auch ein Klimaproblem. Wird die Produktion nicht deutlich reduziert, könnten dabei bis 2050 nach Berechnungen des Zentrums für Internationales Umweltrecht rund 56 Gigatonnen CO_2 entstehen. Das ist etwa ein Zehntel des verbleibenden CO_2-Budgets, das festgelegt wurde, um das Klimaziel von Paris[35] zu erreichen. […]

Plastik ist in Verruf geraten[36].

Kein schlechter Zeitpunkt also, um Plastik zu verbieten. Doch verschwinden werden nur bestimmte Produkte. Was von 2021 an von dem Verbot betroffen ist, wurde laut Europäischer Kommission von der „Verfügbarkeit[37] geeigneter und nachhaltiger[38] Alternativen" abhängig gemacht. Für Getränkeflaschen, Luftballons, Reinigungstücher[39], Chipstüten und Zigarettenfilter[40] gebe es keinen oder zu wenig erprobten Ersatz. Darum bleiben

[14] disposable plastic – [15] not necessarily – [16] to break out – [17] to have a second life – [18] to hoard – [19] foamed polystyrol – [20] major customer – [21] tableware – [22] foil – [23] to be infectious longer – [24] the last gasp of sth. – [25] straws – [26] stirrers – [27] cotton buds – [28] decree – [29] Federal Assembly – [30] pro forma – [31] consumer – [32] packaging – [33] delivery chain – [34] throw-away mentality – [35] climate goal of the Paris Climate Summit of 2015 to limit the temperature increase to 1.5° C – [36] to fall into disrepute – [37] availability – [38] sustainable – [39] cleaning wipe – [40] cigarette filters

sie vorerst erlaubt. Für Luftballonstäbe, Wattestäbchen, Trinkhalme und Besteck seien die Optionen hingegen klar: Sie werden in Holz, Pappe oder Papier gefertigt. [...]

Nur: Es ist fraglich, ob Holzbesteck und Co. per se[41] umweltfreundlicher sind. Zwar hat die EU-Kommission eine Ökobilanz[42] in Auftrag gegeben, diese stellt jedem Produkt jedoch nur einen der möglichen Einweg-Ersatzstoffe[43] gegenüber, auch wenn es mehrere Optionen gibt. Zum Beispiel Plastikbesteck nur mit Besteck aus Sperrholz[44] verglichen. Alternativen aus Bambus oder Papier bleiben unberücksichtigt[45]. Bestimmte Faktoren wie den Resourcenaufwand der Entsorgung[46] oder den Herstellungsort der Produkte sowie den davon abhängigen Transportweg nach Europa bezieht sie nicht mehr mit ein. [...]

Der entscheidende Vorteil von plastikfreien Alternativen zeigt sich, wenn sie in die Umwelt gelangen. Sie sind vollständig biologisch abbaubar[47]. Beim Kauf lassen sie sich häufig durch den Hinweis „kompostierbar[48]" erkennen. Aber längst nicht alle Alternativen auf dem Markt seien wirklich plastikfrei, so Braungart [Chemiker und Experte für Kreislaufwirtschaft]. Pappgeschirr oder Papiertrinkhalme hätten häufig einen Kunststoffüberzug[49], um ein zu schnelles Aufweichen[50] zu vermeiden. Holzprodukte seien mit Lacken[51] behandelt.

Solche Alternativprodukte gehören in den Restmüll[52], reines Plastik in die gelbe Tonne. Solange Kunststoff vorschriftsmäßig dort landet, kann er im besten Fall vollständig recycelt werden. Jede Tonne recyceltes Plastik spare 1,6 Tonnen CO_2, sagt Michael Schneider vom Recyclingunternehmen Remondis. [...] Allerdings verwende die Industrie bisher nur rund 15 Prozent recycelten Rohstoffs in der Produktion, so Schneider. [...]

Die Deutsche Umwelthilfe wirft der Bundesregierung vor, die deutsche Verordnung[53] gehe nicht weit genug[54], weil sie Einweg mit Einweg ersetze, statt Mehrwegsysteme[55] zu fördern. Das sieht Michael Braungart ähnlich. Für ihn ist allein der Kreislaufgedanke[56] entscheidend. Folien, die so dünn sind, dass sich das Recycling nicht lohne, müssten biologisch abbaubar sein, fordert er. Für alle anderen Einwegprodukte schlägt er eine Art Pfand[57] vor und Strafen für Firmen, deren Verpackungen in der Umwelt landen. Denn: „Wenn Plastik vollständig wiederverwendet würde, dann wäre Kunststoff jedem anderen Naturmaterial für Produkte wie Einwegbestecke absolut überlegen[58]. [...]

Damit nächsten Sommer der Cocktail nicht direkt aus dem Glas getrunken werden muss, entdecken jetzt Start-ups den Markt für Alternativen. Und einen lokalen, kompostierbaren und CO_2-neutralen Rohstoff ganz ohne Chemikalien: Strohhalme aus Stroh.

Die Zeit, 23 July 2020, p. 20

ANALYSIS

3. Study the German infographics below and on p. 164 and explain the percentage share of the different plastic items in the ocean.

→ Focus on Skills, Mediation, p. 253
→ Focus on Skills, Analysis of Statistical Data, p. 243

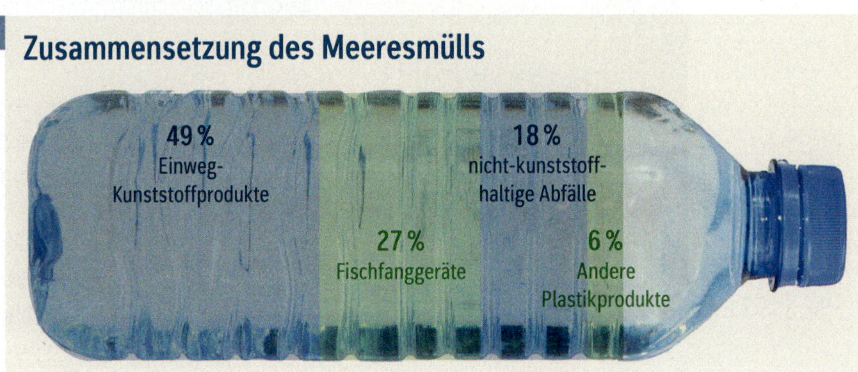

Data: Die Zeit, 23 July 2020, p. 20

Tips on vocab

composition of marine trash ■ disposable plastic products ■ fishing equipment ■ non-plastic trash ■ diverse plastic products

[41] per se – [42] life cycle assessment – [43] substitutes for disposable products – [44] plywood – [45] disregarded, not considered – [46] disposal – [47] biodegradable – [48] compostable – [49] plastic coating – [50] softening – [51] paint, varnish – [52] residual waste – [53] decree – [54] far-reaching – [55] reusable waste system – [56] circulatory system – [57] deposit – [58] to be superior to

2 Müll im Meer

Grundlage für die Daten ist eine repräsentative Auswertung des Mülls an europäischen Stränden: 276 Strände in 17 EU-Mitgliedsstaaten an 4 Meeren (Ostsee, Schwarzes Meer, Mittelmeer, Atlantikküste) im Jahr 2016. Insgesamt wurden 355 671 Gegenstände gefunden und nach Häufigkeit geordnet.

10 Produkte (siehe rechts) machen

86%

der Einweg-Kunststoffprodukte im Meer aus.

Tips on vocab

a plastic/styrofoam tray ■ plastic foil ■ top ten ranking ■ fastenings ■ lids ■ cotton buds ■ bags for crisps/sweets ■ toiletries ■ tampons ■ wipes ■ cutlery ■ straws ■ stirrers ■ balloons ■ balloon sticks ■ food containers ■ fast food packaging

Data: Die Zeit, 23 July 2020, p. 20

3

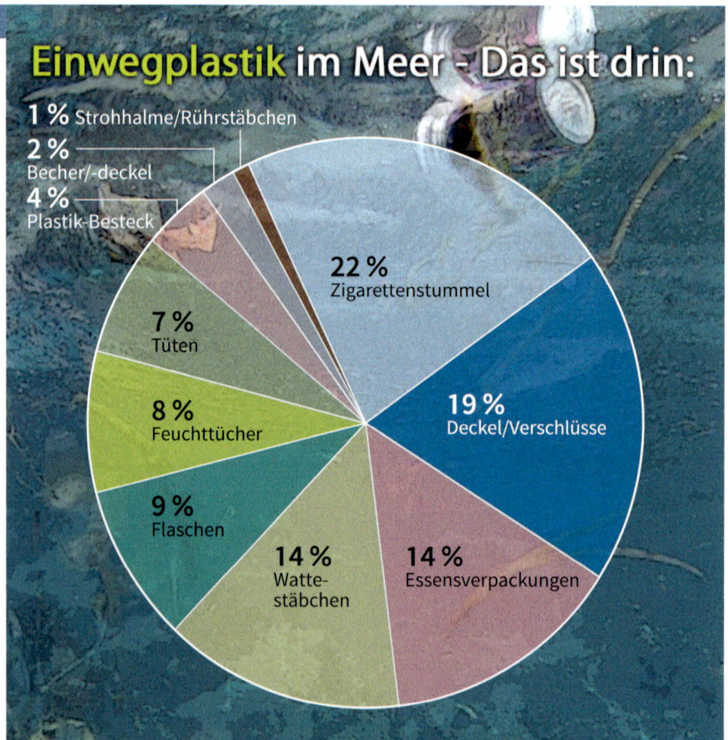

Data: European Commission; Visualisation: DOMKE/WDR mediagroup GmbH

Tips on vocab

disposable plastic ■ pie chart ■ cigarette stubs ■ lids ■ fastenings ■ food packaging ■ cotton buds ■ wipes ■ plastic cutlery ■ cups ■ straws ■ stirrers ■ percentage shares

4. Compare your findings from task 3 to the information given in the article from *Die Zeit*:
- Is banning the plastic items listed in the article sufficient (*ausreichend*) to tackle the problem?
- Against the shocking reality presented in the WWF video clip (cf. Awareness task) – what immediate action must be taken?

ACTIVITIES

5. Scenario:
Your American friend Timothy has set up an environmental club at his high school. He heard that the German government has enacted a law that prohibits the production and sale of disposable plastic products. Unfortunately, his German is not good enough to understand German newspaper articles. Therefore, he has asked you to give him further information for his club.
You have come across the various materials at hand and now plan to compile a short video clip yourself that contains the relevant information.

Step 1:
Team up in groups of 3 – 4 students and collect visual and textual information about these aspects:
- The danger plastic poses to the climate
- The prohibition of plastic items in Germany
- The advantages of plastic-free products
- The advantages of recycling plastic
- New innovative products

Step 2:
Decide on the genre of your video clip, e. g. a detective story, a fairy tale, a documentary, an eco-thriller, etc.

Step 3:
Compile and edit your video clip(s) and
a) present and discuss them in class,
b) email your video clip(s) to your American friend Timothy to help his environmental club.

GRAMMAR / LANGUAGE

6. Collect words, phrases and expressions in connection with the following topics:
- disposable plastic
- marine pollution
- climate change
- recycling
- environmental protection

WES-121500-027

Collect relevant words from the texts you have dealt with in this unit and use your (online) dictionary for further help. Arrange your findings in clusters, then compare your results with a partner. Use worksheet 27.1 for your notes.

Resulting from excessive production, the irresponsible handling and disposal of articles made of plastic has become a major threat to the environment as well as to animals and humans alike. This has led to an ongoing debate about how to tackle this disaster.

Angela Hengsberger

Warum Kleidung aus Plastikmüll nicht für saubere Meere sorgen kann

G-Star kooperiert mit Musik-Star Pharrell Williams

Die niederländische Jeansmarke G-Star hat [...] mit Parley und dem Künstler Pharrell Williams Kleidung[1] aus Plastikabfällen entwickelt. Das von Williams geförderte[2] BioTech-Startup Bionic Yarn schafft den Plastikmüll aus dem Meer, der wiederum als Rohstoff[3] für die *Raw for the Oceans*-Kollektion dient. Die Kooperation war derart erfolgreich, dass Pharrell Williams mittlerweile Miteigentümer[4] von G-Star geworden ist.

Aus alten Fischernetzen[5] werden Bademode[6] oder Strümpfe[7]

Nicht nur große, bekannte Labels nutzen Plastikabfälle, um neue Kleidung herzustellen. Auch ganz junge und kleine Marken upcyceln Müll aus dem Meer. Die 2015 von Barbara Gölles and Andrea Kollar gegründete Bademodenbrand *Margaret and Hermione* nutzt Fischernetze, die im Meer treiben[8] und dort Schaden anrichten, als Ausgangsstoff für ihre Kollektion. Die Netze werden zunächst zu Garn[9] und weiter zu Bademodestoffen verarbeitet.

Kunert, Strumpfspezialist aus Immenstadt im Allgäu, bietet seit Januar 2017 Feinstrumpfhosen[10] an, die zu 100 Prozent aus alten Fischernetzen gemacht sind. Rohstoff für die Textilien ist dabei die Garnneuheit Econyl. Dieses Nylon-Garn, das aus Plastikabfällen aus dem Meer gewonnen wird, hat einen weiteren Vorteil: Es kann unendlich[11] oft recycelt werden, wie der italienische Hersteller Aquafil verspricht.

Ein Lebenszyklus ohne Ende

Genau diese Eigenschaft des Garns wird in Zukunft für alle Rohstoffe eine wichtige Rolle spielen müssen: ein Produkt kann künftig nicht mehr einen Lebenszyklus[12] mit einem Ende haben. Das Müllproblem lässt sich nachhaltig[13] nämlich nur lösen, wenn dieses Ende gleichzeitig der Anfang für ein neues, genauso hochwertiges[14] Produkt ist. Anders gesagt: Wenn aus Pet-Flaschen T-Shirts hergestellt werden und diese T-Shirts am Ende auch wieder Restmüll[15] sind, dann löst dieser Weg das Abfallproblem nicht. Diese Tatsache betonte etwa auch Andreas Röhrich, Leiter der Entwicklungsabteilung[16] des internationalen Wäscheherstellers Wolford, in einem Interview mit LEAD Innovation. Wolford arbeitet gemeinsam mit 11 anderen Firmen an einem kompostierbaren[17] BH[18]. Dieses Produkt, dem 2019 eine ganze Wäschelinie folgen soll, wird aber nicht nur nach seinem Lebenszyklus zu wertvollem Kompost[19]. Retourniert der Kunde die Textilien, dann kann ein Garnhersteller [...] [daraus] wieder ein Polymer machen, das als Rohstoff für ein neues Textilteil dient.

Von der Wiege zurück zur Wiege

Cradle-to-Cradle nennt sich dieser Ansatz. Dieses Konzept ist nichts geringeres als die Vision einer völlig abfallfreien Wirtschaft, in der gesundheits- oder umweltschädigende[20] Stoffe keine Verwendung mehr finden. Alle Materialien sollen sich entweder in den natürlichen Kreislauf reintegrieren lassen (so wie bei der Kompostierung[21] von Unterwäsche). Oder aber, Rohstoffe wie Metall oder eben Kunststoff, lassen sich unendlich oft für den gleichen Zweck verwenden. [...]

Fazit: Warum Kleidung aus Plastikmüll nicht für saubere Meere sorgen kann

Anders als Glas oder Metall war Plastik von Anfang an als Rohstoff für den Einweg-Gebrauch[22] gedacht. Seit der Erfindung des vielseitig verwendbaren Materials haben sich jedoch imposante Müllberge angesammelt, von denen ein großer Teil auf und in dem Meer schwimmt. Diesen Müll wieder zu verwerten, ist ein löblicher Ansatz. Selbiger hilft allerdings nur dann weiter, wenn aus einer Wiederverwertung eine Immerwiederverwertung wird. Die Kunststoffindustrie wird sich also möglichst bald zu einer Kreislaufwirtschaft wandeln. Dass dies machbar ist, zeigen bereits erste Erfolge, wie der kompostierbare BH von Wolford oder auch die Faser Econyl.

https://www.lead-innovation.com/blog/warum-kleidung-aus-plastikm%C3%BCll-nicht-f%C3%BCr-saubere-meere-sorgen-kann, 12 September 2018 [08.01.2020]

M **1.** Mediate the online article above which was published by Lead Innovation Management, a Germany-based marketing and management agency.

Tip: You will possibly need the information given in the article for the debate later on.

[1] clothes – [2] to promote – [3] raw material – [4] co-owner – [5] fishing net – [6] beach fashion – [7] hosiery – [8] to drift – [9] yarn – [10] pantihose – [11] indefinitely – [12] lifecycle – [13] sustainable – [14] premium – [15] residual waste – [16] research and development (R&D) – [17] compostable – [18] bra – [19] compost – [20] environmentally damaging – [21] composting – [22] single use, disposable use

Ocean. Now!

In Your Face: 50 Beaches – 50 Faces

In Your Face is a collective project with international participants. Over five months, ocean lovers collected microplastic samples which are now presented as a 'beauty mask' on the faces of well-known people. The project's plan is to ban microplastics in cosmetics and cleaning products.

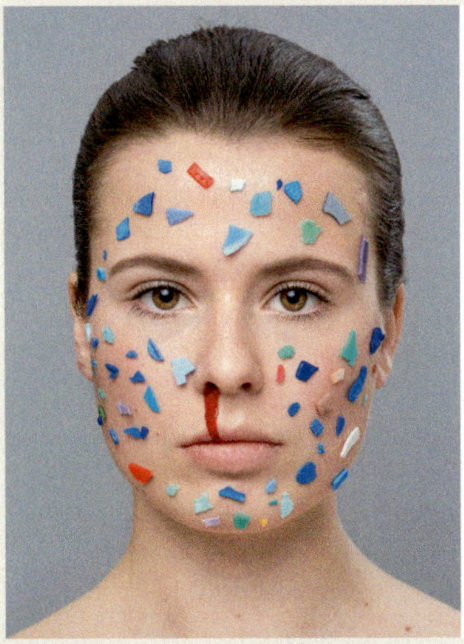

Luisa Neubauer, Aktivistin bei #FridaysForFuture Deutschland

Was bedeutet dir der Ozean?

Dieter:
Plastik gehört ebenso wenig ins Meer wie Senf und Ketchup in einen Teller Milchreis.

Luisa:
Wem das Klima am Herzen liegt, kommt an den Ozeanen nicht vorbei. Klimaschutz heißt auch Meeresschutz.

OCEAN. NOW!

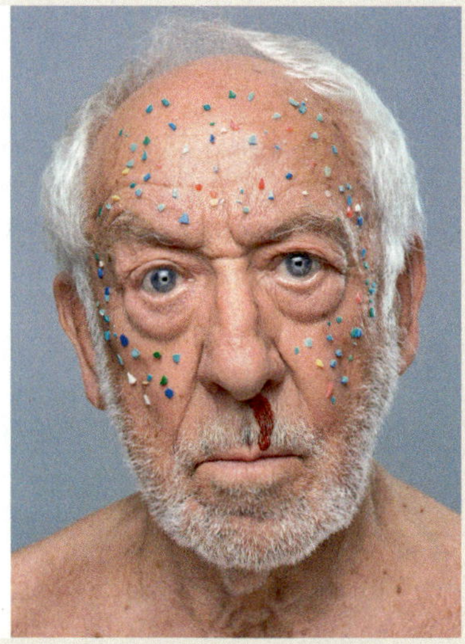

Dieter Hallervorden – Schauspieler, Theaterleiter

2. Organize and prepare a debate on the controversial issue of how to deal with microplastics.

Step 1: Divide the class into different groups, with each group representing a specific viewpoint.

- the car industry
- the packaging industry
- environmentalists/climate activists
- marine researchers
- doctors
- the petrochemical industry

Step 2: In your group, do research on your chosen topic, collecting information for your argumentation.
→ Focus on Skills, Doing Research and Citing Sources, p. 262

Step 3: Remember that a debate is a formal type of discussion with a specific structure and strict rules. Use the information given in the checklist for your preparation.

Checklist

elements …	function …
• form debate teams • choose a moderator	→ each team has to take a clear position a) stating arguments in favour of sth. b) challenging the arguments of the other side c) substantiating their own position with arguments for or against the resolution
• each team names a first speaker	→ avoiding chaos → supporting clearly structured statements
• each team's speaker gives an opening statement	→ clarifying the topic and viewpoint
• the moderator monitors the time allowed to debaters • the moderator takes questions from the audience	→ providing clear structure and order → focusing on the essentials
• each team's speaker holds a two-minute closing statement	→ summing up the topic from their perspective → appealing to the audience
• the audience makes the final decision	

environment		
above/below sea level	how far above/below the surface of the sea land is situated (measured in m/km)	*über/unter dem Meerespiegel*
to become extinct	to no longer exist, to cease to exist	*aussterben*
biodegradable [baɪəʊdɪˈgreɪdəbl]	a substance that can change into a harmless natural state by using bacteria	*kompostierbar*
carbon footprint	the effect of sb.'s behaviour on the environment	*CO_2-Bilanz*
climate change	a permanent (usually worsening) change in weather conditions	*Klimawandel*
climate crisis	the severe point the environment has now reached, which will get much worse if measures are not taken	*Klimakrise*
drought [draʊt]	long period of dry weather when there is not enough water	*Dürre*
environmentally-friendly	not harmful to the environment	*umweltfreundlich*
fossil fuel	fuel such as coal or oil, formed over millions of years from the remains of animals or plants	*fossile Brennstoffe (z. B. Öl, Kohle)*
global temperature	the average temperature across Earth, which is rising rapidly	*globale Temperatur*
greenhouse effect	the phenomenon where carbon emissions trapped in the atmosphere cause a gradual rise in the global temperature (= global warming)	*Treibhauseffekt*
ice sheet	a large chunk of ice that covers the land around it	*Eisschild, Inlandeis*
to melt	to change from a solid into a liquid	*schmelzen*
natural disasters	catastrophic events like floods, hurricanes and earthquakes, partly as a result of climate change	*Naturkatastrophen*
ozone layer	a layer of gases in the sky that prevents harmful radiation from the sun reaching the Earth	*Ozonschicht*
power station	a large plant where electricity is produced	*Kraftwerk*
to predict	to anticipate what will happen in the future	*vorhersagen, voraussagen*
raw material	material in its natural state before it is processed	*Rohstoff*
to recycle sth.	to break sth. down so it can be remade into sth. new	*recyceln*
to reduce sth.	to make sth. less or smaller in price, size, quantity	*verringern, reduzieren*
to reuse sth.	to use sth. again and again, not just once	*wiederverwenden*
(ir-)reversible	sth. that can (not) be changed back	*(nicht) umkehrbar*
rising sea levels	one of the consequences of global warming and melting ice sheets	*steigende Meerespiegel*
sustainable	sth. that can last in its current state for a long time	*nachhaltig*
pollution		
acid rain	rain containing harmful quantities of acid (*Säure*) due to industrial pollution	*saurer Regen*
air pollution	a large quantity of harmful substances in the air	*Luftverschmutzung*
atmosphere	the layer of air surrounding the earth	*Erdatmosphäre*
carbon dioxide [daɪˈɒksaɪd]	the gas produced when animals breathe out, when carbon is burned in air or when animal or vegetable substances decay; contributes to greenhouse effect	*Kohlendioxid*
chemicals	artificial, sometimes toxic, substances	*Chemikalien*
emission	a (harmful) gas or substance that is sent into the air	*Schadstoffausstoß*
excess packaging	more packaging than is necessary/useful	*unnütze/überflüssige Verpackung*
fertilizer	a substance that is put into the soil to make plants grow	*Dünger*

fuel	liquid used mainly for producing power in the engines of cars, aircraft, etc.	*Brennstoff, Benzin*
fumes	large clouds of smoke	*Abgase*
landfill	a place where waste is buried between layers of dirt	*Mülldeponie*
lead [led]	a soft grey heavy metal that melts easily and is poisonous	*Blei*
light pollution	an excessive amount of artificial light	*Lichtverschmutzung*
living conditions	the conditions under which people live	*Lebensbedingungen*
marine pollution	the pollution and waste that is found in the sea	*Meeresverschmutzung*
meltdown	the state when the material inside an atomic reactor overheats and burns through its container, allowing dangerous radioactivity to escape	*Kernschmelze*
mercury	heavy, dangerous, silver-white metal; found in increasing concentrations in fish	*Quecksilber*
microbeads	small manufactured solid plastic particles	*Mikroperlen, Mikrobeads*
microplastics	very small pieces of plastic	*Mikroplastik*
nanoplastics	the smallest possible pieces of plastic	*Nanoplastik*
noise pollution	an excessive amount of sound	*Lärmbelastung*
the Great Pacific Garbage Patch	a huge floating mass of plastic waste in the Northern Pacific Ocean, also known as the Pacific trash vortex	*der große pazifische Müll-strudel*
pollutant	a substance that makes sth. dirty or unsafe to use	*Schadstoff*
pollution	the process of making sth. (air/water) dirty with unnatural substances that harm people, wildlife and the entire eco-system	*Verschmutzung*
radioactive waste	dangerous material left in the process of producing nuclear energy and difficult to dispose of	*radioaktiver Abfall*
reusable	the quality of being able to be used more than once	*wiederverwendbar*
single-use plastic	plastic that is only used once and then thrown away	*Einwegplastik*
substance	a particular type of solid, liquid or gas	*Substanz*
sulphur dioxide ['sʌlfə daɪ'ɒksaɪd]	a poisonous gas that is a cause of air pollution in industrial areas	*Schwefeldioxid*
sulphuric acid [sʌl'fjʊərɪk 'æsɪd]	a powerful acid	*Schwefelsäure*
waste	garbage, litter	*Müll*
	ecology/energy	
agriculture	the practice of farming	*Landwirtschaft*
alternative energy sources	using the sun, wind and water instead of nuclear and fossil fuels (*fossile Energie*) to generate electricity	*alternative Energiequellen*
biodiversity [baɪəʊdaɪ'vɜːsɪti]	the range of different species living in an area	*Biodiversität*
carbon emission	carbon dioxide that planes, cars, factories etc. produce, which is harmful to the environment	*Kohlenstoffausstoß*
conservation	the protection of animal species and ecosystems	*Erhaltung, Naturschutz*
coral reef	an ecosystem in the sea primarily made of coral	*Korallenriff*
deforestation	the act of cutting down trees in an area, either to use the wood or to clear the space	*Entwaldung, Abholzung*
ecosystem	a term that refers to living organisms, their environment, and the relationship between them	*Ökosystem*
food chain	a system to rank who eats what in the natural world	*Nahrungskette*

global warming	the increase in temperature of the earth's atmosphere, caused by the increase of particular gases, esp. CO_2 (greenhouse effect)	*globale Erderwärmung*
infinite resource [ˈɪnfɪnət]	sth. that is in unlimited supply	*erneuerbarer Rohstoff*
organic	used to describe sth., usually food, that is grown without chemical or artificial products	*biologisch*
palm oil	a substance used in beauty and food products that is a major cause of deforestation	*Palmöl*
pesticide	a chemical used on crops to protect them from insects	*Pestizid*
pollinator	an insect, usually a bee, that helps the pollination of plants, so that they can regrow and produce a harvest	*Pollenspender, Bestäuber*
to pose a threat to sb./sth.	to have the potential to put sb./sth. in danger	*für jdn./etw. eine Bedrohung darstellen*
power cut	a failure or interruption of the electricity supply	*Stromausfall*
renewable energies	harnessing the energy of natural, infinite resources such as wind or solar power to generate electricity	*erneuerbare Energien*
slash-and-burn method	a method of deforestation used to quickly clear land where trees are cut and burnt straightaway	*Brandrodung*
species	the technical name for a type of living organism	*Art, Spezies*
vegan	sb. who does not eat any animal products	*Veganer/-in*
vegetarian	sb. who does not eat meat or fish, but does eat some animal products, like eggs and dairy products	*Vegetarier/-in*
water supply	the local water resources available for use	*Wasserversorgung*
wave energy	energy produced using the movement of sea waves	*Wellenenergie, Wellenkraft*
wind turbine	similar to a windmill, with rotating blades producing electricity by being turned round by wind power	*Windrad*
WWF (World Wildlife Fund)	the world's largest conservation organization	*weltweit wichtigste Umwelt-organisation*
	(mass) consumption	
bargain hunting	looking for things to buy that are cheap	*Schnäppchenjagd*
capitalism	a societal structure based on the ability to make profit	*Kapitalismus*
chain	a large, wealthy company that has lots of offices/stores in difference places/countries	*Handelskette*
competitive	in a situation of fighting off rivals, wanting to be more successful than others	*konkurrenzorientiert, Wett-bewerbs-*
consumerism	a state where goods are constantly bought and sold	*Konsum*
discount	a reduction made to the cost of a product	*Nachlass, Rabatt*
(un)ethical	(not) good and fair for everyone	*(un)ethisch*
excessive	too much, unnecessary	*übermäßig, überschüssig*
to export sth.	to transport sth. (usually goods) to another country	*etw. exportieren*
Fairtrade	a way of monitoring whether sth. has been produced ethically in compliance with the Fair Trade Agreement	*fairer Handel*
fashion victim	a person who feels that they must follow the latest fashion trends and always buy new clothes to keep up, even if they do not suit them	*jd., der immer nach dem neuesten Modetrend gekleidet sein möchte*
fast fashion	the constant, rapid production of masses of clothes in a way that harms the environment and the workers	*Fast Fashion*
globalization	the phenomenon where the world has grown more interconnected, with increased travel and technology	*Globalisierung*

greenwashing	a phenomenon where large corporations claim to be environmentally friendly for good publicity but in reality are damaging the environment	*Greenwashing*
to hold sb. accountable	to make sure that sb. faces the consequences of their actions	*jdn. zur Verantwortung ziehen*
to import sth.	to bring sth. (usually goods) into one country from another	*etw. importieren*
independent business	a smaller business that often operates on a local level, is more ethical and better for the environment	*selbstständiges Geschäft*
locally produced	sth. that has been made in the local area with minimum transportation required	*lokal produziert*
to meet the demand for sth.	to produce or deliver enough of sth. to satisfy the need/ desire for it	*den Bedarf decken*
overproduction	when an unnecessary amount of sth. is made	*Überproduktion*
the #PayUp movement	a social movement organized to hold multi-billion-dollar brands accountable for their working conditions	*#PayUp Kampagne*
price reduction	asking for less than the original price	*Preissenkung*
refund	repayment made for damaged goods	*Rückerstattung*
(ir-)responsible consumption	consumption that is (not) mindful of its consequences for others and the environment	*(nicht) verantwortungsbewusster Konsum*
second-hand	sth. that has been owned before, not brand new	*gebraucht*
slave labour	forced work done by people treated like slaves	*Sklavenarbeit*
surplus	a greater amount than needed	*Überangebot, Überschuss*
unnecessary	not needed/wanted, or more than is needed/wanted	*unnötig*
to waste	to use/produce/buy more of sth. than is necessary, with the result that some ends up as rubbish/in landfill	*verschwenden*
work ethics	working conditions that involve moral principles (e. g. no exploitation, fair wages, safe workplace etc.)	*auf ethischen Grundsätzen basierende Arbeitsbedingungen*

Youth Culture and Role Models in the Digital Age

Jeff Koterba, Omaha World Herald, 22 August 2013

Tips on vocab

to work at a computer ■ to do one's homework online ■ to stare at the screen ■ to have a grumpy/irritated (*genervt*) facial expression ■ to boss sb. around ■ to control sb.'s (online) activities

START-UP ACTIVITIES

1. Share your ideas in a round-robin activity. What do you associate with the term "cyber surveillance"?

2. Look at the cartoon. The boy working at the computer puts "cyber surveillance", "NSA spying" and parents monitoring their children's homework on the same level. Do you think he has a point there? Give reasons for your views.

[1] **cyber surveillance** the careful watching of a person's internet use and activities, esp. by the police or military, because of a crime that has happened or is expected – [2] **to intimidate sb.** to frighten or threaten sb. – [3] **NSA** (National Security Agency) a US government organization responsible for checking foreign communications, esp. those that could be a threat to the country's safety and security, as well as protecting its own electronic communications – [4] **to monitor sb./sth.** to watch and check a person or situation carefully for a period of time

How to Deal with "Haters"

1 What is a "Hater"?

"Hater" is a label used to refer to people who use negative and critical comments and behavior to bring another person down by making them look or feel bad. These hurtful and negative comments can be delivered in person, online, or in texts and apps. Often, the comments and behavior are repeated over time. Haters are often anonymous[1] (especially online) but they can also be acquaintances[2], peers[3], or people who were once considered friends. Hateful, critical behavior is another form of bullying or cyberbullying. Like bullying, hater behavior is something that a person does – it is not who they are, and it can be changed.

Often, haters pick on people whom they perceive[4] as being different from themselves. Being the focus of negative and critical comments can be upsetting and trigger[5] feelings of anger, hurt, and confusion, and cause the person being criticized to question their self-worth and behavior. If the negative comments are posted online, it can also make someone afraid to use their social media accounts or feel ashamed of what is happening there.

Many children and teens don't want to be a part of negative behavior like name calling, criticizing, bullying, and cyberbullying. Dealing with haters isn't that different from dealing with bullying and cyberbullying. Teens who feel overwhelmed[6] by all the drama on social media will often unfriend or unfollow people online to disengage[7].

2 How to Deal with Haters

Ignore it. Walk away. Don't react or respond to negative comments. If it continues, there are other things you can do. If someone threatens you, report it to a parent, teacher, or other trusted adult!

Block online haters. If someone is making negative or hateful comments on your posts or account, or is cyberbullying, block them. If they're threatening you, tell your parents, report it to the platform, and take screenshots.

Be kind and respectful, even to haters. It shows that you're in control of your emotions and that you aren't letting negativity bring you down.

Stick with supporters. Having a friend nearby if you think you might encounter[8] a hater not only makes it less likely that an incident might happen, but also means you'll have positive reinforcements[9] just in case.

Remind yourself that comments from a hater are a reflection of them and aren't really about you. People who feel good about themselves don't need to put others down.

Understand criticism can be a sign of pain. People sometimes lash out[10] because they have other life struggles. Negative comments may have nothing to do with you.

Acknowledge[11] your feelings. Talk to a trusted adult or friend and get some encouragement and support.

Keep being you. Keep moving forward, pursuing[12] your interests, and being who you are.

https://www.stopbullying.gov/cyberbullying/how-to-deal-with-haters, 9 October 2019 [18.12.2020]

3. Read the definition of the word 'hater' and the various pieces of advice given on how to deal with haters.
- Explain in your own words what the specific characteristics of haters are and what motivates them to bully others.
- What do you consider to be the most relevant advice given in the second part of the text?

4. Team up in groups of four students and

@ WES-121500-028

a) research the information given on how to stop cyberbullying and access the websites provided on the webcode.
b) evaluate the advice and tips given there and discuss whether (or not) you assess this information to be practicable and useful.

5. Initiate a 'Stop Cyberbullying' campaign at your school and design posters which provide
- useful information and tips,
- visuals to illustrate the information and make your poster (and message) more appealing.

[1] **anonymous** [əˈnɒnɪməs] – [2] **acquaintance** *Bekannte(r)* – [3] **peer** a person who is the same age or has the same social position or the same abilities as other people in a group – [4] **to perceive** to see, to consider – [5] **to trigger** to cause sth. to start – [6] **overwhelmed** helpless, powerless – [7] **to disengage** to stop being involved in sth., to separate from sth. – [8] **to encounter** to meet unexpectedly – [9] **reinforcements** additional support – [10] **to lash out at sb./sth.** (*phr. v.*) to suddenly attack sb. or sth. physically or verbally in an angry way – [11] **to acknowledge** to accept the existence of sth. – [12] **to pursue** to try to do or achieve sth.; *etw. (z. B. einen Plan) verfolgen*

The Duke of Sussex (Prince Harry)

The Power of the Invisible Role Model

AWARENESS

The Duke of Sussex, better known as Prince Harry, is the second son of Charles, Prince of Wales, and Diana, Princess of Wales. After years of trying to come to terms with his mother's death, and serving in the British army, he finally seems to have found his role in life. In 2014, he launched the *Invictus Games*, a paralympic-style sporting event, which he – along with numerous non-profit organizations and charities – is also a patron of. Prince Harry particularly supports the empowerment of youth, the preservation of (African) wildlife and nature as well as injured servicemen and -women and veterans of war. In May 2018, he married the African-American actress Meghan Markle, and their first child, Archie Mountbatten-Windsor, was born in May 2019.

Everybody has (had) certain role models in life, whether they are famous celebrities, public figures or just 'everyday' people. Reflect on what you consider to be relevant characteristics of a person that make them role models for others. Pick 3 – 5 traits from the box below and explain why they are most important to you.

confidence • leadership • courage • concern • uniqueness • communication • respect • humility • knowledge • well-roundedness • doing good things • willingness to admit mistakes • passion • inspiring others • having a clear set of values • commitment • selflessness • tolerance • trust • overcoming obstacles • integrity • ambition • success • efforts to improve • creativity • optimism • hardworking • empathizing • sincerity • generosity • determination • joy • love • positivity • responsibility • persistence

COMPREHENSION

WES-121500-028

In a shared listening activity, team up with a partner and be ready to listen to the speech at least twice. The webcode provides you with the link to Prince Harry's speech.

1. In a **first listening**, get a general understanding of Prince Harry's speech and the aspects he mentions. Jot down some notes that you consider to be relevant information.

Tips on vocab

mentoring the act of supporting and advising sb. with less experience to help them develop ▪ **to percolate** to spread slowly ▪ **quintessential** (*fml.*) being the most typical example or most important part of sth. ▪ **to be struck** here: to be deeply impressed – **impactful** having a powerful effect on sb./sth. ▪ **to mimic** to copy the way sb. speaks, move or behaves ▪ **measure** (*fml.*) here: equal ▪ **to acknowledge** to accept, admit or recognize sth. ▪ **internal state** the condition inside a person's mind ▪ **inspirational** filling you with hope or encouragement ▪ **aligned** here: being together and connected ▪ **North Star** here: sb. who guides you and leads you through life ▪ **to collaborate** to work together with sb. ▪ **alchemy** (*lit.*) a process that is so effective that it seems like magic ▪ **to occur** to happen ▪ **in sync** (*infml.*) reaching the same or related stage at the same time; to understand each other very well ▪ **mutually** *gegenseitig* ▪ **to pledge a commitment** *sich einer Verpflichtung verschreiben* ▪ **to unlock** to make sth. more active and productive ▪ **conscious** *bewusst* ▪ **to inspire** to fill sb. with confidence and a desire to do sth. ▪ **mentee** a person who is helped and guided by a mentor

2. Exchange your notes with your partner and briefly summarize **the gist** of the speech to each other.

3. Listen to Prince Harry's remarks **a second time**, now paying attention to **details** and taking notes on the aspects listed below.
- the impact of a role model
- Harry's role as a father
- leading by example
- Harry's mother, Princess Diana
- the need for mentors and mentoring

→ Focus on Skills, Listening Comprehension, p. 225

WES-121500-028 Additionally, you can use worksheet 28.1 for a detailed listening comprehension.

ANALYSIS

4. Examine and analyse the relevant rhetorical devices* Prince Harry employed in his speech and explain how they serve to appeal to the audience and call them to action.

Step 1:
Despite the fact that Prince Harry delivers his speech to honour the work of the young people present, his speech is clearly argumentative and aims at conveying his beliefs and convictions and influencing the listeners. Therefore, it is important to have a look at the **train of thought*** and **line of argument*** to better understand the structure and strategy of his speech. Following the topical order of the speech, filter out essential aspects and arrange them in a flow chart that illustrates the logical order of the arguments.

Example:

paying compliments … enthusiasm … optimism …	… invisible role model …	
… each move matters …		Princess Diana …
	… a mentor …	Conclusion: …

Step 2:
WES-121500-028 Now, focus on the most relevant rhetorical devices* in the speech as well as their function and effect. Use worksheet 28.2 for your respective notes.

→ Focus on Skills, Analysis of a Political Speech, p. 242
→ Focus on Skills, Analysis of a Non-Fictional Text, p. 237

Tip: Do not waste time identifying all the possible devices you could refer to but focus on the most relevant rhetorical devices* the speaker uses to convey his **message** and **appeal** to the audience. Think about what *you* would tell people if you wanted to motivate them, e. g. telling them
- how great they are,
- how successful they have already been,
- about positive examples,
- about your personal experience,
- that you need their help (calling them to action).

5. If necessary, listen to the speech another time, then complete your notes in the grid. Remember to add evidence from the speech and to identify the function and effect of the respective devices.

Tip: Of course, the predominant intention of most speeches is to influence and appeal to the audience. However, you are required to be more precise and go into detail in order to explain the function of certain elements and aspects of the speech.

Tips on vocab

- The speaker gives an overview of …
- The parts of the speech can be subdivided into thematic units …
- The choice of words gives the speech the character …
- The phrase/choice of words suggests …
- The speaker establishes a relationship between …
- He/She supports his/her view with …
- His formulations imply …

Tips on vocab

The speaker …
- … enlarges on the situation of …
- … emphasizes/praises the progress made …
- … honours … for …
- … appeals to the listeners' understanding …
- … wants the audience to adopt his view on …
- … aims to get the listeners to act/to take action …
- … uses techniques of persuasion …
- … appeals in an emotional way …
- … alludes to his mother …
- … uses emotive language, like …
- … frequently uses …
- … uses stereotypes …
- … intends to …/… has the intention of …

6. Finally, using your results from the flow chart and the grid, write an analysis of the speech of about 350 words. Use the Tips on vocab boxes above for further help.

Tip: Make sure to paraphrase the speaker's remarks, using indirect speech.
Remember to
a) mainly use the simple present for your analysis and
b) give precise evidence from the speech to support the accuracy of your analysis.

Example:
On 2 July 2019, Prince Harry, the Duke of Sussex, delivered an honorary speech at the Diana Award National Youth Mentoring Summit, in which he emphasized the power of …
Prince Harry expresses his gratitude to …. He then continues to describe …, referring to …

7. Team up with a partner and work on the cartoons below. First, describe the cartoons to each other and explain how they deal with the importance of role models.
Then, relate the cartoons to Prince Harry's understanding of a role model – what similarities and differences can you detect?
→ Focus on Skills, Analysis of Cartoons, p. 244

1

"I want to be a role model."

2

ACTIVITIES

8. You are the editor of an online youth magazine and your boss has asked you to interview Prince Harry against the background of
a) his speech on the power of role models,
b) his situation of being a role model himself.
Your interview will be played in a podcast on the youth magazine's website later.

@ **Tip:** Use the information given in Prince Harry's speech and do further research on his life to ask more specific and investigative questions.

→ Focus on Skills, Doing Research and Citing Sources, p. 262

Step 1:
Take notes on the most interesting and relevant topics of Prince Harry's speech, e. g.
- what motivated him to become patron of so many NGOs and charities,
- what it feels like to be a father,
- the importance of his mother, Princess Diana, for people today, so many years after her death.
- etc.

Step 2:
Now, formulate your questions using the help given in the Info boxes on pages 67 and 130.

Examples:
- What motivated you to launch the *Invictus Games*, one of your most important projects?
- How has your view on role models changed since you became a father in 2018?
- How does it feel to be a father?
- How important is your mother, Princess Diana, for you today?

→ Focus on Skills, Writing an Interview, p. 269

Step 3:
Before asking your interview questions, think about a 'door opener', i. e. a few friendly and welcoming introductory remarks to make your interview partner feel more comfortable and relaxed.

Tip: Although Prince Harry is still a royal, he has always wanted to meet people as equals. Therefore, be polite and respectful rather than too formal and 'stiff'. You want your interview to be relaxed and appealing to your audience.

Step 4:
Together with a partner, first exchange your questions and ideas for the interview. Then, think about possible answers Prince Harry might give and complete your interview.

Tip: In order to make the interview more realistic, employ linguistic devices and communicative strategies such as
- 'fillers'
- feedback phrases to emphasize that you are listening closely,
- turn-taking phrases to bring in another person,
- avoiding judgmental comments,
- expressing yourself indirectly by using conditional forms,
- using question tags,
- making suggestions.

→ Focus on Language, Conversation and Discussion, p. 254
→ Focus on Language, Connectives and Adverbs, p. 251

Tips on vocab – fillers

- last but not least
- in answer to that point
- in general
- to put it more clearly/precisely
- it seems obvious to me that …
- it appears to be evident
- what I'd like to say is …

Step 5:
Finally, act out your interview, with one of you being the interviewer and the other Prince Harry. Use your smartphone to record your podcast.

Step 6:
Present your podcasts in class and discuss your results.

GRAMMAR / LANGUAGE

9. Your school has a Chinese partner school and you are doing an e-twinning project. Your Chinese e-twinning partner is not really fluent in English and has difficulties in understanding the details of Prince Harry's speech. However, he or she is very interested in the empowerment of youth, and wants to know more about Prince Harry's speech.
Write your friend an email in which you focus on essential parts of the speech. Use **indirect speech** to transmit Prince Harry's formulations as precisely as possible. Remember to **backshift tenses** where necessary.

Tip: Think about appropriate introductory verbs, phrases and sentences and do not overuse the verbs "say" and "think".

Tips on vocab

Prince Harry …
described ■ gave a vivid illustration of ■ explained ■ pointed out ■ uttered ■ emphasized ■ praised ■ highlighted ■ honoured ■ referred to ■ remarked ■ appealed to

Examples:
- Prince Harry emphasized that it was a pleasure to be there that afternoon …
- The Duke of Sussex highlighted that he could feel the inspiration that was marked by …

→ Indirect Speech, p. 293
→ Tenses, p. 300

Sebastian Meineck

Vorbilder[1] für Jugendliche im Netz

AWARENESS

Social media platforms like YouTube, Instagram, TikTok and Twitch have become extremely popular among teenagers.

Discuss in class which platforms and social media celebrities you like or dislike – and why.

Für Kinder und Jugendliche sind YouTuber die Popstars von heute, sie werden wie Idole angehimmelt[2]. Internetberühmtheiten können eine ähnliche Vorbildfunktion einnehmen wie eine große Schwester oder ein großer Bruder.

Eltern werden es kaum schaffen, einen kompletten Überblick über alle großen Influencerinnern und Influencer zu erhalten. Neben YouTube bringen auch die Social-Media-Plattformen Instagram, TikTok und Twitch eigene Promis[3] hervor. Auf YouTube gibt es allein in Deutschland bereits mehr als 90 Kanäle, die mehr als zwei Millionen Abonnenten haben.

Gemessen daran[4] ist der durch „Die Zerstörung der CDU" einer breiten Öffentlichkeit[5] bekannt gewordene Rezo nur ein mittelgroßer YouTuber: Seine Videokanäle haben die Zwei-Millionen-Abo-Marke noch nicht geknackt[6]. Wer wirklich verstehen will, was die eigenen Kinder gerade begeistert[7], muss wohl immer wieder das Gespräch darüber suchen, wer gerade gehypt wird, und sich bestenfalls ein paar Videos gemeinsam anschauen. Trotzdem gibt es einige hervorstechende[8] Persönlichkeiten, die YouTube nachhaltig[9] prägen[10], beispielsweise Knossi, Katja Krasavice und Tanzverbot. Viele von ihnen sind keine optimalen Vorbilder, ihre Themen reichen vom Online-Glückspiel[11] bis zur Sex- und Pornowelt. Das ist aber kein Grund, ihre Videos pauschal[12] abzulehnen[13]. Wenn Sie diese zehn YouTuberinnen und YouTuber kennen, bekommen Sie einen guten ersten Eindruck von den aktuell wichtigsten Gesichtern in YouTube-Deutschland.

Julien Bam

Knossi

Shirin David

1 MontanaBlack: Wahr gewordener Jungstraum

Wer ist das? In vielen Videos sieht man Marcel Eris, besser bekannt als MontanaBlack, mit Muskelshirt[14], Cap und Energy Drink in seinem abgedunkelten[15] Zimmer. Er spielt Spiele wie „Call of Duty" und kommentiert die Chat-Nachrichten seiner Live-Zuschauer. Seine Biografie „MontanaBlack – Vom Junkie zum YouTuber" stand im Jahr 2019 zwischenzeitlich auf Platz eins der Bestsellerliste[16] für Sachbücher[17]. In dem Buch berichtet Eris, wie er mit Drogen sein Leben ruiniert hat und kriminell wurde – und wie sich auch dank YouTube alles geändert hat. Heute hat er 2,6 Millionen Abonnenten auf YouTube und gehört zu Deutschlands meistabonnierten[18] Streamern auf der Livestreaming-Plattform Twitch.

Was ist der Reiz seiner Videos? Was man von Eris' Leben im Internet sieht, ist wie ein wahr gewordener, stereotyper Jungstraum. Den ganzen Tag mit Games verbringen dürfen, eine Zimmerwand voll mit Caps, einen Lamborghini in der Garage, zu jedem Thema einen Spruch parat[19]. Wenn Eris mit seiner sonoren[20] Stimme davon erzählt, wie er von den Drogen runterkam[21], will man ihm einfach nur anerkennend[22] auf die Schulter klopfen[23].

Was sollte man beachten? Monte, wie ihn seine Fans nennen, ist mehrfach durch rassistische und sexistische Äußerungen aufgefallen[24]. In einem Livestream 2018 machte er unter anderem ein Wortspiel[25] mit dem N-Wort[26] und wurde mit einer temporären Sperre[27] auf Twitch bestraft. 2019 sagte er in einer Live-Übertragung mit Bezug auf eine frühere Beziehung den Satz „Frauen sind wie Hunde", angeblich nur um auszudrücken, dass

[1] role model – [2] to adore – [3] celebrity – [4] in comparison – [5] wider public – [6] to exceed – [7] to be enthusiastic about – [8] prominent – [9] strongly – [10] to influence – [11] online gambling – [12] generally – [13] to reject – [14] muscle shirt – [15] dimmed – [16] bestseller list – [17] non-fiction book – [18] most subscribed – [19] always ready to make a clever remark – [20] full and loud – [21] to get off – [22] approvingly – [23] to give sb. a pat on the back – [24] to get sb.'s attention – [25] play on words – [26] N-word (referring to 'nigger' or 'negro') – [27] ban/suspension

Freiraum in einer Beziehung wichtig sei. Erst später sagte Eris, dass der Ausdruck metaphorisch[28] gemeint sei und der Vergleich „vielleicht ein bisschen zu viel" gewesen sei. Auch wer etwas gegen Schimpfwörter[29] hat, ist bei Eris schlecht aufgehoben. […]

2 Bibi: Heile Konsumwelt

Wer ist das? Bianca Claßen, bekannt als Bibi, ist nicht zu verwechseln[30] mit Dagmar Kazakov, bekannt als Dagi Bee. Obwohl Bibi und Dagi vieles gemeinsam haben: Beide Influencerinnen wurden durch Kosmetik und Beauty-Videos für Mädchen und junge Frauen berühmt, beide verkaufen eigene Drogerieprodukte[31], beide gehören zu den meistabonnierten YouTuberinnen Deutschlands. Seit dem Herbst 2018 gibt es für die 5,9 Millionen Abonnenten auf Claßens Kanal ein weiteres zentrales Thema: Mit ihrem Ehemann Julian Claßen, bekannt als Julienco, bekam sie ihren Sohn Lio. Im Frühjahr 2020 folgte das zweite Kind.

Was ist der Reiz ihrer Videos? Wenn das Leben von MontanaBlack wie ein wahr gewordener Jungstraum wirkt, dann wirkt Bibis Leben wie ein wahr gewordener, stereotyper Mädchentraum. Über Jahre hinweg konnten Zuschauerinnen und Zuschauer Bibi beim Erwachsenwerden[32] zuschauen: Von Schmink-Tutorials über die Hochzeit mit dem geliebten Julian bis hin zum ersten Kind. Mit mehreren Videos pro Woche schafft es Claßen, im Alltag ihrer Fans präsent zu sein, als wäre sie eine echte Bezugsperson[33].

Was sollte man beachten? Claßen preist ihren Fans Produkte ihrer eigenen Kosmetik-Marke Bilou an, zum Beispiel 200 Milliliter Duschschaum[34] für rund vier Euro. Auch grundsätzlich nimmt Konsum und Geldausgeben eine zentrale Rolle in der dargestellten, heilen Familienwelt[35] ein. […]

3 Knossi: Hyperaktiver Stimmungsmacher

Wer ist das? Jens Knossalla, kurz: Knossi, ist ein Entertainer, der schon mehrfach im Privatfernsehen[36] aufgetreten ist, etwa in Scripted-Reality-Shows[37]. Außerdem war er in Videoformaten rund ums Pokern zu sehen. Auf Twitch gehört er mit MontanaBlack zu den meistabonnierten deutschen Streamern. Besonders bekannt ist er für seine Live-Streams beim Online-Glücksspiel[38]. Der Twitch-Kanal richtet sich einem Banner zufolge zwar an Erwachsene, Zusammenschnitte[39] von Knossis Streams erscheinen aber ohne Altersbeschränkung[40] auf YouTube. Viel Aufmerksamkeit[41] erhielt Knossi im Juli auf Twitch mit einem „Angelcamp" genannten Live-Event, an dem auch der Rapper Sido beteiligt war.

Was ist der Reiz seiner Videos? Knossi tut all das, was Kinder gern tun: brüllen, bis der Kopf rot wird, herumspringen und toben[42], alle Gefühle rauslassen. Kaum ein deutscher YouTuber ist so hyperaktiv[43] und überschwänglich[44] wie Knossi. Schon das allein hat Unterhaltungswert. Er trägt außerdem gern eine Krone, als wäre jeden Tag Kindergeburtstag. Wenn er beim Online-Casino einen Gewinn erzielt, flippt[45] Knossi vor Begeisterung aus. Seine Energie kann anstecken[46].

Was sollte man beachten? Ein modernes Männerbild vermittelt die laute, selbstbezogene[47] Kunstfigur Knossi nicht. Wer ihn zu Hause nachmacht, könnte anderen schnell auf die Nerven gehen. Die Videos von Knossi erwecken zudem den Eindruck, Glücksspiel sei eine alltägliche Art, Spaß zu haben. Dabei kann Glücksspiel süchtig machen[48], und man kann rasend schnell sein Erspartes verlieren. […]

4 Shirin David: Weibliches Idol im deutschen Hip-Hop

Wer ist das? Barbara Shirin Davidavičius, bekannt als Shirin David, ist eine deutsche Rapperin. Auf YouTube, wo sie 2,7 Millionen Abonnenten hat, wurde sie durch Unterhaltungsvideos groß; im Jahr 2017 war sie Jurorin[49] der RTL-Show „Deutschland sucht den Superstar". Inzwischen setzt David den Fokus auf ihre Musikkarriere und zählt zu den berühmtesten Rapperinnen Deutschlands, ihr Debütalbum „Supersize" war 2019 zwischenzeitlich auf Platz eins der Deutschen Charts.

Was ist der Reiz ihrer Videos? Den Wechsel zur Musikkarriere haben schon viele YouTuberinnen und YouTuber versucht, Shirin David ist er mit Erfolg gelungen. Noch immer sind populäre Solokünstlerinnen im Rap eher die Ausnahme[50], vor allem in Deutschland. Wer ein weibliches Idol im deutschen Hip-Hop sucht, kommt an Shirin David kaum vorbei. Lieder wie „Gib ihm" strotzen[51] vor Selbstbewusstsein[52] und erinnern an Nicki Minaj und Cardi B.

Was sollte man beachten? Mit Reichtum protzen[53] und einen optimierten Körper haben: Über die Werte,

[28] metaphorically – [29] swear words – [30] to mix sb./sth. up – [31] drugstore products – [32] to grow up/growing up – [33] sb. you can admire – [34] shower foam – [35] perfect family – [36] private TV – [37] scripted reality show – [38] online gambling – [39] compilation – [40] age limit – [41] attention – [42] to cavort – [43] hyperactive – [44] exuberant – [45] to freak out – [46] to be contagious – [47] self-centred – [48] to be addictive – [49] juror – [50] exception – [51] to be overflowing with sth. – [52] self-confidence – [53] to show off

die Shirin David in ihren Musikvideos transportiert, lässt sich diskutieren. Ihr Lied „90-60-111“ richtet sich gegen den Schlankheitswahn[54] und spielt auf die vermeintlichen Idealmaße „90-60-90“ an. Einerseits ist das ein Statement dafür, dass nicht nur sehr schlanke Körper schön sind – andererseits sind auch „90-60-111“ für die meisten Menschen unrealistische Maße. […]

5 Julien Bam: Tänzer, Sänger, Multitalent

Wer ist das? Julien Zheng Zheng Kho Budorovits, bekannt als Julien Bam oder einfach nur „Ju“, ist einer der kreativsten YouTuber Deutschlands. Seine Videos sind eine Mischung aus Musik, Comedy, Tanz und Parodien. Ende 2019 hat Julien Bam seinen Hauptkanal mit 5,7 Millionen Abonnenten aber bis auf Weiteres[55] eingestellt[56] und veröffentlicht seitdem auf seinem Zweitkanal Unterhaltungsvideos mit deutlich weniger Produktionsaufwand[57]. Bam ist auch als Synchronsprecher[58] zu hören, etwa als Stimme von „Sonic the Hedgehog“ im gleichnamigen Kinofilm[59].

Was ist der Reiz seiner Videos? Die Videos von Julien Bams Hauptkanal stachen immer wieder durch extrem hohe Produktionsqualität hervor. Ein Höhepunkt ist die Videoreihe „Songs aus der Bohne“, eine mehrteilige Comedy-Geschichte mit hochwertig produzierten Songparodien[60] und Gastauftritten[61] von YouTube-Größen. Julian Bam gelingt es außerdem, Motive aus Kindergeschichten in seiner Musik unterzubringen, ohne dass es peinlich[62] wird: So hat Bam schon Rapvideos über den „Sandmann[63]“ und die „Zahnfee[64]“ veröffentlicht.

Was sollte man beachten? Wer Ohrwürmer[65] vermeiden möchte, sollte die Musik von Julien Bam besser nicht hören, vor allem nicht „Mach die Robbe“. Im Allgemeinen könnten die Videos von Bam wohl problemlos im Jugendprogramm[66] eines Fernsehsenders[67] laufen. […]

Diese zehn YouTuber sollten Eltern kennen […] Der Spiegel, Sebastian Meineck, 19.08.2020
https://www.spiegel.de/netzwelt/web/jugendliche-im-netz-diese-zehn-youtuberinnen-und-youtuber-sollten-eltern-kennen-a-af853bf9-3070-4c03-8d1c8286530aa631 [19.08.2020]

COMPREHENSION

1. Scenario:

Your school is participating in an international forum that is examining and discussing

- the advantages and potential benefits of social media platforms,
- the potential risks and dangers of social media platforms,
- the various influences social media platforms have,
- the celebrities who are often role models for teenagers.

M Mediate the German magazine article and write an outline for the editors of the online forum.

Tip: Although you are given quite a few annotations, be careful not to translate the magazine article word for word. Use the annotations to get **a general idea** of how to **mediate** and **contextualize** the article with regard to the addressee.

Step 1:

Read the article and look for relevant information on the following topics:

- the importance of YouTubers and influencers to young people
- the potential risks and negative influences
- the most relevant topics of YouTubers/influencers
- how YouTubers/influencers become successful and make a media career
- role models for young people

Step 2:

M Now sort your findings and mediate them into English. Fill in the respective English words, phrases and expressions and complete the grid on the following page.

[54] obsession with being thin – [55] for the time being – [56] to discontinue – [57] production costs – [58] dubber – [59] feature film – [60] song parody – [61] guest appearance – [62] embarrassing – [63] sandman – [64] tooth fairy – [65] catchy song – [66] youth channel – [67] TV channel

the importance of YouTube to teenagers	potential risks & negative influences	most relevant topics
• like an older brother or sister	• online gambling	• …
fascination for teenagers	**success & media careers of YouTubers and influencers**	**role models for young people**
• …	• selling merchandise	• …

Tip: You can use the annotations and a dictionary for specific technical terms – but try to formulate and paraphrase difficult expressions in your own words as much as possible. The Info box on paraphrasing on page 85 will give you additional help.

→ Focus on Skills, Mediation, p. 253

Step 3:
Remember that you are asked to mediate the magazine article for an international online forum. You want to inform them about the examples and information given in the German article.

Tip: First, read up on how to write an outline.
- Focus on the relevant information given in the article.
- Avoid lengthy explanations.
- Structure your outline in visual as well as thematic paragraphs to give it more clarity.

Step 4:
Using your notes and answers, write an outline on YouTube role models and influencers, mediating the German magazine article into a coherent text of about 250 – 300 words.

Tip: Begin your text with a few introductory words and remember to include the source of the information (name of the magazine, author, title of the article, publication date, etc.).

Example:
Dear …,
Only recently I found a most interesting and comprehensive magazine article about how YouTubers and social media influencers are role models … The article, entitled …, was published … on …

ANALYSIS

2. Examine how the German article reports on the topic and pay attention to specific formulations and their function and message.

Examples:
- … die Popstars von heute … Eltern werden es kaum schaffen …
  → addressees: parents and grown-ups; (indirect) appeal to parents
- Wer es wirklich verstehen will … die eigenen Kinder … muss wohl …
  → giving advice to parents
- … keine optimalen Vorbilder … vom Online-Glückspiel bis zur Sex- und Pornowelt …
  → warning of potential risks and dangers; urgency to get informed

WES-121500-029

3. Compare the German magazine article to the online article by Kat Tenbarge, which is provided on worksheet 29.1.
- What further information on YouTubers and influencers and their impact on teenagers does the article provide?
- Who do you think are the potential addressees of these articles? And do you consider the information given to be useful?

Discuss in class.

→ Focus on Language, Conversation and Discussion, p. 254

ACTIVITIES

4. The article "Vorbilder für Jugendliche im Netz" predominantly portrays social media celebrities who focus on gaming, shopping, music and entertainment in general.
In addition to the outline of the article you write in task 1, provide further information for the international online forum on the German chemist, science communicator and YouTuber Mai Thi Nguyen-Kim and her YouTube channel maiLab.

Tip: As you are writing for an international online forum, your text should be informative and factual. Accordingly, you should avoid judgmental, positive or negative emotive words and formulate your text as objectively and matter-of-factly as possible.

Step 1:

@ Do research on Mai Thi Nguyen-Kim and collect information about
- her personal and professional background,
- her YouTube channels *maiLab* and *The Secret Life of Scientists*,
- her work as a TV presenter,
- the various awards she has won.

→ Focus on Skills, Doing Research and Citing Sources, p. 262

Step 2:
Structure your research results, e. g. by sorting them chronologically.

Tip: Use the tips given in the Tips on vocab box to formulate your text as objectively as possible.

→ Focus on Skills, Basic Types of Non-Fictional Texts, p. 237

Step 3:
Explain to the participants of the online forum why Mai Thi Nguyen-Kim is such a positive example of a YouTuber who not only 'entertains' but also informs and communicates relevant messages to teenagers.

Tips on vocab

Factual language
- avoid giving personal statements/ opinion/comments
- focus on facts
- use passive forms
- use a clear sentence order
- use the simple present
- avoid repetitions
- use specific adverbs and connectives and avoid overused conjunctions like: and, then, next
- do not use metaphorical language

Step 4:
Finally, write an additional text of about 150 words, and add it to your previous information.

GRAMMAR / LANGUAGE

WES-121500-029

5. Read the article about YouTubers and influencers provided on worksheet 29.1.
Decide whether to use the adjective or adverb and cross out the incorrect alternative.

→ Adjectives and Adverbs, p. 289

M **6.** Mediate the sentences below, which were left out of the magazine article, into English.
Use the **passive voice** whenever possible to make your formulations less personal.
- MontanaBlack hat inzwischen seine Casino-Streams beendet und nennt sie einen Fehler.
- Hinter dem Lebensstil von Bibi liegen Werte, die man hinterfragen kann.
- YouTuber kritisieren Shirin David für *blackfishing*; sie hatte sich wie eine schwarze Frau gestylt und geschminkt.
- Das Musikvideo „Santa der Boss" von Julien Bam stellt Tänzerinnen im Minirock als reine Dekoration dar.
- Rebekah Wing legt den Schwerpunkt ihrer Videos auf reine Unterhaltung.

→ Passive, p. 298

Jeanne Ryan

Nerve

AWARENESS

Step 1:

@ Do research and try to find the official film trailer of *Nerve* and watch it.

Step 2:

The subtitle to the film *Nerve* is "Watcher or Player?"
Team up with a partner and take notes on the 'dares' the protagonists of the film have to perform.

Step 3:

What overall atmosphere does the film scene convey? Pay attention to the use of:

- colour
- sound
- special effects (high-angle shots, close-ups, etc.)

→ Focus on Skills, Analysis of a Film Scene, p. 239
→ Focus on Facts, Camera Operations, p. 232

Step 4:

What do you think about this kind of game and its participants? Discuss in class whether (or not) the thrill and (possible) fame are worth taking these risks for.

Jeanne Ryan's young adult techno thriller *Nerve* deals with the high school junior Vee and her partner Ian, who get drawn into performing more and more risky 'dares' for the online game Nerve. This excerpt is taken from the first chapter of the novel, when Vee starts participating in the game and with the help of her friend Tommy uploads her first reel (*Rolle*).

1 I'm the girl behind the curtain. Literally. But after I open the grand drape[1] for Act Two, I'll have forty minutes to kill, no more costume changes or makeup to coordinate unless an actor needs a quick repair. I take a deep breath. For opening night, things have gone smoothly, which worries me. Something always goes wrong the first show. It's tradition.

I debate between heading to the girls' dressing room, where the talk will be about guys, or staying out in the hallway, where I might actually run into one, well, one in particular. Since the guy in question has a cue[2] in ten minutes, I choose the hallway and pull out my phone, even though Ms. Santana, our drama coach, has us under threat of death to keep them off during all performances.

Nothing new on my ThisIsMe page. Not surprising, since most of my friends are in the play or the audience. [...]

Along with the message, I post a picture I took before the show of my best friend, Sydney, star of the play, and myself. The photo's like something out of those contrast books from preschool, she, the golden Hollywood Barbie hovering[3] next to me, the retro Blythe doll[4], with pale skin, dark brown hair, and eyes a little too big for my face. But at least the metallic shadow I borrowed from the cast's makeup kit makes them look bluer than usual. [...]

As I'm debating what further measurements[5] to enter, a familiar laugh booms out of the guys' dressing room, followed by its owner, Matthew, who sidles up next to me so our shoulders are touching, well, my shoulder to his football-team-honed[6] biceps.

He leans so his mouth is inches from my ear, "Thirty-four B[7], right?"

Ack, how did he read my phone so fast? I shift it out of his vision. "None of your business." More like 32A[8], any-

[1] **grand drape** the front curtain in a theatre that reveals or conceals the stage from the audience – [2] **cue** a signal for sb. to do sth., here: a signal to tell the actors to come on stage – [3] **to hover** *in der Luft schweben* – [4] **Blythe doll** a fashion doll with an oversized head and large eyes – [5] **measurements** *(Körper)Maße* – [6] **to hone** to make sth. perfect – [7] **thirty-four B** 75B – [8] **32A** 70A

way, especially tonight with my filmy[9] bra[10] that doesn't claim to perform miracles.

He laughs. "You were about to share it with total strangers, why not me?"

I flick off the display. "It's just for this dumb[11] ad, not a real person". [...]

He reaches around me and slips the phone from my fingers. [...]

We huddle next to each other as he selects various slips and bikinis. Every time I try to pull the phone away, he laughs and tugs[12] it back. I try a different tactic, nonchalance[13]. It almost works when I surprise him with a quick swipe[14]. Not fast enough to get the phone away, but at least I hit the right part of the screen, closing the dress-up site. It's replaced with an ad for that new game called NERVE, which is basically truth or dare[15], without the truth part. Under a banner that says LOOK WHO'S PLAYING! pop up three thumbnail[16] pictures of kids completing various missions.

2 Matthew's eyebrows rise. "Hey, let's check out this girl doing the pretend-to-shoplift dare."

He tilts the phone so we can watch a video of a multi-pierced female stuffing bottles of nail polish down her camo[17] pants. Um, even if she's just pretending, it seems like a felony[18] to stick any merchandize[19] down those pants. And how does she get through airport security with all those safety pins along her jawline[20]? As if she hears my snarky[21] thoughts, she turns to the camera and gives it the finger[22]. The image zooms in on her wolflike features, causing my shoulders to stiffen. With a smirk[23], she marches out of the store and into the parking lot, where she uses the polish to paint a crimson XXX on her forehead.

The clip fades to black and Matthew clicks below it to give the girl a four out of five star rating.

"I'd have only rated her a three, if that. The dare was to pretend to shoplift, not actually do it," I say. "What kind of idiot would record herself breaking the law?" [...]

He hands the phone back to me and is already ten feet away when I notice that he's updated my ThisIsMe status from *single* to *promising*. My heart does a little jump. [...]

3 Footsteps approach and Tommy Toth, who designed the sets and presides over all the tech stuff, peeks into the room. [...]

He follows me. "You okay?"

I fold a pair of Matthew's pants that he left hanging over a chair. "Sure. It's just been a busy week."

He stretches his arms upward. "Yeah, between the two of us, we're covering most of the crew duties."

Yep, the backbone[24]. No applause, though. No roses either. I blink my eyes dry and turn to face him. "You did a great job, Tommy. No one else could've designed the sets the way you did." The stage transforms from a war-torn Afghani village to a Tokyo dance club in one minute flat. It's multicultural play.

He shrugs.

"Don't be so modest. You deserve as much attention as the actors."

"There are benefits to not being center stage."

My eyebrows must go to my hairline. "Name one."

"Privacy."

I laugh, which comes out between a grunt and a snort[25]. "That's a benefit?"

He shrugs again. As I finish up with the costumes, my phone buzzes. I pull it out to find a text from my mom, reminding me to be home in forty minutes. Sigh. The leash[26] is a-yanking[27]. When I delete the message, I see that Matthew left the link to the NERVE site up. The game he knew I wouldn't attempt. [...]

4 Standing next to Tommy, I click through the game site. It lists a number of dares people can do to apply for the live rounds, along with pop-ups promising instant fame, and a video clip of a few of last month's grand prize winners attending a movie premiere. Two of the girls flash the serious bling[28] that they won for their dares. Lucky ducks[29].

I scan through the list. Most of the dares seem awful, but there's one to go to a coffee shop and dump water on yourself while shouting, "Cold water makes me hot." Sounds kind of stupid, but less dangerous than stealing nail polish, or even pretending to. I check my watch. Gotta-Hava-Java[30] is between here and home. If I was quick enough, I could do it. That would take the "little"

[9] **filmy** very thin and often transparent – [10] **bra** (*abbr.*) brassiere; *BH* – [11] **dumb** (*infml.*) stupid – [12] **to tug** to pull sth. quickly – [13] **nonchalance** calm behaviour that suggests that you are not interested; *Lässigkeit* – [14] **swipe** *ausholende Armbewegung* – [15] **dare** sth. difficult or dangerous that you do because sb. asks you – [16] **thumbnail** here: very small – [17] **camo** (*infml.*) camouflage; *Tarn-* – [18] **felony** serious crime – [19] **merchandize** goods – [20] **jawline** *Kieferpartie* – [21] **snarky** (*infml.*) *abfällig* – [22] **to give sb. the finger** (*infml.*) *jdm. den Stinkefinger zeigen* – [23] **smirk** *Grinsen* – [24] **backbone** *Rückgrat* – [25] **snort** *Schnauben, Prusten* – [26] **leash** *(Hunde)Leine* – [27] **a-yanking** (*infml.*) pulling sb./sh. with a quick movement – [28] **bling** (*infml.*) *Modeschmuck* – [29] **lucky duck** (*infml.*) *Glückspilz* – [30] **Gotta-Hava-Java** (= must have a Java coffee) name of a coffee shop

out of Matthew's vocabulary, which he includes with my name even when he texts, something he's been doing since we started play rehearsals[31]. Cute, flirty stuff, especially late at night.

I eye Tommy. "You wanna do something out of the ordinary?"

His cheeks get pink. "You're not going to apply for the game, are you?"

"No way. It's pretty late to get picked, anyway. But wouldn't it be fun to try a dare? Just to see what it feels like?"

"Uh, not really." He blinks rapidly as if his contacts[32] are getting ready to call it a night. "You realize it would be posted online for the world to see, and since nobody has to pay to watch the prelim[33] dares, that could be a lot of people?"

"Yeah, that's kind of the point."

He cocks[34] his head. "You sure you're feeling all right?"

I march to the cabinet to lock up the spray bottle. "I'm fine. You don't need to come with me. I just thought it would be fun."

"Maybe it would be." He nods, clearly thinking it over. "Okay, I'll video you."

Oh yeah. I'd totally forgotten that I'd need someone to capture the dare. I grab my purse and head past him, feeling all Lara Croft[35]. "Great. Let's go." [...]

5 We enter the coffee shop and my heart races when I see that it's packed. It's one thing to choose a dare from a list on your phone, another to be performing it. Performing, ugh, that's the problem. Like for the school play audition[36] I ran out of, or those World Studies[37] reports I sweated through in front of the class. Why on earth is someone like me playing a game like this?

I inhale, picturing Matthew kissing Sydney on stage, while I watch on the sidelines. Obviously, I'm doing this to prove something. Thank you, Intro to Psych.

Tommy finds a seat at a community table near the center of the shop and sets our things down. He fiddles with his phone. "The NERVE site says I have to capture this on a live feed straight to them so we can't edit the footage[38]. I'll start as soon as you're ready."

"Okay." I creep to the back of the line, fighting the weird sensation that I'm losing control of my legs. It takes all of my concentration to place one leaden[39] foot in front of the other, as if I'm wading across a swimming pool of syrup. Breathe, breathe, breathe. If only the coffee fumes weren't so strong. The ventilation in here sucks[40]. My hair and clothes will reek[41] long after I leave. Will Mom notice? [...]

I wave at one of the baristas in an attempt to get his attention. He just smiles and continues pumping espresso. The clock on the wall says 9:37. Crap, twenty-three minutes until curfew[42] and I just realized I'll need to take Tommy back to his car before I can go home. I push my way toward the counter, causing a few angry comments. Once they see what I'm up to, maybe they'll shut up. No one wants to mess with a nut job[43]. At the corner of the counter stands a pitcher[44] of ice water and a stack of plastic cups. I fill one up and move to a spot near Tommy, trying not to spill it despite my trembling arms and legs.

Nine thirty-nine. [...]

I stare at the clock, suddenly feeling a sense of tunnel vision. Everything around me goes dark. All I see is the clock, pulsing like Edgar Allan Poe's[45] Tell-Tale Heart[46]. This is ridiculous. It's just one cup of water and one line to recite. Syd would pour a whole pitcher while singing her favorite number from *Les Mis*[47]. Of course, I'm not her.

The racing of my heart progresses to pounding, and my head feels light. Every molecule in my body wants to run. Or scream. Or both. I tell myself to breathe. The dare will be over in a minute. Just a few moments more of enduring this terror. I wipe my cheek. As the clock on the wall moves to 9:40, I clear my parched[48] throat.

Can I do this? The question repeats itself even as I raise the cup over my head. Amazingly, my arm still works. In a voice barely above a whisper, I say, "Cold water makes my hot." I pour a few drops on my head.

Tommy squints[49] like maybe he didn't hear me.

I raise my voice, which comes out in a crackle and say, "Cold water makes me hot!" I pour the rest of the cup

[31] **rehearsal** *Probe* – [32] **contacts** *Kontaktlinsen* – [33] **prelim** an exam that acts as a preparation for a more important exam to follow – [34] **to cock one's head** *den Kopf neigen* – [35] **Lara Croft** main protagonist of the video game *Tomb Raider* – [36] **audition** a short performance that an actor, musician, dancer, etc. gives in order to show they are suitable for a particular play, film, show, etc. – [37] **World Studies** the study of political, economic and social situations in the world – [38] **footage** *Bild-/Filmmaterial* – [39] **leaden** ['ledən] *bleiern* – [40] **sth. sucks** (*sl.*) sth. is very bad – [41] **to reek** to smell very strongly of sth. unpleasant – [42] **curfew** the time at which sb. is supposed to be at home – [43] **nut job** (*sl.*) sb. who is silly, crazy or strange – [44] **pitcher** *Krug* – [45] **Edgar Allan Poe** (1809–1849) American writer and poet, best known for his poetry and short stories of the macabre – [46] **Tell-Tale Heart** (1843) short story which describes a murder, the dismembering of a body in a bathtub and then it being hidden under the floorboards – [47] **Les Mis** (*Les Misérables*) a 2012 musical based on the French historical novel of the same name (1862) by Victor Hugo – [48] **parched** dried out – [49] **to squint** *blinzeln*

over my head. The icy shock clears my brain. Oh my God, I did it. And now I'm standing here soaked[50], wishing harder than I ever have for the ability to disappear.

6 A nearby woman yelps[51] and jumps away. "What the heck?[52]"

"Sorry," I say as water drips from my nose. I know I should be doing something, but my body is paralyzed. Except for my eyes, which take in a million details at once, and all of them seem to mock[53] me. With conscious effort, I break my immobility spell and wipe my face with the back of my hand while some guy nearby snaps my picture. I give him a dirty look and he snaps another.

Tommy puts the phone down, staring at me with wide eyes. "Uh, Vee, oh boy, your shirt –" He points at my chest[54] with a look of horror. I start to look down but am interrupted by a barista who runs around me with a mop. He sneers at the puddle toward my feet. [...]

Tommy catches up to me and holds my jacket. "Put this on, now!"

I look at my shirt under the outside light and catch my breath. What I hadn't considered before pouring the water on myself was that my blouse was white cotton. And that my bra was a thin silk blend[55]. Me, the costume coordinator, who works part-time at a clothing store, should have realized the effect of dumping water on these fabrics. I may as well be wearing a wet T-shirt. On camera.

Oh my God, what have I done?

from *Nerve* by Jeanne Ryan. Simon & Schuster UK Ltd., London, pp. 9 ff.

COMPREHENSION

1. In a **first reading**, try to understand **the gist** of the excerpt and
a) find an appropriate heading for each part,
b) do the comprehension tasks to gain a **general** understanding of the text.
WES-121500-030 Use worksheet 30.1 for your notes.

2. In order to get a **detailed understanding** of the excerpt, **read it a second time** and do the comprehension tasks provided on worksheet 30.2. WES-121500-030

ANALYSIS

3. Explain Vee's true motivation for participating in the dares in *Nerve*.

4. **Part 5** of the excerpt is composed like a 'mini drama' and has all the relevant dramatic components: an exposition, rising action, a climax, falling action and a resolution.
Together with a partner, visualize the development of the action in a graph and take short notes on the relevant stages of the development.

5. Examine the stylistic devices that are used to dramatize the action in **part 5** and **part 6**. Pay particular attention to
- specific verbs and phrases,
- repetitions,
- questions,
- numbers.

WES-121500-030 Explain their function and effect, using worksheet 30.3 for your notes.

6. Read the excerpt from the BBC article about "Selfie deaths" and "seeking the perfect picture" (p. 189) and compare it to Vee's motivation for participating in the dares in *Nerve*. What makes "being in the picture" so important to (young) people?

[50] **soaked** extremely wet – [51] **to yelp** to make a sudden, short high sound – [52] **What the heck?** *Was zum Teufel?* – [53] **to mock** to make fun of sb. – [54] **chest** *Oberkörper* – [55] **blend** a mixture of different things

7. **Step 1:**
M
After reading the German online articles about TikTok's "Blackout Challenge" (pp. 189 f.), take notes about these aspects in English:
- How does the Blackout Challenge work?
- What happened to 10-year-old Antonella?
- What do experts demand governments do to protect children?
- How did Italy's data protection authorities react?
- What did TikTok promise to do?

Step 2:
Obviously, many teenagers, and even children like Antonella, are attracted to presenting themselves on social media platforms doing certain challenges or dares.
Speculate about and critically examine the possible reasons that drive young people into doing these potentially dangerous dares.

ACTIVITIES

8. *After Vee's first dare in the coffee shop ...*
Write a continuation of the excerpt and think about what the protagonist(s) might experience next.

Step 1:
Together with a partner, develop ideas of further events that might happen.

Examples:
- Matthew has seen Vee's dare and suddenly shows up ...
- When Vee gets home, her mother ...
- The next day, Vee's best friend Sidney ...

Step 2:
Think about possible complications that might occur in order to flesh out your story and make it more exciting, e. g.:
- all of a sudden the police show up in the coffee shop ...
- the next dare Vee is offered is about ...

Step 3:
Before you start working out and writing a scene, think about its possible structure, and roughly sketch out the possible plot.

Step 4:
Note that the creative writing task requires you to imagine what the characters introduced in the excerpt might do or say and put yourself in their position. Accordingly, you have to adapt to the characters' way of thinking, speaking and (re-)acting as shown in the text.

Examples:
- Tommy is rather careful and hesitant, but tries to help Vee.
  → *Vee, come on, you don't need that ... Let's leave ...*
- Vee is scared but wants to impress Matthew and does not want to be called "little" any longer
  → *What if Matthew thinks I'm just shy and boring?*

Step 5:
Now write a continuation of the text.

Tip: Be careful to follow the structural pattern of the scene.
- Combine dialogue/monologue and descriptions/explanations/comments.

- You could use different typefaces, e. g. bold print (*Fettdruck*), italics (*Kursivschrift*), capitalization (*Großbuchstaben*).
- Your text could have a funny, surprising, tragicomic or sad and melancholic ending.

→ Focus on Skills, Continuing of a Fictional Text, p. 264

GRAMMAR / LANGUAGE

9. Vee is already making plans for the future and thinks about the impression she might make on Matthew, whereas Tommy is sceptical about Nerve and the impact it has on people.
Use different types of **conditional sentences** (if-clauses) to express their hopes and concerns.

Examples:
- If Matthew sees the dare, he will … (type I)
- If Vee hadn't been so careless, her mother wouldn't have … (type III)

→ If-Clauses (Conditional Sentences), p. 292

Selfie deaths: 259 people reported dead seeking the perfect picture

The quest[1] for extreme selfies killed 259 people between 2011 and 2017, a 2018 global study has revealed.
Researchers at the US National Library of Medicine recommend that 'no selfie zones' should be introduced at dangerous spots to reduce deaths.
These would include the tops of mountains, tall buildings and lakes, where many of the deaths occurred.
Drowning, transport accidents and falling were found to be the most common cause of death.
But death by animals, electrocution[2], fire and firearms also appeared frequently in reports from around the world.
In July this year, 19-year-old Gavin Zimmerman fell to his death while taking selfies on a cliff in New South Wales, Australia.
[…] News reports like this were analysed to compile the study.
They found that selfie-related deaths are most common in India, Russia, the United States and Pakistan and 72.5% of those reported are men.
Previous studies were compiled from Wikipedia pages and Twitter, which researchers say did not give accurate results.
The new study also showed that the number of deaths is on the rise.
There were only three reports of selfie-related deaths in 2011, but that number grew to 98 in 2016 and 93 in 2017.
However, the researchers claim that the actual number of selfie deaths could be much higher because they are never named as the cause of death.
"It is believed that selfie deaths are underreported and the true problem needs to be addressed," it says.
"Certain road accidents while posing for selfies are reported as death due to Road Traffic Accident.
"Thus, the true magnitude[3] of the problem is underestimated[4]. It is therefore important to assess the true burden, causes and reasons for selfie deaths so that appropriate interventions[5] can be made."

https://www.bbc.com/news/newsbeat-45745982, 4 October 2018 [02.02.2021]

„Blackout-Challenge": Zehnjährige stirbt nach TikTok-Mutprobe[1]

In Italien würgte[2] sich eine Zehnjährige mit einem Gürtel, offenbar, um an einer „Blackout-Challenge" teilzunehmen. Sie starb. Der Fall löst nun eine Debatte aus.
Auf Sizilien ist eine Zehnjährige mutmaßlich infolge einer Internet-Mutprobe bei TikTok ums Leben gekommen. Das Mädchen namens Antonella hatte sich Medienberichten zufolge in Palermo zu Hause mit einem Gürtel bewusstlos[3] gewürgt. Nachdem eine Schwester das Mädchen entdeckt hatte, brachte die Familie es am Mittwochabend ins Krankenhaus. Dort stellten Ärzte

[1] **quest** an attempt to achieve sth. difficult – [2] **electrocution** *Tod durch Stromschlag* – [3] **magnitude** the large size or importance of sth. – [4] **to underestimate sth.** *etw. unterschätzen* – [5] **intervention** *Eingriff, Einschreiten*

[1] dare – [2] to strangle – [3] unconscious

den Hirntod[4] des Kindes fest, wie eine Sprecherin des Hospitals *Di Cristina* bestätigte.
Justiz[5] und Jugendschutz[6] nahmen Ermittlungen[7] zu den Umständen des Todes auf. In Medienberichten hieß es, das Mädchen habe an einer „Blackout Challenge“ oder „Hanging Challenge“ auf der Video-App TikTok teilnehmen wollen.
Bei so einer gefährlichen Aktion würgen sich Teilnehmerinnen und Teilnehmer und filmen das mit dem Smartphone. Die Bilder zeigen sie in sozialen Netzwerken. Die Polizei untersuche Antonellas Handy, wie die Zeitung *La Repubblica* schrieb.

Bürgermeister fordert Debatte über Handynutzung

Der Tod des Kindes sorgt in Italien für Trauer und aufgewühlte[8] Debatten. Ein TikTok-Sprecher teilte der Nachrichtenagentur[9] ADN-Kronos zufolge mit: „Wir stehen für die zuständigen Behörden[10] bereit, um bei den Ermittlungen zu helfen.“ Das Unternehmen versuche, Aufrufe zu lebensgefährlichem[11] Verhalten zu stoppen.
Der Bürgermeister Palermos, Leoluca Orlando, schrieb auf Facebook, er und vermutlich die ganze Stadt stünden unter Schock. Eine Debatte über die Beziehungen junger Menschen zum Smartphone und zu sozialen Netzwerken sei überfällig[12] – „besonders in Zeiten der Pandemie, die uns immer stärker in die digitale Kommunikation hineingetrieben[13] hat.“
Experten fordern, gesetzliche Verschärfungen[14] zum Umgang von Kindern mit Handys und sozialen Netzwerken zu erwägen. Es gibt seit Jahren im Netz und in vielen Ländern *Challenges*. Manche dieser Herausforderungen sind nicht nur vermeintlich[15] lustig, sondern auch extrem gefährlich.

https://www.spiegel.de/panorama/justiz/tiktok-mutprobe-in-palermo-zehnjaehrige-stirbt-nach-blackout-challenge-a-30e0f990-0785-4ad7-b954-81f42c1bafad, 22 January 2021 [05.02.2021]

Nach Tod von Zehnjähriger: TikTok verspricht Italiens Datenschutzbehörde[1] bessere Alterskontrollen

Ein Mädchen, das offenbar wegen einer Internet-Mutprobe ums Leben kam: Diese Nachricht aus Sizilien ging um die Welt. Italiens Datenschutz-behörde hat sich mit TikTok auf Konsequenzen geeinigt.
Die Video-App TikTok, die viele junge Nutzerinnen und Nutzer hat, hat den Behörden in Italien verbesserte Alterskontrollen und den Rauswurf[2] von Nutzerinnen und Nutzern unter 13 Jahren zugesagt[3]. Ergänzend zu diesen Maßnahmen starte TikTok am Donnerstag eine Informationskampagne, die sich sowohl an Eltern als auch an Kinder richtet, berichtet die Datenschutzbehörde *Garante* in Rom. TikTok hat in einem eigenen Blogpost von Mittwoch eine Einigung[4] mit der Behörde bestätigt.
Vor rund drei Wochen war eine Zehnjährige in Palermo auf Sizilien gestorben – vermutlich im Zuge einer gefährlichen Internet-Mutprobe für die App. Die italienische Datenschutzbehörde hatte TikTok daraufhin ein Ultimatum gestellt.
Die App werde ab dem 9. Februar den Zugang für alle Nutzer in Italien blockieren und ihn erst nach einer Neueingabe[5] der Geburtsdaten wieder freigeben, erläuterte die Behörde jetzt. Wer unter 13 Jahre sei, dessen Nutzerkonto werde gesperrt[6].

Nutzer können sich gegenseitig melden[7]

Die TikTok-Verantwortlichen[8] hätten zudem zugesagt, das Alter der App-Nutzer in Zukunft verstärkt mit künstlicher Intelligenz zu kontrollieren, heißt es. Ein kürzlich freigeschalteter[9] Button ermögliche es TikTok-Nutzern zudem, andere Anwender zu melden, bei denen sie den Verdacht[10] haben, diese seien noch keine 13 Jahre alt.
Die 13-Jahre-Altersgrenze, um die es nun geht, ist nicht neu: TikTok ist schon lange offiziell erst ab 13 Jahren nutzbar. Nun geht es offenbar mehr darum, dass diese Regelung in der Praxis auch wirklich durchgesetzt wird – von den App-Betreibern, aber auch mithilfe von Eltern, die über jene Altersgrenze aufgeklärt werden sollen.
Viele junge Nutzer und Nutzerinnen von Apps wie TikTok machen sich bei der Anmeldung gern älter. Dieses Problem betrifft auch konkurrierende Dienste[11]. Experten gehen aber davon aus, dass Internetfirmen durch eine Analyse der hochgeladenen Videos und durch das Verhalten im Netz das ungefähre Alter von Nutzern durchaus abschätzen[12] können.

https://www.spiegel.de/netzwelt/netzpolitik/tiktok-verspricht-italiens-datenschutzbehoerde-bessere-alterskontrollen-a-0091bd40-da5a-4d9d-ba12-87b56ff41623, 4 February 2021 [05.02.2021]

[4] brain death – [5] judiciary – [6] youth protection – [7] investigation – [8] agitated – [9] news agency – [10] public authorities – [11] life-threatening – [12] overdue – [13] to drive sb. into sth. – [14] tightening – [15] allegedly

[1] data protection authority – [2] expulsion – [3] to promise – [4] agreement – [5] new entry – [6] to block – [7] to report – [8] executives – [9] to release sth. – [10] suspicion – [11] competing services – [12] estimate

Taylor Lorenz

Teens Are Being Bullied 'Constantly' on Instagram

AWARENESS

Step 1:

Form groups of four students and
a) describe the cartoons to each other,
b) explain the cartoons' messages and what they specifically criticize.

1

2

Tips on vocab

to crouch in front of a locker ■ to stare into one's smartphone ■ to have a blank facial expression ■ to be frustrated

Tips on vocab

to pillory sb. (*an den Pranger stellen*) ■ to hold sb. captive/prisoner ■ to be locked up ■ to bend down ■ to be desperate ■ to be publicly exposed

Step 2:

State whether (or not) you share the views on the potential dangers described and criticized by the cartoons. In a four-corners activity, choose one of the statements (= corners) and explain why you have chosen it.

1
Privacy is dead, and social media hold smoking gun.
Pete Cashmere

2
Social media is addictive precisely because it gives us something the real world lacks: It gives us immediacy, direction, a sense of clarity and value as an individual.
David Amerland

4
Social tools are not just about giving people a voice, but giving them a way to collaborate, contribute and connect.
John Stepper

3
Engage, Enlighten, Encourage and especially ... just be yourself!
Social media is a community effort, everyone is an asset.
Susan Cooper

[1] **trolling** (*sl.*) the act of leaving an insulting message online in order to seriously annoy sb. – [2] **doxing** (*sl.*) to publicly identify or publish private information about sb., especially as a form of punishment or revenge

Harassment[1] on the platform can be uniquely[2] cruel, and for many it feels like there's no escape.

1 No app is more integral to teens' social lives than Instagram. While Millennials relied on Facebook to navigate high school and college, connect with friends, and express themselves online, Gen Z's networks exist almost entirely on Instagram. According to a recent study by the Pew Research Center[3], 72 percent of teens use the platform, which now has more than 1 billion monthly users. Instagram allows teens to chat with people they know, meet new people, stay in touch with friends from camp or sports, and bond by sharing photos or having discussions.

But when those friendships go south[4], the app can become a portal of pain. According to a recent Pew survey, 59 percent of teens have been bullied online, and according to a 2017 survey conducted by Ditch the Label, a nonprofit anti-bullying group, more than one in five 12-to-20-year-olds experience bullying specifically on Instagram. "Instagram is a good place sometimes," said Riley, a 14-year-old who, like most kids in this story, asked to be referred to by her first name only, "but there's a lot of drama, bullying, and gossip[5] to go along with it."

Teenagers have always been cruel to one another. But Instagram provides a uniquely powerful set of tools to do so. The velocity[6] and size of the distribution mechanism allow rude comments or harassing images to go viral[7] within hours. Like Twitter, Instagram makes it easy to set up new, anonymous[8] profiles, which can be used specifically for trolling. Most importantly, many interactions on the app are hidden from the watchful eyes of parents and teachers, many of whom don't understand the platform's intricacies[9].

"There is no place for bullying on Instagram, and we are committed to fostering[10] a kind and supportive community. Any form of online abuse on Instagram runs completely counter to the culture we're invested in – a platform where everyone should feel safe and comfortable sharing their lives through photos and videos," an Instagram spokesperson told *The Atlantic* in September. This week, the company also announced a set of new features aimed at combatting bullying, including comment filters on live videos, machine-learning technology to detect bullying in photos, and a "kindness camera effect to spread positivity" endorsed[11] by the former *Dance Moms* star Maddie Ziegler.

Still, Instagram is many teens' entire social infrastructure; at its most destructive, bullying someone on there is the digital equivalent of taping[12] mean flyers all over someone's school, and her home, and her friends' homes.

2 After a falling-out[13] with someone formerly in her friend group last year, Yael, a 15-year-old who asked to be referred to by a pseudonym, said the girl turned to Instagram to bully her day and night. "She unfollowed me, blocked me, unblocked me, then messaged me days on end, paragraphs," Yael said. "She posted about me constantly on her account, mentioned me in her Story, and messaged me over and over again for weeks."

Yael felt anxious even just having her phone in her pocket, because it reminded her of the harassment. "Every time I logged on to my account, I didn't want to be there," she said. "I knew when I opened the app, she would be there. I was having a lot of anxiety[14] over it, a lot of stress."

But still, she hesitated to quit the app entirely. Her friends on Instagram serve as a source of support. Also, quitting wouldn't stop her tormentor[15] from talking about her, and she'd rather know what the girl was saying. "You know someone's talking about you, they're posting about you, they're messaging about you, they're harassing you constantly," she said. "You know every time you open the app they're going to be there."

Because bullying on your main feed[16] is seen by many as aggressive and uncool, many teens create hate pages: separate Instagram accounts, purpose-built and solely dedicated to trashing[17] one person, created by teens alone or in a group. They'll post bad photos of their target, expose her secrets, post screenshots of texts from people saying mean things about her, and any other terrible stuff they can find. [...]

The scariest thing about being attacked by a hate page, teens say, is that you don't know who is doing the attacking. "In real-life bullying, you know what's doing it," said Skye, a 14-year-old. "Hate pages could be any-

[1] **harassment** *Belästigung, Schikane* – [2] **uniquely** extremely – [3] **Pew Research Center** an American think tank based in Washington – [4] **to go south** (*infml.*) to fail – [5] **gossip** *Gerede, Getratsche* – [6] **velocity** speed – [7] **to go viral** used to describe something that quickly becomes very popular or well known by being posted on the internet – [8] **anonymous** [əˈnɒnɪməs] – [9] **intricacy** [ˈɪntrɪkəsi] the quality of having a lot of complicated details – [10] **to foster** to take care of sb./sth. – [11] **to endorse** to make a public statement of support for sb./sth. – [12] **to tape sth.** *etw. anheften, ankleben* – [13] **falling-out** (*infml.*) argument; *Streit* – [14] **anxiety** [æŋˈzaɪəti] a feeling of nervousness and worry – [15] **tormentor** *Peiniger* – [16] **feed** a web page, screen, etc. that updates (= changes) often to show the latest information – [17] **to trash** to criticize very strongly

one. It could be someone you know, someone you don't know – you don't know what you know, and it's scary because it's really out of control at that point. Teachers tell you with bullying [to] just say 'Stop,' but in this case you can't, and you don't even know who to tell stop to." [...]

3 On Instagram, it's easy to see what people are up to[18] and whom they're hanging out with. For teenagers who are acutely aware of social status, even a seemingly innocent group photo can set a bully off[19]. Teens say that tagging[20] the wrong friend in a photo can unleash[21] a bully's wrath[22]. Every location tag, comment, Story post, and even whom you follow or unfollow on your finsta (a secondary Instagram account where teens post more personal stuff) is scrutinized[23].

"Lots of bullying stems from jealousy, and Instagram is the ultimate jealousy platform," Hadley said. "People are constantly posting pics of their cars, their bodies. Anything good in your life or at school goes on Insta, and that makes people jealous."

Many high schools have anonymously run "confessions"-style Instagram accounts where users submit gossip about other students at school. [...]

Rory, a 15-year-old, said that confessions accounts had gotten so out of control at her high school that administrators had banned taking photos of other students on campus. "People at my school would ... expose drama or make up[24] stuff, Photoshop people's faces, bully them basically. It's all anonymous."

But Rory said that the no-picture rule hasn't really curbed[25] bullying. [...]

In Rory's case, Instagram has been both the catalyst[26] and the medium for bullying. When she was 13, she was featured on[27] the official Instagram account of Brandy Melville, a popular teen clothing brand.

"Tons of people from my school saw it immediately and started to make memes[28] of me, calling me anorexic[29]," she said. "Then there were others suggesting I wasn't thin enough. On their finstas, people were posting these mean things, people I thought I was friends with. I would block their finstas and they would tag my main account."

But even in the midst of the worst bullying, teens say they're wary[30] of logging off. Rory is still active on the platform, though she only uses one account.

"Everyone has friends from Instagram," said Liv, a 13-year-old. "Everyone makes friends that way. It's inevitable[31]. Everyone does it." Some teens did say they'd deactivate or take a break if their parents forced them to, but quitting forever "wasn't an option." [...]

https://www.theatlantic.com/technology/archive/2018/10/teens-face-relentless-bullying-instagram/572164/, From The Atlantic. 10 October 2018 [18.12.2020]

COMPREHENSION

1. This text, taken from the magazine *The Atlantic*, is relatively complex, i. e. it is quite long and employs some formal language.
Therefore, **before** you start **reading the article**, **read the headline** on page 191 and try to anticipate what the article will be about, e. g.:
- Instagram and problems connected with it
- examples of teenagers who are bullied
- certain kinds of bullying
- etc.

→ Focus on Skills, Understanding Complex Texts, p. 230

WES-121500-031 **2.** In order to fully understand the text, do the comprehension tasks on worksheet 31.1.

Tip: Read the text part by part. After each part, do the respective tasks on the worksheet.

[18] **to be up to sth.** (*infml.*) to be doing sth., often sth. bad or illegal, usually secretly – [19] **to set sb. off** (*phr. v.*) to cause sb. to start doing sth. – [20] **tagging** the activity of marking digital information with a name, etc. to show that it is of a particular type or is connected with a particular person, group or subject – [21] **to unleash** to set free – [22] **wrath** [rɒθ] (*fml.*) anger – [23] **to scrutinize** to examine sth. very carefully in order to discover information – [24] **to make sth. up** (*phr. v.*) to invent sth. such as an excuse or story – [25] **to curb** to control or limit sth. that is not wanted – [26] **catalyst** an event or person that causes great change – [27] **to feature sb./sth.** to include sb./sth. as an important part – [28] **meme** [miːm] an idea, image, video, etc. that is spread very quickly on the internet – [29] **anorexic** *magersüchtig* – [30] **wary** not completely trusting or certain about sb./sth. – [31] **inevitable** certain to happen

ANALYSIS

3. Compare your findings and ideas from the awareness task to the information given in the article. Does the article give a comprehensive picture and overview or are there substantial parts missing? If so, which ones?

4. "Instagram is many teens' entire social infrastructure; [...] bullying someone there is the digital equivalent of taping mean flyers all over someone's school, and her home, and her friends' homes". (ll. 48 ff.) Explain and discuss the extent to which teenagers today
   a) are dependent on social media like Instagram and
   b) can be socially isolated and stigmatized through social media.

ACTIVITIES

5. "... we are committed to fostering a kind and supportive community [...] a platform where everyone should feel safe and comfortable sharing their lives through photos and videos ..." (ll. 35 ff.). Against the background of this statement and the shocking amount of bullying taking place on Instagram, write a formal letter to Instagram's CEO in which you
   a) complain about the unacceptable situation and
   b) demand that the company take immediate measures to guarantee the safety of the platform in order to protect the users who are still under age.

Tip: Although you should generally aim at expressing your thoughts straightforwardly and frankly, try to use a more neutral language register and avoid becoming too informal so as not to appear biased or judgmental. Use your dictionary to find appropriate words and double-check certain formulations if you are not sure about them.

Step 1:
Read up on how to write a **formal letter** (or email).
→ Focus on Skills, Writing a Formal Letter, p. 267

Step 2:
Begin your letter by referring to the magazine article and/or an observation that you have made.

Example:
I read your article published in *The Atlantic* on ... with great interest. As a teenager and user of social media platforms myself I would like to ...

Tip: In order to make a friendly approach, try to show a certain understanding of the company's view but nevertheless express your view on the topic clearly and in a balanced and factual way.

Tips on vocab

- I was really surprised/shocked/concerned to find out that ...
- It is absolutely astonishing to see that ...
- Tragic examples from all over the world reveal that ...
- With all due respect, it has to be said that ...
- When it comes to holding somebody responsible one has to see that ...

Step 3:
Structure the body of your letter clearly and avoid unnecessary repetition. Include examples, arguments and references to support your view.

Step 4:
Conclude your letter with a summarizing sentence and an outlook on the issue, e. g. by asking a (rhetorical) question or making a suggestion on possible alternatives.

Example:
I would like to conclude my letter/email by expressing my general appreciation of how difficult it is to control … However, there are children and teenagers who need the protection of … and so, you should consider …

GRAMMAR / LANGUAGE

6. Based on your results in task 2, write a **summary** of the magazine article in about 200 words, using **indirect speech** and **paragraphing** passages.

Tip: Remember to predominantly use the **present tense** for your summary and write an **introductory sentence** that contains

- the title and the type of text,
- the author's name,
- the date/year of publishing,
- the problem/topic the text deals with,
- important features.

Example:
The article "Teens Are Being Bullied 'Constantly' on Instagram" published in the US magazine … on … deals with Instagram and how teenagers …
→ Focus on Skills, Writing a Summary, p. 231
→ Indirect Speech, p. 293

Denise Witmer

Why Teens Need Privacy from Their Parents

AWARENESS

Step 1: First, reflect on what you associate with the word 'privacy' in general and what 'having privacy' means for you and your life.

Step 2: Next, complete the sentence "Privacy is …" and write your answers on slips of paper which you attach to the board.

Step 3: Discuss your various views and ideas in class.

The article below is taken from the *VeryWell* website, which provides health and wellness information. It was launched in 2016 and its content is created by numerous health experts whose comments are reviewed by approved physicians. The text is addressed to parents who fear losing control of their children's lives.

1 The desire for more privacy is a natural part of growing up. As teens get older, they begin facing big challenges, like learning what kind of person they are, where they fit in, and what they want to do in life. Their brains also are rapidly developing; they are gaining new thinking skills and developing new social interests. As a result, it is only natural that they would crave[1] more privacy and space as they work these things out. For parents, this time period can be a huge adjustment[2] as well. After all, there are so many unknowns with your teen that it can be unsettling[3] at times; but it is important to recognize that wanting more privacy does not necessarily mean your child has something to hide. Being more protective of information about themselves goes hand in hand with the development of independence and autonomy[4]. Only when there is extreme secrecy[5] should this be considered a potential red flag[6]. By understanding the relationship between privacy and trust, why you should usually respect your teen's privacy, and when it is appropriate to snoop[7], you will be able to raise a healthy, trustworthy, and independent teen.

2 The Link Between Privacy and Trust

As teens grow up, they want to be trusted to do more things than they did when they were younger. They also want to be thought of as mature[8], responsible, and independent. Giving teens some space and privacy can work wonders for their development. Not only do they feel trusted, but they also feel capable[9] and confident[10]. Remember, too, that teens also endure[11] physical changes that make privacy at this age imperative[12]. A child who always felt comfortable changing clothes in front of their parent may no longer want to disrobe[13] with them in the room. They also may lock their bedroom door or the bathroom door to ensure that their privacy is respected. This is a normal part of growing up and not a reason for concern[14]. Teens may also feel more comfortable asking questions or confiding[15] in a same-sex parent about certain issues. This is especially true if they need guidance about romantic relationships or the physiological[16] changes they're experiencing. When teens are given the privacy they need, it helps them become more independent and builds their self-confidence. As their parent, strive[17] to strike a balance[18] between knowing what your teen is doing, trusting your teen to have some private matters, and knowing when to step in. […] Teens either feel like their parents don't trust them or that they expect teens to behave like school-age children. If this is your experience, take a step back and determine[19] where you can give your teen more space and

[1] **to crave** to have a strong desire for sth. – [2] **adjustment** the activity of becoming more familiar with a new situation; *Anpassung* – [3] **unsettling** making sb. feel nervous and worried – [4] **autonomy** [ɔ:ˈtɒnəmi] independence – [5] **secrecy** *Geheimnistuerei* – [6] **red flag** a sign of danger – [7] **to snoop** (*infml.*) to find out private things, especially by looking secretly around a place – [8] **mature** behaving like an adult and being emotionally balanced – [9] **capable** able to do things skilfully – [10] **confident** being certain of your abilities – [11] **to endure** to suffer sth. unpleasant, difficult or painful – [12] **imperative** extremely important or urgent – [13] **to disrobe** (*fml.*) to get undressed – [14] **concern** *Beunruhigung* – [15] **to confide in sb.** *sich jdm. anvertrauen* – [16] **physiological** *körperlich* – [17] **to strive** to try very hard to do sth. – [18] **to strike a balance between sth.** (*idm.*) *einen Mittelweg finden* – [19] **to determine** to decide what will happen

privacy without compromising[20] their need for safety and guidance from you. […]

3 Finding the Right Balance

One way to determine where those boundaries[21] exist is to ask yourself what you really need to know and what you do not need to know. For instance, you need to know where your teen is going, who they are going to be with, and when they will be home.

But you do not need to know what they discussed with their friends. Of course, some teens are willing to share this information, but if your teen is not willing to share much about their night, don't be too alarmed and don't demand it. The key is knowing what you absolutely have to know as a parent and the things you can allow your teen to keep private.

Other ways you can give your teen privacy include:

- Allowing them to see the doctor privately if that is their preference
- Asking before getting something out of their wallet[22] or backpack
- Giving them time alone
- Knocking on the door before going into their room
- Leaving their cell phone alone and not snooping through texts and emails
- Leaving their journals[23] and notebooks alone
- Letting them have private conversations with their friends or siblings[24] without demanding a lot of details
- Respecting the privacy of their room by not going through their things

4 Earning Privacy Through Responsibility

Of course, the best way to determine how much privacy and freedom your teen is ready for is to gauge[25] how responsible they are with their obligations[26]. In other words, do they get to school on time, do their homework, respect their curfew[27], and complete their chores[28]? If they are able to complete these things without a lot of nagging[29] from you, you can probably loosen[30] the reins[31] a little bit.

Overall, there should be a direct link between the amount of responsibility and honesty that kids have shown and the amount of privacy they are allowed to have. And, if your teen messes up or violates your trust, allowing them a little less privacy for a period of time is a logical consequence.

5 Online Privacy

A teen's need for privacy on social media is similar to their need for privacy IRL[32]. As a parent, it is your responsibility to mentor and guide them to make sure they know what behavior is safe and appropriate. You should also role-model appropriate social media use by not posting photos and information about your teen on your own feeds[33] without their permission[34].

When it comes to their social media use, teens need to earn your trust just like other privileges. But once they have earned that trust, it's fair to give them their privacy so they can continue to mature and become more independent.

6 When to Invade a Teen's Privacy

There are times when it may be appropriate to snoop on your teen. For instance, if you overhear them talking about dating violence, see them crying over an Instagram post, or you find a JUUL[35] in their pocket while doing laundry, it is time to pry[36] a little bit. Your job as a parent is to keep your kids safe. These types of things are red flags that something harmful is happening in their lives. […]

For instance, if you notice signs of depression, issues with sleep, or unexplained marks[37] or bruises[38] on their body, it is time to take action. Other red flags include losing interest in hobbies, becoming withdrawn, stopping socializing[39], or showing signs of drug or alcohol use.

That said, snooping shouldn't be your first move in these circumstances. First, try to communicate with your teen about the changes you are seeing. […] Then, listen to what your child says.

If all you get in response is a shrug[40] or "I don't know," consider having your child talk to a counselor[41]. Meanwhile, if your teen mentions suicide, wanting to die, or that life is just not worth it, forget snooping and seek medical help right away.

https://www.verywellfamily.com/why-does-my-teen-need-privacy-2609615 23 March 2020 [18.12.2020]

[20] **to compromise** to endanger; *aufs Spiel setzen* – [21] **boundary** a limit of sth. – [22] **wallet** *Geldbeutel* – [23] **journal** diary; *Tagebuch* – [24] **sibling** *Geschwister* – [25] **to gauge** ['geɪdʒ] to calculate – [26] **obligation** duty; *Verpflichtung* – [27] **curfew** (*US*) a time by which a child must be home in the evening – [28] **chore** a necessary but sometimes unpleasant task – [29] **nagging** complaining or criticizing – [30] **to loosen** *lockern* – [31] **rein** *Zügel* – [32] **IRL** (*abbr.*) in real life – [33] **feed** a webpage or screen that gives the latest information – [34] **permission** *Erlaubnis* – [35] **JUUL** (*abbr.*) a brand of e-cigarettes – [36] **to pry** to snoop – [37] **mark** *Fleck* – [38] **bruise** *Bluterguss* – [39] **to socialize** to spend time, when you are not working, with friends – [40] **shrug** *Achselzucken* – [41] **counselor** sb. whose job is to provide advice, help or encouragement

COMPREHENSION

1. **Step 1:**
Team up with a partner and read the text paragraph by paragraph.

Step 2:
After each paragraph, summarize the most relevant information to each other.

2. Basically, the article recommends that the readers try to find the right balance between **privacy, secrecy, trust** and **control**.
WES-121500-032
Find the information given on these aspects in the text and complete the grid provided on worksheet 32.1.

Tip: Some of the information given in the text refers to different aspects, e.g. privacy and trust.

ANALYSIS

3. Examine which stylistic devices the author has employed in order to
   - serve as a mediator between teenagers and parents,
   - convey a feeling of sympathy and understanding of both sides,
   - win the readers' (= parents') confidence.

   Focus particularly on the use of
   - personal pronouns (you – they) as patterns of solidarity and identification,
   - adjectives and adverbs,
   - keywords and key phrases.

   → Focus on Skills, Analysis of a Non-Fictional Text, p. 237

4. Describe the cartoons below and on p. 199 and
   a) explain their message,
   b) explain how they present the parents' and the teenagers' perspective,
   c) relate the cartoons' message to the information given in the text on how to find the right balance between trust and privacy.

   → Focus on Skills, Analysis of Cartoons, p. 244

1

Tips on vocab

to complain about sb./sth ■ to search sb.'s private belongings ■ to be/feel permanently surveilled/supervised ■ surveillance ■ to be too trusting ■ to share one's private life/personal data on social media platforms

2

"I can't keep track of him, but I trust Google can."

Tips on vocab

to keep track of sb. ■ to control sb. ■ to crouch in an armchair ■ to play with one's smartphone ■ to be out of control ■ to track sb. ■ to be concerned

ACTIVITIES

5. Write a comment in response to the article in which you critically state whether (or not) you agree with the recommendations given to the parents and present your view of the matter.

Tip: A comment falls into the category of non-fictional texts. Its argumentative character aims at influencing the reader directly and requires a clear structure and the use of rhetorical devices.

a) Read up on **forms of argumentative texts**.
   → Focus on Facts, Basic Types of Non-Fictional Texts, p. 227

b) The skills page Writing a Comment will help you to structure your text.
   → Focus on Skills, Writing a Newspaper Commentary/an Editorial/a Blog Post, p. 266

Step 1:
Think about a concise (*prägnant, knapp*) and strong introduction, in which you raise a controversial question or refer to a disputed example or event. You can also make a (provocative) first remark or statement on a disputed matter.

Step 2:
In the main part of your text, state and describe the pros and cons of your topic.

Tip: Do not just state your opinions, but include valid arguments and examples that support your view. If you are not sure about the matter, do further research and find events, quotations, etc. that serve as examples.

Step 3:
Decide on the structure of your argumentation:
- listing structure,
- progressive structure,
- antithetical structure,

and sort your material accordingly.
→ Focus on Facts, Basic Types of Non-Fictional Texts, p. 227

Tip: Use the general pattern of **introduction – main part – conclusion** for your comment.

- **introduction** (answering the w-questions who – what – where – when – why and attracting the reader's attention)
- **main part** (presenting arguments)
- **conclusion** (briefly summarizing the main ideas)

Tips on vocab

I consider it to be right/wrong to say … ■ I believe that … ■ I hold the view that … ■ To my mind … ■ I have the impression that … ■ As far as I know … ■ I am sure about/of … ■ I have doubts about … ■ I doubt that … ■ It seems possible that … ■ It is rather unlikely … ■ The author seems to … ■ I (dis-)agree with … ■ The author has reason to believe … ■ I share/do not share the author's view on … ■ I would like to clarify … ■ The author's opinion/statement contrasts with/contradicts …

Tip: Use connectives and linking phrases to make your text more fluent.

Tips on vocab

furthermore ■ for example ■ yet ■ however ■ as well as ■ perhaps ■ because of this ■ having said that ■ on the contrary ■ beyond that ■ moreover ■ in order to ■ despite ■ bearing in mind ■ on the other hand

Step 4:

Write the comment in a coherent text of about 300 words, and express your views on the matter.

Tip: Remember to refer to the text and employ quotes to substantiate your arguments.

→ Focus on Skills, Writing a Newspaper Commentary/an Editorial/a Blog Post, p. 266

GRAMMAR / LANGUAGE

WES-121500-032

6. Complete the table provided on worksheet 32.2 and find the corresponding verb, noun and/or adjective.

The Origin of Gender

AWARENESS

Step 1: Take a look at the tilt painting, which depicts a so-called reversible figure, i. e. a two-dimensional drawing or painting which can be seen from (at least) two different perspectives. The front and back figures appear to switch places. What can you see?

Tip: The painting contains four different heads.

Step 2: Explain and discuss your findings in class.

WES-121500-033 **Tip:** You can access the weblink and watch the painter Martin Mißfeldt paint the picture.

Four Faces: Old or Young Man or Woman? Oil on canvas painting by Martin Mißfeldt, 2019

COMPREHENSION

WES-121500-033

1. Together with a partner, watch the video clip which is provided on the webcode, and try to get a **general understanding** of what is said about
   a) the difference between gender and sex,
   b) how different societies at different times have distinguished between male and female.

WES-121500-033

2. **Step 1:**
   In a second viewing, get a more specific understanding of the details and use worksheet 33.1 for your notes.

   Step 2:
   Compare your findings with a partner and make additions and/or corrections where necessary.

ANALYSIS

3. Watch **part 6** (04:38 – 05:58) and **part 7** (06:00 – 07:38) of the video clip again and explain
   a) how the categories 'race' and 'class' were linked with gender,
   b) how workplace politics influenced gender role attitudes in the 18th and 19th centuries.

ACTIVITIES

4. **Prepare a presentation on "The Origin of Gender" and compile a cross-lined concept map to visualize the different societal concepts and developments.**

Step 1:
Use your findings from tasks 2 and 3 and include the following keywords in your concept map/visualization:

- binary – two genders/categories
- gender and sex
- sex: biological and physical traits of the body
- gender: (societal) roles, identities, ideas, behaviour
- cultural conditioning vs. biological determinism
- gender and language(s)
- alternative gender models
- ancient Greece
- the influence of the Enlightenment in Europe
- class and race – gender and sex
- gender and gender norms in modern societies

Tip: In addition to keywords and phrases, use visual symbols to express and visualize concepts and relationships.

Note: A concept map is different from a mind map. Concept maps help to organize and structure concepts, developments and ideas and interconnect them.
→ Focus on Skills, Concept Maps, p. 252

Step 2:
In order to gain a general idea or overview of the matter, watch the video clip again and pay attention to the pictorial elements employed that help to illustrate and visualize the complex content.

Step 3:
For your **presentation**, take notes of the most relevant information on cards.

Tip: Follow the structure of worksheet 33.1 and use a transcript of the video clip for more details.

Step 4:
Integrate the concept map into your presentation and take short breaks to give yourself and the audience time to think, follow the explanations and understand the various aspects.

Step 5:
Finally, give your presentation and use the concept map as a visual support.
→ Focus on Skills, Concept Maps, p. 252
→ Focus on Skills, Presentation, p. 261

GRAMMAR / LANGUAGE

5. **Step 1:**
WES-121500-033
Typically male or female?!
In order to avoid verbal stereotypes and clichés, team up with a partner and reflect on the adjectives that are commonly associated with male or female behaviour or traits. Do the tasks provided on worksheet 33.2.

Step 2:
Compare and discuss your categories in class.

The Harmful Influence of Gender Stereotypes in Adverts and Social Media

AWARENESS

Most people want to be attractive and present their 'best self'.

Step 1:

Team up with a partner and tell each other

a) what you (do not) like about how you look and what you would want to change,

b) what you think is good-looking about your partner.

Ellen Scott

Rankin Project *Selfie Harm* Shows What Happens When Teenagers Are Asked to Edit Their Selfies for Social Media

We're probably all guilty of tweaking[1] our photos to show our best selves, whether it's taking 34 selfies to get the perfect shot or applying the most flattering[2] filter.

But the rise of apps designed specifically for easily editing pictures of yourself normalises taking those tweaks to another level.

Apps such as FaceTune let you slim your nose, blur out[3] spots, and make your eyes look bigger.

With those options available, and with so many people taking them up, what's happening to our sense of self? How is this affecting how we think we should look?

Rankin's new project, *Selfie Harm*, explores this.

Rankin photographed 14 teenagers, then handed them the images to edit and filter until they felt the picture was 'social media ready'.

Not one girl left her photo unedited.

Instead, the teenagers slimmed their jawlines[4], made their noses smaller, and brightened their skin.

'People are mimicking[5] their idols,' says Rankin, 'and all for social media likes.

'It's just another reason why we are living in a world of FOMO[6], sadness, increased anxiety[7] and Snapchat dysmorphia[8]. It's time to acknowledge the damaging effects that social media has on people's self-image.'

The photo series forms part of a new project called *Visual Diet*, which sees M&C Saatchi[9], Rankin and MTArt[10] Agency team up to explore how the images we consume are affecting our mental health.

The website reads: 'In the age of the influencer, we're increasingly force-fed[11] thousands of images every day.'

'Hyper-retouched, sexually gratuitous[12], bite-sized[13] images are served up fast and fleeting[14]. They often leave us feeling hollow[15] and inadequate[16].'

'These are the empty calories. The visual calories we gorge on[17] because they're there. Our appetite for this type of content is insatiable[18]. It is visual sugar and we are addicted.'

'Consuming too much of this content seriously harms your mental health.'

What can we do about all this?

Well, neither *Selfie Harm* nor *Visual Diet* has revealed the secret cure just yet.

https://metro.co.uk/2019/02/05/rankin-project-shows-happens-teenagers-asked-edit-selfies-social-media-8441410/, 5 February 2019 [06.02.2021]

[1] **to tweak** to make slight changes to improve sth. – [2] **flattering** making sb. look more attractive – [3] **to blur out** to make sth. become less clear – [4] **jawline** the outline of the chin – [5] **to mimick** to imitate – [6] **FOMO** (*abbr.*) the fear of missing out – [7] **anxiety** the state of feeling nervous or worried – [8] **dysmorphia** a condition in which a part of the body grows larger than normal – [9] **M&C Saatchi** an international advertising agency – [10] **MTArt** talent agency for visual artists – [11] **to force-feed** to use force to make sb. eat or drink – [12] **gratuitous** done without any good reason and often with harmful effects – [13] **bite-sized** very small, easy to take in – [14] **fleeting** lasting only a short time – [15] **hollow** empty – [16] **inadequate** not good enough – [17] **to gorge on sth.** to eat a lot of sth. until you are too full to eat any more – [18] **insatiable** always wanting more

Step 2:

With the rising popularity of selfies, there has been an increase in the number of apps which help edit pictures and optimize your looks. Read the text on p. 204 about Rankin's project *Selfie Harm*.

- What motivated him to start the project?
- What does he think about 'optimizing one's self-image'?

Step 3:

Look at the photos below.

- What have the teenagers changed in order to improve their looks?
- Do you think that the new image is more attractive? What would you have changed, if anything at all?

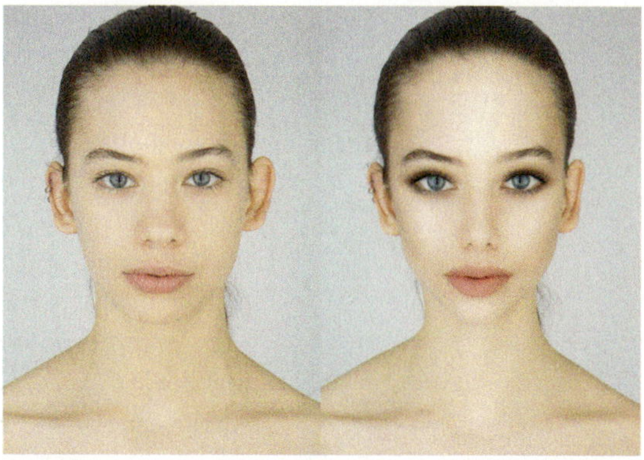

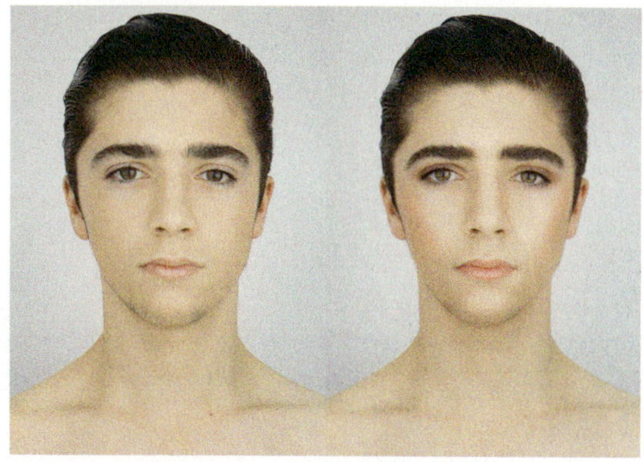

Step 4:

How would you edit *your* image to be 'social media ready'?

Step 5:

@ WES-121500-034

Access the links provided on the webcode. Then, do further research on Rankin's project and prepare short presentations in class.

→ Focus on Skills, Doing Research and Citing Sources, p. 262

'Harmful' Gender Stereotypes in Adverts Banned

Influencers, social media and advertisers not only tell us how to look but also have enormous influence on how we think we have to behave and which (societal) roles we have to take on. Thus, they transport ideals and stereotypes of social and gender roles. Some time ago, the UK Advertising Standards Authority (ASA) decided to ban adverts featuring 'harmful gender stereotypes'.

1 A ban on adverts featuring "harmful gender stereotypes" or those which are likely to cause "serious or widespread offence[1]" has come into force.

The ban covers scenarios such as a man with his feet up while a woman cleans, or a woman failing to park a car. The UK's advertising watchdog[2], the Advertising Standards Authority (ASA) – the organisation that administers the UK Advertising Codes – introduced the ban because it found some portrayals could play a part in "limiting people's potential".

It said it was pleased with how advertisers had responded.

The new rule follows a review of gender stereotyping in adverts by the ASA, which cover both broadcast and non-broadcast adverts, including online and social media.

The ASA said the review had found evidence[3] suggesting that harmful stereotypes could "restrict the choices, aspirations[4] and opportunities of children, young people and adults and these stereotypes can be reinforced

[1] **offence** *Anstoß, Ärgernis* – [2] **watchdog** an organization that checks that companies are not doing anything illegal or ignoring standards or people's rights– [3] **evidence** *Beleg, Hinweis* – [4] **aspiration** sth. that you hope to achieve

by some advertising which plays a part in unequal gender outcomes".

"Our evidence shows how harmful gender stereotypes in ads can contribute to inequality in society, with costs for all of us. Put simply, we found that some portrayals in ads can, over time, play a part in limiting people's potential," said ASA chief executive Guy Parker.

2 'Stereotypes'

Blogger and father of two Jim Coulson thinks the ban is a good idea. He dislikes adverts that perpetuate[5] stereotypes about dads being "useless".

"It's the small things though that build up, and the small things are what inform the subconscious[6]," he told the BBC.

"That's the problem ... that adverts rely on stereotypes. We know why they do it, because it's easy."

But columnist Angela Epstein disagrees, and thinks that society has become "over-sensitive".

"There's a lot of big things we need to fight over – equality over pay, bullying in the workplace, domestic violence, sexual harassment[7] – these are really big issues that we need to fight over equally," she told the BBC.

"But when you chuck in[8] the fact that women are doing the dishes [in advertisements], it's not in the same sphere. When we lump[9] it all together and become desensitized[10], we devalue[11] those important arguments we need to have."

3 'Lack of diversity'

As part of its review, the ASA brought together members of the public and showed them various adverts to gauge[12] how they felt about how men and women were depicted.

One of them was a 2017 television advert for Aptamil baby milk formula, which showed a baby girl growing up to be a ballerina and baby boys engineers and mountain climbers.

The ASA found some parents "felt strongly about the gender-based aspirations shown in this advert, specifically noting the stereotypical future professions of the boys and girls shown.

"These parents queried[13] why these stereotypes were needed, feeling that they lacked diversity of gender roles and did not represent real life."

At the time it was released, the campaign prompted complaints but the ASA did not find grounds for a formal investigation as it did not break the rules.

However, Fernando Desouches, managing director of marketing agency New Macho, which specialises in targeting men, said this was an example of a past advert that would not pass the new ASA legislation.

He said it showed how easy it can be for "deeply entrenched[14] views on gender to come through in an ad that purports[15] to be caring and nurturing of future generations." He was "unsurprised it generated a backlash[16]".

Other situations likely to fall foul[17] of the new rule include:

- Adverts which show a man or a woman failing at a task because of their gender, like a man failing to change a nappy[18] or a woman failing to park.
- Adverts aimed at new mothers which suggest that looking good or keeping a home tidy is more important than emotional wellbeing.
- Adverts which belittle[19] a man for carrying out stereotypically female roles.

[5] **to perpetuate** (*fml.*) to cause sth. to continue – [6] **subconscious** *das Unterbewusstsein* – [7] **harassment** *Belästigung* – [8] **to chuck sth. in** (*phr. v., infml.*) to add, to include – [9] **to lump together** (*infml.*) to put all together – [10] **desensitised** *abgestumpft* – [11] **to devalue** to make sth. seem less important than it is – [12] **to gauge** ['geɪdʒ] to find out, to measure – [13] **to query** to ask questions, esp. in order to check if sth. is true or correct – [14] **entrenched** established firmly so that it cannot be changed – [15] **to purport sth.** (*fml.*) to pretend to be or to do sth., esp. in a way that is not easy to believe – [16] **backlash** a strong negative reaction by a large number of people – [17] **to fall foul of sth.** to break a rule or law, esp. without intending to – [18] **nappy** *Windel* – [19] **to belittle** to make sb./sth. seem unimportant

However, the new rules do not preclude[20] the use of all gender stereotypes. The ASA said the aim was to identify "specific harms" that should be prevented.
So, for example, adverts would still be able to show women doing the shopping or men doing DIY[21], or use gender stereotypes as a way of challenging their negative effects.
The ASA outlined the new rules at the end of last year, giving advertisers six months to prepare for their introduction.
Mr Parker said the watchdog was pleased with how the industry had already responded.
The ASA said it would deal with any complaints on a case-by-case basis and would assess[22] each advert by looking at the "content and context" to determine if the new rule had been broken.

https://www.bbc.com/news/business-48628678, 14 June 2019 [16.01.2021]

The Critics ...

[...] Critics said the new rules were too draconian[1] and that banning even the most innocuous[2] use of gender stereotypes showed the watchdog had gone too far.
"It is concerning to see the ASA take on the role of the morality police," said Geraint Lloyd-Taylor, an advertising expert at the law firm Lewis Silkin. "It has let its zeal[3] to enforce[4] the new rules override its common sense in this first batch[5] of rulings.
"The ASA seems to be out of sync[6] with society in general. As it stands, the ASA's definition of 'harm' is unworkable and urgently needs to be clarified. I hope that these advertisers seek an independent review of the latest decisions."
Clearcast, the body[7] responsible for vetting[8] ads before they are broadcast, also expressed its frustration at the decisions. "We are naturally disappointed," it said. "The ASA's interpretation of the ads against the new rule and guidance goes further than we anticipated and has implications for a wide range of ads."

Mark Sweney, https://www.theguardian.com/media/2019/aug/14/first-ads-banned-for-contravening-gender-stereotyping-rules, 14 August 2019 [16.12.2020]

COMPREHENSION

1. Read the introductory part of the article *'Harmful' Gender Stereotypes in Adverts Banned* and point out
- which general criteria the ASA used for their decision,
- why certain ads were or are considered to be particularly harmful.

2. State why stereotypes are potentially dangerous.

3. Read the third part of the article and present examples given in the text of "deeply entrenched views on gender".

4. Describe why critics are deeply disappointed about the ASA's decision.

ANALYSIS

WES-121500-034

WES-121500-034

5. **Step 1:**
Watch the video clips provided on the webcode and take notes on how the TV ads use stereotypes to convey their message. Use worksheet 34.1 for your notes.

[20] **to preclude** (*fml.*) to make impossible – [21] **DIY** (*abbr.*) Do It Yourself – [22] **to assess sth.** here: to judge the nature and quality of sth.

[1] **draconian** (*fml.*) extremely severe – [2] **innocuous** completely harmless – [3] **zeal** great enthusiasm and eagerness – [4] **to enforce** to make people obey a law – [5] **batch** *Bündel* – [6] **out of sync** (*infml.*) not synchronized, not in agreement – [7] **body** here: *Gremium* – [8] **to vet** to examine sb./sth. carefully to make certain that they are acceptable or suitable

Step 2:
Explain in what ways the stereotypes
- have remained the same or similar since 1954,
- have changed since 1954,
- are still being used in a more implicit and hidden or less obvious way.

WES-121500-034

6. Examine and juxtapose (*gegenüberstellen*) the arguments given by the ASA and the critics in favour of or against banning stereotypical adverts. Use worksheet 34.2 for your notes.

stereotypes in adverts	
the ASA's view	**the critics' view**
• adverts can cause serious offence … • …	• too draconian • …

ACTIVITIES

7. Create adverts that critically deal with or even mock (*sich lustig machen*) gender stereotypes.

Step 1:
Form groups of four students and select a product or service of your choice that you want to advertise. This can be a product that already exists or something you invent.

Step 2:
Decide on how you want to deal with the matter, e. g. in a funny or satirical way or in a serious or even shocking way.

Tip: You can use your smartphones and film a short video clip or design posters.

Step 3:
In your team, think about slogans, power words and generally, the text you will need for your advertising copy (*Werbetext*). Write a script which contains e. g.
- a dialogue
- a voice from the off promoting something or telling a story
- etc.

Step 4:
After completing your advert, present it in class, and then discuss your various ideas.

GRAMMAR / LANGUAGE

8. In German adverts, employing words and expressions from foreign languages is relatively common. However, many of the words that sound 'cool' (can) have a different meaning from the one intended and can be quite embarrassing.
Turn the German words on worksheet 34.3 into correct English words and expressions and use a dictionary for help if necessary.

WES-121500-034

Torsten Landsberg

Masculinity and Gender Roles Are Undergoing Change

AWARENESS

Step 1:
Divide the class into two groups, with two students always working with one of the cartoons.

Step 2:
Together with your partner,
a) describe the cartoon to each other, using the help given in the Tips on vocab box,
b) explain the underlying message and how the cartoonist mocks and criticizes stereotypes of femininity and masculinity.

Step 3:
Pair up with two students who have dealt with the other cartoon and exchange your findings and results.

Step 4:
Discuss whether (or not) you share the cartoonists' views and criticisms.

1

"You missed a spot."

2

"Do you ever worry you've had to sacrifice your femininity to succeed in the male business world."

Tips on vocab

a messy kitchen ■ dirty cupboards and floor ■ a man eating a sandwich ■ a woman dressed in a business outfit ■ to be annoyed/critical/angry

Tips on vocab

to urinate standing up ■ urinal ■ to wear high heels/ a business costume ■ to stand next to each other ■ to wear make-up ■ to pretend to be masculine

Traditional gender roles are no longer valid[1], but men are dealing with the new expectations of masculinity in different ways. From vulnerability[2] to metrosexuality[3], gender is transforming.
As the popular German tongue-in-cheek[4] song by Herbert Grönemeyer goes: "When is a man a man?" Men's role in society is transforming and their social dominance is under threat[5]; women no longer accept less pay for doing the same job as a man and demand representation in the upper echelons[6] of politics and the economy.
Even the way we talk about gender roles is changing. After all, it makes sense to use gender neutral terms to refer to professions practiced by both men and women.

[1] **valid** socially acceptable or accepted – [2] **vulnerability** *Verletzbarkeit* – [3] **metrosexuality** the characteristics of a man who is interested in fashion and appearance – [4] **tongue-in-cheek** meant ironically – [5] **under threat** in danger – [6] **echelon** a rank or position within an organization, company or profession

Fortunately, there are men who find this completely normal and long overdue[7] while also actively supporting these demands. For many fathers it has become quite normal to play a bigger role in childcare or to take parental leave[8]. It wasn't so long ago that this was frowned upon[9].

The number of men turning to psychologists or masculinity coaching is on a steady rise as men question what it really means to be a man. It seems Grönemeyer was right when he sang: "Men are so vulnerable."

This transformation has, however, led to a transformation for some. The Victorian[10] ideals of traditional gender roles may have largely been rolled back, but social expectations of the so-called "stronger sex" have not. A man can still be expected to provide a shoulder to cry on, and he is often the family provider[11], even if he no longer has to hunt wild animals with a club[12].

"A fundamental reevaluation of masculinity began in the early 1970s," psychologist Stephan Grünewald explained to DW[13]. Germany was particularly impacted by this change after two world wars. "Hard like Krupp steel – this should no longer be the dominant image of men who were now expected to be sensitive and empathetic[14]."

There is nothing bad to be said about the person who is able to empathize with others. The modern man is also able to admit weaknesses, even flaws[15] and defeats – unlike a certain man in Washington[16].

In his book *How Germany Ticks*, Stephan Grünewald writes about the "performance crisis" of men. "Many men strongly define themselves according to what their partner expects, and no longer articulate their own wishes. They believe that this is how they can receive and hold onto love."

But what they get is the opposite. Grünewald's market research institute Rheingold carried out in-depth interviews which showed that women were irritated[17] by dutiful[18] obedience[19]. "They complain that men are like jelly and don't stand up for anything."

"Many men have a hard time articulating their own desires and ideas to their partner," says the psychologist. "Ideally, the man is self-confident and develops his own position, but he also puts it up for discussion." These personal conflicts may take effort, "but they lead to compromises and further increase sexual attraction".

A typical family in the 19th century

The tension between productive conflict on the one hand and patriarchal[20], even despotic[21] relationships on the other don't just exist in the private sphere, but are also present on the global political stage. "We're seeing a roll-back movement," says Stephan Grünewald – there is a longing for strong leaders who take decisive action, an image which is still closely associated with masculinity.

One last bastion[22] of the male sphere of influence is the workplace. In studies, men talked about brimming with[23] "functional potency" in the workplace, but when the conversation turned to the private sphere, the confidence waned[24]. "The workplace is still a place of refuge for many men," Stephan Grünewald says. What's left when their families don't want them having a post-work beer at the bar?

Men's appearances have also changed. Or at least there is more flexibility and acceptance when it comes to choos-

[7] **overdue** late; *überfällig* – [8] **parental leave** *Elternzeit* – [9] **to frown upon sth.** (*phr. v.*) to disapprove of sth. – [10] **Victorian** related to the time when Queen Victoria was queen of Great Britain and Ireland (1837 – 1901), old fashioned – [11] **family provider** person who earns a living for the family – [12] **club** *Keule* – [13] **DW** (*abbr.*) *Deutsche Welle* – [14] **empathetic** having the ability to imagine how sb. else feels – [15] **flaw** a fault, mistake or weakness – [16] **a certain man in Washington** here: Donald Trump – [17] **irritated** annoyed – [18] **dutiful** *pflichtbewusst* – [19] **obedience** doing what you are told – [20] **patriarchal** ruled or controlled by men – [21] **despotic** having unlimited power over other people, and often using it unfairly and cruelly – [22] **bastion** *Bollwerk* – [23] **to brim with** to be full of – [24] **to wane** to become less

ing one's style. And that doesn't have to stop at painting one's fingernails or wearing high heels as does Mark Bryan, an American living in a small German town, an act which won him 200,000 new Instagram followers.

Pop culture has opened up new ways for men to aesthetically[25] express themselves. He can now wear pink and can maybe even correctly identify the particular shade as mauve[26]. But for those heterosexual men with a flair for fashion who feel the need to distinguish themselves from homosexual men, there is a modern fitting label: metrosexual.

Men today shave their bodies, but then grow a bushy beard which they tend to[27] with an array[28] of beard care products.

The discovery of and care for one's body is not just a question of vanity[29] however. Skin as tough as leather is a "fascist ideal," Stephan Grünewald explains. "Skin represents flexibility and sensitivity. The more one takes care of himself, the more self-confident he is and can open up on other levels."

https://www.dw.com/en/masculinity-and-gender-roles-undergoing-change/a-55585195, 13 November 2020 [18.12.2020]

COMPREHENSION

1. In a paired reading activity, **read the article on your own first** and try to **understand the gist** of it. Then, summarize the article to your partner and clarify possible questions.

2. Now, **read the article a second time** and complete the sentences below, using evidence from the text.
   a) Gender roles are drifting and men are dealing with …
   b) Men's social dominance is under threat because …
   c) Many men and fathers think that …
   d) Victorian ideals of the 'stronger sex' have changed but …
   e) Two world wars have led to …
   f) The modern man is able to …
   g) The term the 'performance crisis' of men means …
   h) Some women are irritated about men because …
   i) The world is seeing a roll-back movement, which means that …
   j) The workplace is very important for men because …
   k) Fashion and pop culture have helped men …

ANALYSIS

3. Examine the author's train of thought* and explain what reasons and ideas are given to support the hypothesis that "masculinity and gender roles are undergoing change".
   → Focus on Skills, Analysis of a Non-Fictional Text, p. 237

Info

- **Train of thought** is the way a series of ideas is gradually developed and structured.
- **Line of argument** is the way different reasons are gradually developed and structured to convince a reader of a particular point of view.

[25] **aesthetically** in a beautiful or artistic way – [26] **mauve** [məʊv] a pale purple colour – [27] **to tend to sb./sth.** (*phr. v.*) to care for or look after sb./sth. – [28] **array** variety or collection – [29] **vanity** *Eitelkeit*

ACTIVITIES

4. Write a *Letter to the Editor* in response to the article and express your view as young men and women on how masculinity and gender roles are changing.

Step 1:
If necessary, do further research on the development of gender roles and the (changed) understanding of femininity and masculinity.

Step 2:
As a *Letter to the Editor* falls into the category of a formal letter, read up on the basic elements of a formal letter or email.
→ Focus on Skills, Writing a Formal Letter, p. 267

Tip: Remember that in a *Letter to the Editor*, the writer
- responds to an article he or she has read and states his or her opinion on the matter,
- expresses his or her criticism of or support for a position taken by the publication,
- comments on a current issue or a problem of public interest,
- corrects a perceived error or misinterpretation.

Step 3:
Begin your letter by referring to the article at hand and/or an observation that you have made.

Example:
I read your comprehensive article published in … on … with great interest … As a young man/woman myself, I think that … . However, I would like to point out that …

Tips on vocab
- I was really surprised to find out that …
- I read a fascinating article about …
- Much to my surprise, you write that …
- What would it be like if …?
- It is absolutely astonishing to see that …
- From my own experience …

Step 4:
Structure the body of your letter clearly and avoid unnecessary repetition. Include examples, arguments and references to support your view.

Tip: In order to improve your fluency and make your English sound more natural, you might want to use certain phrases and connectives. But be careful not to overdo it – you do not want to produce empty phrases.
→ Focus on Language, Connectives and Adverbs, p. 251

Step 5:
Conclude your letter with a summarizing sentence and an outlook on the issue, e. g. by asking a (rhetorical) question or making a suggestion on possible alternatives.

Example:
I would like to finish by emphasizing that … To my understanding, men and women should …
→ Focus on Skills, Writing a Letter to the Editor, p. 273
→ Focus on Language, Conversation and Discussion, p. 254

GRAMMAR / LANGUAGE

WES-121500-035

5. Brush up your vocabulary on gender roles, femininity and masculinity and complete the acrostics provided on worksheet 35.1.

Caroline Eitel, Martin Spiewak

Der große Unterschied

AWARENESS

Girls and boys in Germany have the same legal right to education and making the best of their talents and likings. And, of course, there are girls who are excellent at maths and science, and boys who score higher in languages, literature and art than girls. However, reality shows that there are differences between

- the subjects (most) girls and boys prefer,
- boys' and girls' performances in subjects like maths, languages, literature and art.

From what you know about your friends and/or students in your grade and class, what differences do you know of and what do you consider to be the reasons for these differences? Discuss in class.

1

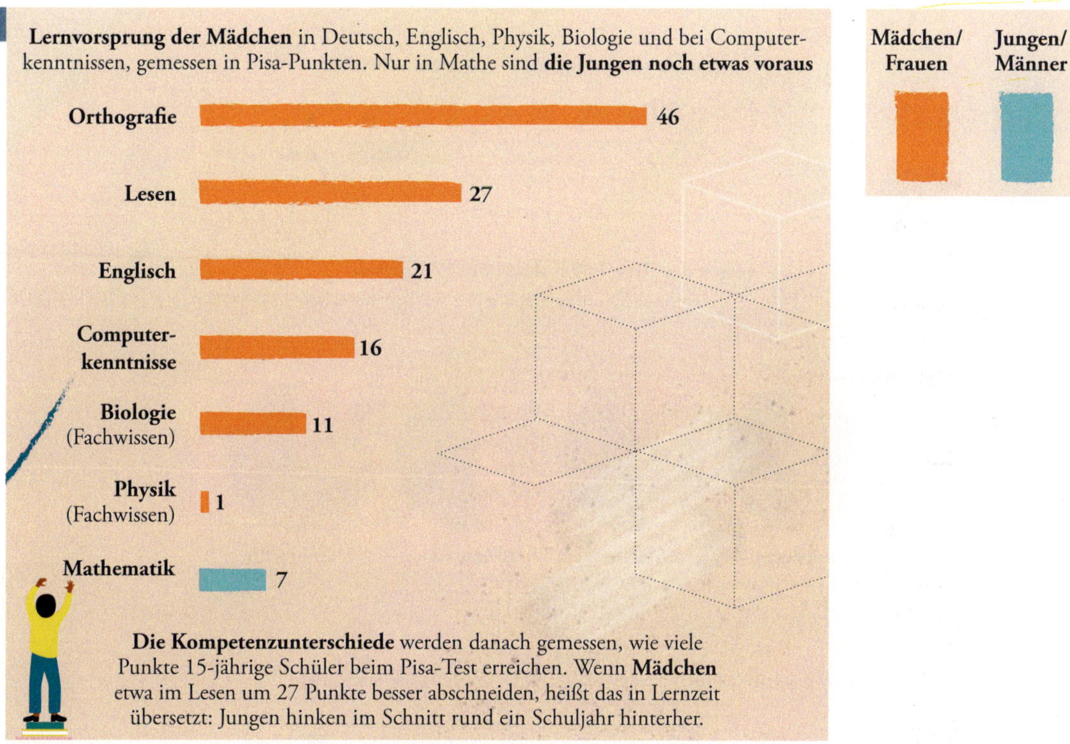

2

Tips on vocab

1 bar chart ■ spelling ■ computer literacy ■ physics ■ (to measure) differences in skills ■ to score better/worse than … ■ on average ■ to lag behind ■ significant differences ■ … times as much as

2 to have deficits in … ■ first day at school ■ enrolment ■ pre-school language classes ■ to lack language skills ■ to be less fluent in … ■ to lack a core knowledge of …

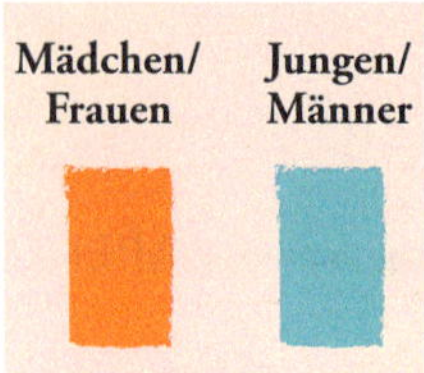

3

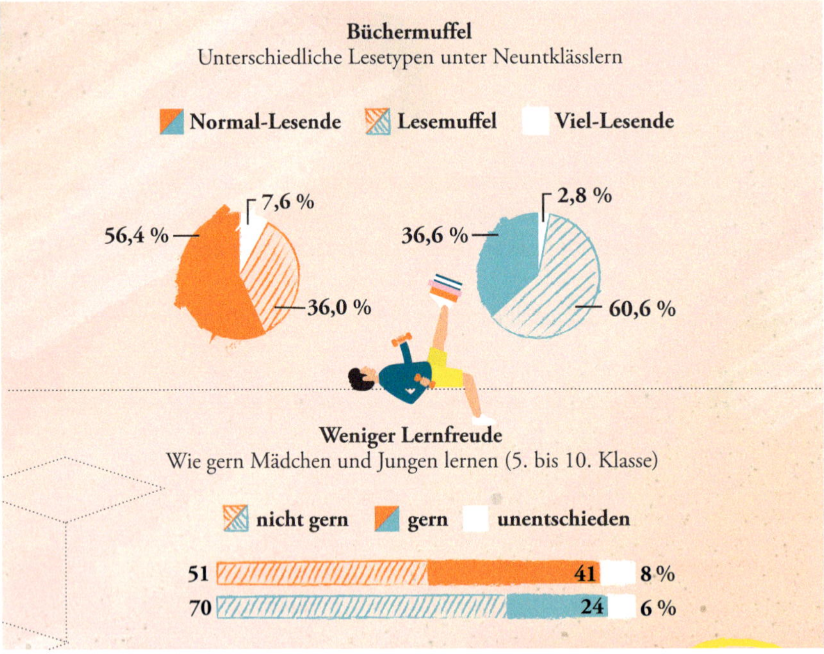

4

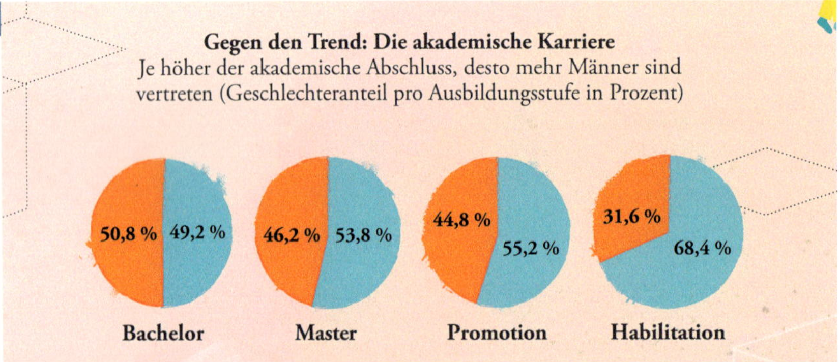

5

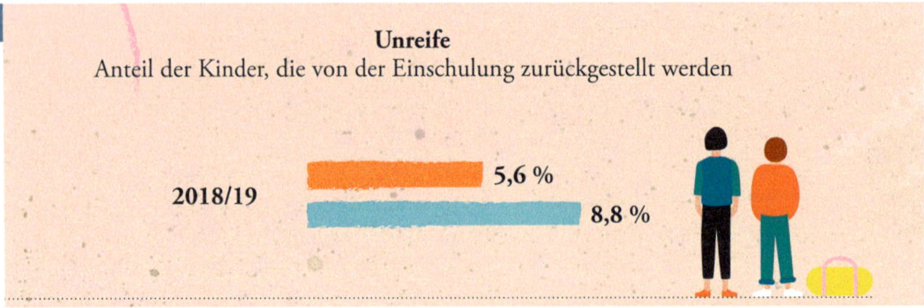

Tips on vocab

3 pie chart ■ to hate reading ■ bookworm ■ to binge-read ■ different types of readers ■ to read more than average ■ joy of learning

4 pie chart ■ academic career ■ to have an academic degree ■ level of education ■ percentage-wise ■ doctorate ■ PhD ■ habilitation (qualification for a professorship at a university in Europe)

5 bar chart ■ immaturity ■ school enrolment ■ first day at school ■ to keep sb. back from starting school

6

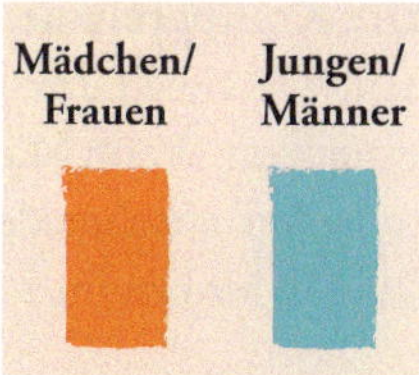

7

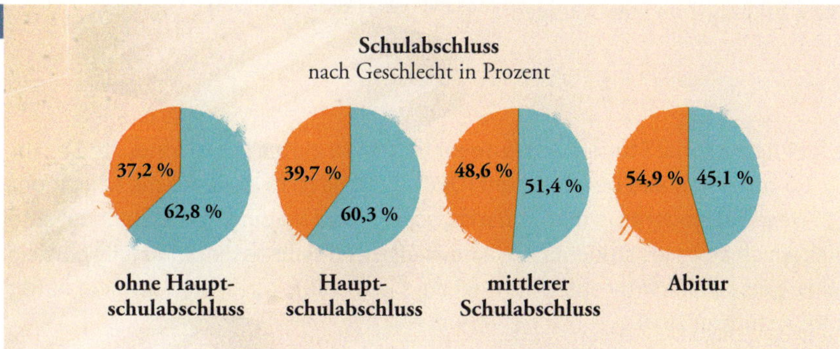

8

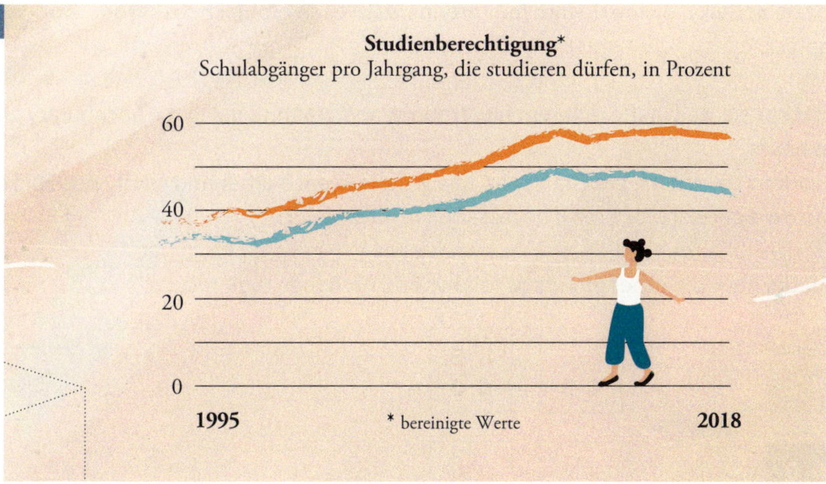

Tips on vocab

6 bar chart ■ to stay longer at home ■ to be hesitant about leaving home ■ living with your parents ■ average age of leaving home ■ not flying or leaving the parental nest

7 pie chart ■ graduation ■ school-leaving certificate ■ secondary school qualification ■ A-levels ■ to show striking differences ■ to differ by … per cent

8 line graph ■ university entrance qualification ■ to qualify for ■ to be close to ■ to be comparable to ■ to be more or less than 50 per cent ■ more than half of

Die Kompetenzunterschiede werden danach gemessen, wie viele Punkte 15-jährige Schüler beim Pisa-Test erreichen. Wenn **Mädchen** etwa im Lesen um 27 Punkte besser abschneiden, heißt das in Lernzeit übersetzt: Jungen hinken im Schnitt rund ein Schuljahr hinterher.

Warum fallen Jungs zurück?
Jungen sind nicht dümmer als Mädchen. Vielmehr sind es Verhalten und Einstellungen[1], die ihrem Schulerfolg im Wege stehen, vermuten Bildungsforscher[2]. Jungen sind im Schnitt nicht so motiviert und diszipliniert beim Lernen, im Unterricht verhalten sie sich häufiger so, dass sie vom Stoff[3] weniger mitkriegen[4]. Hinzu kommt: Mädchen sind sprachlich stärker[5] und haben ausgeprägtere[6] soziale Fähigkeiten – Kompetenzen, die heute wichtiger sind als früher.

Text and graphics from "Der große Unterschied" by Martin Spiewak and Caroline Eitel. DIE ZEIT, 47/2020, https://www.zeit.de/2020/47/geschlechterunterschiede-jungen-schulabschluss-jobchancen-bildung, 12 November 2020 [10.01.2021]

COMPREHENSION

The Programme for International Student Assessment (PISA) is a global study conducted by the Organization for Economic Co-operation and Development (OECD), intended to evaluate the education and school performance of 15-year-old students in mathematics, science and reading. It is a triannual study, first performed in 2000, which assesses students' key knowledge and skills essential to fully participate in society. In Germany, girls significantly outperformed boys in reading, but scored lower in mathematics than boys in the PISA study of 2018.

1. In a **group puzzle activity**, divide up into four groups, with each group choosing and working with two of the infographics.

2. Mediate the data presented in the different illustrations and graphics using the vocabulary given in the Tips on vocab boxes.
M Describe the various bar charts, pie charts and line graphs to each other and clarify possible questions. Additionally, use a dictionary for help if necessary.

3. The groups should now join other groups as follows and exchange their results.

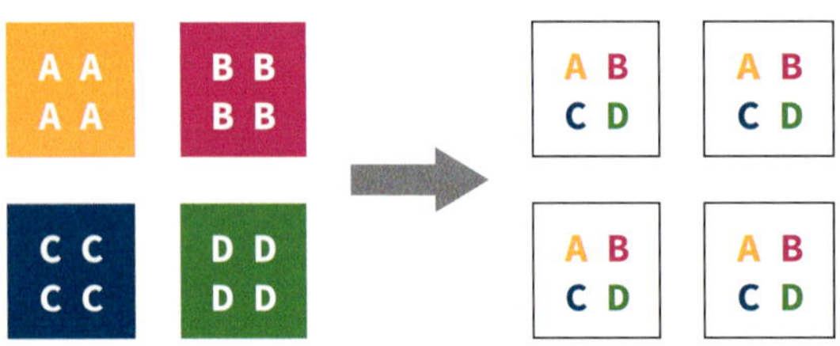

ANALYSIS

4. The short text at the top of this page gives explanations and reasons for
M the striking differences. Mediate and explain the explanations given.

5. Take another, closer look at graphic no. 4, whose data runs counter to the other trends. Explain the reversed situation here and try to find reasons why more men pursue an academic career than women.
→ Focus on Skills, Analysis of Statistical Data, p. 243

Tips on vocab
- compared with …
- in comparison to …
- in contrast, men …
- in contrast to the previous trend, …
- men outperform women … by … %
- by far …

[1] attitude – [2] education researcher – [3] subject matter – [4] to pick up – [5] more gifted in languages – [6] more distinct

ACTIVITIES

6. Scenario:
In comparison to other nations, Germany ranks above average, but countries like China, Estonia, Canada, the UK, Australia and Norway score (significantly) higher in the PISA study of 2018. However, according to media reports, British students, and particularly girls, are extremely afraid of failure; about 22.4% of British girls have developed emotional disorders and anxieties by the age of 19. In December 2019, the British newspaper *The Guardian* critically commented that "children are not guinea pigs trained for PISA".
Your English friend Nathan has asked you what the situation is like in German schools. He feels that British students are put under enormous pressure to perform and wants to know about how you view the situation.
Write him an email in which you
a) include the information given in the infographics and
b) give your view on the matter.

M

Step 1:
Go through the results of tasks 2 and 3 again and **select the most relevant information**. Leave out less relevant details.

Tip: As the heading of the material indicates, the focus is put on the striking differences in the school performance of girls and boys in Germany. Accordingly, you should leave out information given on minor differences.

Step 2:
M
Following the assignment, select and mediate the relevant information given in the infographics first, using the language help given in the Tips on vocab boxes.

Step 3:
Now, consider your opinion of
a) the various data and explanations given and
b) your personal situation and experience at school.

Tips on vocab

- The overall trend shows that …
- The PISA study mirrors the situation of …
- There seems to be a (wide) gap between …
- Personally, I (do not) agree with …
- I am critical of … and doubt that …
- To my mind, teachers should …
- What a pity that …

Step 4:
Do not forget to
a) write a few short introductory remarks to your friend, like thanking him for writing, asking him how he is, etc.,
b) close your email with a complimentary close (and/or an emoji) and your name.

Step 5:
Finally, write an email of about 250 words to your friend Nathan.

GRAMMAR / LANGUAGE

WES-121500-036

7. Worksheet 36.1 provides you with statements in response to the PISA study and the infographics. Turn these sentences into the **passive voice** to make them less personal.
→ Passive, p. 298

4 Units – 4 Topics – 4 Articles

After having worked with various units, topics and material provided in the *Approach*, you will have gained a lot of knowledge and skills to do a project that applies all these aspects.

A newspaper front page or template as well as an example of a front page from the British quality newspaper *The Guardian* give you an overview of the core elements of a front page.

A so-called **template** (= a particular model for arranging information or images in a document, etc. that you can copy and use for your own purposes) of a typical newspaper front page illustrating the various elements

Champions League Spurs revival sets up all-English final

Plus: The battle for quieter restaurants

The Guardian

Climate crisis 'may force UK towns to be abandoned'

Environment Agency warns huge numbers are under threat from coastal and river floods

'We can't win a war against water by building away climate change with infinitely high defences'

Girl is first patient saved by GM virus treatment

The **front cover** of an issue of the British daily newspaper *The Guardian*, published on 9 May 2019

Compiling a Newspaper Front Page

1. Form four teams of students, one team for each unit/topic of the *Approach*.
Discuss and decide in class whether each of the four teams compiles one complete front page or whether you distribute the space available on one front page among the whole class so that each group completes one fourth of the page.

Step 1:
You can use the texts and material provided in the Students' Book/*Approach*, and/or do further research on your chosen topic, decide what kind of article you are going to write and what other material (photos, infographics, further texts, etc.) you will need.
→ Focus on Skills, Doing Research and Citing Sources, p. 262

Step 2:
Brush up your knowledge of the characteristics of newspapers and what to consider when writing a newspaper article.
Additionally, you can use the information given in the checklist below and in the template on the opposite page.
→ Focus on Facts, The Press, p. 229
→ Focus on Skills, Writing a Newspaper Article, p. 270

2. Write your newspaper article(s) and arrange them on the front page of your newspaper.

Tip: You should use a computer to typeset your articles and (roughly) plan the arrangement of the various elements you want to use.

3. Display your front page(s) in class and compare, discuss and evaluate the various articles, further materials, etc.

Checklist

elements ...	... function ...
• masthead	→ newspaper's name printed in special type
• lead (paragraph)	→ usually set in bold (*Fettdruck*), italics (*Kursivschrift*) or larger text
• columns of writing	→ articles, reports, etc.
• by-line	→ journalist's name and job title
• cut	→ photo or illustration
• index	→ alphabetized table of contents of the newspaper
• photo credit	→ reference to the source of a photograph or illustration
• banner	→ headline that runs across the full page, used for important news or scandals
• classified ads	→ advertisements in small type, often submitted by individuals or small traders
• editorial (leader)	→ article that represents the newspaper's opinion
• subhead	→ one- or two-lined headline at the head of a paragraph to structure the text
• anchor	→ light-hearted, human interest story placed at the bottom of front page

role models		
to be tricked into buying (expensive beauty and fashion products)	to be talked into doing sth.	*verleitet werden (teure Kosmetik- oder Modeprodukte) zu kaufen*
celebrity	a famous person, esp. in the entertainment business	*Berühmtheit*
to copy a lifestyle	to try and live in the same way as sb. else	*einen Lebensstil nachahmen*
to empower sb.	to give sb. the (literal or metaphorical) power to do sth.	*jdn. ermächtigen*
to encourage sb.	to support sb. in a way that helps them achieve sth.	*jdn. ermutigen*
to have an influence on sb.	to affect the way sb. thinks and acts, either with positive or negative consequences	*einen Einfluss auf jdn. haben*
idol	sb. who is hugely admired, even worshipped	*Idol*
to idolize sb.	to admire sb. to the point you almost worship them	*umschwärmen*
influencer	sb. who makes money by promoting a certain lifestyle or certain products online on social media	*Influencer*
to inspire sb.	to positively encourage other people to do/believe sth.	*jdn. inspirieren*
invisible role model	sb. who sets a good example and inspires others without receiving praise, credit or publicity for doing so	*unsichtbares Vorbild*
to lead by example/ set a good example	to act in a way that shows others how to act when you are in a leadership position or position of responsibility	*mit gutem Beispiel vorangehen*
to look up to sb.	to admire, respect sb.	*zu jdm. aufblicken*
mentor	sb. whose role is to encourage and support people younger or less experienced than them	*Mentor/in, Betreuer/in*
to motivate sb.	to give sb. the motivation to achieve sth.	*jdn. motivieren, bewegen*
to reach your full potential	to have the opportunity to achieve everything you are capable of	*das volle Potenzial ausschöpfen*
reality check (*infml.*)	an event or experience that makes sb. see the truth	*Augenöffner*
role model	sb. who (younger) people look up to as a positive example for how they should live their lives	*Vorbild*
gender roles/gender stereotypes		
androgynous [æn'drɒdʒənəs]	not clearly male or a female	*androgyn*
biological determinism	the belief that our behaviour is caused by biological factors such as hormones, genetics, etc.	*biologischer Determinismus*
bisexual	being sexually attracted to people of both male and female sex	*bisexuell*
convention	the way sth. is done that most people in a society expect and consider to be right	*Konvention, Gewohnheit*
cultural conditioning	the belief that our behaviour is caused by external, cultural factors such as societal convention	*kulturelle Bedingtheit*
to emancipate sb.	to liberate or free sb.; to give sb. equal opportunities	*jdn. emanzipieren*
femininity	qualities that are considered to be typical of women	*Weiblichkeit*
gay	(esp. men) sb. attracted to people of the same sex	*schwul*
gender	social construct relating to the performance of roles, traits and ideas perceived as masculine or feminine; in the past, this was closely linked to one's biological sex	*Gender, (soziales) Geschlecht*
gender binary	the concept that there are only two genders, man and woman, and everyone is either one or the other	*eine binäre Geschlechterordnung*
gender fluidity	the state of identifying as no single gender, but having attributes associated with several genders in constant flux, i. e. some days more masculine than others	*Gender Fluidität, nichtbinäre Geschlechtsidentität*

gender neutral term	terminology that does not assume sb.'s gender, e.g. police officer instead of policeman	*geschlechtsneutraler Begriff*
gender pay gap	the difference between how much a man and a woman are paid for doing the same work	*Lohnlücke*
gender socialization	the specific (and often different) ways in which boys and girls are educated socially, with different expectations for how they ought to behave	*Geschlechtssozialisation*
heterosexual	to be sexually attracted to people of the opposite sex	*heterosexuell*
homosexual	to be sexually attracted to people of the same sex	*homosexuell*
legal emancipation	having the legal rights and independent responsibilities of an adult person	*rechtliche Gleichberechtigung*
lesbian	a woman who is sexually attracted to other women	*lesbisch, Lesbierin*
LGBTQIA+ community	the community of everyone who does not identify as heterosexual (Lesbian, Gay, Bi, Transgender, Queer/Questioning, Intersex, Asexual/Aromantic/Agender/Allied + all others)	*LGBTQIA+-Gemeinde, -Gemeinschaft*
macho (*adj.*)	trying to behave in a way that is thought to be typical of a man	*Macho-Verhalten, Macho-Gehabe*
masculinity	qualities that are considered to be typical of men	*Männlichkeit*
non-binary	a state of being neither solely masculine nor feminine	*nonbinär*
(biological) sex	biological and physical factors that determine sb. as male or female	*(biologisches) Geschlecht*
stereotype	an expectation or pre-judgment of a group of people	*Stereotyp*
toxic masculinity	a type of masculinity that encourages damaging behaviour and perpetuates negative stereotypes	*toxische Männlichkeit*
traditional gender roles	the typical, slightly outdated, expectation for how masculinity and femininity should be expressed	*traditionelle Geschlechterrollen*
transgender	sb. who identifies as the gender opposite to their biological sex	*Transgender*
to transition	to change from one form to another	*übergehen, wechseln*
XX/XY chromosomes	specific biological traits that determine sex: XX chromosomes are female and XY male	*XX/XY Chromosome*
	digital life, social media & communication	
to block sb.	to prevent sb. from accessing your social media or contacting you online	*jdn. blockieren*
blog	an online platform for writing, like a diary	*Blog*
to communicate with sb.	to exchange information, news, ideas, etc. with sb.	*mit jdm. kommunizieren*
cyberbullying	a specific type of bullying that takes place online	*Cybermobbing*
to edit a photo	to make adjustments to a photo so it looks 'better'	*ein Foto bearbeiten*
(main) feed	what you see as you scroll through social media	*Feed*
to follow sb. on social media	to make sure that you can keep up to date with sb. online and see their posts on your feed	*jdm. folgen*
FOMO (Fear Of Missing Out)	a feeling that drives you to constantly check social media because you do not want to miss sth. interesting	*Angst, etw. zu verpassen*
to go viral	to quickly become popular and widely shared online	*rasend schnell bekannt werden*
group chat	a group where lots of people can communicate online	*Gruppenchat*
hate page	a site or account specifically designed to bully sb.	*Hass-Seite*
hater	sb. who intends to bully people and be cruel online	*Hasser, Neider*
to message sb.	to write directly to sb. online	*jdm. eine Nachricht senden*

to photoshop sth.	to digitally edit a photo using online tools	*photoshoppen*
(online) platform	a digital service that enables direct social interaction	*Onlineplattform*
to post sth. online	to put sth. (a photo/tweet/blog etc.) on the internet	*im Internet veröffentlichen*
to report sb.	to complain about sb.'s behaviour on social media	*jdn. zur Anzeige bringen*
to share sth.	to pass sth. you have found online to sb. else	*etw. weitergeben*
to subscribe to sth.	to sign up to see specific posts/videos/emails	*etw. abonnieren*
to tag sb. in sth.	to mark sb. as identifiable in a post/photo/tweet	*jdn. markieren*
virtual	the state of taking place online rather than in person	*virtuell*
wireless communication	a system of sending and receiving signals and messages without wired connection	*drahtlose Kommunikation*
	technology, electronic & digital media	
anonymous [əˈnɒnɪməs]	unable to be identified, nameless	*anonym*
artificial intelligence	the ability of computers to learn to do complicated tasks	*künstliche Intelligenz*
to bookmark sth.	to save a website or online page in a place that is easy to access at a later point	*ein Lesezeichen bei einer Internetseite setzen*
cookies	information stored on your device that monitors how you use the internet and notes the content you see	*Cookies*
data [ˈdeɪtə] **protection authority**	experts on data protection issues and (how to avoid) breaches of privacy	*Datenschutzbehörde*
digital lifestyle	a way of life heavily influenced by electronic media	*digitaler Lebensstil*
GDPR (General Data Protection Regulation)	the official EU rules concerning the storing and sharing of private data, designed to uphold privacy and security	*DSGVO (Datenschutz-Grundverordnung)*
to go live (*coll.*)	to start recording sth. in 'real time' so that it is seen or heard as it is actually happening	*live gehen, auf Sendung gehen*
to invade sb.'s privacy	to breach/disturb sb.'s privacy without having permission to do so	*in jmds. Privatsphäre eindringen*
live coverage	a report on TV or the radio that takes place in 'real time'	*Direktübertragung*
manual	file/booklet giving information on how to do or use sth.	*Handbuch*
operating system	a set of programs inside a computer that controls the way it works	*Betriebssystem*
privacy	the right to keep personal matters and data secret	*Privatsphäre, Datenschutz*
source (of information)	the place where sb. finds information	*Quelle, Informationsquelle*
(to keep sb. under) surveillance	the act of carefully watching or observing sb., often if they are suspected of having committed a crime	*Überwachung*
URL (= universal resource locator)	general way of accessing an internet address	*Internetadresse*
user-friendly	easy to work with	*benutzerfreundlich*
verified	confirmed to be authentic or true	*geprüft, verifiziert*
virus	a piece of code designed to cause faults in a computer or damage the data stored on it	*Computervirus*
wi-fi	wireless local area network	*WLAN, drahtloses lokales Netzwerk*

Skills & Competences

Language and grammar

(Identifikation sprachlicher Mittel und kommunikativer Strategien; Grammatik)

Listening Comprehension

"Okay, if you think it will help you be a better listener."

Language learning is dependent on good listening. Therefore, it is important to **learn to adjust one's listening to various situations** in order to be able to interact well in spoken communication. These situations can be listening to a song, an interview, (watching and) listening to a film, or listening to somebody in a conversation. Usually, you already have a lot of background knowledge, e.g. about the topic, the person, and of course, you already know a lot of the vocabulary used in the spoken text you are supposed to listen to. Before you start **taking notes**, make use of the following strategies that can help you to understand texts more easily.

Strategies that can help to understand texts

a) Predicting

This technique helps you to mentally prepare yourself for the text.

- Try to imagine what the text will be about by judging from the title/headline.
- Try to make predictions about the rest of the text after the first sentence or the first part of the text.

b) Listening for the main idea

- Try to understand the gist of the text by paying attention to key nouns, people's names, official place names, etc.
- Try to find answers to the w-questions (who?, what?, where?, when?, why?).

c) Drawing inferences – intelligent guessing

- Make use of German words that are very similar to English words (e.g. mouse – *Maus*, mile – *Meile*, house – *Haus*, etc.). However, watch out for false friends (e.g. become ≠ *bekommen*, chef ≠ *Chef*, etc.).
- Make use of other foreign languages that you know and link them to anglicized words (e.g. French *la qualité* – quality, *la circonstance* – circumstance, etc.).
- Listen for internationally-used English words (e.g. *crew*, *team*, *display*, *design*, etc.) and relate them to the possible contents of the text.
- Connect (parts of) words that you already know to words in the text that sound similar (e.g. to teach – *teacher*, to grow – *growth*, etc.).
- Double-check your guessed meaning of the word by relating it to the context.

d) The given-new strategy

- Pay attention to certain keywords employed in the text that emphasize an additional aspect given in a sentence (e.g. *The weather was warm* ***but*** *rainy.*). Further keywords or phrases are: ***before***, ***after***, ***although***, ***such as***, ***another***, ***as you know***, ***to sum up***, ***conclusion***, etc.

Strategies that can help to process and memorize the information

While listening

- The audio text will be presented to you (at least) twice.
- While listening a **first time**, try to get a **general understanding** and just jot down a few keywords which will help you to memorize **the gist** of what is said.
- When listening a **second time**, pay attention to details and take further notes.
- Do not be worried if you do not understand each word. Contextualize and try to understand the main idea of the sentence/group of sentences.

Note-taking – mind mapping – summarizing

- Use your notes taken while or after listening to order and (re-)arrange your understanding of the text.
- Relate your findings to other contexts.
- Draw a mind map of your notes and try to find further useful details from the text.
- Write a summary using your notes and try to explain the text you listened to in your own words.

→ Focus on Skills, Writing a Summary, p. 231

Basic Types of Fictional Texts

1. Narrative texts	**a) Novels** • are extended and complex works of fiction written in prose. • contain a variety of characters, action and a greater complication of plot. • present a sustained exploration of the milieu, the characters, their motives. • can vary greatly in form, style and content; one less complex form is the novella (e. g. John Steinbeck, *Of Mice and Men* or *Cannery Row*). • have certain subclasses, e. g. the social novel (e. g. Harriet Beecher-Stowe, *Uncle Tom's Cabin*), the coming-of-age story (e. g. Mark Twain, *Tom Sawyer and Huckleberry Finn*; Paul Auster, *Moon Palace*). **b) Short stories** • are written in prose and are shorter and less complex than a novel. • are mostly confined to one setting, a limited number of characters and events. • often employ an open plot with an abrupt opening and ending. • do not put focus on the development of a character but on a significant incident or decisive moment that reveals strengths and weaknesses of characters, mostly presented as a snapshot of life. • are told from the point of view of a narrator. • place maximum significance on the few things mentioned, which are aimed at producing a certain effect in the reader's mind. • emerged in the USA in the 19th century in response to the development of the newspapers, which required shorter forms of text; Edgar Allan Poe (1809 – 1849) is often regarded as the originator of the short story; other famous writers of short stories include Ernest Hemingway, Annie Proulx and T. C. Boyle. **c) Fables** • are short texts in which animals represent human types (→ the beast fable). • are a form of allegory exemplifying an abstract moral thesis or principle of human behaviour. • are didactic and are intended to teach the reader a moral lesson. • Two famous writers of fables are James Thurber and George Orwell.
2. Dramatic texts	**a) Plays** • are designed for performance in a theatre. • require actors who take on the roles of different characters, performing the actions and speaking dialogues or monologues. • usually contain stage directions included by the playwright, telling the actors how and where to move on stage as well as giving information about how to arrange the stage, what props, sound effects or lighting to use. → Focus on Facts, Drama and Theatre, p. 234 **b) Screenplays/scripts** • are written works, especially for film or television. • consist of numbered scenes which show action and dialogue descriptions. • have numbered slug lines telling the reader that the story has changed in location and time (e. g. INT. WAREHOUSE – NIGHT; EXT. STREET – DAY) → Focus on Facts, Screenplays and Storyboards, p. 228
3. Poetry/ lyrics	**a) Poetry** • is a type of literature that is not prose, in which ideas, experiences and feelings are expressed in compact, imaginative and often musical language. • may be arranged in lines and may contain patterns of rhyme and rhythm. • often contains figures of speech and imagery to appeal to the readers' and listeners' emotions and imagination. **b) Lyrics** • are a set of words that accompany music, either spoken or sung. → Focus on Skills, Analysis of Lyrics and Poetry, p. 241

Note: Explanations of the respective technical terms can be found in the Literary Terms section, pp. 274 ff.

Basic Types of Non-Fictional Texts

The four basic types of non-fictional texts

1. Descriptive texts: the author wants to inform in a relatively balanced and neutral way (e. g. description of a landscape, a place, a person, an object)

2. Narrative texts: the author wants to inform the reader about a development or a sequence of events; the report (objectively or subjectively) gives answers to the questions *who? what? where? when? why?* and *how?* and often presents further details. Reports are often made livelier by fictional elements, such as a detailed description of people or the way people are affected by an event (e. g. travel report, report on the development of a situation)

3. Expository texts: complicated and difficult facts are presented and explained in a matter-of-fact way; the structure/pattern of such texts is called **topical order** (a sequence of points follows a statement of the topic at the beginning of the text, e. g. explanatory notes, scientific reports, factual texts, descriptions of historical events)

4. Argumentative texts: the author tries to influence the reader directly; this text type tends to be more critical and appellative, using persuasive arguments (e. g. commentary, criticism, review, essay, sermon, pamphlet, political speech); these texts usually deal with controversial topics; reasons are given for and/or against the matter and are arranged in a well-planned order

Forms of argumentative texts

structure	type 1	type 2	type 3
introduction	Presenting a topic and giving opinions on the problem	Presenting a topic and giving opinions on the problem	Presenting a topic and giving opinions on the problem
↓	arguments ↓	arguments ↓	arguments ↓
main part	supporting facts	counter-arguments and refutation to stress the author's position	argument → counter-argument argument → counter-argument argument → counter-argument etc. (mainly used in disputes and debates)
↓	↓	↓	↓
conclusion	conclusion	conclusion	conclusion

A non-fictional text that puts forth a personal view has a **unity of thought**, and usually follows a clear **structure** (line of thought, train of thought, line of argument).
Here are some of the most common **compositional patterns for structuring texts**:

listing structure:	**method:** enumerating, numbering of facts, ideas, arguments **effect:** clarity and coherence through parallel arrangement
progressive structure:	**method:** using a clearly-defined starting point; developing in a cause-to-effect or problem-solution arrangement **effect:** clarity through unity and logical coherence
antithetical structure:	**method:** contrasting and juxtaposing of facts, ideas and arguments **effect:** clarity and emphasis through comparison and contrast

Screenplays and Storyboards

The process of making a film is very complex and requires a number of preparatory arrangements such as **scriptwriting**, **shooting**, **editing** and finally **distributing the film** to the audience. Usually, it involves a large number of general staff and specialists and can take up to several years to complete. Here are two of the most relevant preparatory steps.

Screenplay

- A screenplay or script is a written work for film or television. It can be an original work or an adaptation from an existing work like a novel, short story, etc.
- A screenplay focusses on **describing** the literal, **visual aspects of the story**, rather than the internal thoughts of its characters.
- The major components are **action** and **dialogue**. The description of the 'action' is always written in the present tense.
- One page of a screenplay usually equates to one minute of screen time.

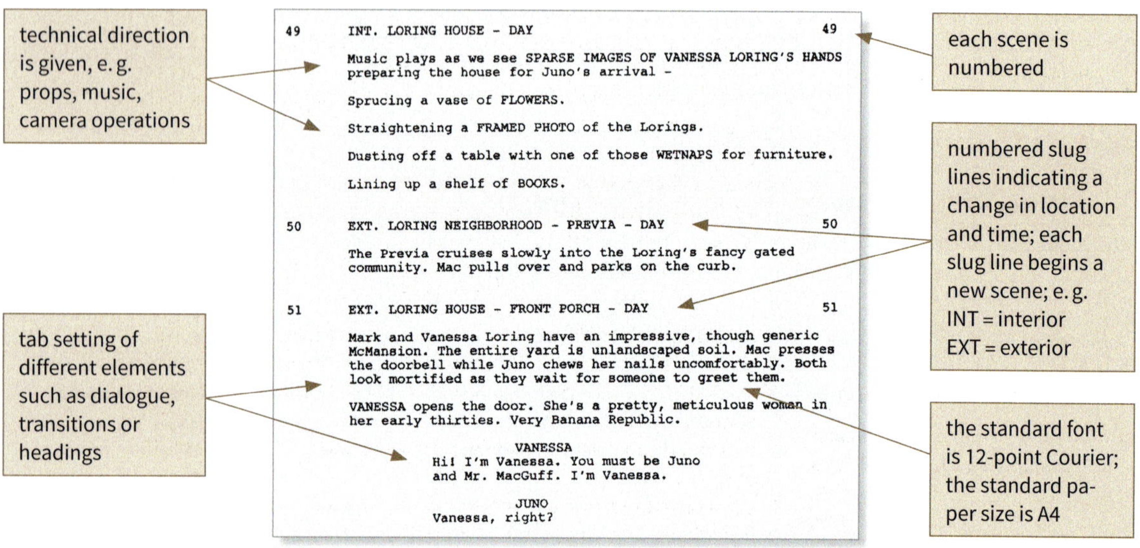


```
49     INT. LORING HOUSE - DAY                                    49

       Music plays as we see SPARSE IMAGES OF VANESSA LORING'S HANDS
       preparing the house for Juno's arrival -

       Sprucing a vase of FLOWERS.

       Straightening a FRAMED PHOTO of the Lorings.

       Dusting off a table with one of those WETNAPS for furniture.

       Lining up a shelf of BOOKS.

50     EXT. LORING NEIGHBORHOOD - PREVIA - DAY                    50

       The Previa cruises slowly into the Loring's fancy gated
       community. Mac pulls over and parks on the curb.

51     EXT. LORING HOUSE - FRONT PORCH - DAY                      51

       Mark and Vanessa Loring have an impressive, though generic
       McMansion. The entire yard is unlandscaped soil. Mac presses
       the doorbell while Juno chews her nails uncomfortably. Both
       look mortified as they wait for someone to greet them.

       VANESSA opens the door. She's a pretty, meticulous woman in
       her early thirties. Very Banana Republic.

                          VANESSA
                Hi! I'm Vanessa. You must be Juno
                and Mr. MacGuff. I'm Vanessa.

                          JUNO
                Vanessa, right?
```

Diablo Cody, Ivan Reitman: Juno: The Shooting Script. Newmarket Press, New York 2007, p. 20

Storyboard

- Storyboards are **graphic organizers** that display images in sequence in order to pre-visualize a film as it is to be seen through the camera lens.
- Before the shooting of the film begins, each storyboard maps out the **director's vision of where the camera will be placed** for action sequences in a film.
- A storyboard helps the director to find potential problems or brainstorm further ideas.
- Technical details are described either in picture form or additional text; often, there are arrows or instructions that indicate movement.

The Press

An overview of different newspaper, magazine and online formats

(online) newspapers	characteristics	tips on vocab
British quality newspapers: *The Times, The Guardian, The Daily Telegraph, The Sunday Telegraph, The Financial Times, The Observer, The Independent*, etc. **Scottish quality newspapers:** *The Scotsman, The Herald*, etc. **American quality newspapers:** *The New York Times, International Herald Tribune, The Wall Street Journal, The Chicago Tribune, The Washington Post, USA Today, The Los Angeles Times*, etc.	• headlines on the front page are smaller in size and more informative and factual • proportionally more text than photos and in smaller print • more informative/credible coverage • articles are in-depth, present facts, dates/numbers/statistics; are more balanced • use of quotations from credible people • language is more objective/precise/elaborate/formal • information is based on serious research; analysis; hard news • objectivity through a variety of perspectives and credible sources • offer critical comments on issues	■ to publish a newspaper ■ accuracy ■ informative (-ness) ■ visual material ■ thought-provoking ■ ironic/satirical ■ column ■ to cover a subject/topic ■ editorial ■ to generate sth. ■ source of information ■ to be in/to hit the headlines ■ headline-grabbing ■ sophisticated ■ special feature ■ current affairs ■ to focus on sth.
British tabloids/popular newspapers: *The Sun, Daily Star, Daily Mirror, Daily Express, Daily Mail*, etc. **American tabloids/popular newspapers/'supermarket tabloids':** *Chicago Sun-Times, New York Post, World Weekly, Examiner, Newsday, Globe*, etc.	• use of banner headlines in bold type • more sensationalist and play on people's emotions • often one-sided and exaggerated reporting • no sharp line between fact and fiction, fact and opinion • use of subjective, often informal language to appeal to the readership's emotions • often lack of reliable sources of information • doubtful/dubious/debatable sources of information • focus on 'less serious' content, e. g. crime stories, celebrities, etc.	■ to skim a newspaper ■ entertaining ■ biased ■ prejudiced ■ gossip ■ attention-grabbing ■ to hound sb. ■ to invade sb.'s privacy ■ exaggeration/to exaggerate ■ superficial/superficiality ■ inaccuracy ■ (political) leanings
British magazines/periodicals: *Cosmopolitan, The Economist, New Scientist, New Statesman*, etc. **American magazines/periodicals:** *TIME, Esquire, Cosmopolitan, Forbes, Reader's Digest, Newsweek, People, O – The Oprah Magazine, Vanity Fair, The New Yorker, Harper's Magazine*, etc.	• periodical publications • published (bi-)weekly, monthly, etc. • printed in colour on glossy paper • financed by advertising • two broad categories: consumer magazines and business magazines • often contain cartoons/reviews • sometimes essays or preprints of books by famous journalists/authors	■ to incorporate ■ supplements ■ subscription/to subscribe ■ circulation ■ editor ■ publisher ■ compilation of a front page

Further important components and formats of newspapers and magazines

- **advice column/agony aunt**: a part of a newspaper or magazine in which a person (not necessarily an expert) gives advice to readers about their personal problems
- **human interest story**: a feature story that presents people and their problems in an emotional way that attracts interest and evokes sympathy in the reader; often criticized as 'soft', sensationalist or manipulative news
- **letter to the editor**: a letter sent to a publication about issues of concern to its readers; usually appears in the same specific place (e. g. at the beginning of a newspaper or magazine); comments on or is related to a current or previous edition; can be critical or praising
  → Focus on Skills, Writing a Letter to the Editor, p. 273
- **blogs:** informational or discussion websites, often in the format of diary-style entries (posts) and shared on social media websites; in authoritarian regimes, bloggers are often driving forces in exposing political scandals and challenging pro-government media

Understanding Complex Texts

A text can be complex for different reasons:

- A **historical document** or a **historical play** (e. g. Shakespeare) that contains words with a different spelling and meaning than in contemporary English (e. g. "thee", "thou" → Elizabethan English).
- A **legal text** which is written in formal English and contains many technical terms (e. g. The Declaration of Independence, the Civil Rights Act, the Bill of Rights, etc.).
- A **very long** text without obvious paragraphs or sections (e. g. the scene of a play, etc.).
- A **scientific text** written in formal English, employing technical terms/academic language.
- A **literary text** containing a lot of **implicit meaning** (e. g. figurative language, symbols, allusions, etc.), lapses in time (*Zeitsprünge*), multiple points of view, etc.
- A text **requiring a lot of life experience** from the reader (e. g. cultural, historical, literal background knowledge, etc.) and expecting the reader to 'read between the lines' to understand the underlying references.

Step 1: Before reading

- Read the title of the text and try to **anticipate what the text will be about**. Take notes and/or make a mind map of the topic, the plot or possible arguments the text might deal with.
- If the text is about a scientific or historical topic, you can **do some research in advance** in order to get a first overview of the matter.
- If the text is fictional, e. g. a play or novel, try to **get information on the respective topic** of the text and/or the author/playwright first.

Step 2: While reading

- Be prepared to **read the text at least twice**:
  - In a **first reading**, try to get a **general understanding** (w-questions).
  - In a **second reading**, focus on **details in connection with the assignments** you are given.
- **Annotate the text** and **use different colours** for different aspects (e. g. blue – contents/plot; red – characters/stylistic devices; orange – structure/line of thought; green – allusions, references; etc.).
- **Highlight** or **underline** relevant information, e. g.
  - names of people/places,
  - main ideas/arguments,
  - special vocabulary/technical terms,
  - unknown vocabulary,
  - statistical data/numbers,
  - references/allusions.

  Tip: Do not underline whole sentences but focus on essential keywords, arguments, etc.
- **Make notes in the margin.** For example:
  - Divide the text into paragraphs/thematic units.
  - Write a summarizing headline or sentence of each paragraph/thematic unit.
  - Write your own definitions or explanations of difficult terms.
  - Translate ideas into your own words (paraphrasing); use a dictionary if necessary.
  - Ask questions about aspects you do not understand or you are critical about.
  - Distinguish between information/facts given and personal remarks or evaluations made in the text.
  - Comment on ideas/arguments of the author or thoughts/dialogues of characters in a play/novel.
  - Identify the message of the text and the author's intention.

Tip: Make sure that you have **understood the assignments correctly** and focus on the aspects you are required to examine, to explain or to comment on or evaluate. (→ Standardized Terminology for Tasks, pp. 10 ff.)

Step 3: After reading

- **Sort and structure your notes** (e. g. by numbering them) and make sure that you do not distort (*verfälschen*) the information given in the text.
- **Use your pre-reading** research on the matter and cross-check the information given in the text. You can use it for your evaluation or analysis as well.

Writing a Summary

A **summary or an abstract** (*Zusammenfassung, Inhaltsangabe*) is common in all forms of writing and is aimed at **highlighting the major points** of a piece of writing and outlining the most important facts. Furthermore, it helps you to obtain a better **orientation and understanding of the structure and contents of a text** which you need for additional analysis and evaluation.

General aspects

A summary ...

- gives the **most relevant facts** and the overall meaning of a text,
- must not contain your own thoughts and opinions,
- begins with an **introductory sentence**,
- is about 150 – 200 words long, depending on the length of the text that is to be summed up,
- **must not contain direct speech or quotations**,
- should be **factual**,
- leaves out irrelevant details,
- should usually be written in the **present tense**,
- should present the events in **chronological order** (→ no suspense),
- closes with a sentence that **sums up the main message of the text and its intention**,
- prepares the analysis part of your composition – it must not analyse the text but **strictly focuses on depicting** *(wiedergeben)* **the text** in your own words.

Your composition

Before writing:

- **Underline** the most relevant aspects and facts given in the text.
- **Divide the text into paragraphs**/thematic units and **find a suitable headline** for each paragraph.
- Make sure that you understand everything – if necessary, **crosscheck the meaning of words** and **expressions** in your dictionary.
- Do not underline every detail but focus on the **most important information/striking keywords.**

→ Focus on Skills, Understanding Complex Texts, p. 230

While writing:

- **Use the present tense** for your text.
- Write an **introductory sentence** which answers the **w-questions** and informs about the **source** of the text: author, title of the text, type of text, topic, place and year of publication, information about whether the text is an excerpt or is abbreviated.
- Do not copy the words and expressions used in the text but **use your own words and/or try to find synonyms to paraphrase** the main aspects. Use your dictionary to find alternative formulations.
- **Do not quote** from the text and **do not use direct speech**.
- **Do not refer to any specific lines** in the text.
- **Use formulations** to state what the text/author writes about or wants to express.
  Example: *The author makes remarks on ...; The author/narrator expresses his/her concerns about ...*
- Be careful to not just follow the chronology of the text, but **restructure it and focus on key aspects/focal points** (*Schwerpunkte*).
- **Do not use short forms**.
- **Use standard English** for your summary even though the text you are to summarize may be written in informal English or in verse, etc.

After writing:

- **Proofread your text** and check for grammatical correctness, punctuation and spelling. Make sure that you have used the **present tense**.

Camera Operations

Camera perspectives/camera positions

over-the-shoulder shot: taken with the camera behind a person, looking over his or her shoulder; usually used in dialogue scenes

reverse-angle shot: shot opposite to that in the preceding scene, showing the dialogue partner

overhead shot (bird's eye view): makes an object less prominent or gives orientation

Camera movements

static shot: camera does not move; aims at evoking a calm, quiet, peaceful state

to pan left/right (*horizontal schwenken*): used for orientation or to follow a person

to tilt up/down (*vertikal schwenken*): used to indicate height or to follow a person/an object (e.g. leaf, water, snowflake, etc.)

to zoom in/away from sth./sb.: zooming in can focus on important details; zooming out can establish the context of the whole situation

tracking shot: camera is on a vehicle (= 'dolly') moving on the ground, following a moving character or object, or is moved freely (**hand-held camera or steady cam**); used to indicate the steady movement through the setting

crane shot: camera moves flexibly in all directions on a crane; camera might also pan or tilt

Field size/camera distance

long shot (*Totale*): people/objects shown from a distance; usually to introduce a new setting (see establishing shot)

full shot: shot of the whole body/ object and not much else; to emphasize action and the constellation of characters

medium shot: upper body/part of an object; usually to show one or two characters in action

close-up (*Nahaufnahme*): head, face and shoulders of a person are shown; focus is on the expression of the face *(Mimik)* e. g. to show emotions

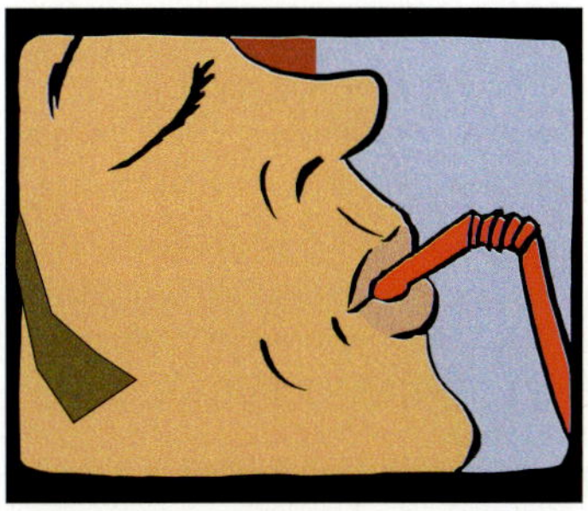

extreme close-up (*Detailaufnahme*): detailed shot of parts of the face/ the object; often used to create suspense

point-of-view shot: a shot seen through a character's eyes; e. g. an establishing shot at the start of a scene

Camera angle

high-angle shot (bird's eye view, shot from above): used to make people seem smaller, weak, helpless, humiliated, less important

low-angle shot (worm's eye view, shot from below): used to make people seem bigger, stronger, superior, self-confident, powerful, threatening

eye-level shot (straight-on angle): relatively neutral and restrained

Drama and Theatre

Drama

A **play** is written to be performed by **actors** in a theatre, in a film, on television or on the radio. Traditionally, a play is composed of **acts** (units that reflect the main stages in the development of the action), which are further subdivided into **scenes** (= sequences of continuous, uninterrupted action). Modern plays may just present a sequence of scenes. More reduced forms are **one-act plays**. One of the basic elements of drama is a **conflict between opposing characters (= protagonist/antagonist)**, or contrasting ideas, attitudes and interests. Conflict creates tension and **dramatic action**, which unfolds in **dialogues** and/or **monologues**. Good dialogues or monologues must capture the personalities, social positions, attitudes, thoughts and emotions of the characters. **Stage directions** given by the **author/playwright** help the director and the actors perform the play on stage. Such directions may be rather short and leave room for individual interpretation, while others are very detailed and indicate the precise design and arrangement of the **setting** (= time and place), **scenery, props** (= properties, i. e. furniture, decoration, etc.), the characters' appearances, movements, gestures, ways of speaking, or the **sound and lighting** to be used.

Drama is the generic[1] term for the genre. The most important subclasses are:

- the **traditional tragedy**, which develops dramatic action like this:

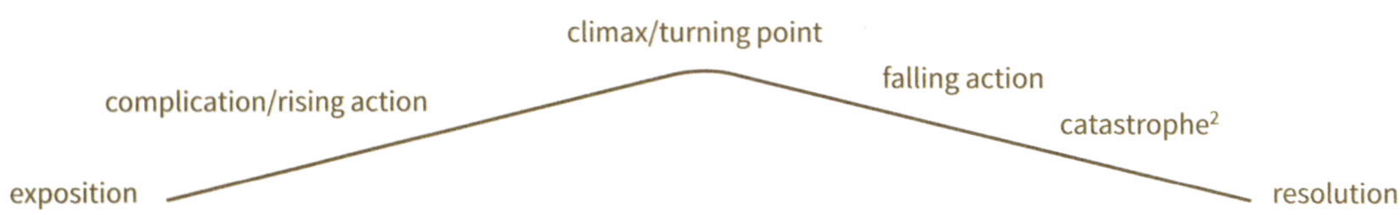

- the **traditional comedy**, which develops dramatic action like this:

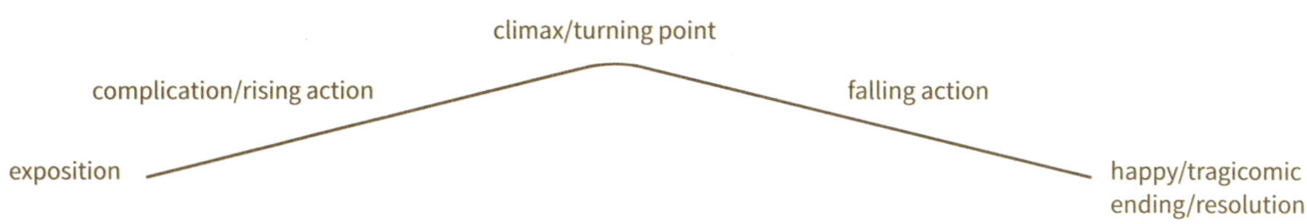

Theatre

Here are some of the important elements of a theatrical stage:

Note: Explanations of the respective technical terms can be found in the Literary Terms section, pp. 274 ff.

[1] **generic** shared by, including or typical of a whole group of things; not specific – [2] **catastophe** [kəˈtæstrəfi]

Analysis of a Fictional Text

The three basic types of fictional texts

a) Narrative texts (novel, short story, fable)
b) Dramatic texts (play, screenplay/script)
c) Poetry/lyrics (poem, song)

Step 1: Analysis of the general meaning

In a written examination, you are given clear assignments that follow the pattern comprehension – analysis – comment/(re-)creation of text. Accordingly, when you begin writing your analysis, you have already gained an overview of the given text and most likely written a summary or a similar type of text which focuses on the content and/or the structure of the text you are required to work with.
In your **analysis**, however, you are required to closely examine and explain not what is said but how certain stylistic devices help to support what the author/playwright/poet wants to express.

Do not repeat the introductory sentence (w-questions) you are required to write for the comprehension part of your paper/essay. Instead, begin your analysis with a sentence that picks up on relevant aspects of the comprehension part, leads on to the analysis and connects both parts. Additionally, you can formulate a hypothesis on the assumed message/intention of the text.

Tips on vocab

- As pointed out in the first part of my paper/essay, the author's intention is … therefore he/she employs …
- Against the background of the author's intention to … you can see that he/she uses certain stylistic devices to …
- Given the fact that … you can see that …
- The specific point of view taken by the narrator, is underlined/emphasized by …
- Continuing the writer's ideas of … there are several stylistic devices that reveal/show how …

Step 2: Analysis of basic elements

Usually, in a written examination, you are given specific aspects/keywords to help you focus on relevant stylistic devices. However, it is important and helpful to get a general overview of the stylistic elements in order to acquire a deeper understanding and connect certain aspects.

a) **Before** you start writing your analysis, read the given text again and highlight/underline the stylistic devices you are asked to analyse. Take notes in the margin on the meaning/function/effect of these devices.

b) **Identify the structural and narrative/stylistic devices** and show what **effect and function** they have. Use the **4-step method**:

1. **Identify** the device in the text.
2. Use the **correct technical term** for it. (Do not say 'word', but noun, adjective, verb, pronoun, metaphor, etc.)
3. Refer to the **precise line(s)** where you found the device (→ quote).
4. Take notes on the **possible meaning/effect/function** of the device; i.e. *how* the device supports the message of the text or the author's intention.

→ Focus on Skills, Writing an Analysis, p. 248

The following grid contains some terminology and tips on what to look for in the given text. More vocabulary and phrases can be found in:
→ Stylistic Devices, p. 284
→ Focus on Language, Vocabulary for Text Analysis, p. 249

narrator, narrative situation, point of view, mode of presentation	• first-person narrator • witness/observer narrator • third-person narrator • objective/reliable narrator • subjective/unreliable narrator • limited point of view • unlimited/omniscient point of view • panoramic presentation • scenic presentation • relation of acting time and narrating time
structure	• How is the text structured? • What time span does the narration cover? • What is the relation between acting time and narrating time ? • Which conflict is the story based on? • How does the action develop – or stagnate? • Are there any leitmotifs?
characters	• flat/round characters • protagonist vs. antagonist • minor character(s) • hero(ine) • anti-hero • outward appearance • behaviour • relationship to other characters • direct or indirect characterization
setting (= time and place)	scenery, mental climate, basic mood, social environment, atmosphere • Does the scenery/setting itself imply any symbolism? (e. g. thunderstorm = danger, large city = liveliness, anonymity, etc.) • What is the effect on the audience? • What intention might the author/playwright have had?
language/style	• level of speech • manner of speaking • style • syntax • choice of words • inner monologue • chain of associations • stream of consciousness • register

c) **Always remember to quote** from the text to demonstrate the accuracy of your paper/essay.
→ Focus on Skills, Analysis of a Non-Fictional Text, Section b, p. 238

Step 3: Concluding your analysis

An analysis has to be factual, therefore
- use the simple present as the predominant tense,
- avoid judgmental and evaluating formulations and adjectives,
- give your analysis a clear structure and avoid repetition.

Conclude your analysis by
- summarizing and highlighting your results in one to two sentences,
- connecting your analysis results and verifying your hypothesis.

Tips on vocab

- Taking the various results/aspects into consideration, one can say/conclude that …
- Concluding, it has to be said that …
- In conclusion, …
- The author's/writer's/playwright's/poet's intention is …
- … to convey a specific message
- to imply that …

Analysis of a Non-Fictional Text

Step 1: Analysis of structure and content

A non-fictional text usually aims at
- informing the reader about a certain topic/situation,
- persuading the reader to take action, to do something,
- conveying a certain message.

Accordingly, non-fictional texts usually
- **follow a clear structure** (e. g. introduction – main part – conclusion),
- provide the reader with **arguments** and/or **examples** which are presented in a specific **train-of-thought** or **line of argument**.

In your analysis, you are required to closely examine and explain how arguments, along with certain stylistic devices, are used to convey a specific message to the reader.
In preparation of your analysis,
- read the given text closely and clarify unknown words to make sure you have understood everything correctly,
- identify and specify the theme/topic/subject of the given text,
- identify the characteristics of the title (provocative, ironic, funny, etc.),
- divide the text into thematic units and relate these parts to the heading and the whole text,
- clarify the line of argument, the train of thought (the general structure of the text),
- determine the message of the text and the basic characteristics of the text (type).

→ Focus on Facts, Basic Types of Non-Fictional Texts, p. 227

Tips on vocab

- At the beginning, the author/writer formulates the (provocative) hypothesis …
- Right from the beginning, the author/writer aims at … /raises the question of …
- The author/writer implies that …
- After introducing …, the author/writer continues by … /focuses on …
- In order to illustrate his/her point of view, the author/writer refers to/alludes to …
- The author/writer uses techniques of persuasion to …

Step 2: Analysis of stylistic devices/use of language

a) While reading the text, **identify** and underline/highlight the **stylistic devices** and use the **4-step method** (p. 235) to take more specific notes on the function and effect of these devices.
The following grid offers you a choice of stylistic devices to give you ideas of what to look for in the text. More detailed explanations of these devices and further vocabulary for your analysis can be found in:

→ Stylistic Devices, p. 284
→ Focus on Language, Vocabulary for Text Analysis, p. 249

register (= ***Sprachebene***)	**choice of words**	**style**	**tone**	**rhetorical devices**
slang	denotations	plain	humorous	alliteration
colloquial	connotations	sober	playful	anaphora
everyday English	keywords	natural	colloquial	allusion
written language	figurative/literal meaning of words	matter-of-fact	conciliatory	reference
(in)formal	emphatic/negative function of words	clear	depressive	antithesis
poetic	euphemisms	precise	serious	ellipsis
sophisticated	synonyms	concise	solemn	hyperbole
familiar		vigorous	ironic	irony
technical terms		fluent	satirical	metaphor

register (= *Sprachebene*)	choice of words	style	tone	rhetorical devices
• scientific • religious • metaphorical	• abstractions	• passionate • elegant • artificial • stilted • wordy • colourless • cliché-ridden • snappy • lengthy • clumsy • spontaneous • trite • expressing doubt/certainty	• sarcastic • warm-hearted • aggressive • whining • reproachful	• paradox • personification • simile • symbol • understatement • exaggeration • parallelism • employment of leitmotifs • repetition • juxtaposition • (rhetorical) question • quotation • enumeration • appeal • comparison • digression from the main topic • grammatical tense • illustration • superlative • personal pronouns (we – they, I – you, our – their, them – us)

b) **Remember to include quotes** to demonstrate the accuracy of your paper/essay/analysis. Here are some examples of how to do it correctly:

- When **referring** to an important part of the text without quoting the words, give the page(s) and/or line(s): e.g. *The politician tells the audience about his plans for the future (ll. 12 – 16).*
- You can **integrate the quotation** into your sentence: e.g. *The environmentalists demand "the immediate abolition of plastics" (l. 59), which means that …*
- You can use a **full quotation**: e.g. *In the first part of the speech, the politician explains: "We must stop global warming". (ll. 12 f.)*
- Note the **abbreviations**:
  - one page or line: p. 17/l. 24
  - more pages or lines: pp. 12 – 16/ll. 23 – 30
  - the following page(s), line(s): f./ff. (e.g. pp. 15 f. or pp. 20 ff.)
- **Omissions** of any kind are indicated by square brackets and three dots: […]. Remarks or **changes from the original text** are indicated by square brackets: *He* [the politician] *demands …*

Step 3: Evaluation of the text

- Be careful not to give a *personal* comment/judgment about whether (or not) *you* like/dislike what is said in the text.
- Finish your analysis with some **concluding sentences** in which you
  - summarize and highlight your results,
  - state briefly whether/to what extent the text/author succeeds in addressing the reader(ship).
  - state briefly whether (or not) the text is well-structured/convincing/effective/appropriate.

Be careful to refer to specific lines/paragraphs and include quotations.

Analysis of a Film Scene

General tips on viewing and analysing a film

- Watch the film scene at least twice.
- Work systematically and concentrate on the devices employed in the scene in a certain order.
- Take notes while or immediately after each viewing of the film scene.
- Whenever you identify and specify a certain narrative technique and/or cinematic device used in a film scene, explain and illustrate its function and effect on the viewer.
- In order to explain the use and function of cinematic devices precisely and correctly, make use of technical terms.
  → Literary Terms Section, pp. 274 ff., and Focus on Facts, Camera Operations, pp. 232 f.
- When viewing and analysing a film scene, it is not possible to explain and demonstrate every single detail; therefore, you should focus on the most striking and relevant devices employed in the scene.

Step 1: Focus on narrative techniques

guiding elements	function
• **setting**: What is the time and place of the action? What is the atmosphere like?	→ orientation for the viewer → general exposition
• **plot:** What happens and why?	→ drawing the viewers into the action, evoking and raising interest
• **suspense**: Which questions are raised and remain unanswered?	→ evoking the viewers' curiosity and keeping them interested
• **appearance of characters**: What do(es) the character(s) look like?	→ evoking interest, sympathy, antipathy, etc.
• **body language**: What is/are the character(s)' movements, gestures, postures, facial expressions?	→ revealing character traits, quirks, etc.
• **language/communication**: What choice of words and tone do(es) the character(s) use? How do they interact?	→ exposition of the intellectual background, demonstration of the characters' relationship(s)

Step 2: Focus on cinematic devices

cinematic device	function
• **camera operations**: Which field sizes, camera angles, camera positions, camera movements, etc. are employed?	→ transferring narration into film/images/pictures
• **visual symbols**: Which visual symbols (e. g. cross, blood, tombstone, eagle) are employed?	→ visual leitmotifs serve as links and help to express/ to intensify a deeper contextual meaning
• **film music/sound**: What kind of music/what (background) sounds are employed?	→ to show/emphasize a mood, to create suspense, to foreshadow, etc.
• **(special) effects**: What further effects (e. g. slow motion, voice-over narration) are employed?	→ to intensify the action, to reveal thoughts, to suggest speed, etc.

Step 3: Explanation of the function of the scene (in the context of the film)

- Place the scene in the context of the film.
- Explain and give examples of how the scene
  a) moves the action forward and creates suspense,
  b) presents an unexpected turning-point in the action,
  c) reveals a new character trait of the protagonist,
  d) introduces (a) new character(s),
  e) defines (a) relationship(s) between characters.

Analysis of a Screenplay

"Whatta you mean 'minor script changes?' It's supposed to be a western."

A screenplay or film script is a written work for a film or TV programme. Basically, a film script depicts the **movement, actions, expressions and dialogues of characters** and gives **technical directions and instructions**, e. g. concerning the camera operations. The action is always written in the present tense. Here are further characteristic features of film scripts that you should consider in your analysis.

Format and style

- A screenplay **focuses on what is audible and visible** on screen.
- Screenplays have a **specific layout and codified**[1] **notations**[2] of technical or dramatic elements, e. g. scene transitions[3], changes in the narrative perspective, sound effects, emphasis on dramatically relevant objects, emphasis on characters speaking from outside a scene. These notations are always **written in capital letters**.
- **Different scene elements** are visualized by **tab settings**[4], e. g. dialogue, scene headings, transitions or parentheticals[5].
- The **beginning** of a scene is usually marked with "FADE IN:", the **ending** with "FADE TO BLACK."

Slug lines[6]

One of the **most relevant and unique features** of screenplays are slug lines; they are always written in **capital letters** and are usually divided into three parts.
Part 1 ... determines the **general setting** of a scene, e. g. inside (interior = INT.) or outside (exterior = EXT.).
Part 2 ... determines the **location** of the scene, e. g. SUSAN'S APARTMENT – KITCHEN, JIMMY'S CAR, etc.
Part 3 ... determines the **time** of the scene, e. g. DAY, NIGHT, DAWN, LATE NIGHT, etc.
If a character starts inside and then walks outside during a scene, a new slug line is needed which begins with CONTINUOUS[7].

Examples: • INT. ALICE'S HOME – BATHROOM – NIGHT • EXT. PARK – DAY/MORNING

Further characteristics:
- each slug line begins a new scene
- slug lines are numbered consecutively[8]
- any change of time or location requires a new slug line
- each slug line is in a line of its own, flush with the left margin[9] and are completely typed in capital letters.

Common abbreviations used in scripts

ELS	extreme long shot	**2-S or 3-S**	two-shot or three-shot	**VO**	voice-over
MLS	medium long shot	**INT**	interior	**OSV**	offscreen voice
LS	long shot	**EXT**	exterior	**DIS**	dissolve[10]
MS	medium shot	**BG**	background	**MIC**	microphone
MCU	medium close-up	**POV**	point of view shot	**VTR**	videotape
CU	close-up	**ZI or ZO**	zoom in or zoom out	**ANNCR**	announcer
ECU	extreme close-up	**SOT or SOF**	sound on tape or sound on film	**SUPER**	superimposition[11]
OS	over-the-shoulder shot	**SFX or F/X**	special effects (sound or visual)	**Q**	cue[12]

→ Focus on Facts, Screenplays and Storyboards, p. 228

[1] **to codify** *festschreiben* – [2] **notation** *Bezeichnung* – [3] **transition** *Übergang* – [4] **tab setting** *Tabellator* – [5] **parenthetical** *Einschub* – [6] **slug line** a line of abbreviated text; master scene heading – [7] **continuous** *andauernd* – [8] **consecutive** *fortlaufend* – [9] **flush with left margin** *linksbündig* – [10] **to dissolve** *sich auflösen, verschwinden* – [11] **superimposition** *Einblendung, Überlagerung* – [12] **cue** *Stichwort, Regiesignal*

Analysis of Poetry and Lyrics

Poetry (from the Greek "poiesis" = making, creating) is a type of literature in which **ideas, experiences and feelings are expressed** in compact, imaginative, and often musical language. Poets arrange words in ways designed to touch readers' senses, emotions and minds. Lyrics are a set of words that accompany music, either by speaking or singing. The word *lyric* derives from the Greek word "lyrikos" (meaning 'lyrical'). Most poems and lyrics are written in lines that may contain patterns of rhyme and rhythm to help convey their meaning. They often use **figures of speech and imagery to appeal to the readers' and listeners' emotions and imagination**. The poet or songwriter usually invents a speaker from whose point of view the feelings, ideas, experiences, etc. are expressed. Poems and songs may be divided into stanzas (groups of lines) or sections and can greatly vary in structure, theme and atmosphere.

general meaning/ content	• What situation/topic is presented? • What is the theme? Are there any (striking) leitmotifs? • What is the author's/singer's intention? What is the message of the poem/song? • What kind of register of English has been chosen (poetic, colloquial, archaic, slang, etc.)? • What is the melody like (harmonious, rhythmical, tuneful, staccato, etc.)?
formal analysis: a) structural devices	• Examine – the structure of the poem/song (stanzas, lines, (lack of) punctuation, refrain(s), break(s), enjambements, chorus, etc.), – the use of repetition and/or enumeration/parallelism, – the use of contrast(s)/antithesis, – the use of an illustration (= an example to make an idea clear), – the rhyme scheme (e. g. pair rhyme aa bb cc; cross rhyme abab; enclosed rhyme abba), – the use of free verse.
b) sense devices	– (How) are objects and ideas/thoughts brought together? – What type(s) of sentence(s) is/are used (hypotactical/paratactical sentences, questions, commands, etc.)? – Are there allusions/references to a certain topic (e. g. nature, city, love, etc.)? – Check on the use of simile (a direct comparison: "like, as"), metaphor (an implied comparison without a connective word: "an ocean of tears"), personification (something non-human is given human characteristics: "the frosty cliffs were asleep"), or symbol (an object that also stands for some abstract idea: a red rose → symbol of love, beauty). – the use of grammatical tenses, – the speaker's point of view, – the use of hyperbole/exaggeration.
c) sound devices	• Examine – the use of alliteration/anaphora, – the use of rhyme and/or assonance (= imperfect rhymes), – the use of a particular rhythm, beat, – the use of onomatopoeia (= words that imitate a sound: buzz, cuckoo, etc.), – the instrumentation, beat, vocal/instrumental type of music, vocals, etc. **→ Show how these devices support, stress/emphasize the meaning/content of the poem/song (→ function/effect).** **→ Show how style and content are connected.** **→ Show how sound and lyrics match and support each other.**
d) final comment and evaluation	Try to classify the given poem/song (refer to other poems/songs by the same author or authors of the same background). Evaluate the poem/song (Is the poem/song convincing? Has the author/singer succeeded in conveying his/her message? etc.). What do you consider to be the final message of the poem/song? What do you consider to be the effect on the reader/listener?

Note: Explanations of the respective technical terms can be found in the Literary Terms Section, pp. 274 ff.

Analysis of a Political Speech

General aspects of political rhetoric

The purpose of most political speeches is persuasion rather than information. There is always a (hidden, underlying) message involved, often related to certain attitudes and values of the speaker. A political statement intends to affect the listeners by making use of diverse structural and rhetorical devices. In order to understand and evaluate a political speech, you should consider the following aspects:

first (general) impression:	• topic, subject matter, general tone, issues and purpose of the speech
contents and structure:	• salient and striking topics, important aspects • organization of the text, arrangement of parts (e. g. introduction, main part or body, conclusion) • train of thought, composition, line of argument
circumstances of the speech/political context:	• time and place/medium (e. g. TV, radio, face-to-face, Internet) • position of the speaker (president, leader of a political party, leader of a protest movement, etc.) • audience (mass audience, a limited group of people) • occasion (election campaign, protest demonstration, political debate, informal gathering) • genre and type (presidential address to the nation, sermon, speech at a demonstration, campus speech, testimony)
formal and stylistic devices: **a) language**	• keywords and phrases • word groups/clusters related to a certain topic • different registers for different addressees (e. g. sophisticated language to address wealthy and/or educated people, use of dialect, etc.) • choice of words (colloquialisms, slang expressions, poetic expressions)
b) grammar	• sentence structure/syntax (use of main/sub-clauses) • use of grammatical tenses (indirect references to history, future, etc.)
c) rhetoric	• use of rhetorical questions • use of contrast and opposites (positive/negative, familiar/alien, near/distant, etc.) • use of key symbols, slogans, stereotypes • abstractions and generalizations • use of pronouns (I, us, we – you, they: patterns of identification and solidarity or the opposite) • metaphors, personifications • allusions and references to history (American Dream, important political/historical issues, good/bad times, tradition, future, etc.); quotations • repetitions (alliteration, anaphora); parallelisms • comparisons, numbers, factual information • irony, exaggerations, simplifications • imperatives, emotionally-loaded words • concentration on essential points vs. wordy elaboration • insertions
d) manner of speaking/voice	• volume, tempo, stress, intonation, abrupt changes, pauses, rhythm
evaluation:	→ Comment on the personal integrity of the speaker, the general political circumstances, the impact on the listeners. → Compare the speech/speaker to other political speeches/speakers. Was he/she convincing?

Note: Explanations of the respective technical terms can be found in the Literary Terms Section, pp. 274 ff.

See also: → Focus on Skills, Writing an Analysis, p. 248
→ Focus on Skills, Analysis of a Non-Fictional Text, p. 237

Analysis of Statistical Data

different types

population	2010	2020	2030
USA	309 m	331 m	350 m
China	1,3 bn	1,44 bn	1,46 bn
India	1,15 bn	1,38 bn	1,51 bn

A table gives raw data as the basis for analysis and consists of a grid with numbers arranged in lines and columns. Typically, it aims to present data in an ordered way, thus making the information easy to understand.

general aspects

- How reliable/trustworthy is the source?
- Are the numbers up-to-date?
- Consider why a chart/graph/table has been chosen as the means of visual representation.
- Are the figures absolute numbers or percentage figures – and what is the function of this presentation?
- What do the numbers/data suggest?
- Turn the percentage figures/data into words and compare them.
- Relate the data to the given context.

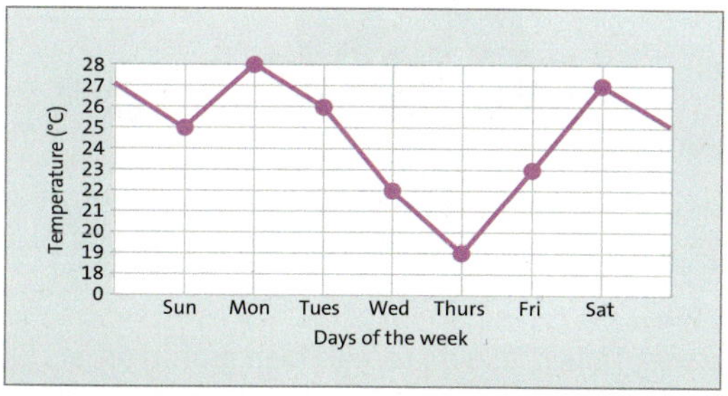

A (line) graph presents one or more lines in a system of coordinates/axes – a horizontal and a vertical axis. It shows the development of figures/variables over a period of time (trends, tendencies).

useful terms and phrases

■ to reach a peak/a low point/an all-time high/low of … ■ to remain constant/stable ■ to go through a period of growth ■ to increase/rise/grow/go up ■ to decrease/fall/drop/go down ■ a fall/decline/drop/decrease ■ an increase/a rise/growth ■ to grow … by 10 %/at a certain rate ■ a rise of 8 %/in temperature/to €25 ■ steep/strong/rapid … growth ■ a gradual/steady/continual … fall ■ a slight/barely noticeable … rise

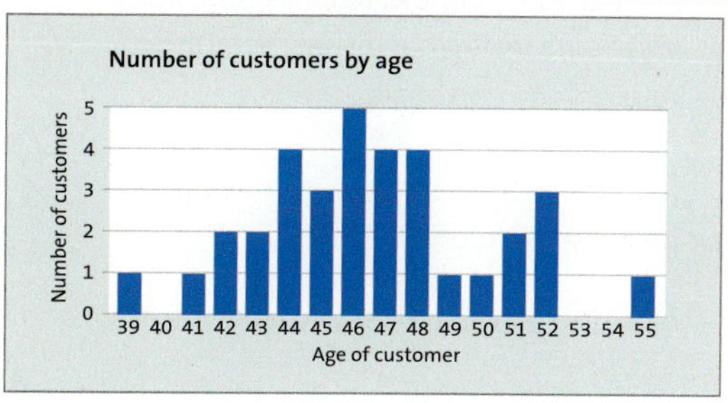

A bar chart shows differences between various things. It presents bars of different heights in a system of coordinates. The bars can be arranged horizontally or vertically.

useful terms and phrases

■ in comparison with/compared with ■ in contrast to ■ to achieve an average/below-average/above-average figure ■ to be at the top/bottom of the ranking ■ to rank first/second … last ■ the highest/lowest figure/score ■ no/little/a big difference between A and B (… with regards to … last year …) ■ the figures are identical/similar to … ■ the vast majority of/only a minority … ■ to experience a sudden rise/drop ■ after a brief recovery …

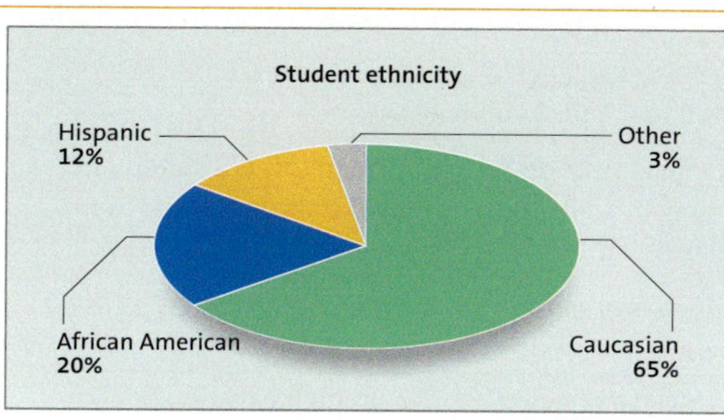

A pie chart shows percentages of a whole. It consists of a circle/pie divided into different sections/segments.

useful terms and phrases

■ the pie chart is divided into … ■ segments/sections ■ each segment represents … ■ the share of 5 % of the total amount is about 2 million euro … ■ the biggest/the smallest section ■ the whole circle represents/stands for … ■ the chart reveals the share of … ■ percentage-wise ■ a marginal percentage of … ■ an infinitely small amount of …

Analysis of Cartoons

A cartoon is a **comic or satirical drawing** in a newspaper, magazine, a blog or on the internet that aims at
- making people aware of certain problems or topics,
- humorously criticizing a current, historical, political or social event.

It usually consists of a drawing (**pictorial part**) and speech bubbles and a comment or a caption (= a short title) which is most frequently placed underneath (**textual part**). However, all the elements are not necessarily used in a single cartoon.

Step 1: Author and source

- What is the title or caption of the cartoon (if existing)?
- What artist drew the cartoon (if known)?
- Where did the cartoon appear (newspaper, magazine, internet, street art/graffiti, etc.) and when?

Tip: Find out about the political/social/historical background of the cartoonist and the medium where the cartoon appeared, for instance, a newspaper or magazine like *The Economist* or *New York Times*. Also do research on graffiti artists like *Banksy*, who places his graffiti in urban areas, on the walls of houses, on subway trains, etc.

Step 2: Descriptive level

- Describe the people, objects and the setting in the cartoon in detail. What action is taking place?
- **Tip: Structure your description**: What do you see e. g. in the foreground, centre, background, etc.?
- What visual elements are employed, e. g. colours or a black-white contrast, what visual metaphors?
- What (political, historical, social) events or issues may have inspired the cartoon?

Step 3: Symbolic/figurative level

Cartoonists (often) employ pictures and words to express their personal opinions.
- What tools are used to convey a certain message?
- What do the symbols used stand for?
- What person/group does the cartoon focus on?

irony	The recognition of the difference between reality and appearance. In **verbal irony**, there is a contrast between what is said and what is actually meant. **Situational irony** refers to a situation in which the opposite of what you expect to happen actually happens.
parody	In literature, a text that imitates and slightly changes another well-known text in order to ridicule it, comment on it or trivialize it.
caricature	A character whose traits have been exaggerated to create a comic effect.
sarcasm	A bitter or aggressive remark used to express mockery or disapproval; often this is a statement which conveys the opposite of its literal meaning. In contrast to irony, which is gentle and more subtle, sarcasm is bitter and usually openly expressed.
pun	An expression involving a play on words, in which one word has two different meanings, so that a sentence can be understood in two different ways.
allusion/reference	An allusion or reference to e. g. a well-known (historical) person or event, politics, popular culture, the arts or a statement from a famous work of literature.

stereotype/ labelling	A word or phrase that describes a person in a way that is too general and often not true (*jdn. abstempeln*); cf. cliché
hyperbole [haɪˈpɜːbəli]	A figure of speech that contains an exaggeration
symbol	An element of imagery in which a concrete object stands not only for itself but for some abstract idea or larger concept as well (e. g. rose → love)
visual/pictorial metaphor	The representation of a person, thing or idea by a visual image, e. g. Uncle Sam for the United States, an elephant for India, an orange for sunshine, etc.
black humour	Humorous effects resulting from grotesque, morbid or macabre situations. Black humour aims to shock and disorient readers, making them laugh in the face of anxiety, suffering or death.

Non-fictional texts usually

- **follow a certain structure** (e. g. introduction – main part – conclusion),
- provide the reader with **arguments** and/or **examples** which are presented in a specific **train-of-thought** or **line of argument(ation)**.

Tips on vocab

the cartoonist alludes to … ■ in the background/foreground of … ■ in the centre of … ■ contradiction between … ■ contradictory ■ discrepancy between … ■ eyecatching/eyecatcher ■ to establish a connection between … and … ■ to highlight … ■ to give the impression that … ■ the literal meaning of sth. ■ the symbolic meaning of sth. ■ to convey a message ■ to refer/allude to …

Step 4: Meaning and evaluation

- What is the message of the cartoon?
- To what extent do you think the cartoon is effective in conveying its message?
- How convincing is the pictorial presentation?

→ Focus on Language, Vocabulary for Text Analysis, p. 249

Analysis of Photos

To help you analyse visuals or images, here are some steps for you to follow:

Step 1: Production

- When and where was the image taken?
- Who created the image (e. g. a professional photographer, a private person, an advertising agency, etc.)?
- Was the picture arranged or was it a snapshot?
- Is the picture presented in the original version or has it e.g. been photoshopped?

Step 2: Image

- **Describe the visual elements of the image and how they are arranged.**
  - What is being shown? (e. g. surroundings, people, facial expressions, gestures, posture, clothing, accessories, etc.)
  - What are the main visual components and how are they arranged?
    Tip: In order to get a better overview of the various elements, their arrangement and relationship to each other, make a rough draft before you start to describe them.
  - Where is the viewer's eye drawn to in the picture – and why? (eye-catching/visually-dominant elements)
  - What use is made of colour?
- **Explain the function and effect of visual elements and symbols.**
  - What medium is the image taken from (e. g. film, advert, photo campaign, Internet, etc.)?
  - Is the image contradictory?
  - What visual symbols are employed and what is their function and effect?
  - State whether they imply a deeper, symbolic meaning.
  - Point out whether they appeal to the viewer/the target audience/the addressee(s).

Step 3: Addressing the audience

- **Identify and explain the message of the photo/picture.**
  - Who does the image address?
  - Is there a particular target group (e. g. a snapshot of a demonstration, etc.)?
  - What relationship is created between the image and the viewer?
  - Is more than one interpretation possible?
  - How might different viewers interpret the image and its message?
  - What emotions does the image appeal to?
  - Is there a strategy behind the image? If so, which one?
  - Are there any political/cultural/social implications?
  - Are there any historical/political/religious references?
- **State whether the visual/image/picture is effective and convincing in its message.**

visual elements:
- dancing children → motion/vitality
- a street scene → everyday life
- b/w photo → focus on contrast

visual metaphor: black and white child playing together → overcoming racism

surroundings: street in New York City

snapshot: a glimpse of reality

use of contrast: black and white

function: emotional appeal to the viewer and (indirect) political message

Helen Levitt. New York, 1940s

Characterization of a Figure in Literature

Fictional characters can be presented in a number of ways. In general, a character in a fictional text is developed through action, description, language and ways of speaking.

Types of characters

relevance within the text and characteristics	
• **protagonist** (the main character around whom most of the work revolves)	• **major characters** (main characters who dominate the story)
• **antagonist** (the person who the protagonist is against; often the villain)	• **minor characters** (less important persons who support the main character(s) by letting them interact or reveal their personalities, etc.)
• **the modern hero** (the average man/woman)	• **dynamic character** (changing and developing, with different traits)
• **the anti-hero** (often dishonest, graceless or inept person who struggles in life; the loser)	• **static characters** (unchanging, often stereotypical)
• **the tragic hero** (e.g. *Macbeth*; person who ends tragically as a result of character flaws)	• **round character** (three-dimensional, with different and changing facets to the personality)
• **romantic hero** (a character with a strong will and personality who goes against established norms; often this figure experiences melancholy, isolation and unfulfilled or unhappy love)	• **flat character** (one-dimensional, often stereotypical)
• **the Hemingway hero** (a character who has been at war, drinks too much, a loner, a 'cowboy')	

Types of characterization in literature

- In a **direct characterization of a character** the narrator or one of the other characters **tells** the readers/audience what the character's personality is like.
- In an **indirect characterization** the writer **shows/presents** the character talking and acting, which reveals the character's personality. Indirect characterization can be achieved through:
  a) **speech** (What does the character say, how does he/she communicate and interact with others?)
  b) **thoughts** (What is revealed through the person's private thoughts, e.g. in a monologue, soliloquy, diary entry, etc.?)
  c) **effect on others/on the character** (How does the person react/respond to others? Does he/she have any relationships? How do others react to the person?)
  d) **actions** (What does the person do, how does he/she behave?)
  e) **looks** (appearance, body language, gestures, facial expression, etc.)

How to write a literary characterization

Step 1: Collect the facts and clues given in the text and move from the outward features and characteristics to the inward nature of the character:

- **personal data** (name, age, sex, nationality)
- **attitudes/views** (thoughts, dreams, emotions)
- **relationships** (social background, family, friends)
- **outward appearance** (body, face, clothes, etc.)
- **behaviour** (toward other characters, actions)

Step 2: Draw your conclusions about the person's character and relate your findings to the text by referring to specific lines. Use the simple present for your characterization.

Step 3: Follow the 'introduction – main part – conclusion' pattern in your characterization. Write an introductory sentence that answers the w-questions.

Tip: Remember **to quote** from the text to prove the accuracy of your paper/essay/analysis.

→ Focus on Skills, Writing an Analysis, p. 248
→ Focus on Language, Vocabulary for Text Analysis, p. 249
→ Literary Terms, pp. 274 ff.

Writing an Analysis

Writing a text analysis usually follows a standardized pattern, regardless of what kind of text or material you are required to analyse, e.g. a fictional or non-fictional text, a political speech, an excerpt from a play or a cartoon.

General aspects

Before writing:

- **Read the assignment carefully** and make sure that you have understood what exactly you are required to do. Pay particular attention to the **standardized terminology** (*Operatoren*), which tell you what to focus on. (→ Standardized Terminology for Tasks, pp. 10 ff.)
- Pay attention to **additional keywords** given in the assignment, e.g. which (stylistic) aspects of the text or which features of a character you are expected to analyse in particular.
- Read the text as often as necessary to **understand it thoroughly**. Underline and/or highlight the parts that are significant and important with regard to the assignment. Note down your observations and make notes in the margin of the text. Use your dictionary to crosscheck that you have understood expressions and formulations in the text correctly.
- Find the **main issue or message** that the text addresses and the **writer's position** in this regard.

While writing:

- Check for **features/references to lines to support your findings**, e.g. arguments, line of argument, choice of words, facts and numbers given, quotes from further experts, etc.
- Prepare a **draft outline** (*Entwurf, Konzeption*) of the text you want to write. Do not write every single sentence line-by-line but take notes on:
  a) how you want to structure your composition, b) which textual references and quotes you want to use and c) what background knowledge you want to use and refer to.
- Pay attention to details: do not cover everything but focus on the most relevant/striking aspects.
- **Avoid wordy and generalized explanations** and repetitions and be **specific and precise**.
- Do not include your personal opinion or beliefs on the matter but be **factual and neutral**.

After writing:

- **Proofread** your analysis and crosscheck that you have not forgotten anything from your draft outline. Check for grammatical correctness, punctuation, spelling and that your composition is written in the **present tense**.

Your written analysis

Introduction

- Formulate a **connecting sentence at the beginning** in which you refer to a relevant aspect from your comprehension task. Briefly state that the writer for example uses a specific line of argument to underline his ideas.
  Example: *As I have pointed out in the first part of my composition, the writer XY aims at persuading the reader of his critical view of the USA. In order to emphasize his position he uses several persuasive techniques which will be explained in the following.*
- Give a **concise** (*kurzgefasst*) **outline of the structure** of the text, referring to the writer's train of thought and/or line of argument and the general message of the text.
- **Do not repeat** the introductory part from your first assignment (w-questions).

Main part

- Use the **three-step method** for your analysis:

Step 1: quote from the text	Step 2: use the correct technical term	Step 3: explain the function
"... some citizens, many people, the whole world ..." (ll. 10 f.)	→ climax, parallelism	→ emphasis on numbers and amounts involved

Vocabulary for Text Analysis

When you are asked to analyse and interpret a text, you should express yourself precisely and appropriately. Therefore, it is important to use a specific terminology that employs **technical terms** (e. g. stylistic devices) and a variety of formulations that make your text more fluent and less repetitive.

The following words and phrases are related to the most relevant aspects of an analysis.

introduction	author
• The text deals with/is about … • The theme of the text is … • The text is composed of/consists of … • Two/three … different parts can be distinguished … • The first part runs from line … to line … • At the beginning of the text, … • The author begins by saying … • At the end of the text,/Finally,/Lastly, … • The first part forms the introduction … • The main/central/principal idea is … • In the conclusion, the author states that … • In the final part, the author …	• The author thinks/says/believes that … • According to the author, …/In his/her view, … • The author illustrates his/her point of view with … • The author makes a comment on … • The author is convinced that … • The author's judgments are (un)realistic/not objective/ unfounded/well-founded … • The reader can sympathize with the author's view on … • The author expresses doubts/questions … • The author makes remarks on … • The intention/aim/objective of the author is … • The author portrays credible characters. • The author gives a detailed/vague description of …
text/plot/story	**characters**
• The story is told from the perspective of … • The plot is set in … • The text is written in an ironic tone. • The text contains comical elements. • The setting of the action is unreal/imaginary. • The action becomes more/less intense … • The situation seems quite absurd… • Suspense is created because/by … • The ending of the story is believable …	• The main/principal character in the story is … • The author characterizes him/her as … • He/She has many positive traits … • His/Her behaviour is marked by … • Another essential quality is … • He/She shows his/her superiority by saying that … • He/She is characterized as … • The protagonist lacks … • As far as his/her outward appearance is concerned, … • He/She plays an important/a secondary role …
structure	**action**
• The exposition gives information about … • The first scene introduces … • The starting point for the action is … • The conflict reaches its climax in … • The turning point is indicated by … • The crisis is in act … • In the last scene, … • This play/story has a happy/tragic ending.	• The action takes place in … • The action develops in … stages … • The action progresses fast … • The scene contains a flashback. • The action is interrupted by … • This is one of the central scenes … • The development of the action is slowed down by …
purpose (of texts)	**vocabulary**
• The author wants to arouse the reader's interest. • The text appeals to … • He/She tries to manipulate … • He/She wants the reader to become aware of … • The text addresses young/poor/… people … • It is the author's objective to create a feeling of … • The author attempts to influence the reader by … • The advert suggests to the reader that …	• The vocabulary contains many colloquial expressions/ technical terms … • This word/term expresses fear … • This word has a negative meaning/negative associations … • This phrase suggests … • These phrases are examples of spoken language. • The choice of words gives the text its romantic/ technical/… character. • These expressions are typical of …

criticizing the author	further useful expressions
• I (dis-)agree with the author on … • I do not understand why he/she … • I consider it to be wrong/difficult to … • This … cannot be taken seriously … • I would like to comment on … • It must be pointed out that … • This statement contradicts his/her view of … • There is a contradiction in … • It goes without saying that … • It is essential that … • This raises the question as to why he/she … • What really matters is … • This problem has nothing to do with … • This is of no importance/significance for … • As far as … is concerned, … • From this point of view, … • Generally speaking, … • As a matter of fact, … • In theory, …, but in reality, …	• To give an explanation for … • The author pretends to know … • The author describes the characteristics of … • The article is based on … • The author makes an allusion to … • This sentence reveals the true character of … • He/She appeals to emotions rather than … • He/She quotes some experts as an example of … • The article relates … to … • The text conveys the impression that … • The writer establishes a relationship between … • The author's theses are … • He/She supports his thesis with … • His/Her outlook on life is … • He/She takes a positive/negative view of … • The author generalizes about … • This is a great simplification of …

- When you analyse or interpret a text, you should use **Standard English**.
- You should generally use the **present tense** when you describe, explain or analyse specific aspects of the text.
- Be careful not to imitate the tone or the language of the text. When you write about a text written in colloquial English, you should still use Standard English in order to appear **impersonal and objective.**
- Try to **vary the beginnings of your sentences** by employing different connectives.
- Even when you express your personal opinion about a text/the author, etc., your choice of words should be appropriate and respectful. It can be helpful *not* to begin sentences with "I …" or "I think …" but to **focus on the text, the author**, etc. (*The article gives the impression that …, The author seems to intend to …*). This appears much more impersonal and academic.
- **Do not overdo it by being too formal** or stilted. Your text should reflect your view and stance on the matter.
- Be careful **not to use short forms** (don't, doesn't, there's, haven't, you're, etc.) in the tasks that are related to the **comprehension, analysis and comment/evaluation** of texts. They should only be used in creative writing tasks, e. g. in an informal conversation, diary entry, or interior monologue, when you are asked to express your thoughts in a more informal way. However, when you write e. g. a letter to the editor, you should use formal English.

Note: Explanations of the respective technical terms can be found in the Literary Terms Section, pp. 274 ff.

Connectives and Adverbs

In order to improve your style and speak and write more fluently, you should employ connectives and adverbs. **Try to vary the beginnings of your sentences** and use sub-clauses to express your opinion and thoughts in a more diversified way.

listing/order	**adding/reinforcing**[11]
first, second, third; firstly, secondly, thirdly; for one thing … (and) for another (thing); to begin with; to start with; initially/in the first place; then; finally; to conclude[1]; last but not least	also; as well; too; furthermore; moreover; then; in addition to; above all; what is more; again; equally; generally speaking
comparison/similarity[2]	**summary/conclusion/consequence**
equally; likewise; similarly; in the same way; compared to …; both; but while the first …; although; though	then; all in all; to sum up; in conclusion; accordingly; as a result; briefly; consequently; generally speaking; hence; it follows that; taking everything into account; thus; therefore
exemplification[3]	**reformulation**
namely; for example (e. g.); for instance; that is (i. e.); that is to say	or rather; to put it another way; in other words
alternative	**contrast**
alternatively; on the other hand	on the contrary; in contrast; by contrast; on the one hand … on the other (hand); compared to; although; likewise
concession[4]	**reason and purpose**
besides; however; nevertheless; still; though; in spite of that; on the other hand; despite this; admittedly[5]	as; because of; consequently; for this/that reason; hence; in order to; on account of; since; so; that explains why; this is why; therefore
emphasis[6]	**condition**
as a matter of fact; at any rate; clearly; evidently[7]; ideally; undoubtedly[8]	as long as; even if; if; in any case; on condition that; provided that; unless
your own opinion	**contrasting point of view**
from my point of view; in my opinion; in my view; the way I see it; to my mind; to my way of thinking	alternatively; but; despite/in spite of (the fact); except for; however; in contrast to; instead of; nonetheless; on the contrary
reference[9] **to sth./sb.**	**assumption**[12]
according to; as for; the former; the latter; with reference to; referring to; with regard to; concerning	assuming that; given that; presumably; probably; granted that; allegedly[13]; seemingly; on the face of it; supposedly[14]
toning down[10] **arguments**	**emphasizing arguments**
a little (worrying); almost; fairly; hardly; more or less; somewhat; on second thought; at first sight	actually; absolutely; (not) at all; badly (needed); completely; extremely; entirely; indeed; not in the least; perfectly; really; seriously; thoroughly; totally; utterly[15]; very

[1] **to conclude** to come to an end – [2] **similarity** the state of being like sth./sb. but not exactly the same – [3] **exemplification** illustration, giving an example – [4] **concession** *Zugeständnis* – [5] **admittedly** accepting that sth. is true – [6] **to put emphasis** *Betonung, Nachdruck* – [7] **evidently** clearly, obviously – [8] **undoubtedly** *zweifellos* – [9] **reference** sth. that you connect or relate to sth. else – [10] **to tone down sth.** to express an opinion in a less extreme or critical way – [11] **to reinforce sth.** to make a feeling/an idea stronger – [12] **assumption** *Annahme, Vermutung* – [13] **allegedly** *angeblich* – [14] **supposedly** *angeblich, vermutlich* – [15] **utterly** totally, very much

Concept Maps

Concept mapping is a **communication tool and visualizing technique** that uses visual symbols to express and **structure** ideas, concepts, thoughts, knowledge and the **relationships** between them. In a concept map, **each term is connected to another** and linked to the original idea, word or phrase. Concept maps can be simple or detailed, linear, branched, radiating or cross-linked.

A concept map is different from a mind map, which is created around a single word or text placed in the centre, to which associated ideas are added, e. g. with branches and sub-branches. A mind map is a good tool for brainstorming ideas quickly and spontaneously, whereas a concept map helps to organize and structure results or ideas.

Use of concept maps

- **note-taking and summarizing** concepts, their relationships and hierarchy
- **communicating** complex ideas and arguments
- **detailing the structure** of an idea, train of thought or line of argument
- **mapping, visualizing, structuring** and **presenting** group results/knowledge
- **comparing and connecting** ideas or concepts
- **revising** knowledge (repetition of a topic)
- as part of a placemat activity in order to **structure and compare results**

Examples

- **a linear concept map** (e. g. flow chart) depicts how one concept or idea leads to another

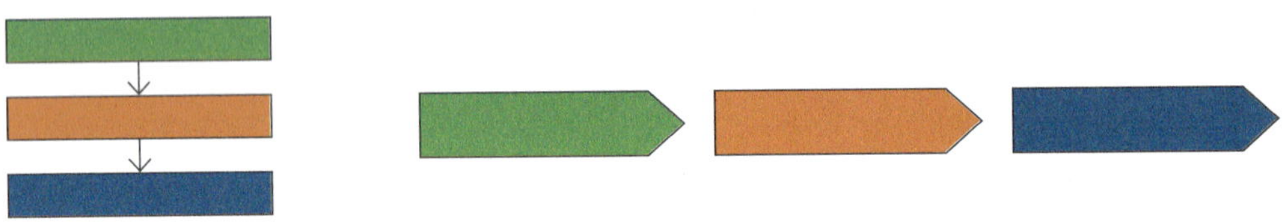

- **a hierarchical concept map** presents information in a descending/ranking order of importance

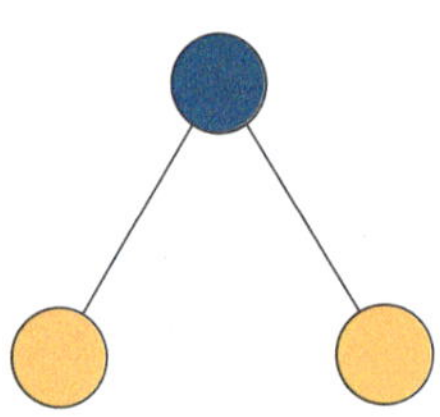

- **a spider concept map** has a central idea and outwardly radiating sub-ideas or topics

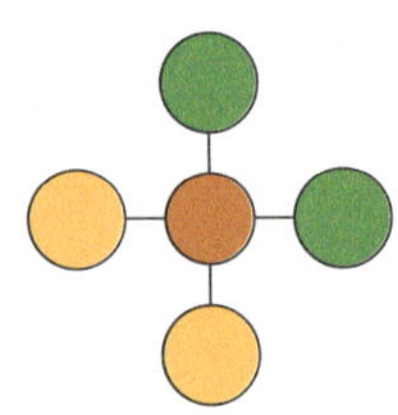

- **a cross-linked concept map** uses descriptive words or phrases and visualizes their relationship with a labelled arrow

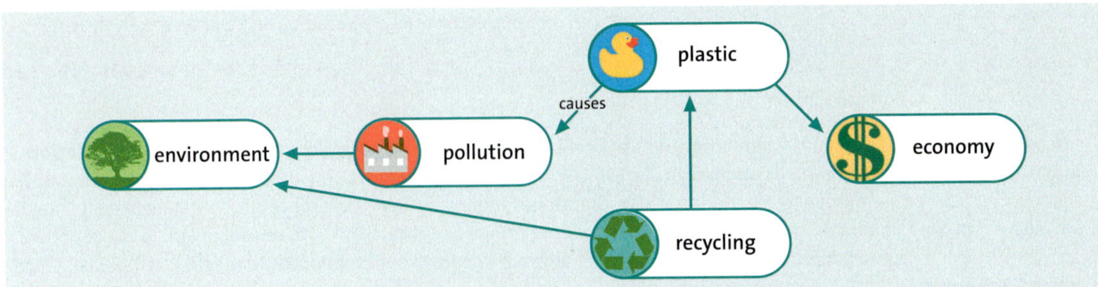

Mediation

Mediating a text means translating a written or recorded text from one language into another (e. g. German → English, English → German). In general, the person who is mediating must **consider the addressee(s), the meaning of the text/message, as well as cultural and situational aspects**.
When you are in a foreign country, you are constantly confronted with information and facts that you have to read or listen to: road signs, brochures, maps, (radio) announcements, advertisements, commercials, films, flight/train schedules, websites, letters, instructions, prescriptions, people talking to you, etc.
In a written examination you must consider the following aspects when asked to mediate a text:

How to mediate a text in a written examination

- **Select the most relevant information** from the text you are asked to mediate. Leave out less important details.
- **Focus** on the information **your communication partner** needs to know or what is important for the **topic**.
- Give an **analogous rendition** (*sinngemäße Wiedergabe*) of the text, not a literal translation.
- **Consider** the **addressee** (e. g. his/her cultural background).
- Take **situational aspects** into account (private, professional, etc.).
- Give **additional information** and explanations if necessary (on geography, culture, politics, etc.).
- **Consider** the **type of text you are required to write** (*Zieltextformat*) (a blog, a formal/informal letter, etc.).
- **Use compensation strategies** (paraphrasing, synonyms, etc.).

Criteria for evaluation

- Has the **purpose and intention** of the text been conveyed?
- Has the **addressee** been considered appropriately?
- Have the **assignments and standardized formulations** (*Operatoren*) been taken into consideration?
- Have the **characteristics of the type of text** (*Zieltextformat*) been considered?
- Is the text **formulated in your own words**?
- Do the **style and choice of words** match the intention of the text?
- Does the **construction of sentences** vary (e. g. use of linking words and connectives)?
- Is the text **grammatically correct** (grammar, spelling, punctuation, word order)?

10 tips to help mediate a written or recorded text

1. Do not translate the text word for word.
2. Listen to/watch out for keywords and the most relevant/useful/appropriate information.
3. Leave out minor details and irrelevant information (→ summarizing).
4. Try to understand the gist of the text and put it into your own words (but do not change the facts!).
5. Sometimes there are words that cannot be translated into German/English because they imply cultural differences (e. g. homecoming, gap year, cheerleading or *Schützenfest*, *Abigag*, etc.). In such cases, give examples to illustrate the situation, or add information on the cultural background if necessary.
6. Do not interpret or evaluate the text, just mediate it.
7. Express difficult passages more simply; technical terms should be replaced by everyday language.
8. Make use of paraphrases (e. g. a cheerleader is a girl who …).
9. If you do not know a word, use a synonym (= word or expression that has the same or nearly the same meaning as another in the same language).
10. If you cannot think of the right word, try simply using the opposite with 'not' (generous – not mean).

→ Proverbs can reveal a great deal of cultural background. Try to find the equivalent proverb rather than trying to translate literally (e. g. *vom Regen in die Traufe* → out of the frying pan and into the fire).

→ Beware of false friends, i. e. English words that sound or look like German ones but **differ** in meaning (e. g. become, actual, sensible, etc.).

Conversation and Discussion

opening a conversation	expressing your opinion/giving an opinion
You should always start a discussion with some kind of introductory phrase: • I saw an interesting programme on TV last night …/ I read a fascinating article in the newspaper yesterday about …/What do you think about …? • Have you ever thought about …/What would it be like if …? • I was really surprised to find out that … • Did you know that …? • Do you mind if I join you? • Excuse me, … • (I'm) sorry (to trouble you), but … • Have you got time to …?	• In my view, … • In my opinion, … • As I see it, … • To my mind, … • If you ask me, … • I am sure/certain that … • I think/believe/feel that … • It seems to me that … • There should be …/ought to be … • I would like to …/I wouldn't like to … • It would be a good idea to … (because …)
making suggestions/recommendations	**including your conversation partner**
• If I were you, I would … • The best thing would be to … • You'd better … • Why don't you …? • How about …? • Have you tried/thought of … (+ gerund)? • You should/could …	*Sometimes in a discussion, you may find that you are monopolizing the conversation, and you would like to know what your partner thinks:* • So what do you think, … (+ name)? • How do you feel about that? • What is your view on this (matter)? • What is your opinion about/of/on …?
interrupting your conversation partner	**changing the subject**
Sometimes it is the other way round. Your partner is monopolizing the discussion and you want to have your say: • Can I jump in here? • Can I just make a point? • Perhaps I can interrupt you there. • I'd like to get in on that, if I may. • Do you mind if I say something on that point? • Wait a minute … • (I'm) sorry to interrupt, but … • Sorry, may I interrupt you for a second … • Sorry, but did you say …? • Can I just say/add that … • Yes/You're right/I agree, but … • I hope you don't mind, but …	*These expressions help you to bring in further aspects:* • (Oh) by the way, … • Before I forget,… • I just thought of something … • There's something else I wanted to ask you/say … • Oh, now I know what I wanted to say/ask you … • I know this has got nothing to do with what we are talking about, but … • Could I just say … (before I forget …) • Let's also consider … • While I think of it, …
holding the floor	**returning to the original subject**
Sometimes you notice that someone is trying to interrupt you, but you have not finished what you want to say, so you try to carry on: • If I might just say this. • Do you mind if I just finish what I was saying? • I'd just like to finish making this point and then it's over to you. • Let me just add one more thing. • This is my final point. • Would you please let me finish (this sentence/thought)?	*Sometimes people stray from the main issue of a debate and it is necessary to get back to the topic:* • As I was saying, … • (Now) what was I saying/what were we talking about? • To get back to what we were talking about, … • Let's get back to … • (Yes, well) anyway, … • Let's get back to the point … • But we are digressing … • Where were we before we got onto this topic?

defending yourself	expressing surprise
If someone attacks you in a discussion, you can say: • That's not what I said/meant at all. I was merely pointing out that … • You've got that all wrong. What I said was … • You're putting words in my mouth. • You are distorting what I actually said.	• I don't believe it/that! • That's strange/funny … • Are you (being) serious? • Are you pulling my leg? • Really? • You can't mean that seriously!/You can't be serious! • I doubt it/that/whether … • Are you kidding me?
ending a discussion/a conversation	**using fillers**
When you feel that you have effectively finished your discussion, that the conversation is not getting anywhere or that you have exhausted the topic, you can finish off: • We'll just have to agree to disagree on that point. • Further discussion is pointless, so let's end there. • We've heard some interesting points/some new ideas, so let's stop there and go away and think about them. • I can understand you better now, even though I don't completely agree with you. • Well, anyway … • Would you excuse me now, please? • Sorry, but I've got to go now. • I'd love to stay and discuss this further, but … • It's been a very interesting discussion. However … • Perhaps we can continue this another time. • Look after yourself. • Take care.	• Well, … • Actually, … • You know/see … • Let's see … • I/you mean … • Now let me think/see … • In fact, … • I wonder … • The thing is … • I see what you mean. • Right then. • Let's say …
expressing complete agreement	**expressing partial agreement**
• You're absolutely right. • I completely agree with you on that point. • Precisely/Exactly. • So do I./Me too. (agreement with a positive statement) • Nor do I./Me neither. (agreement with a negative statement) • That's what I think, too.	• You're right up to a point. • That might be the case/true. • You could be right. • You've got a point. • Maybe that's true. • That's true enough.
partial disagreement	**complete disagreement**
• Do you really think so? • Are you sure? • That's an exaggeration. • That's not necessarily the case/true. • It's not as simple as that. • I wouldn't quite say that. • I can't imagine that. • I find that hard to believe.	*Careful with this one! You do not want to make enemies, do you? Try not to be abrupt or too direct:* • That is definitely not the case. • I'm 100 % certain of that. (disagreement with a previous negative statement) • That's not true at all. • You're quite wrong there. • I totally disagree with you.

Job Interview

"Well, I guess a master's degree is a master's degree, even if it *is* in skateboarding."

How to prepare yourself for an interview

- **Research** the company where you will have the interview, e. g.
  - the company's history and background (founder, etc.),
  - make sure to use the company's correct name,
  - the company's range of products and/or services.
- **Think of possible questions** you might be asked and **prepare suitable answers**.
- **Rehearse a job interview** with a friend and have them ask you questions (some that you have prepared *and* some surprise questions).
- **Evaluate** the 'mock interview' with your friend:
  - Which answers turned out well and which ones need to be improved?
  - What impression did your friend have of you (body language, nervousness, friendliness, etc.)?
- Think of **questions that you want to ask** the interviewer. Your questions should reveal that you already know something about the company and its management and structure (cf. Tips on vocab below).
- **Dress** nicely, neatly and **appropriately**.
- In case you are to have an **online** job interview, make sure that your digital devices and especially your microphone are working properly and check that your camera is in the right position (→ eye-level). Depending on where you are when you have the interview, you might want to blur or change the background image.
- **Arrive early** so that you have time to collect your thoughts and appear calm and relaxed.

Tips on vocab

the company's corporate culture/identity ■ challenges/innovations for the future ■ plans for future expansion ■ approach taken towards managing employees ■ management philosophy

What to do during the interview

- **Smile and maintain eye contact** with your interviewer. **Be positive** and try to convey that you are enthusiastic and energetic.
- If the interviewer tries to lighten the interview with some **small talk, be prepared to chat** with him/her.
- **Speak clearly and slowly.** Do not rush through your answers, and give yourself time to think before you answer. You do not want to convey the impression of being thoughtless or superficial.
- Do not hesitate **to ask the interviewer to repeat** or explain his/her question.
- Think about how to present yourself in an individual and unique way, and emphasize your personal strengths and particular qualities and qualifications. Do not simply tell the interviewer what he/she wants to hear or play up to somebody (*jdm. nach dem Mund reden*) but make your personal statements and standpoints clear.
- **Do not simply answer questions with "yes", "no" or "I don't know".** The interview is your chance to express your thoughts and convince the interviewer that you are the best choice for the job.
- But: be careful not to talk too much – **keep your answers clear and concise**.
- If there is still time (or the interviewer asks you to do so) **you can ask the questions** that you prepared.
- **Thank your interviewer** at the end.

Tips on vocab

I didn't have any difficulty finding you. The map your secretary sent me was very helpful. ■ As you can see from my CV … ■ … perhaps you would like me to tell you something about my experience in … ■ Is there anything specific you would like to know about me? ■ Could you tell me more about …? ■ Thank you very much for seeing me. ■ Thank you for your time.

After the interview

- After a short time (approx. 2 weeks), **send a follow-up mail/letter** thanking your interviewer.
- **Express your interest** in the company again.
- Ask politely **when you can expect a reply**/a decision.

Tips on vocab

What happens next? ■ When can I expect to hear from you? ■ When will a decision be made? ■ When are you likely to make a decision? ■ I had an interview for the position of a … two weeks ago and would like to enquire whether a decision has been taken yet.

Oral Examination

Oral exams are a lot like job interviews, so you can prepare for these in the same way that job applicants prepare – predict likely questions and practice the answers. In general, an oral exam is an opportunity for you to **demonstrate your knowledge, your presentation and speaking skills as well as your ability to communicate**. Examinations can be formal or informal, but in either case you must listen carefully to the questions and answer them directly.
The **formal exam** usually consists of a set of prepared questions, and the evaluation criteria usually follow a right/wrong format. In contrast, **informal exam questions** are more open, answers are usually longer and evaluated based on problem-solving, analysis, method as well as communication and presentation skills.

Preparing for the exam

- **Collect all the material** that is likely to be covered in the exam and **try to predict essay-type questions**, i. e. questions that require a more complex answer and include a wider range of aspects. If you work with a textbook, you can use the table of contents to find possible topics.
- **Write down possible questions** on an index card. Then practice answering each possible question out loud.
- Make **a list of vocabulary terms and phrases** in connection with the possible questions.
- Then select three index cards at random (*stichprobenartig*). Pretend to be the examiner and ask a question that **connects the three aspects together**. This will help you to make connections between the different topics.
- If you are a **visual learner**, you may want to draw images to boost your memory.
- **Turn off electronic equipment.**

During the exam

- Some oral exams begin with a presentation by the student. For an introduction, **give some indication of what the topic or problem is about** and why it is important.
- Give the examiner **your full attention** and look interested. Maintain **good posture** and **eye contact**.
- **Listen carefully** to the questions and make sure that you **understand exactly** what is being asked. If a short answer is requested, keep it short. If more detail is desired, give a longer response.
- Give yourself a moment to **think before you answer**. If you do not know the answer right away, feel free to take time to think. If you are able to use a blank sheet of paper and a pencil, take notes and/or draw the images you created as memory boosters.
- If you do not understand the question, **ask the examiner to reformulate, rephrase or repeat** it.
- If you cannot answer a question, **state directly that you do not know the answer** and go on.
- **Do not simply answer with "yes" or "no"**; demonstrate your knowledge by explaining aspects and backing up your answers with two or three key points or examples.
- If you are asked to describe, analyse and discuss a picture or cartoon, use the **present tense** or **present progressive** for your description. Describe the picture/cartoon **systematically** (e. g. from the foreground to the background, from right to left, etc.).
- If you need a moment to decide what to say, you can stall with formulations like "If I remember correctly", "That reminds me of …" or "If that is the case …", etc.
- If you are being evaluated together with a partner or in a group, **remember to interact with your partner(s)** and respond to his/her/their remarks. (→ Focus on Language, Conversation and Discussion, p. 254)

Follow-up

- Reflect on your performance (e. g. where you did well or poorly).
- Note how you could do better next time.
- Speak with the examiner if you have questions on the material and/or your performance. Ask if there is anything that you should have answered that would have improved your performance.

Telephoning and Videoconferencing

Telephone conversations, especially business conversations, usually follow a certain pattern and are often made to request information or to ask for clarification.

Common pattern of business telephone conversations

- Someone answers the phone and asks if she/he can help.
- The caller makes a request – either to be connected to someone or for information.
- The caller is connected, given information or told that the requested person is not in the office at the moment.
- If the person is not in the office, the caller is asked to leave a message.
- The caller leaves a message or asks other questions.
- The phone call ends.

"Call the tech. Our new video-conferencing equipment needs adjustment."

Tips to slow down native speakers on the phone

Usually, one of the biggest problems is that native speakers, especially businesspeople, tend to speak very quickly on the phone. However, it is important that both sides understand each other. Therefore, you should try to slow the speaker down:

- Immediately ask the speaker **to speak slowly**.
- When taking note of a name, date or other important information, **repeat** each piece of **information** as the person speaks.
- **Do *not* say you have understood if you have not.**
- Ask the person to repeat what they have said until you have understood.
- If all else fails and the person does not slow down, **begin speaking in your own language to signal that there is a lack of communication.**
  Usually, the person will understand that communicating in a different language, especially on the phone, is difficult. However, be careful not to offend the speaker and **be polite and friendly**.

Videoconferencing

Videoconferencing has become an indispensable tool of modern communication and allows people to communicate with each other through dynamic face-to-face interactions. According to psychologists, 55 % of communication is body language, 38 % the tone of your voice and 7 % is the actual words spoken that convey meaning. Therefore, it is important to follow certain rules to communicate successfully in video conferences.

Video etiquette

- Be on time.
- Make sure you have a good internet connection.
- Test some time in advance that everything is working properly and you are connected to your interlocutor (*Gesprächspartner*).
- Sit up straight.
- Smile and greet those participating at the beginning.
- Be careful not to overdo gestures in front of the camera.
- Avoid touching your face, tugging at your earlobes or chewing your lower lip – you might appear insecure on camera.
- Nod your head periodically to show the viewers that you hear them properly and are listening.
- Follow the schedule in order to demonstrate efficiency.

- Avoid distraction when you are videoconferencing. Do not check your emails, go onto a social network or check news.
- Remember that this is a professional meeting, so dress and behave accordingly.
- Do not forget to summarize what you have discussed.

Tip: Watch Amy Cuddy's TedTalk on how "Your body language may shape who you are". https://www.ted.com/talks/amy_cuddy_your_body_language_may_shape_who_you_are, June 2012 [20.02.2021]

Here is some useful vocabulary when participating in a video conference.

Tips on vocab

Welcome! Hello everyone! ■ Today, I'm going to talk to you about … ■ I'd like to address the topic of … ■ I'd like to give a brief breakdown of … ■ I'd like to give you some background information on … ■ A good example of this is … ■ Let me elaborate further on … ■ This ties in with … ■ Based on your findings, … ■ I'd like to illustrate this point by showing you … ■ Let's summarize briefly what we have looked at. ■ I'd like to recap the main points. ■ I want to mention the following issues. ■ This leads me to my next point.

Important phrases for telephone calls and voicemails

Tips on vocab – Telephone call

Introducing yourself
- *Hello, this is Susan/my name is Susan …*

Asking who is on the phone
- *Excuse me, who is this?*
- *Can I ask who is calling, please?*

Asking for your communication partner
- *Could I speak to …?*
- *Can I/May I speak to …? (more formal)*
- *Is Susan in? (informal idiom)*
- *Can I have extension 255?*

Connecting someone
- *I'll put you through (= connect you).*
- *Can you hold the line?*
- *Can you hold on a moment?*

How to reply when someone is not available
- *I'm afraid … is not available at the moment.*
- *The line is busy. (the extension is being used)*
- *Mr Johnson isn't in …*
- *Mr Johnson is out at the moment.*

Taking a message
- *Could/Can/May I take a message?*
- *Could/Can/May I tell him/her who is calling?*
- *Would you like to leave a message?*

Tips on vocab – Leaving a message/voicemail

Introduction
- *Hello, this is Susan.*
- *Hello, my name is Susan Smith. (more formal)*

Stating the time of day/the reason for calling
- *It's eight in the morning. I'm calling/phoning to*
- *find out if …/to ask whether …/to see if …/to let*
- *you know that …/to tell you that …*

Making a request
- *Could you call/phone/ring me back?*
- *Would you mind calling me back?*
- *Could you tell … to call me back?*

Leaving your telephone number
- *My number is …*
- *You can reach me at …*
- *Call me at …*

Finishing the call
- *Thanks a lot, bye.*
- *I'll talk to you later, bye.*

Giving a Speech

Why giving a speech is good for you

- You learn to **speak effectively** in **different situations** and to audiences of **different backgrounds** and **levels of knowledge** and improve your **general speaking abilities**.
- The ability to speak well enough to **interest, influence or persuade people** is a major asset for your future life.
- You **gain self-confidence** by learning to overcome and manage nervousness and excitement.
- You learn **different techniques** of **using and varying your voice** and tone of speaking.
- You learn to control your **body language** and to **choose the right words** in the respective situation.
- You learn to **listen to people** in order to speak more effectively to them.

Non-verbal communication

The **major tools** you will use as you speak are **your voice and your body language**. Here are some aspects that will help you to check yourself and be better prepared for a speech:

Voice:

- Is my voice (too) loud or (too) soft?
- Do I speak (too) slowly or (too) quickly?
- Is my voice monotonous?
- Do I articulate clearly or do I mutter?
- Will my accent be a problem for my audience?
- Do I forget to breath or do I gasp when I speak?

→ Try to **speak naturally and clearly**, and check (ask your audience) whether you can be heard.
→ **Do not shout**, because this is hard on the voice and uncomfortable for the listener.
→ Go in advance to the **room** in which you will be speaking and **familiarize yourself with its layout**.
→ Try to **vary your speech** by raising and lowering your voice, stressing and emphasizing keywords.
→ **Mark your script or notes** using a highlighter on the points you want to stress.
→ **Make pauses in your talk** and give the audience and yourself time to think and reflect (e. g. use visual aids and ask if there are any questions).

Body language:

- Do I rush into the room or walk in confidently and determined (*entschlossen, bestimmt*)?
- Do I look down, hunch my shoulders and shuffle my feet (lacking confidence)?
- Do I look at the audience and smile at them before starting to speak (eye contact)?
- Do I look comfortable and businesslike?
- Do I look (too) casual or nervous?
- Do I use my hands and arms to indicate or reinforce a detail of my speech?

→ **Smile at the audience** to make them feel welcome and to **establish a good relationship**.
→ **Tell yourself that it will be a good, friendly and supportive audience** to calm yourself down.
→ **Show a cheerful**, enthusiastic **and positive state of mind**.
→ **Make eye contact** with the audience; this gives the audience the impression that you are trustworthy and honest.
→ **Put your script at the right distance** for **reading and look** up at the audience occasionally.
→ Do **not fold your arms in front of you** or put your hands in your pockets.
→ **Open your hands to show an outgoing and friendly nature** – a clenched fist indicates aggression.
→ Do not move backwards and forwards all the time while talking – you will make the audience nervous and distract them.
→ **At the end** of your speech, **leave the audience with a smile** and do not flop back in your chair with a look of exhaustion or irritation. Do not forget: The last impression will stay in the audience's mind!

For further information: → Focus on Skills, Presentation, p. 261

Presentation

"...and in conclusion: all you need is Love!"

Five good reasons for giving a presentation

- Presentations get a discussion going.
- Presentations offer a variety of perspectives.
- Presentations provide good practice for oral examinations.
- Presentations are a good opportunity for students who can present themselves better verbally than in writing.
- The ability to give presentations is a skill required in many occupations.

Preparing a presentation

- Have a clear focus – decide on the **key messages/information** that you want to get across.
- Be selective – identify the most relevant points.
- **Avoid overloading the audience** with everything that you know.
- Make use of the **postcard technique**:
  a) Divide up your presentation into sections.
  b) Give each section a heading.
  c) Write one heading and a few easy-to-read prompt words on each postcard.
  d) Number the postcards in the order that you want to present these points.
  → These postcards will structure your talk and give you confidence.
- **Prepare audio-visual aids**, e. g. transparencies/an overhead projector, a PowerPoint presentation, a CD and CD player, a large poster, etc. Do not overdo it, however, your talk should take centre stage and not your technical equipment.
- **Do not simply read out** what is on your transparencies or posters, etc.; paraphrase and explain them.
- **Practise your presentation** several times, going slowly and timing yourself. If your presentation is too long, shorten it. Talk slightly more slowly than in normal speech. Use a clock to time yourself.
- Provide a handout for each person.
- Use audience response systems like Slido or eduVote, which is an interactive tool for voting or asking live questions. Alternatively, the visual storytelling and presentation software Prezi enables users to pan between topics, zoom in on details and pull back to reveal context during a presentation.

Giving a presentation

- Greet the audience, introduce yourself and smile at them. This creates a friendly and more relaxed atmosphere.
- Wait until everybody is quiet before you start speaking.
- Tell your audience whether you would prefer questions during the presentation or at the end.
- **Speak more slowly and loudly than usual.**
- Look up and **make eye contact** with at least two people in your audience.
- Do not apologize for anything you have not done or you feel could be better. Act as though you are confident and well-prepared. This way you will win your audience's attention and confidence.
- At the beginning, briefly outline your topic by summing up what you are going to say and in which order.
- Go through your cards. Pause and take a breath after each point.
- If you use difficult words or technical terms, write them on the board or on a flipchart and explain them to your audience.
- At the end, briefly sum up what you have said.
- End your presentation with a pithy (= *prägnant*) last line.
- Thank the audience for paying attention and ask them if there are any questions they want to ask.

→ Focus on Skills, Giving a Speech, p. 260

Doing Research and Citing Sources

Before you start your research, you should check these aspects:

1. Read the assignment carefully – make sure that you understand what *exactly* your research task is.
2. Start a file in which you collect all your findings and research results.
3. Formulate research questions and aims.
4. Collect keywords and topics that can be used for your research.

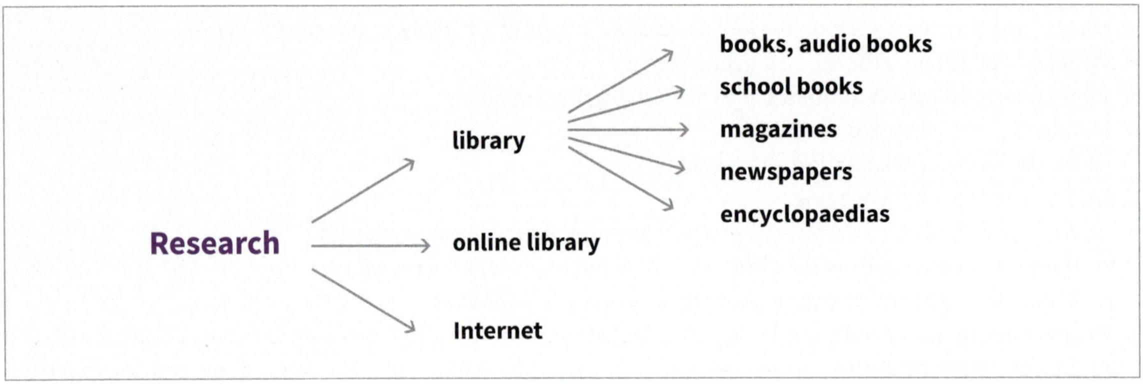

Indicators to check the quality/validity/reliability of the websites used

- The website has an author.
- The website has an impressum/copyright.
- The author is an expert in the respective subject matter/the author is recommended by other experts.
- The website is published by or related to a well-known organization, university, public institution, etc.
- The information provided on the website is relevant and up-to-date.
- The intention of the website is obvious; there is no hidden advertising or links to commercial websites (→ integrity, respectability).
- If there is any advertising, it is clearly distinguishable from the factual content of the website.
- The text is written in Standard English (few or no orthographic mistakes, colloquialisms, etc.).
- The author refers to his/her sources.
- There is more than *one* opinion.
- The opinions of others are respected.
- Statistical data and/or visuals are related to the text and are relevant (not just decorative elements).
- There are further links to other trustworthy websites/suggested reading.
- The website is designed appropriately for teenagers/children (in terms of contents, colours, graphics, animation, etc.); it displays appropriate pictures, videos, audio samples, etc.
- The website has a clear structure.
- The content of the website and the information given can be double-checked on other websites; there are references/links to other authors and/or other websites.
- The target group and the purpose of the website (e. g. commercial, educational, etc.) can be clearly identified.

Citing sources

In order to demonstrate the quality and credibility of your work, you need to name the sources that you have used. There are different citation styles. Here are some examples of how to cite different sources correctly:

Books

title of the book in italics

publishing company

page(s) where the quotation can be found

***Gun Love* by Jennifer Clement. Hogarth, New York 2018, pp. 25 ff.**

first name of author or editor (ed.)

surname

place and year of publiction

Articles from magazines/newspapers

title of the article in quotation marks

"Social media addiction is not natural or normal – but is it really a disease?" by Roisin Kiberd. *The Guardian*, 19 March 2020, p. 1

first name of the author

surname

name of magazine or newspaper in italics

date of publication

page(s) where the article can be found

Internet

title of the article in quotation marks

"When Social Media Is Really Problematic for Adolescents" by Perro Klass. https://www.nytimes.com/2019/06/03/well/family/teenagers-social-media.html, 3 June 2019 [24.02.2021]

URL[1] (name of the website)

publication date of the article

date when <u>you</u> printed/used/quoted the website (*Abrufdatum*) in square brackets

Films

title of the film in italics

film company

***Green Book*. Directed by Peter Farrelly. Entertainment One (Fox), USA 2019**

director of the film

place and year of release

[1] **URL** (*abbr.*) uniform/universal resource locator (the address of a World Wide Web page)

Continuing a Fictional Text

Types of fictional texts you might be required to continue are:
- **narrative texts** (novel, short story)
- **dramatized texts** (drama, play, one-act play)
- **film scripts** (screenplays)

Possible assignments

The assignment to continue a fictional text will usually be part of the task of working creatively with the text subsequent to the comprehension and analysis of a text. Accordingly, this task requires you to use your previous results and continue, complement or pad the text at hand with further details. You could be asked to:

- **rewrite** a scene/dialogue **from a different narrative perspective**, e. g. by choosing another character or by creating and adding a new character
- **rewrite** a scene/dialogue and **change the ending**, e. g. by turning the happy ending into a tragic ending or vice versa
- **elaborate on unspoken thoughts** of a character, e. g. by writing an interior monologue or a diary entry
- **continue a scene** from a play/screenplay or **a chapter** from a novel
- **change the genre of the text**, e. g. by turning a descriptive part in a novel into a scene in a screenplay or into dialogue with two or more characters interacting
- **change time and place** of the text and continue the scene/dialogue, etc. after a lapse of time, e. g. after 20 or more years when one of the characters has grown up, has aged and is looking back at his/her life

Your composition

Step 1: Be aware of the characteristic features of the literary genre and the type of text you are required to work with creatively. Here are some examples:

narrative texts		dramatized texts		film script
novel	**short story**	**classical drama**	**modern play**	**screenplay**
• narrator/narrative perspective • character(s) • panoramic/scenic presentation • main/sub-plot • stream of consciousness/interior monologue • development of action/plot • disruptions/lapses in time/ foreshadowing/flashback, etc. • spoken/everyday English, informal English	• immediate beginning • open ending • exceptional incident in everyday life • spoken English	• protagonist/antagonist/hero • dialogue/monologue/soliloquy • stage directions • acts/scenes • spoken English • development of a conflict • often linear development • happy/tragic ending/resolution	• everyday character(s) • internal conflict • current topics, e. g. society, politics, crisis, war, etc. • stage directions • disruptions/ lapses in time • spoken English	• slug lines • dialogue/monologue • action • focus on visual aspects • technical directions (props, music, camera operations) • spoken English

Step 2: Employ the above-mentioned **formal characteristics of the respective genre** in your text.

Step 3: The **stage directions** require you to briefly characterize the speaker's intentions, emotions or behaviour. In order to avoid overusing verbs like "think", "say" or "give", use a dictionary to find alternative formulations, e. g. to reflect, to boast, to complain, to whine, to mutter, to whisper, to shout, to consider, to offer

Step 4: Make **the characters interact** and not just deliver monologues. They can use feedback phrases or questions (Oh, really?; You don't say!), interrupt each other (Are you sure?; Are you suggesting that ...?), etc.

Writing a Review

Review of a book or film

Step 1: Plot/characters/theme

- Briefly summarize the plot of the book/film (approx. 150 words). 'Who/where/when/what/why'-questions should be answered.
- Include the type of film (e. g. feature film, western) /book (e. g. historical novel), title, author/director, publishing/release year, edition, special features.
- Briefly describe the main characters and how they are related.
- Briefly outline the basic theme(s) and leitmotif(s).
- Describe the overall atmosphere.

Step 2: Narrative/cinematic aspects

- Point out striking narrative qualities (e. g. point of view, metaphorical language, structure of the plot).
- Refer to any striking cinematic devices that create/reinforce the atmosphere of the film.
- Mention which actors were chosen for the respective roles.
- Explain what the book's/film's message and the author's/director's intention may be.

Step 3: Evaluation

- Say what you like or dislike about: the plot, structure, directing, camera work, sound, special effects, casting and performance of the characters/actors.
- Explain whether the book/film has successfully conveyed any/its core message.
- Comment on the actors: Have they successfully personified and typified the characters?
- Consider and quantify shortcomings/weaknesses and strengths of the book/film.
- If the film is a literary adaptation: How well has the story been adapted? – Is there anything missing (in comparison to the novel or in comparison to other books/films by the same author/director)?

Step 4: Conclusion

- Is the film worth viewing?/Is the book worth reading?
- Would you recommend the book/film? – What was your favourite part of the book/film?
- Do not just follow the chronological order of the text but also focus on **relevant aspects, stylistic devices, characters**.
- Be careful to **quote correctly**. (→ Focus on Facts, Basic Types of Non-Fictional Texts, p. 227)

Conclusion

- End your text by **referring to your introduction** and formulating a **concluding sentence** in which you refer to the message or the type of the text (again).
- **Do not evaluate** the text. Stay factual and concise.

Tips on vocab

- The film/novel/story is set in …/ directed by…
- The starring role is played by …/The protagonist is …
- On the whole, I would (not) recommend …
- The film/novel leaves much/nothing to be desired …
- The film /novel touches upon the problem of …
- The film will keep you at the edge of your seat …
- The film /novel clearly points out how…
- The film/book/story is thought-provoking …
- In view of the fact that …
- The plot resolves around/centres on …
- The plot is rather (un-)convincing …

Writing a Newspaper Commentary/an Editorial/ a Blog Post

A newspaper commentary/an editorial/a blog post

In contrast to a newspaper report, **a commentary, an editorial or a blog post presents the newspaper's opinion on an issue**. Editorial writers build on an argument and try to influence the reader's opinion, **criticize** a certain issue or try to **clarify a complicated or controversial** matter. Sometimes they ask people to take action. In a nutshell, editorials are **opinionated news stories** which are **personalized** and which **evaluate** issues or events.

Structure

- **headline**
- **introduction, body, paragraphs, conclusion**
- **an objective explanation of the issue**
- **opinions from the opposing viewpoint**
- **opinions of the writer**
- **alternative solutions to the problem or issue being criticized**
- **a solid and concise conclusion**

"Sleaze, please."

How to write a newspaper commentary/an editorial/ a blog post

Step 1: Choose a significant topic that would interest readers.

Step 2: Do research and collect information, facts, statistical data, interview people, etc.

Step 3: In an introduction, state your opinion briefly, e.g. *Have you ever thought about … ? Taking into account that … Looking at the latest results of … one should … I think that …*

Step 4: Explain the topic/issue objectively and explain why this topic is important, e.g. *Looking at the facts/ numbers we have to realize that … therefore, it is our responsibility to …*

Step 5: Give the opposing viewpoint first with its quotations and facts, e.g. *On the contrary one might think that … the numbers suggest that … on the surface, the situation appears to be …*

Step 6: Refute the opposing viewpoint and develop your case:
- present at least three arguments
- the strongest argument should come last
- back up your arguments by facts, e.g. statistics, quotations, expert information
- if you comment on a text, refer to the text with quotes to substantiate your arguments

Step 7: Repeat key phrases to reinforce an idea, e.g. *Let us get back to … Let us take a closer look at … This situation requires a clear judgment … We have no option but to …*

Step 8: Employ rhetorical devices to make your article more convincing (comparison, antithesis, metaphorical expressions, etc.).

Step 9: Give a (realistic) solution to the problem and encourage constructive criticism and pro-active reaction.

Step 10: Sum up the information and highlight important points and solutions. Refer back to your introductory remarks and statement. Your conclusion should have some punch, e.g. *If we do not take action against dangerous and poisonous food, who will?*

→ Focus on Facts, Basic Types of Non-Fictional Texts, p. 227

Tips on vocab

In my opinion … ■ As far as I understand … ■ In my view … ■ I am convinced that … ■ I might be wrong but … ■ I approve the view that … ■ I'm of the same opinion … ■ I agree/ disagree with … ■ I can imagine that … ■ I disapprove of … ■ I'd like to emphasize … ■ I am of mixed opinions on this … ■ I like/support the idea that … ■ the main reason is that … ■ another point/argument is that … ■ not only … but also … ■ another problem/aspect is … ■ on the one hand … on the other hand …

Writing a Formal Letter

Business letter/letter of complaint – layout

Tel: +49(0)6131 123456
Fax: +49(0)6131 1234567
tobymueller@web.de

Gartenweg 20
55116 Mainz
Germany

15 May 2022

Your ref: TBS/1234

Digital World Inc.
8607 Main Street
Cornerstone, NJ 23657
USA

Attention: Ms Goldwell, Customer Services

Dear Ms Goldwell

My Order No. CF-23405 – Smartphone "Stay Connected", black, dated 4 March 2022

The above-mentioned smartphone was delivered to me today and on opening the package I found that

- the touchscreen is badly scratched
- the GPS navigation does not work properly
- applications cannot be downloaded
- the headset is missing

Obviously the smartphone was poorly packed and roughly handled in transit and something must have gone wrong in production and while packaging the phone.

Needless to say, I cannot use the phone and thus would like to return it at your expense.

I am looking forward to hearing what you have to say about the matter and would welcome an immediate replacement of the damaged article.

Yours sincerely

Tobias Müller
Tobias Müller

Enc.: Copy of the packaging slip and invoice

---

letterhead with postcode, telephone and fax numbers and email

reference initials

date

inside address, including street, ZIP code, country

attention line

salutation
- *Dear Sir or Madam* → used if name is unknown
- *Miss* → unmarried woman (old use)
- *Mrs* → married woman
- *Ms* → unclear if the woman is married or not
- *Mr* → man
- no comma at the end of the salutation

subject line (optional)
- after salutation in the UK
- before salutation in the USA
- in bold type
- capitalized

body of the letter
- begin with a capital letter
- paragraphs are separated by a free line

complimentary close
- *Yours sincerely* → most common use
- *Yours faithfully* → formal, only used if the name of the addressee is unknown
- *(Best) Regards, Best wishes* → friendly
- signature, name, position of the signatory

enclosure (*Anlagen*)
- Enc (singular), e. g. *order form*
- Encs (plural), e. g. *cheque, folder*

Basic types of business letters

- **Enquiry:** a request for or question about information about sth. (*Anfrage*)
- **Offer:** a voluntary but conditional promise given by a buyer or seller to another for acceptance (*Angebot*)
- **Order:** a request to make or supply goods (*Bestellung*)
- **Reminder:** a request for an overdue payment that should have been paid by an earlier date (*Mahnung*)
- **Letter of complaint:** a request to deal with and solve a problem, e. g. delay in delivery, unsatisfactory or defective goods, wrong goods, etc. (*Beschwerdebrief, Reklamation*)

Writing a Handout

A handout is a useful tool that serves as a memory aid (= *Gedächtnisstütze*) for the listeners of a presentation and helps them to follow the presenter's line of argument or train of thought.
It should provide a short overview of the presentation, the most relevant facts, keywords and data, and may include some interesting or provocative statements for the audience to consider.

Structure

1. Heading
- name of school/college/university
- subject/course
- name of teacher/lecturer/professor
- name of student

2. Main part/body

a) title/topic of the presentation
b) introduction of the topic, e. g. main ideas, the central theme (= *roter Faden*)
c) depiction of the most relevant aspects in keywords; structuring elements such as bullet points, subheadings, etc.
d) conclusion and results of the project/coursework/presentation

3. List of references/indication of sources
- bibliographical references (e. g. books, essays, etc.)
- references to Internet websites, links, etc.

→ Focus on Skills, Doing Research and Citing Sources, p. 262

Example

Karl Kraus Gymnasium
Subject: English
Teacher: Mr/Ms …
Student: Katharina Müller 10 May 2022

The British Empire

Outline/overview:

1. Introduction/definition	4. The Impact on India
2. Historical background	5. Gandhi
3. The Raj	6. Conclusion

1. Introduction/definition
- British expansion …
- …

2. Historical background
- Queen Elizabeth I …
- …

3. …

List of references

Bibliographical references:

Darwin, John, Unfinished Empire: *The Global Expansion of Britain*, Penguin, London 2013, pp. 40 f.

Internet:

www.bbc.co.uk/history/british/modern/endofempire_overview_01.shtml [03.04.2021]

Writing an Interview

In a written examination you might be required to **write an interview as a creative writing task** in addition to the comprehension and the analysis tasks. Your written interview text should be written in such a way that it can serve as a script or draft (*Vorlage*) for an interview you are asked to conduct. In general, an interview is a conversation between two (or more) people, (an) **interviewer(s)** and an **interviewee**, where (usually pre-formulated) questions are asked by the interviewer(s) to obtain information, facts or statements on a certain topic. In journalism, interviews are used to collect information, or present views and assessments to viewers or listeners. Interviews are also important in qualitative research, e. g. when interviewing an expert in some field.

Types of interviews

- **informal, conversational interview**
  No pre-formulated questions are asked; the interviewer stays as open and adaptable to the interviewee's personality, response and priorities as possible.
- **general interview**
  The focus is on collecting more general information from the interviewee; the interviewer pre-formulates questions but stays open to the interviewee's focus and priorities on a certain matter.
- **standardized, open-ended interview**
  The same, standardized and pre-formulated questions are asked of different interviewees. This method allows for rather fast interviews that can be easily analysed and compared.
- **closed, fixed response interview**
  All interviewees are asked the same pre-formulated questions and are asked to choose questions from the same set of alternatives they want to answer.

The interviewer

Although the general aim of an interview is to elicit (*hervorlocken*) information from an interviewee by strategically and skilfully posing questions, the interviewer should follow certain rules. He/She should be **neutral**, **unemotional** and **unbiased**.

Technique and structure

- **introducing the topic**; the reason for the interview/the occasion; introduction of the **interviewee(s)**, their background, position and reason for being interviewed, e. g. *Good afternoon … today our topic is … I would like to welcome our special guest … who is an expert in …*
- asking a **well-structured** sequence of (pre-formulated) questions
- **listening and reacting** to the interviewee(s) in order to achieve more focus and attention to detail
- asking **follow-up questions** throughout the interview to
  a) enable the interviewee to elaborate on certain topics and to gain more comprehensive information
  b) to clarify complicated or confusing aspects, e. g. *What do you mean by saying …? Could you elaborate on … and give us some more details on …?*
- asking **precise and respectful questions** in order not to offend the interviewee or make him/her become defensive or unwilling to share
- making the interviewee(s) feel comfortable and respected by **avoiding interrupting** him/her/them whenever possible
- **ending the interview** by
  a) summarizing the result of the discussion or the views taken by the participant(s),
  b) thanking the participant(s), e. g. *I am sorry to say that our time is up. Thank you, … it has been most comprehensive … informative … It has been a pleasure to have you with us.*
- using **spoken English** (not formal, but avoiding colloquial English or slang)

Writing a Newspaper Article

In general, (print or online) newspaper reports aim **at informing their readership** about events that have happened in their local area, or about national and international news. Newspaper reports usually **provide answers** to questions (who, what, where, when, why, how). They should be **easy to read, objective and present reliable, unbiased facts and information** and should be written in a snappy and concise style. However, the style of an article and the language register (formal, informal) depends on the type of newspaper the article is published in, e. g. a quality paper, a popular paper, etc. (→ Focus on Facts, The Press, p. 229).

Types of newspaper articles

- **local news** (focussing on the neighbourhood/the region)
- **national news** (focussing on one's country)
- **international news** (world news)
- **a feature article** ('soft news', e. g. about a celebrity; a person who does volunteer work in the community; a movie review, etc.; it is **not** considered a news story)
- **editorial** (an article that contains the writer's, publisher's or editor's opinion on an issue)
- **a column** (an article written by the same person on a regular basis, about subjects of interest to him/her, current events or community happenings; it is not considered a news story)

General structure / layout

- **headline** (catching the reader's attention)
- **sub-headlines** (structuring the article)
- **columns/paragraphs** (structuring the article; all paragraphs relate to the main idea/topic)
- **pictures, photos, graphics, visuals,** etc. (illustration, proof)
- **first paragraph** (introduces the main point of the story (who?); introduces the main idea (what?))
- **following paragraphs** (provide answers to the other questions (where?, when?, why?, how?); develop the main idea)
- **paragraphs** (short, punchy, not too long)
- **information** (clear, concise, factual)
- **language** (precise, clear sentence structure, explanation of technical terms)
- **grammatical tense** (usually past tense – when an event has already taken place)
- **references** to a) what people said (quotations/direct speech; reported speech),
  b) sources, other articles on the topic, etc.

How to write a newspaper report

Step 1: Select your target group (e. g. students, readers in a small town, a neighbourhood, etc.).

Step 2: Find a subject of interest (e. g. the costs of schoolbooks or field trips; the quality of clothes, etc.).

Step 3: Do research on the matter (e. g. interviewing people, Internet research, etc.).

Step 4: List your potential sources. They shoud be reliable and credible (e. g. authority, expert, celebrity, hero, witness, ordinary people, etc.).

Step 5: Write your lead-in (the introductory paragraph).

Step 6: Write the rest of your article and
- structure it into paragraphs of 4 – 5 lines,
- develop a clear train of thought and line of argument,
- employ references to prove the reliability of your information.

Step 7: Find a suitable title for your report. It should be lively and catchy and announce the topic in a concise way. Try to evoke your reader's interest by asking a question (*Why is ethical fashion so expensive?*) or using an exclamation mark (*No Boring Lessons Any Longer!*).

Note: The information given in a newspaper article should be true, objective and original.

Writing a Speech Script

In your written examination, you might be asked to write a speech in response to a text you analysed or on an issue related to the text at hand. A good speech always has a clear and distinct structure and follows clear-cut lines of argument and trains of thought.

Structure

Introduction

In order to **win your audience's attention** and **attract their interest** you can start by

- saying sth. thought-provoking,
- saying sth. controversial,
- citing an interesting quotation or
- telling a joke.

After having gained their attention, you should **introduce yourself** and **the subject** you are going to talk about. Additionally, you can make a positive remark/pay a compliment to the place where you are speaking, the audience, etc. – this will help you to bond with your audience.

Tips on vocab

Good evening, ladies and gentlemen. ■ Dear friends … ■ I feel deeply honoured to speak to such an illustrious audience. ■ Let me first thank you for inviting me to this impressive meeting. ■ It is a great pleasure to be here to talk to you. ■ As … said, it is never too late to take action. ■ Wouldn't it be wonderful if we managed to … ■ Let me assure you …

Main part/body of the speech

This is the longest part of your speech and should therefore have a clear structure, following a topical order, a line of argument or a train of thought.

- Start with a **thought-provoking** and **important thought** or argument.
- Decide on which pattern you want to choose for the **body of your speech**:
  a) **progressive structure** (developing on a cause-to-effect or problem-solution arrangement)
  → effect: clarity, unity and logical coherence
  b) **antithetical structure** (contrasting and juxtaposing facts, ideas, arguments)
  → effect: clarity and emphasis through comparison and contrast
- **Support your arguments** with
  a) information (e. g. statistical data, facts),
  b) examples,
  c) quotations (e. g. of experts, political authorities, etc.),
  d) references to similar situations.
- **Work in some rhetorical devices**, e. g. alliteration, repetition of relevant phrases/words/numbers, contrast, comparison, climax, rhetorical questions.
- **Use linkers and connectives** to vary the beginning of your sentences and to connect your thoughts and arguments.

Conclusion

This part of your speech is very important because it gives you the opportunity to end with a punch and/or an appeal that will stay in your audience's mind.

- Give a **concise summary of the most relevant points** of your speech.
- Finish with a **punchy remark, a call for action** or sth. personal to **reinforce your line of argument**.
- Relate your finishing remarks to the beginning of your speech in order to **round off your speech**.

Tips on vocab

Let me quote … again, … ■ (to put it) in a nutshell … ■ to put it bluntly … ■ Let us be honest, shouldn't we … ■ Now that you have realized the importance of … ■ I put my trust in you to … ■ I have absolutely no doubt that you will make the right decision. ■ Let us roll up our sleeves and get to work.

→ Focus on Skills, Giving a Speech, p. 260
→ Focus on Skills, Presentation, p. 261
→ Focus on Skills, Analysis of a Political Speech, p. 242

Writing a CV and a Letter of Application

your own address in the top right-hand corner

date of writing

reference number or keywords related to the position

address in full, as on envelope

Use "Madam or Sir" if you do not know the name of the person.

introductory paragraph; reason for your letter; start with a capital letter

body of letter; your qualifications; reason(s) why you want the job

If you started with "Dear Madam or Sir," end with "Yours faithfully".
If you know the surname, e. g. "Dear Ms. Brown," end with "Yours sincerely".

Sign your name and print it in full afterwards.

Tel: +49 (0)6131 123456

Gartenweg 20
55116 Mainz
Germany

15 May 2022

Your ref: TBS/1234

Roots & Shoots
The Jane Goodall Institute
1595 Spring Hill Road
Vienna, VA 22182
USA

Dear Madam or Sir,

I am writing to apply for an internship at your institute.
Please find enclosed a copy of my CV.

Since graduating from St. Thomas Grammar School, I have gained experience in working with various environmental groups as well as in a zoo. I have also had the opportunity of working in an animal shelter and have experienced the importance of giving more to these animals than just medical treatment.

I would welcome the opportunity to work in one of your camps and look forward to your response.

Yours faithfully

T. Müller

Tobias Müller

Enc. CV

Curriculum Vitae

Name	Tobias Müller
Address	Gartenweg 20 55116 Mainz
Telephone No.	+49(0)6131 123456
Mobile	+49(0)1723456789
Email	tobymueller@web.de
Nationality	German
Date/place of birth	25 July 2005, Mainz
Profile	a highly motivated and creative graduate from a grammar school with experience in animal care
Education	
2015 – 2022	Grammar School (A-Level)
2011 – 2015	Elementary School
Employment/	practical work as an animal caretaker/ keeper in a zoo and at an animal shelter
Interests	judo, tennis, music

- only refer to your most relevant qualifications or skills
- if possible, you can include references (= people that can be contacted in order to give a judgment of your qualifications, experience, character, etc.)
- enclose photocopies of relevant certificates
- begin with the most recent employment/qualification and work backwards

Tips on vocab

I noted with interest … ▪ I am writing in response to … ▪ With reference to your advertisement in … ▪ As you can see from my CV, … ▪ I am currently studying at … ▪ Having gained a degree in …, ▪ This position interests me because … ▪ I would be grateful for the opportunity to … ▪ I have extensive experience in … ▪ I am available for an interview … ▪ If you consider my qualifications to be suitable …

Writing a Letter to the Editor

A letter to the editor is a **formal letter** that has **different functions**:
A reader …
… **responds to an article** in a newspaper/magazine/on the Internet he/she has read and **states his/her opinion on the matter**.
… **expresses his/her criticism or support** of a stance taken by the publication.
… responds to **another reader's letter** to the editor.
… **comments on a current issue** or a problem of public interest.
… **remarks on materials** that have appeared in a (previous) publication.
… **corrects** a perceived **error or misinterpretation**.

Tips for writing

- **Read the publication thoroughly** and underline/highlight key phrases and the most relevant parts.
- Pay attention to the **focus and the standardized terminology** used in **your assignment**, e.g.: Write a letter to the editor and assess the author's view of immigration to Great Britain.
- **Name the article** you are responding to in the first sentence of the body of your letter or in a subject line.
- Include your **name, address and email address (phone number)** at the top of your letter to give the editor the opportunity to verify your identity.
- Since your letter may be edited, **get to the point and be concise** (*knapp und präzise*) and focused. Do not write a lengthy argument.
- Limit your letter to **two or three paragraphs**:
  a) **Introduce** the subject matter and briefly state your opinion/objection (*Einwand*).
  b) Include a few sentences (**arguments, examples**) to support your view.
  c) End with a **concluding remark** and a clever, punchy (*ausdrucksstark*) line.
  Keep in mind that a letter to the editor is a formal letter. Use **Standard English** and write in **a matter-of-fact style**, using clearly structured arguments. Avoid informal and insulting (*beleidigend*) or offensive language and do not be overly emotional.
  Start your letter like this:
  Dear Editor/Sir/Madam,
  I am writing in response to the article …
- **If you do not want your name published**, state so clearly, e.g. in the last paragraph.
  Example: *Please note, I do not want my (full) name published with this letter.*
- **Proofread** your letter to check for poor grammar and spelling errors.
- **Submit** your letter by email (if possible) to enable the editor to cut and paste your letter.

Tips on vocab

to have a good/positive opinion about sb./sth. ■ to (strongly) (dis-)agree with sb. about sth. ■ to approve of sb./sth. (*billigen*) ■ to advise sb. to do sth. (*raten, beraten*) ■ to acknowledge that … (*anerkennen*) ■ to show one's solidarity with … ■ to argue in support of sb./sth. (*sich aussprechen für …*) ■ to take a negative view of sb./sth. ■ to refute sb.'s arguments (*entkräften, widerlegen*) ■ to express criticism of … ■ to call sth. into question ■ to express doubts about sb./sth. (*jdn./etw. anzweifeln*) ■ to protest against ■ to have reservations about (*Vorbehalte haben*) ■ to disassociate oneself from sb./sth. (*sich distanzieren von*) ■ to make remarks on ■ to make observations about ■ to maintain/claim that … (*behaupten*)

→ Focus on Skills, Writing a Newspaper Commentary/an Editorial/a Blog Post, p. 266
→ Focus on Skills, Writing a Formal Letter, p. 267
→ Focus on Skills, Writing a Review, p. 265

This compilation (*Zusammenstellung*) of literary terms is designed to help you understand the meaning of terms and phrases used in connection with literature and the analysis of literary (and non-literary) texts. The terms and phrases are assorted into different categories and genres to help you select the correct and specific term and/or phrase.

Fiction/Fictional Texts

Narrative texts

Structure and plot

allegory ['æləgəri]	a text that may be understood on a superficial or factual level and a deeper, more philosophical level; the characters are often personifications of abstract ideas (evil, love, etc.)
climax	the moment when the conflict is most intense
conflict	a struggle between different forces which produces suspense
dénouement [ˌdeɪˈnuːmɑ̃ː] (resolution)	the final outcome, when the conflict is resolved
epigram	a short, witty statement which may be written in prose or verse
exposition	the very beginning of a fictional text which introduces the main character(s), the theme, the setting and the atmosphere
falling action	a reduction of suspense
flashback	an episode/event which interrupts the chronological order of a text and goes back in time to show what happened earlier
foreshadowing	hinting at later events
internal conflict	a struggle between two opposing views/values which takes place in a character's mind
(leit)motif ['laɪtməʊtiːf]	a theme/expression/object which recurs throughout the text and which refers to a certain person, situation or atmosphere
open ending	the conflict remains unresolved → the reader is left to reflect on possible resolutions
plot	the author's selection and structure of action as a set of events connected by cause and effect that are meant to create suspense
rising action	an increase in suspense
setting	place and time of a story/play
surprise ending	a sudden and unexpected turn of fortune/action
suspense	a feeling of tension/expectation
tension	the emotional strain caused by a conflict

Narration

acting time	the time from the beginning to the end of an episode in a text; this is usually longer than the narrating time because the writer can describe the passing of years in just a sentence; *erzählte Zeit*
interior monologue	a technique used within the stream of consciousness; a special kind of scenic presentation, often not in chronological order
mode of presentation – panoramic presentation – scenic presentation	the way the writer narrates events; *Darstellungsart* – the narrator tells the story as a condensed series of events, summarizing in a few sentences what happens over a longer period of time – the narrator shows an event in detail as it occurs, using dialogue, depicting thoughts and emotions, describing a scene, etc.
narrating time (= reading time)	the time it takes to relate an episode in a text (= reading time); it depends on the mode of presentation; *Erzählzeit*

narrator – omniscient [ɒmˈnɪsiənt] narrator – third-person narrator – first-person narrator – witness/observer narrator – objective/reliable – subjective/unreliable	person who tells the story (*not* the author!) – a narrator who seems to know everything – a narrator who stands outside the story and describes events in the third person – a narrator who is a character in a story; this is a limited point of view – a narrator who is a character in a story (protagonist or minor character) – a narrator who the reader can trust – a narrator who the reader is critical of
point of view/viewpoint – unlimited point of view – limited point of view	the perspective from which the characters, topics and events are presented (*not* the author's!) – the reader can examine the action/characters from various angles – e.g. a first-person narrator who only has limited insight into the action/characters
stream of consciousness [ˈkɒnʃəsnəs]	the presentation of experience through the mind of one character in a text

Tips on vocab

- In the exposition/the expository part, the reader gets information about …
- The author introduces the characters/setting/plot by describing …
- The main part comprises the chapters …
- In part …, the author develops his/her idea of …
- The final part contains the denouement/resolution.
- The conflict is solved in the final part.
- The text contains narrative passages and parts written in dialogue.
- The story/novel is an (auto-)biographical account of …
- The story/novel contains satirical/comical/humorous elements.
- The author indicates/does not indicate the place and time where and when the action takes place.
- The action develops in several stages.
- The author maintains suspense/irony … throughout the story.
- The ending of the story/chapter … is plausible/implausible because …

Drama

act	the major division of a drama; an act consists of scenes
comedy	a play which deals with a (light) topic in a more amusing way; it always has a happy ending
comic relief	a comic episode in a serious drama which aims at relieving tension by amusing the audience
dialogue	two or more people speaking to each other in a text
monologue	an extended speech by one character in a text; it might be addressed to other characters or the audience
one-act play	a short play consisting of only one act
play	any dramatic work intended to be presented on stage, in film or on TV
scene	a subdivision in a play
setting	the place and/or time in which an action takes place
short play	a short play which takes about 30 minutes to perform
soliloquy [səˈlɪləkwi]	a speech delivered by a character alone on stage (used to reveal the character's thoughts, feelings or motives to the audience)
stage directions	a playwright's notes about how the play is to be performed
tragedy	a play in which the protagonist undergoes a series of misfortunes until he or she finally falls; the hero(ine) experiences a reversal of fortune, i.e. from happiness to misery

Characters

antagonist	the opponent of the protagonist
anti-hero(ine)	a protagonist who does not have the qualities of a typical hero, and is either more like an ordinary person or is morally bad and does not fit into society
characterization – direct characterization – indirect characterization	the way of presenting a character in a text – the narrator or another character describes the character; alternatively, the character may describe him- or herself – the reader/audience learns about the character through action and dialogue
flat character	a minor character who does not develop in the course of the action
hero(ine) [ˈhɪərəʊ; ˈherəʊɪn]	the principal male or female character in a drama; he/she is usually in conflict with another character, fate and/or society
minor character	a character of less importance for the course of the action
protagonist	the main character in a play
round character	a character who develops in the course of action and therefore has the ability to change

Tips on vocab

- The playwright aims at provoking the audience … by …
- The conflict develops in several stages …
- The exposition indicates the time, place and circumstances of the action …
- The conflict reaches its climax in …/when …
- In scene … the conflict builds up …
- There are subplots to the main plot …
- The action progresses fast …
- The scene is full of retarding elements …
- The (development of the) action is slowed down/interrupted by …
- The ending is delayed …
- The (dramatic) action is reinforced by …
- The stage directions give information on/about …
- The protagonist/hero is torn between/in conflict with …
- The playwright shows the hero's motives for …
- The playwright describes the character's social background.
- The playwright takes the action to extremes by …

Poetry

anapaest [ˈænəpiːst]	metrical foot of three syllables (unstressed – unstressed – stressed): e. g. *underneath* – –ˈ–
concrete poem	a type of poem in which the words form a shape or picture
connotation	additional meaning of a word beyond its dictionary definition, for example, due to the associations that are formed through personal experience
dactyl [ˈdæktɪl]	metrical foot of three syllables (stressed – unstressed – unstressed): e. g. *merrily* ˈ– – –
denotation	the actual definition of a word (its dictionary definition)
end rhyme	a rhyme at the end of two lines
enjambement [ɪnˈdʒæmbmənt] (= run-on line)	a sentence which runs from one line to another without a break
foot	a group of stressed and unstressed syllables within a line of poetry which forms a metrical unit
free verse	a poem written without a particular rhyme scheme or regular metre
iamb [ˈaɪæm(b)]	metrical foot of two syllables (unstressed – stressed): e. g. *become* –ˈ–

iambic pentameter	*fünffüßiger Jambus* –'– – –
imagery ['ɪmɪdʒəri]	term for the use of images created by words that are used to appeal to the reader's imagination → often metaphors and/or similes
line	a structural unit in a poem; it is usually classified by a certain number of feet
metre	the regular rhythmic patterns of a poem/the arrangement of words according to stressed and unstressed syllables
poem	a composition which contains a structured line sequence and a special arrangement of words, a special rhythm, the use of imagery
rhyme	using words that repeat syllable sounds
rhyme scheme [skiːm] – rhyming couplets – alternate rhyme – embracing rhyme	the arrangement of rhymes in a poem – two consecutive lines with the same rhyme: aa bb – lines with the rhyme scheme: ab ab – lines with the rhyme scheme: abba
rhythm	the arrangement of stressed or unstressed syllables in writing
sonnet ['sɒnɪt] – quatrain – couplet	poem consisting of 14 lines, usually written in iambic pentameter; e. g. the Shakespearean sonnet consists of three quatrains and a couplet with the rhyme scheme abab cdcd efef gg – a stanza of four lines (e. g. in a sonnet) – two successive rhyming lines (e. g. at the end of a sonnet)
speaker	the fictional person who is imagined as saying the text of a poem (*not* identical with the poet!)
stanza	a major division in a poem consisting of several lines
trochee ['trəʊkiː]	metrical foot of two syllables (stressed – unstressed): e. g. *happen* '– –
verse	a stanza in a poem or song; poetry written in metre

Tips on vocab

- The poem comprises/consists of/is composed of … stanzas
- The stanzas have three or four lines each.
- In stanza/line …, the poet expresses …
- The speaker of the poem is …
- There is a correspondence between line/stanza … and …
- There is a break between …
- The stanzas are of equal length.
- The lines have … syllables.
- The lines are composed of small syntactic units.
- The subject of the poem is …
- The motif of (love) … is taken up again/emphasized by …
- In the course of the poem …
- The poet expresses himself in an indirect way …
- The poet conveys a message to the reader …
- The images in the poem have a symbolical meaning/have to be taken symbolically.
- The poet employs several figures of speech/rhetorical figures …
- The musical character of the poem is caused by its rhythm/its melodic language …

Lyrics/Songs

genre of music	a particular type or style of music, e. g. jazz, rap, funk, heavy metal, protest song, etc.
instrumentation	selection and combination of the musical instruments that are used in a song, e. g. electronic instruments, percussion, violin, etc.
onomatopoeia [ˌɒnəˌmætəˈpiːə]	words that imitate a sound associated with the thing being named, e. g. buzz, cuckoo, hum, etc.
registers of English	the words, style and grammar used, e. g. poetic, formal, slang, non-standard, in order to express a certain message or set of values
rhythm, beat	the regular pattern of long and short notes in music
vocals	the part of a piece of music that is sung, for example, by a lead singer or a choir

Tips on vocab

- The song contains social criticism.
- The song is poetical.
- The song is a folk song about/from …
- The singer/songwriter/composer is …
- … wrote the lyrics/composed the music …
- The structure of the song is …
- The song consists of … verses …
- The … verse is followed by a refrain.
- Each part of the song comprises … verses.
- The music goes together with the lyrics.
- The music underlines/emphasizes the tone … atmosphere …
- The singer's voice is …/… sounds …
- The singer is accompanied by a guitarist/pianist/percussionist/an orchestra.
- The change in the rhythm indicates/underlines that …
- The central motif/theme of the song is …

Non-Fiction/Non-Fictional Texts

Text type

argumentation	an argumentative text deals with ideas and/or controversy; it expresses a clear opinion and gives reasons/arguments to support it
description	a descriptive text aims at describing things/developments, etc.
exposition	in an expository text, the writer explains a rather complex problem in a precise and objective way
instruction	an instructive text gives advice about a particular matter; it typically includes commands and recommendations

Text form

comment	a kind of argumentation in which the writer/speaker gives his/her opinion on a certain topic
editorial	a comment, usually written by the editor-in-chief, that gives his/her opinion on a certain topic of common interest
essay (= literary appreciation)	a text in which the writer expresses his/her personal views on a certain topic; it usually follows a certain compositional pattern, i. e. the use of unity and balance (= statement – development – conclusion)
feature story	a report written to arouse human interest, typically by concentrating on an individual case that many readers can identify with
interview	a dialogue in which someone, usually a journalist, asks another person questions on a topic of common interest; may appear in a newspaper, on TV, etc.
lead story	the most important or prominent news story in a magazine/newspaper
letter to the editor	a letter written by a reader to the editor of a magazine/newspaper in order to express a personal opinion on some topic (→ comment)
news story	a report based on facts and background information that deals with a topical event that the public is interested in
report	a text that aims at answering the 'five w's': who?, what?, when?, where?, why?, which can be checked and verified by the reader
review	a short critical evaluation of a work of art (literature, film, etc.)
scientific report	a text written for scientific purposes, usually containing many technical terms (→ report)
sermon	a religious discourse delivered as part of a church service
speech – political speech – laudatory ['lɔːdətəri] speech	a formal talk or an address delivered to an audience – an address delivered for a political purpose, e. g. the inaugural address of a president or a crisis speech – a speech delivered in order to express praise, e. g. when sb. is awarded a prize

Tips on vocab

- The text is taken from …
- The text is an excerpt/extract from …
- The title of the text is …
- The title is followed by the subtitle …
- The subheading clarifies the subject.
- The text is about …/deals with …/focuses on …
- In the text … the different parts can be distinguished …
- The main part/paragraph consists of …
- The author/writer begins by saying …/pointing out …/referring to …
- At the end/Finally/Lastly, the author … concludes … sums up …
- The author/writer concludes/closes the text by stating/declaring …

Structural devices

column ['kɒləm]	*Textspalte*; mostly used in newspapers and magazines
conclusion	the main idea is often re-stated here or the main aspects of the text may be summarized (*kurz zusammenfassen*)
heading/headline	a caption that is written above a text to arouse the reader's interest
introduction	lead-in to the topic, often by referring to the 'five w's' in order to attract the reader's interest and lure him/her into the story
line of argument(ation)	the way different reasons are gradually developed and structured to convince a reader of a particular point of view (→ train of thought)
main part	the part of the text in which the writer demonstrates a topic/explains his/her intention/ discusses a topic or problem, etc.
paragraph	a division of a text dealing with a particular idea that begins on a new line
passage	a short extract from a text that may consist of several paragraphs
subheading	a caption that subdivides a text into logical sections
theme/topic/subject	a central idea in a text which binds all of its elements together
train of thought	the way a series of ideas is gradually developed and structured

Tips on vocab

- The composition/structure of the text …
- The text is composed of/consists of … parts.
- The … part can be subdivided into … parts/subsections …
- The central/principal/main idea of the text is …
- The author/writer develops/explains his/her idea/understanding of …
- The first paragraph runs from line … to line …
- In the final part, the author/writer draws the conclusion that …
- This paragraph/passage of the text shows/reveals the author's intention …
- This paragraph/passage forms a transition to …/leads up to …

The Media

agony aunt/uncle	a person who writes for a newspaper or magazine giving advice in reply to people's letters about their personal problems
feature story/human interest story	a story or part of a story in a newspaper that people find interesting because it describes the feelings, experiences, etc. of the people involved
front page – cover story – special feature – leading article/editorial	the first page of a newspaper where the most important news is printed – the main story in a magazine that goes with the picture shown on the front cover – a special article or report on sb./sth. (*Sonderbeitrag*) – an important article in a newspaper that expresses the editor's opinion about a news item or a particular issue
headline	the title of a newspaper article printed in large letters
Internet – blog – chatroom – website – web forum	an international computer network connecting other networks and computers – a personal record that sb. puts on their website giving an account of their activities and their opinions, and discussing other sites on the Internet, events, etc. – a site on the Internet where people can communicate with each other in real time – a set of interconnected webpages, generally located on the same server, and prepared and maintained by a person, group or organization – a site on the Internet where people can exchange opinions and ideas on a particular issue
letter to the editor	a (mostly critical) letter written by the reader of a newspaper/magazine in response to an article or a story
masthead ['ma:sthed]	– the name of the newspaper at the top of the front page – the part of a newspaper or a news website which gives details about the people who work on it or other information about it
television/radio – broadcasting company/corporation – channel – commercial (break) – documentary [ˌdɒkju'mentri] – factual report – feature film – live coverage – programme – soap (opera)	 – a company whose business is to make and transmit radio and TV programmes – a television station (*Sender*) – an advertisement on the radio or on television – a film, radio or television programme that gives detailed factual information about a particular subject – a report based on facts (*Tatsachenbericht*) – *Spielfilm* – sth. broadcast while the event is actually happening, not pre-recorded (*Direktübertragung*) – sth. that you watch on TV or listen to on the radio (*Sendung*) – a story about the lives and problems of a group of fictional people that is broadcast every day or several times a week on TV or radio
the press – quality newspapers/broadsheets – tabloids/popular newspapers – magazines/periodicals	 – publications that have in-depth articles and present facts that are based on serious research – usually smaller formats that are more sensationalist – periodical publications financed by advertising; printed in colour on quality paper

Tips on vocab

- The article is taken from .../is published in/on ...
- The journalist/correspondent/blogger wrote/edited/posted an article/comment about ...
- The banner headline evokes the readers' interest/curiosity .../attracts the readers' attention ...
- The headline is printed in large letters/is capitalized/is in bold print/in italics.
- The article/text is (sub-)divided into columns.
- The author's source of information is ...
- A typical feature of this article/text is that ...
- The article is reliable/authentic/credible/objective/subjective/biased ...
- The author presents the facts in a tendentious way ...
- The article appeals to the readers' taste for sensations ...
- The author/journalist comments on .../makes comments on ...
- The author expresses his/her personal opinion on/about ...
- The editorial/leading article offers an analysis of ...
- The article/report gives background information on ...

Films

documentary (film)	a film, television or radio programme that gives detailed factual information about a particular subject
docusoap	a supposedly unscripted television programme that shows what happens in the daily life of real people (= reality TV)
feature film	a full-length film that has a story, which is acted out by professional actors, and is usually shown in a cinema or online
screenplay/script – shooting script	the words that are written down for actors to say in a film, and the instructions that tell them what they should do – a script with additional information/details given by the director (e. g. drafts, technical details, arrows to indicate how to move the camera, etc.)
slug lines	numbered lines between the dialogue lines that indicate a change in location and time (e. g. INT, EXT); each slug line begins a new scene
storyboard	a graphic organizer that displays images in sequence (like a picture story) in order to help the film crew to know where the cameras are to be positioned or where/how a character has to stand/move, etc.

Tips on vocab

- The scene is shot from a … camera angle …
- Cinematic techniques …
- The film/scene triggers the viewers' curiosity …
- The film/scene depicts the setting of …
- The film stars …
- The film/scene is a flashback of … /a foreshadowing of …
- The action is intensified by …
- The setting of the film is …
- The protagonist's reaction is shown/presented/filmed in slow motion …
- The scene creates suspense …
- The scene marks the turning-point of …
- In the scene the narrator articulates his/her thoughts in a voice-over.

Stylistic Devices

In literature, and writing in general, **stylistic devices** or **literary terms** are **rhetorical techniques** used to emphasize particular aspects, convey meaning, persuade or trigger emotion in the reader/audience. They also help to create lively, interesting and convincing texts.

A	
abstraction (generalization)	to generalize sth.; to make vague or indeterminate statements
alliteration	the repetition of a sound, usually a consonant, at the beginning of neighbouring words
allusion	indirect reference to a famous event, person or piece of literature
anaphora [ə'næfərə]	successive sentences starting with the same word
antithesis [æn'tɪθəsɪs]	contrast; opposing words, phrases, views, characters, etc.
appeal	a very strong request; e. g. *Come and help us.* (in an appeal by a politician to the public to become active)
C	
choice of words	the decision to use a particular word based on such aspects as style, register, connotation, etc.
comparison	to compare (*vergleichen*) two or more people or things
D	
digression [daɪ'greʃən] from the main topic	the action of moving away from the main subject you are writing or talking about to writing or talking about sth. else
E	
ellipsis	the shortening of sentences by omitting a word or words; used to make poems or texts more compact; e. g. *I ordered the drink, and she [ordered] the food.*
enumeration	the act or process of making or stating a list of things one after another; e. g. *We bought apples, peaches, cherries, …*
euphemism ['ju:fəmɪzəm]	using polite expressions for sth. unpleasant
exaggeration/hyperbole [haɪ'pɜ:bəli]	making sth./sb. sound better, more exciting, dangerous, etc. than in reality
G	
grammatical tenses	the use of different tenses to underline references to the past, present or future
H	
hyperbole (exaggeration)	the use of obvious and deliberate exaggeration; e. g. *We had to wait forever*
I	
illustration	an example that explains sth. or makes sth. clear
image	a word intended to appeal to the reader's imagination and to bring a new perception to an object (→ figurative language, e. g. metaphors, similes)
imperative	a verb form used to give an order; e. g. *Go home!*
insertion	to add thoughts, etc. to what you want to say; *Einschub*
irony	saying the opposite of what you mean
J	
juxtaposition	to place two concepts, characters, ideas or places near or next to each other so that the reader will compare and contrast them

M	
(leit)motif	a theme, expression or object which recurs throughout a text and which refers to a certain person, situation or atmosphere
manner of speaking	a style that is typical of a particular person, e. g. a politician or worker
metaphor ['metəfə(r)]	poetic comparison without using *like* or *as* (e. g. an ocean of love)
P	
paradox	seeming impossible at first glance but recognized as true on second thought
parallelism	repeating similar or identical words/phrases in neighbouring lines/sentences/ paragraphs
personal pronouns	e. g. I – you; we – they; them – us; patterns of solidarity and identification
personification	giving ideas/objects/animals human characteristics (e. g. a smiling moon)
pun	a play on words
R	
reference	a connection to sth. else (→ allusion)
register/level of speech	the words, style and grammar used, e. g. formal/informal English, colloquialisms, slang, non-standard English, etc.; such aspects are typically adjusted according to the addressees but also depend on the linguistic abilities of the speakers
repetition	deliberately using a word/phrase more than once
rhetorical question	question to which the answer is obvious or to which no answer is possible/expected
S	
simile ['sɪməli]	comparison using *like* or *as*
simplification	the process of making sth. less complicated and therefore easier to do or understand
superlative	relating to the superlative of an adjective or adverb; e. g. *the best car, the most highly recommended novel of the year*
symbol	sth. concrete (object, character, event) standing for sth. abstract (cross – Christianity; horseshoe – luck)
syntax ['sɪntæks] – hypotactical structure – paratactical structure	arrangement of words in a phrase/sentence/text – rather complicated and long sentences, involving sub-clauses – a rather simple sentence structure, mostly consisting of main clauses, sometimes connected with the conjunctions *and, or*
T	
tone	the manner or mood, e. g. macabre, optimistic, etc.

British and American English

Though **Americanisms** are spreading rapidly worldwide, there are still a number of differences between American and British English. Here are some well-known examples of basic differences.

British English		American English
pronunciation		
– dance [dɑːns]	→	dance [dæns]
– water [ˈwɔːtə] *t* is spoken 't'	→	water [ˈwɑːtər] *t* is spoken 'd'
– missile [ˈmɪsaɪl] *-ile* syllable is spoken 'ail'	→	missile [ˈmɪsl] *-ile* syllable is spoken 'il'
– art [ɑːt] 'r' is not spoken	→	art [ɑːrt] 'r' is spoken
spelling		
– neighbour	→	neighbor
– offence	→	offense
– centre	→	center
– quarrelling, travelling	→	quarreling, traveling
– to organise	→	to organize
– catalogue	→	catalog
– programme	→	program
grammar		
– Have you got …?	→	Do you have …?
– to get – got – got	→	to get – got – gotten
– to prove – proved – proved	→	to prove – proved – proven
– I have already written the letter. (present perfect)	→	I already wrote the letter. (simple past)

vocabulary

BE	AE	BE	AE	BE	AE
autumn	fall	filling station	gas station	pavement	sidewalk
biscuit	cookie	film	movie	petrol	gas
boot	trunk	flat	apartment	prison	jail/penitentiary
car park	parking lot	ground floor	first floor	rubber	eraser
chemist's	drugstore	handbag	purse	shop	store
chips	French fries	lift	elevator	sweets	candy
company	corporation	lorry	truck	tap	faucet
cooker	stove	motorway	highway/freeway	traffic light	stop light
crisps	chips	note (money)	bill	trousers	pants
dustbin	garbage can	number plate	license plate	underground	subway

English Words That Can Easily Be Mixed Up ⚠

to abuse – *missbrauchen*	**to misuse** – *missbrauchen, zweckentfremden*
to affect [əˈfekt] – *(ein)wirken auf*	**effect** [ɪˈfekt] – *Wirkung*
to borrow – *von jdm. etwas borgen*	**to lend** – *an jdn. etwas verleihen*
classic – *typisch, vorbildlich (klassisch)*	**classical** – *die Antike betreffend (klassisch)*
conscience [ˈkɒnʃəns] – *Gewissen*	**consciousness** [ˈkɒnʃesnes] – *Bewusstsein*
conscious [ˈkɒnʃəs] – *bewusst*	**conscientious** [ˌkonʃiˈenʃes] – *gewissenhaft*
economic – *(volks-)wirtschaftlich*	**economical** – *sparsam*
efficient – *tüchtig, leistungsfähig*	**effective** – *wirksam*
fat – *dick (Mensch, Profit, …)*	**thick** – *dick (Buch), dicht (Haar)*
first – *zuerst (als Erster …)*	**at first** – *zuerst (am Anfang)*
historic – *geschichtlich bedeutsam (historisch)*	**historical** – *historisch (Film, Buch), die Geschichte behandelnd*
industrial – *industriell*	**industrious** – *fleißig*
legible [ˈledʒabl] – *leserlich (Handschrift)*	**readable** [ˈriːdəbl] – *lesenswert*
literal – *wörtlich*	**literate** – *lesen und schreiben können, belesen/gebildet sein*
to loosen – *losmachen, lockern*	**to lose** – *verlieren*
policy – *Politik/Linie (einer Firma, Regierung)*	**politics** – *Politik (Staatskunst)*
practical – *praktisch (veranlagt), handlich*	**practicable** – *brauchbar, durchführbar*
presently – *bald, gleich*	**at present** – *im Augenblick, zurzeit*
principal – *Schulleiter(in) (US)*	**principle** – *Grundsatz*
to raise [reɪz] – *(an)heben, erhöhen*	**to rise** [raɪz] – *(auf)steigen (Sonne)*
receipt [rɪˈsiːt] – *Quittung*	**recipe** [ˈresəpi] – *Kochrezept*
self-confident – *selbstbewusst*	**self-conscious** – *befangen, gehemmt*
tasteful – *geschmackvoll*	**tasty** – *schmackhaft, lecker*
technique [tekˈniːk] – *Art der Ausführung, Technik (eines Künstlers)*	**technology** – *Technik, Technologie*

The Language Register of English

Many English words and phrases have similar meanings, and are, at first sight, synonyms. However, different contexts or situations typically require more or less formal wording. Some synonyms are more appropriate or more commonly used in **formal texts or situations** (e. g. *to proceed*), whereas in more informal, **everyday spoken English**, you would choose another phrase (e. g. *to go ahead*). Formal or *Standard English* is written in formal documents, e. g. essays, business letters, (traditional) literature; it is spoken in business negotiations, news broadcasts, official examinations, etc.

Different registers of English

everyday English	formal English
• I'm sorry/Sorry/Pardon me/Excuse me …	→ I (would like to) apologize …
• In my opinion/view, … The way I see it, … (*spoken*) If you ask me, … (*spoken*)	→ I am of the opinion that … I take the view that … It is my belief that …
• Is it all right/OK if I … Do you think I could …	→ I was wondering whether I could … Would it bother you if I …?
• Why don't we …? Let's … How about …?/What about …?	→ Perhaps we could … You might like/want to … Shall we …?
• Hi! What's up? How are you? How are you doing?	→ How do you do? (formal, only used when meeting sb. for the first time) Pleased/Lovely/Nice to meet you.
• Thanks. I can't thank you enough.	→ I appreciate … I am most grateful …

Colloquialisms

Colloquial language (i. e. informal, relaxed speech) is only appropriate for casual, familiar or informal conversation and is **not used in formal speech or writing**, except for artistic purposes, such as in novels or poetry. Some examples are: *gonna* (going to), *wanna* (want to), *ain't nothin'* (there is not anything), *not the sharpest knife in the drawer* (not very smart/intelligent).

Slang

Slang words are used in **very informal** situations, and usually only by a specific social group, e. g. teenagers, soldiers, etc. or in literature and song texts. Typically, slang words or phrases are **taboo words** and are often meant in a derogatory way (i. e. insulting, disapproving). Here is an example taken from literature:

> I'm trying to sleep when the other cons on my row are waking up. One of them hears me sigh, and tosses some words through his door. "Little? You a fuckin star!"
> "Yeah, right," I say. "Tell the prosecution."
> "Hell, youse'll get the *bestest* fuckin attorneys, hear what I'm sayin?"
> "My attorney can't even speak fuckin English."
> "Nah," says the con, "they dissed his ass, he history. I saw on TV he said he still workin on it, but that's bullshit, he ain't even hired no more. You get big guns now, hear what I'm sayin?"
> from *Vernon God Little* by DBC Pierre, Faber and Faber, London 2003, pp. 197 f.

Adjectives and Adverbs

Adjectives

Adjectives describe the quality of a noun; an adjective tells what sth./sb. is like.

The regular comparison with 'er' and 'est'

This applies to monosyllabic (= one syllable) and disyllabic (= two syllables) adjectives with the endings -er, -le, -ow and -y. Changes in spelling are highlighted in red.

comparative and superlative forms	examples		
→ monosyllabic adjectives:	old	older	the oldest
	low	lower	the lowest
	thin	thinner	the thinnest
	high	higher	the highest
	large	larger	the largest
→ disyllabic adjectives:	happy	happier	the happiest
	easy	easier	the easiest
	narrow	narrower	the narrowest
	simple	simpler*	simplest*
	*can also be used in the comparative form with 'more'/'most'		

The irregular comparison with 'more' and 'most'

This applies to disyllabic adjectives (= two syllables), trisyllabic (= three syllables) and polysyllabic (= many syllables) adjectives with endings **other than** -er, -le, -ow and -y.

comparative and superlative forms	examples		
→ disyllabic, trisyllabic and polysyllabic adjectives:	useful	more useful	the most useful
	modern	more modern	the most modern
	beautiful	more beautiful	the most beautiful
	interesting	more interesting	the most interesting

The irregular comparison

⚠ Pay attention to the irregular forms:	good	better	the best
	bad	worse	the worst
	much	more	the most
	many	more	the most
	little *(klein)*	smaller	the smallest
	little *(wenig)*	less	the least
	far	further	the furthest
	late	later	the latest *(zeitlich)*

Sentences with comparisons

- Linda is (not) as clever as Tom. → *(nicht) so … wie …*
- Susan is more excited than Lucy. → *aufgeregter als …*
- Michael is taller than Bill. → *größer … als …*
- The situation was getting worse and worse. → *schlechter und schlechter*
- The angrier the teacher got, the louder the students became. → *je … desto …*

Adverbs

An adverb quantifies or modifies (= *abwandeln, einschränken, relativieren*) the meaning of a verb, an adjective or a phrase/sentence.
Adverbs typically answer questions like how?/in what way? (**adverbs of manner**), when? (**adverbs of time**), how often? (**adverbs of frequency**), where? (**adverbs of place**), and to what extent? (**adverbs of degree**).
This can be done by using a single word (e. g. slowly, suddenly, etc.) or by using an adverbial phrase or sentence (e. g. behind the wall, during the holidays, much too early, etc.).

There are **two different kinds of adverbs** in the English language:
a) adverbs of time and place that are not formed from adjectives, e. g. here, there, now, then
b) adverbs that are formed from adjectives, by adding the ending '-ly' to the adjective e. g. nicely, beautifully, easily

The formation of adverbs

- attachment of '-ly': easy → easily; simple → simply; whole → wholly
- adjectives with an '-ly' ending: friendly → in a friendly way
- adjectives with an '-ic' ending: automatic → automatically
- adjectives and adverbs that have the same form and meaning: daily, hourly, weekly, monthly, yearly, early, likely, fast, long, far, straight, low

Adjectives that form adverbs with different meanings

adjective	adverb	adverb
right *(richtig)*	right *(richtig)*	rightly *(zurecht)*
hard *(hart)*	hard *(hart)*	hardly *(kaum)*
fair *(fair)*	fair *(fair)*	fairly *(ziemlich)*
deep *(tief)*	deep *(tief)*	deeply *(zutiefst)*
high *(hoch)*	high *(hoch)*	highly *(höchst)*
late *(spät)*	late *(spät)*	lately *(in letzter Zeit)*
most *(am meisten)*	most *(am meisten)*	mostly *(meistens)*
short *(kurz)*	short *(kurz)*	shortly *(in Kürze)*
pretty *(hübsch)*	pretty *(ziemlich)*	prettily *(hübsch)*

Comparison of adverbs

- adverbs that give information about time: attachment of '-er' and '-est'
  e. g. soon – sooner – the soonest; early – earlier – the earliest
- adverbs with an '-ly' ending: 'more' and 'most'
  e. g. easily – more easily – most easily

⚠ irregular forms of comparison		
adverb	**comparative**	**superlative**
well	better	best
much	more	most
little	less	least
badly/ill	worse	worst
near	nearer	nearest/next
far	further/farther	furthest/farthest
late	later	latest/last

The position of adverbs and adverbials in a sentence

- **adverbs of frequency** are usually put between the subject and main verb or between the auxiliary and main verb
  Timothy always works during the summer vacation.
  Timothy has always had a job in the summer.
- **adverbs of manner** are usually put at the end of the sentence
  The student council had prepared the graduation dance carefully.
- **adverbials of place/direction and time** can be placed at the beginning or at the end of the sentence depending on how much they are stressed
  Recently, Susan has started to learn Italian.
  Tim has lived in London all his life. Now, he wants to move to Canada.
  In this neighbourhood, industrial sites have been threatening people's health for a long time.
- when there are **several adverbs and adverbials at the end of a sentence**, the rules are:
  - place/direction before time
    place **time**
    Many students want to volunteer at a camp during the summer holidays.
  - adverbs of manner before place/direction and time
    manner **place** **time**
    Owen went slowly to the door last night.
  - precise time before general time
    place **precise time** **general time**
    Hester arrived at Owen's house at 8 o'clock last night.

Conditional Sentences (If-Clauses)

Conditional sentences are sentences that discuss **possible**, **almost impossible** or **impossible conditions** and their consequences. A conditional sentence has **two parts**: an if-clause (= the condition, *Bedingung*) and a main clause (= the consequence). There are **three types** of conditional sentences.

if-clause (condition)	**main clause (consequence)**
type I – possible conditions	
simple present	**will-future, modal auxiliary, imperative**
If the weather is nice, ...	we will go to the swimming pool.
If the weather is rainy, ...	we will not (won't) go for a walk.
If Hester does not behave at the ball, ...	she may get detention.
If you want to study abroad, ...	you can apply for a scholarship.
If you want to volunteer, ...	check the Internet for organizations first.
type II – almost impossible conditions	
simple past	**would + infinitive**
If Hester asked Owen for a date,	he would be very happy.
If I were you, ...	I would stop drinking so much alcohol.
If I had the opportunity to go abroad, ...	I would go right away.
type III – absolutely impossible conditions	
past perfect	**would + infinitive perfect**
If you had written the application on time, ...	they would have invited you for an interview.
If Hester had not eaten that much, ...	she would not have felt so sick the following day.
	would + infinitive
If you had not eaten all the chocolate, ...	you would not feel sick now.
	⚠ only used when the consequence is related to the present

⚠ Generally, you **must not use will/would** in the if-clause when the **if-clause expresses a condition**.
If you do not pay the bill, you will be in trouble. (If you ~~will not pay~~ the bill, you will be …)
condition — consequence

You can use will/would in the if-clause when you are asking about **someone's willingness** to do something.
If you would help me, that would be wonderful …

Both **if** (*wenn, falls*) and **when** (*dann, wenn*) can be used to introduce if-clauses but they mean different things:

- use **if** if you are unsure whether you will do something or whether something will happen
  If I get a scholarship, I will take part in the exchange.
- use **when** if you are sure about doing something or if something will most likely happen
  When I get that scholarship, I will take part in the exchange.
- **if** can be used in all three types of conditional sentences, **when** is only used in type I clauses.

Indirect Speech

When you report what an author has written in a text or what a character says or thinks, e. g. in a summary, you should *not* use direct speech *at all;* instead, use indirect speech. Write **an appropriate introductory sentence** and do not always use the verb 'say' – vary your formulations.

Here are some alternative verbs for your introductory sentences:
Statements: to say, to tell, to comment (on), to add, to explain, to mention, to remark, to announce, to point out, to describe, to state, etc.
Questions: to ask, to want to know, to wonder whether/if, to doubt whether/if, etc.
Commands/requests: to tell (sb. to do sth.), to order, to demand, to request, etc.

⚠ **Only** if the introductory verb is in the past tense, is there a **backshift of the tenses** of the direct speech.

backshift		**example**	
tenses		**direct speech**	**indirect speech**
present →	past	"Owen works on the farm in the holidays."	He said Owen worked on the farm in the holidays.
past →	past perfect	"Hester loved the boatman from Tortola." "Hester was drinking all night."	Owen explained that Hester had loved the boatman from Tortola. Tom told us that Hester had been drinking all night.
present perfect →	past perfect	"I have applied for the job."	Sally said that she had applied for the job.
will-future →	would + infinitive	"I'm sure the new cars will be more energy-efficient."	The politician said that he was sure that the new cars would be more energy-efficient.
going to-future →	was/were going to + infinitive	"The government is going to fight unemployment."	The President explained that the government was going to fight unemployment.
can →	could	"I'm sorry we can't come."	Michael was sorry that they could not come.
may →	might	"I may fail the exam."	Tim thought that he might fail the exam.

Indirect questions

- you also have to backshift the tenses in indirect questions
- there is **no do/does/did** in indirect questions
- the **word order** in indirect questions is the same as in statements: **s – v – o**
- if you report questions with question words like **who, what, where, when, why,** use **ask/want to know** + **question word**
- *Tom: "What did you write in the test?"* → *Tom wanted to know what I had written in the test.*
- if there is no question word in the direct question, use **if** or **whether** in the indirect question
  Tom: "Do you love Hester, Owen?" → *Tom wanted to know if Owen loved Hester.*

Indirect commands and requests

- are usually introduced with **tell sb. (not) to do sth., ask sb. (not) to do sth., warn sb. (not) to do sth., remind sb. (not) to do sth.,** etc.
- usually require the **infinitive with 'to'** or **'not to'**

		S	V	O	infinitive	
"Don't drink so much."	→	*The doctor*	*warned*	*him*	*not to drink*	*so much.*
Susan: "Can you help me with the report?"	→	*Susan*	*asked*	*me*	*to help*	*her with the report.*

Pronouns and adverbials of time and place in indirect speech

- **pronouns** and **adverbials of time and place** have to be adjusted to the perspective of the person reporting the statement and changed accordingly if necessary

Hester: "Can I use your car, Owen?"

(Owen to his friend)
Hester asked me if she could use my car.
(Hester to her friend)
I asked Owen yesterday if I could use his car.

adverbials of time and place					
direct speech		**indirect speech**	**direct speech**		**indirect speech**
now	→	then, at that time	last night/week/year	→	the day/week/year before
today	→	(on) that day, yesterday, on Monday …	three days ago	→	three days before/earlier
			this evening	→	that evening
tomorrow	→	the next day, the following day, today, …	tonight	→	that night
			here	→	there
yesterday	→	the day before			

- **further changes:** come → go, bring → take, this → that, these → those

German *(zu-)lassen, machen lassen, veranlassen*

- **let + object + infinitive without 'to'** → ***(zu-) lassen, erlauben***
  In a multicultural society, it is important to let people keep the cultural traditions of their homeland.
- **permit/allow + object + infinitive with 'to'** → ***(zu-) lassen, erlauben***
  Some nations allow immigrants to have two nationalities.
- **have/get + object + past participle** → ***machen lassen***
  Before Hester went to the ball, she had her hair done.
  When Pat prepared her project, she got some transparencies made in the copy shop.
- **have/make + object + infinitive without 'to'** → ***veranlassen, zwingen***
  The teacher had his students correct their own mistakes.
  The teacher finds it diffucult to make the students work regularly.
- **get + object + infinitive with 'to'** → ***jdn. dazu bringen, zwingen***
  The United Nations should get the industrial nations to ban underpaid labour in sweatshops.

Infinitive With/Without 'to' and the Gerund

When two main verbs appear together, the second verb will take one of the following three forms:

1. The infinitive without 'to'

- the infinitive without 'to' is used **after modal verbs**, e.g. will, should, can, must, etc. and **certain verbs of permission and causation** (*Verursachung*), e.g. make, bid, let and have (see above)
  He will study at Oxford next year.

2. The infinitive with 'to'

- the infinitive with 'to' is often used after verbs that can refer to **future actions**, e.g. afford, agree, appear, attempt, choose, dare, decide, expect, fail, help, hope, learn, manage, offer, plan, promise, refuse, seem, wish, would like, would love, would prefer, would hate
  The charity organization helps to give seriously ill children a wonderful vacation.
  I hope to work in a charity organization next year.

3. The gerund

The gerund **is a special form of the verb** used like a noun and is formed with the **infinitive** (without 'to') + **-ing**.

- the **gerund** can be the subject of the sentence
  Travelling abroad is fun and broadens your horizons.

- **the gerund** can be the **object after certain verbs and phrases**, e.g. admit, avoid, consider, deny, hate, detest, dislike, enjoy, excuse, finish, imagine, keep (→ continue), love, like, (not) mind, miss, postpone, practice, prevent, regret, resist, resume, risk, stand (→ tolerate), suggest, cannot/could not help, it is no use, it is worth, look forward to
  Sammy did not mind helping in the garden.

- **the gerund** is used **after prepositions**:
  a) **adjective + preposition**, e.g. capable of, famous for, fond of, good at, interested in, proud of
  Bill Gates became famous for founding Microsoft.

  b) **noun + preposition**, e.g. difficulty in, fear of, hope of, intention of, a question of
  President Obama has the intention of motivating people to volunteer.

  c) **verb + preposition (= prepositional verbs)**, e.g. accuse sb. of, apologize for, believe in, count on, depend on, dream of, insist on, object to, prevent sb. from, rely on, succeed in, thank for
  Lucy succeeded in passing the English test.

⚠ However, be careful with the word 'to'. It can function as a preposition.
We are very much looking forward to meeting you next week.

'To' can also be part of the infinitive with 'to' (see above).
They would like to meet us at the airport.

⚠ The verbs like, love, hate, start, begin, continue, intend can often be used with **a gerund** or **an infinitive with 'to'** with **little or no difference** in meaning.

In contrast, the verbs forget, go on, remember, stop, try have **a totally different meaning** when used with a gerund or infinitive.

Phil stopped eating a hamburger. → *Phil hörte auf, einen Hamburger zu essen.*
Phil stopped to eat a hamburger. → *Phil stoppte/hielt an, um einen Hamburger zu essen.*

Modal Auxiliaries

Modal verbs or modal auxiliaries are a special group **of verbs that are different from other verbs** in **four ways**:

a) after modal auxiliaries the **infinitive** is used without **'to'** (cf. p. 295)
b) modal auxiliaries have **no -s on the third-person singular**
c) **modal questions and negatives** are formed without **'to'**
(*Can you help me?, You must not say that.*)
d) modal auxiliaries have **no infinitives** (~~*to may*~~) and **no participles** (~~*caning, musted*~~).
Instead you use **substitute verbs**:

can	→ to be able to (*können*)
	→ to be allowed to (*dürfen*)
must	→ to have to (*müssen*)
may	→ to be allowed to (*dürfen*)
mustn't	→ not to be allowed to (*nicht dürfen*)
needn't	→ not to have to (*nicht müssen, nicht brauchen*)

Modal Auxiliaries with the Perfect Infinitive

- if you want to express that something **probably** happened in the past or that things might have been different in the past, you can use the modal auxiliaries **must, may, should, ought to, could, might, need (not)** with the perfect infinitive (**have + past participle**)
Hester shouldn't have eaten so much.
If you had told me, I could have helped you.
I didn't hear the telephone. I must have been in the garden.

- in **German**, the construction of a modal auxiliary and the perfect infinitive is usually expressed as ***Konjunktiv*** (*hätte sollen, hätte müssen, etc.*)

Further modal auxiliaries:

- **should** is used to make a suggestion to sb./oneself
I should eat more fruit.
- **have to** is used to talk about rules and laws
You have to stop on red.
- **can**, **would**, **may** is used to ask for permission
Can I borrow your bike? (everyday English)
Could I ask a question? (polite, more formal English)
May I have your name, please? (very formal English)
- **used to (+ infinitive)** is used for finished habits and situations (of the past)
I used to have a red car. (Now I have a blue one) *Ich hatte (immer) ein rotes Auto …*
- **would like to** is used to talk about things that people want to do or to be
Would you like some lemonade?
I would like to be taller.

Participles

Participle constructions instead of adverbial clauses

- you can use a present participle in place of an **adverbial clause of reason** (*Kausalsatz*)
  Tess travelled to the USA to learn English. → *Wanting to learn English, Tess travelled to the USA.*
  She failed her final exam because she did too much sightseeing. → *Having done too much sightseeing, she failed the final exam.*
- you can use a present participle in place of an **adverbial clause of time** (*Temporalsatz*)
  When Pat arrived in New York, she noticed she had forgotten her camera. → *Arriving in New York, Pat noticed that she had forgotten her camera.*
- you can use a present participle instead of an **adverbial clause of manner** (*Art und Weise, Modalsatz*)
  Phil spent all his pocket money in order to buy the ticket. → *Phil spent all his pocket money buying the ticket.*

Past participle constructions instead of adverbial clauses

- the past participle is used to express **a passive meaning**
  When the book is read by a professional actor, it sounds much better. → *Read by a professional actor, the book sounds much better.*
- the past participle can be **used as an adjective**
  a used car, mixed feelings, stonewashed jeans, a pleated dress, baked beans

Pairs of useful participial adjectives		
alarming – alarmed	depressing – depressed	frightening – frightened
amazing – amazed	disappointing – disappointed	interesting – interested
amusing – amused	disgusting – disgusted	relaxing – relaxed
annoying – annoyed	embarrassing – embarrassed	shocking – shocked
astonishing – astonished	exciting – excited	surprising – surprised
boring – bored	exhausting – exhausted	terrifying – terrified
confusing – confused	fascinating – fascinated	

⚠ Be careful **not to mix up** these forms.
The book was boring. ***(active)*** **BUT** *Susan was really bored (with reading the book).* ***(passive)***

Passive

tenses	active	passive
simple past	Microsoft developed computer programs.	Computer programs were developed by Microsoft.
past progressive	The UK was accepting more immigrants at that time.	More immigrants were being accepted at that time by the UK.
past perfect	Lincoln's decree had freed the slaves before the war ended.	The slaves had been freed by Lincoln's decree before the war ended.
past perfect progressive	Susan had been watching TV until she fell asleep.	– not used –
simple present	The president gives an inaugural speech after being elected.	An inaugural speech is given by the president after being elected.
present progressive	An Asian-American is playing the role.	The role is being played by an Asian-American.
present perfect	Millions have crossed the border.	The border has been crossed by millions.
present perfect progressive	The reporters have been interviewing President Biden for hours.	– not used –
will-future	More CO_2 will cause increased global warming.	Increased global warming will be caused by more CO_2.
going to-future	The student is going to write the final exam tomorrow.	The final exam is going to be written by the student tomorrow.

Passive – usage

- is used to talk about a general truth or to make a general statement/announcement
  Something should be done to stop global warming.
  People are asked/requested not to smoke in this building.
- is used to emphasize the person/thing/animal being acted on
  Buffalo were almost wiped out in the 19th century.
- is used when writing in a scientific or academic context (research papers, scientific reports, books on art)
  The acid was diluted with water and then filtrated into a glass container. After this, it was heated.
- to be vague about who is responsible
  Mistakes were made.
- when the agent of the action is irrelevant or unknown
  The painting was stolen from the Louvre last year.

You should NOT use the passive:

- when you have to be precise about who caused sth./who is responsible
- when you want to be precise and to the point (passive sentences can sound wordy and vague)

Sentences with two objects:

S	P	O	O
The teacher	explained	the rules	to the student.
The rules	were explained	to the student	by the teacher.
The student	was explained	the rules	by the teacher.
The woman	gave	him	an apple.
An apple	was given	to him	by the woman.
He	was given	an apple	by the woman.

When active is transformed into passive, pronouns in the object case have to be transformed into the subject case too:

me → I
him → he
her → she
us → we
them → they

Relative Clauses

There are two types of relative clauses, **defining relative clauses** and **non-defining relative clauses**.

1. Defining relative clauses

- are used to define a person or thing (in the main clause)
- are needed **to understand what/who (exactly) is meant**; without them the information given in the main clause would be incomplete
- begin with who, that and whose for people and which, that and whose for things
  Who was the girl who/that became pregnant?
  Juno is the girl whose baby is given up for adoption.
  The self-help group which/that wants to help obese people meets once a week.
- are **not separated by commas** from the main clause
- when that, who, which are objects of the relative clause they can be left out (= contact clause)
  The speech (which/that) the President gave was very inspiring.
- a preposition is preferably put at the end of the relative clause rather than at the beginning
  The apprenticeship (that) the girl was looking for had already been taken by someone else.

2. Non-defining relative clauses

- **give extra information** (that make a sentence more interesting or revealing); they **can be left out** without making the sentence incomprehensible
- begin with who, whose for people and which, whose for things
- are **separated by commas** from the main clause to bracket (*einrahmen, einklammern*) the 'non-essential' information
  Owen Meany has always worked on the farm, which is at the end of the road.
- in formal English, the preposition in the non-defining relative clause should be placed in front of who, which, whose; who is then changed to whom **after** a preposition

  Paul Newman, after whom Newman's Own was named, was well known for his charity work.

3. Participle constructions instead of defining relative clauses

- often, participle constructions take the place of defining relative clauses when the relative pronoun is the subject of the relative clause

S		present participle
The woman who adopts the baby is a nurse.	→	*The woman adopting the baby is a nurse.*

- participle constructions using the past participle have a passive meaning

passive		
Two of the babies that were adopted were girls.	→	*Two of the babies adopted were girls.*

Tenses

past tenses	present tenses	future tenses
simple past *I worked* past progressive *I was working/We were working* past perfect *I had worked* past perfect progressive *I had been working*	simple present *I work/He works* present progressive *I am working/He is working* present perfect *I have worked/He has worked* present perfect progressive *I have been working/ He has been working*	future simple: – will-future *I will work* – going to-future *I am going to work/ He is going to work* future perfect *I will have worked* future perfect progressive *I will have been working* simple present, present progressive } with future meaning

Simple present – usage

- for repeated actions (e. g. hobby, habit, daily event)
  Susan goes to band practice every Tuesday.
  Grandmother sends me a cake each Christmas.

- to express general truths, generalizations or scientific facts
  Independence Day is celebrated on July 4th.
  Water freezes at 0 degrees Celsius.

- for scheduled events in the near future
  The train leaves at 4.30.
  The store opens in 10 minutes.

- for states, i. e. non-progressive verbs (e. g. to want, to cost, to seem, to need, to owe, to own, to like, to mind, etc.)
  Susan seems to be eating too much chocolate; she has put on weight recently.
  Mr Miller owns two old houses in the neighbourhood.

- to talk or write about texts, works of art or to write a summary
  The exposition of the novel introduces the main characters, Michael and Elizabeth.
  The painting/sculpture represents Venus rising from the sea.

Present progressive – usage

- stresses the continuing nature of an act, event or condition
  Nora is reading the latest novel by Stephanie Meyer.
  CNN is broadcasting a speech given by the President.

- to describe a picture/cartoon (→ also in combination with simple present and often in the passive voice)
  In the foreground, a couple are sitting on a bench. They are laughing.

Present perfect and simple past – usage

simple past	present perfect
– a state, action or series of actions that was/were completed in the past *When Grandma was a child, she lived in France.* *In 1865, Abraham Lincoln was killed.* *Frank went into the study and wrote an email.*	– describes a state, action or series of actions that began in the past and continue(s) into the present *Lilly has dreamt about Brad Pitt every night this week.* – typically used to suggest that an action still has an effect on sth. in the present *The heat wave has lasted for three weeks.* (→ effect: now everything is dry)

Past progressive – usage

- for actions that were not complete at a past time
  At 8 o'clock, when Owen came home, Hester was reading.

- often used together with the simple past; the past progressive describes the longer action or situation and the simple past the shorter action that happend during the longer action
  While Juno was walking down the road she saw her friend.
  past progressive (was walking) **simple past** (saw)
- for actions that were taking place in the past at the same time (while)
  While the politicians were discussing the matter, the people were protesting violently.

Past perfect – usage

- when somebody is referring to a time before a past event
  When Juno gave up her baby for adoption, she had already contacted the foster parents.
  simple past (gave up) **past perfect** (had already contacted)

Past perfect progressive – usage

- for actions that had been going on for some time in the past before another action happened; to emphasize the duration *(Dauer)* of an action or situation
  The audience had already been waiting for an hour before the band finally started to play.
  past perfect progressive (had already been waiting) **simple past** (started)

Will-future and going to-future – usage

will-future	going to-future
– future facts/things we believe to be true *The President will support public service.* *I am certain you will get a good mark.* *I am sure you will like her.*	– if you are making a future prediction based on evidence in the present situation *Look at the traffic. We are not going to get there on time.* *Be careful! You are going to fall.*
– if you are not certain about the future; with expressions such as **probably, possibly, I think, I hope** *The climate summit will probably find a good solution.* *I hope the CO_2 emissions will be cut.*	
– at the very moment of making a decision *I will apply for the apprenticeship.* →	– once you have made the decision *Tom, can you get me the address? I am going to write my CV and a letter of application.*

Narrative tenses

Narrative tenses are used when you want **to tell a story** or talk about situations or activities that happened at a defined past time. Do not mix past and present tenses when narrating past events – this will confuse the readers/listeners.

simple past	*Everybody knew that Owen Meany did not drink.* *Owen lit a cigarette and asked Hester for a dance.*
past progressive	*Owen and Hester were dancing closely when the teacher entered.* *While they were dancing, the boys were laughing at them.*
past perfect	*We knew that Hester had been in love with the boatman from Tortola.*
past perfect progressive	*Owen and Hester had been dancing togehter all night until the party finally ended.*

Webcodes

All audio/-visual material and worksheets are provided on **webcodes**.
Access the following website www.westermann.de/webcode and enter the respective code or scan the QR-codes.

@ WES-121500-001

@ WES-121500-002

@ WES-121500-003

@ WES-121500-004

@ WES-121500-005

@ WES-121500-006

@ WES-121500-007

@ WES-121500-008

@ WES-121500-009

@ WES-121500-010

@ WES-121500-011

@ WES-121500-012

@ WES-121500-013

@ WES-121500-014

@ WES-121500-015

@ WES-121500-016

@ WES-121500-017

@ WES-121500-018

@ WES-121500-019

@ WES-121500-020

@ WES-121500-021

@ WES-121500-022

@ WES-121500-023

@ WES-121500-024

@ WES-121500-025

@ WES-121500-026

@ WES-121500-027

@ WES-121500-028

@ WES-121500-029

@ WES-121500-030

@ WES-121500-031

@ WES-121500-032

@ WES-121500-033

@ WES-121500-034

@ WES-121500-035

@ WES-121500-036

Acknowledgements

Images

|Alamy Stock Photo, Abingdon/Oxfordshire: Figel, Adam Jan 17.1; Iakobchuk, Viacheslav 206.1; Image Press Agency 115.1; Paralaxis 155.2; Petrychenko, Anton 155.1; RGR Collection 18.1; Science History Images 210.1. |Alamy Stock Photo (RMB), Abingdon/Oxfordshire: Bourdillon, Mark 107.2; Dwyer, Michael 62.1; frans lemmens 121.1. |Andrews McMeel Syndication, Kansas City, MO: MODERATELY CONFUSED © 2012 Jeff Stahler. Reprinted by permission of ANDREWS MCMEEL SYNDICATION for UFS. All rights reserved. 244.1; STAHLER © 2009 Jeff Stahler. Reprinted by permission of ANDREWS MCMEEL SYNDICATION for UFS. All rights reserved. 16.1; STAHLER © 2013 Jeff Stahler. Reprinted by permission of ANDREWS MCMEEL SYNDICATION for UFS. All rights reserved. 176.1. |Art Explosion, Calabasas, CA: 234.1, 265.1, 265.2. |Artizans Entertainment, Edmonton: Mayes, Malcolm 191.1. |Axel Springer Syndication GmbH, Berlin: Infografik WELT-online vom 9.3.2019 80.1, 81.1. |Baaske Cartoons, Müllheim: Plaßmann, Thomas 130.1. |Berghahn, Matthias, Bielefeld: 23.1, 26.1, 75.1, 122.1, 123.1, 129.1, 138.1, 273.1. |Cagle Cartoons, Santa Barbara, CA: Koterba, Jeff 137.1, 172.1; Sack, Steve 145.1; Weyant, Christopher 60.1. |Cartoon Movement, Amsterdam: Osval 34.1; Popa Matumula 135.1. |Cartoonist Group, Santa Fe, NM: Chip Bok Editorial Cartoon used with the permission of Chip Bok and Creators Syndicate. All rights reserved. 98.1; Steve Kelley Editorial Cartoon used with the permission of Steve Kelley and Creators Syndicate. All rights reserved. 191.2. |CartoonStock.com, Bath: Baldwin, Mike 266.1; Baloo - Rex May 256.1; Besley, Rupert 260.1; Brooks, Rosie 16.2; Bucella, Marty 48.1; Cook, Gary 51.1; Farris, Joseph 53.1; Flanagan, Mike 159.1; Jolley, Richard 18.2, 209.1; Jung, Norman 32.1; Kinsella, Paul 228.1; Olsen, Werner 18.3; Steiner, Peter 53.2; Thomas Bros. 240.1; Toos, Andrew 209.2; Tugg 176.2; Wilbur-Dawbarn 102.3; Wildt, Chris 102.2, 199.1, 258.1. |Courtesy of Pest Control Office - Banksy, London: 107.1. |DER SPIEGEL, Hamburg: DER SPIEGEL 29/2019 140.1; SPIEGEL (online), 18.07.2019 141.1, 142.1, 142.2. |DIE ZEIT, Hamburg: Der große Unterschied Martin Spiewak / Carolin Eitel DIE ZEIT 47 / 2020 (12.11.2020) 213.1, 213.2, 213.3, 214.1, 214.2, 214.3, 214.4, 215.1, 215.2, 215.3, 215.4. |Domke, Franz-Josef, Hannover: 36.1, 114.1, 127.1, 152.1, 153.1, 218.1, 243.1, 243.2, 243.3, 252.1; Foto: stock.adobe.com/artisticco 234.2; WDR mediagroup GmbH 164.2. |Duplicon Martin Mißfeldt, Panketal: 201.1. |eToon.com Cartoons, Maple Ridge: Kolarov, Vlad 261.1. |FOCUS Magazin Verlag GmbH, München: FOCUS 18/2019 84.1, 84.2, 84.3, 84.4, 84.5, 84.6, 85.1. |fotolia.com, New York: dikobrazik 286.1, 286.2; Pixel Embargo 231.1. |Getty Images, München: AFP/Celis, Noel 147.1. |Glasbergen, Randy/glasbergen.com, Sherburne: 225.1. |Guardian News & Media Limited, London: The Guardian 09 May 2019 218.2. |Hawkins, Ed, Reading: www.showyourstripes.info 112.1, 112.2. |HEART AGENCY, London: © Tom Gauld 264.1. |Heller, Joe, Green Bay: 198.1. |HONEYLAND, Skopje: Photo by Ljubomir Stefanov © TRICE FILMS 127.2, 127.3. |HUD Exchange, Washington: The U.S. Department of Housing and Urban Development: The 2018 Annual Homelessness Assessment Report (AHAR) to Congress 66.1, 66.2. |Imago, Berlin: Future Image 179.2, 179.3; HOFER 179.1. |iStockphoto.com, Calgary: Alliya23 37.1, 37.2. |Kassing, Reinhild, Kassel: 232.1, 232.2, 232.3, 232.4, 232.5, 232.6, 232.7, 232.8, 232.9, 233.1, 233.2, 233.3, 233.4, 233.5, 233.6, 233.7, 233.8, 233.9, 242.1, 248.1, 262.1. |Kratzer, Max, Oberschleißheim: 82.1. |Ocean. Now! e.V., Berlin: 167.3; Photo: Saskia Uppenkamp 167.1, 167.2. |Picture-Alliance GmbH, Frankfurt a.M.: ANP/van Weel, Koen 174.1; AP Photo/Getty Images/Moore, John 89.1; dpa/Levitt, Helen 246.1. |Rankin Photography Ltd, London: 205.1, 205.2, 205.3, 205.4. |ReadyToManage, Inc., Los Angeles: © 2012, ReadyToManage 45.1. |Save the Children Deutschland e.V., Berlin: Talitha Brauer 73.1. |Shutterstock.com, New York: Russita, Tatjana 257.1. |Shutterstock.com (RM), New York: Moviestore 68.1. |stock.adobe.com, Dublin: anando.a 121.2; Argus 241.1; artisticco 234.3; bsd555 27.2; kmit 163.1; Martin 134.1; raz234 164.1; supanut 27.3. |Stutte, Matthias, Krefeld: 150.1. |Stuttmann, Klaus, Berlin: 39.1, 93.1. |toonclipart - toonaday: © Ron Leishman 270.1. |Tribune Content Agency, London: © 2019 Bill Bramhall All rights reserved. Distributed by Tribune Content Agency 102.1. |United Nations/Department of Global Communications, New York, NY: „I am a Youth of a Small Island - International Competition" by UN DESA / SIDS Unit on 24 Oct 2019 © 2019 United Nations. Reprinted with the permission of the United Nations. Sustainable Development Knowledge Platform (un.org), 28.04.2021 118.1. |Volunteering Matters, London: 28.1. |Work the World, East Sussex: 27.1. |WWF Deutschland, Berlin: 113.1.